LANCHESTER LIBRARY

3 8001 00550 6393

KT-472-282

Lanchester Library

WITHDRAWN

Effective Project Management

Effective Project Management

Traditional, Adaptive, Extreme

Fourth Edition

Robert K. Wysocki, Ph.D.

Wiley Publishing, Inc.

Effective Project Management: Traditional, Adaptive, Extreme, Fourth Edition

Published by
Wiley Publishing, Inc.
10475 Crosspoint Boulevard
Indianapolis, IN 46256
www.wiley.com

Copyright © 2007 by Robert K. Wysocki
Published by Wiley Publishing, Inc., Indianapolis, Indiana
Published simultaneously in Canada
ISBN-13: 978-0-470-04261-8
ISBN-10: 0-470-04261-3
Manufactured in the United States of America
10 9 8 7 6 5 4 3 2 1
1MA/TQ/RR/QW/IN

Coventry University Library

No part of this publication may be reproduced, stored in a retrieval system or transmitted in any form or by any means, electronic, mechanical, photocopying, recording, scanning or otherwise, except as permitted under Sections 107 or 108 of the 1976 United States Copyright Act, without either the prior written permission of the Publisher, or authorization through payment of the appropriate per-copy fee to the Copyright Clearance Center, 222 Rosewood Drive, Danvers, MA 01923, (978) 750-8400, fax (978) 646-8600. Requests to the Publisher for permission should be addressed to the Legal Department, Wiley Publishing, Inc., 10475 Crosspoint Blvd., Indianapolis, IN 46256, (317) 572-3447, fax (317) 572-4355, or online at http://www.wiley.com/go/permissions.

Limit of Liability/Disclaimer of Warranty: The publisher and the author make no representations or warranties with respect to the accuracy or completeness of the contents of this work and specifically disclaim all warranties, including without limitation warranties of fitness for a particular purpose. No warranty may be created or extended by sales or promotional materials. The advice and strategies contained herein may not be suitable for every situation. This work is sold with the understanding that the publisher is not engaged in rendering legal, accounting, or other professional services. If professional assistance is required, the services of a competent professional person should be sought. Neither the publisher nor the author shall be liable for damages arising herefrom. The fact that an organization or Website is referred to in this work as a citation and/or a potential source of further information does not mean that the author or the publisher endorses the information the organization or Website may provide or recommendations it may make. Further, readers should be aware that Internet Websites listed in this work may have changed or disappeared between when this work was written and when it is read.

For general information on our other products and services or to obtain technical support, please contact our Customer Care Department within the U.S. at (800) 762-2974, outside the U.S. at (317) 572-3993 or fax (317) 572-4002.

Library of Congress Cataloging-in-Publication Data:
Wysocki, Robert K.
  Effective project management : traditional, adaptive, extreme / Robert K. Wysocki. — 4th ed.
     p. cm.
  Includes index.
  ISBN-13: 978-0-470-04261-8 (paper/website)
  ISBN-10: 0-470-04261-3 (paper/website)
  1. Project management. I. Title.
  HD69.P75W95 2007
  658.4'04 — dc22

                    2006030048

Trademarks: Wiley and the Wiley logo are trademarks or registered trademarks of John Wiley & Sons, Inc. and/or its affiliates, in the United States and other countries, and may not be used without written permission. All other trademarks are the property of their respective owners. Wiley Publishing, Inc., is not associated with any product or vendor mentioned in this book.

Wiley also publishes its books in a variety of electronic formats. Some content that appears in print may not be available in electronic books.

About the Author

Robert K. Wysocki, Ph.D., has over 38 years' experience as a project management consultant and trainer, information systems manager, systems and management consultant, author, and training developer and provider. He has written ten books on project management and information systems management. One of his books, *Effective Project Management: Traditional, Adaptive, Extreme*, Third Edition, has been a bestseller and is recommended by the Project Management Institute for the library of every project manager. He has over 30 publications and presentations in professional and trade journals and has made more than 100 presentations at professional and trade conferences and meetings. He has also developed more than 20 project management courses and trained over 10,000 project managers.

In 1990 he founded Enterprise Information Insights, Inc. (EII), a project management consulting and training practice specializing in project management methodology design and integration, Project Support Office establishment, the development of training curriculum, and the development of a portfolio of assessment tools focused on organizations, project teams, and individuals. His clients include AT&T, Aetna, Babbage Simmel, British Computer Society, Boston University Corporate Education Center, Computerworld, Converse Shoes, the Czechoslovakian Government, Data General, Digital, Eli Lilly, Harvard Community Health Plan, IBM, J. Walter Thompson, Peoples Bank, Sapient, The Limited, the State of Ohio, Travelers Insurance, and several others.

He is a member of the ProjectWorld Executive Advisory Board, the Project Management Institute, the American Society of Training and Development, and the Society of Human Resource Management. He is former Association

Vice President of AITP (formerly DPMA). He earned a B.A. in mathematics from the University of Dallas, and an M.S. and Ph.D. in mathematical statistics from Southern Methodist University.

Credits

Executive Editor
Robert Elliott

Senior Development Editor
Kevin Kent

Production Editor
William A. Barton

Copy Editor
Luann Rouff

Editorial Manager
Mary Beth Wakefield

Production Manager
Tim Tate

Vice President and Executive Group Publisher
Richard Swadley

Vice President and Executive Publisher
Joseph B. Wikert

Project Coordinator
Adrienne Martinez
Ryan Steffen

Graphics and Production Specialists
Sean Decker
Stephanie D. Jumper
Heather Ryan

Quality Control Technicians
John Greenough
Brian H. Walls

Media Development Specialists
Angela Denny
Kit Malone
Travis Silvers

Proofreading
Techbooks

Indexing
Kevin Broccoli

Contents

Preface to the Fourth Edition

All three of the previous editions of this book have been successful and have grown in value from their predecessors. The fourth edition is no exception, which includes several changes and additions throughout. Perhaps the most significant is the replacement of the case study. There are now two case studies. The first one is covered extensively in Part I with the Traditional Project Management (TPM) approach. The second is covered with Part II and the Adaptive Project Framework (APF) approach. I sincerely hope that the new case studies will further crystallize in your mind how the approaches are used effectively.

Even after four editions I still view *EPM* as a work in process. As I gain further experience with its use and as I hear from you, my faculty users and other professionals, the work will undoubtedly improve.

I would like to think that this edition offers you a complete view of effective project management as it is now practiced and how it should be practiced in the very near future.

Thank you again for adding my book to your project management library. If you have any questions or would just like to comment, you may contact me at rkw@eiicorp.com.

Enjoy!

—Robert K. Wysocki, Ph.D.

Acknowledgments

This acknowledgment is really a special acknowledgment to the teaching faculty of at least 60 universities and colleges all over the globe that have adopted the third edition. Many of them have offered feedback that I find most useful. Many of their suggestions have been incorporated in this fourth edition. I also owe a debt of gratitude to the many consultants and companies across the globe that have used the APF and taken the time to comment on their experiences. To them I give heartfelt thanks.

Introduction

Change is constant! I hope that does not come as a surprise to you. Change is always with you and seems to be happening at an increasing rate. Every day you face new challenges and the need to improve yesterday's practices. As John Naisbett says in *The Third Wave*, "Change or die." For experienced project managers as well as "wannabe" project managers, the road to breakthrough performance is paved with uncertainty and the need to be courageous, creative, and flexible. If you simply rely on a routine application of someone else's methodology, you are sure to fall short of the mark. As you will see in the pages that follow, I am not afraid to step outside the box and outside my comfort zone. Nowhere is there more of a need for change than in the approach you take to managing projects.

Organizational Structures

The familiar command and control structures introduced at the turn of the century are rapidly disappearing. In their place are task forces, self-directed work teams, and various forms of projectized organizations. In all cases, empowerment of the worker lies at the foundation of these new structures. With structural changes and worker empowerment comes the need for everyone to have solid project management skills. One of my clients is often heard saying, "We hire smart people and we depend on them. If the project is particularly difficult and complex, we can put five smart people together in a room and know that they will find an acceptable solution." While there is merit to this line of reasoning, I think project management should be based more on wisely chosen and repeatable approaches than on the creativity and heroic actions of a room full of smart people.

Software Applications

Many of you may remember the days when a computer application had to meet the needs of just a single department. If there was a corporate database, it was accessed to retrieve the required data, which was passed to an applications program that produced the requested report. If there was no data or you did not know of its existence, you created your own database or file and proceeded accordingly. In retrospect, the professional life of systems developers was relatively simple. Not so any more. To be competitive, you now develop applications that cross departmental lines, applications that span organizations, applications that are not clearly defined, and applications that will change because the business climate is changing. All of this means that you must anticipate changes that will affect your projects, and you must be skilled at managing those changes. Many of the flavors of project management approaches in use in corporations are fundamentally intolerant of change. Barriers to change run rampant through many of these approaches. If your process has that property, bury it quickly; that is not the way to be a contemporary project manager.

Cycle Time

The window of opportunity is narrowing and constantly moving. Organizations that can take advantage of opportunities are organizations that have found a way to reduce cycle times. Taking too long to roll out a new or revamped product can result in a missed business opportunity. Project managers must know how and when to introduce multiple release strategies and compress project schedules to help meet these requirements. Even more important, the project management approach must support these aggressive schedules. That means these processes must protect the schedule by eliminating all non-value-added work. You simply cannot afford to layer your project management processes with a lot of overhead activities that do not add value to the final deliverables. I spend considerable time covering these strategies in later chapters.

Right-Sizing

With the reduction in management layers, a common practice in many organizations, the professional staff needs to find ways to work smarter, not harder. Project management includes a number of tools and techniques that help the professional manage increased workloads. Your staffs need to have more room to do their work in the most productive ways possible. Burdening them with overhead activities for which they see little value is a sure way to failure.

In a landmark paper "The Coming of the New Organization" (*Harvard Business Review*, January/February 1988), Peter Drucker depicts middle managers as either those who receive information from above, reinterpret it, and pass it down or those who receive information from below, reinterpret it, and pass it up the line. Not only is quality suspect because of personal biases and political overtones, but the computer is perfectly capable of delivering that information to the desk of any manager who has a need to know. Given these factors, plus the politics and power struggles at play, why employ middle managers? As technology advances and acceptance of this idea grows, we have seen the thinning of middle management layers. Do not expect them to come back; they are gone forever. The effect on project managers is predictable and significant. Hierarchical structures are being replaced by organizations that have a greater dependence on project teams, resulting in more opportunities for project managers.

Changes in the Project Environment

Traditional Project Management (TPM) practices were defined and later matured in the world of the engineer and construction professional, where the team expected (and got) a clear statement from clients as to what they wanted, when they wanted it, and how much they were willing to pay for it. All of this was delivered to the project manager wrapped in a neat package. The i's were all dotted, and the t's were all crossed. All the correct forms were filed, and all the boxes were filled with the information requested. Everyone was satisfied that the request was well documented and that the deliverables were sure to be delivered as requested. The project team clearly understood the solution they would be expected to provide, and they could clearly plan for its delivery. That describes the world of the project manager until the 1950s. By the mid-1950s, the computer was well on its way to becoming a viable commercial resource, but it was still the province of the engineer. Project management continued as it had under the management of the engineers.

The first sign that change was in the wind for the project manager arose in the early 1960s. The use of computers to run businesses was now a reality, and we began to see position titles such as programmer, programmer/analyst, systems analyst, and primitive types of database architects emerging. These professionals were really engineers in disguise, and somehow they were expected to interact with the business and management professionals (who were totally mystified by the computer and the mystics who could communicate with it) to design and implement business applications systems to replace manual processes. This change represented a total metamorphosis of the business world and the project world, and we would never look back.

In the face of this transformation into an information society, TPM wasn't showing any signs of change. To the engineers, every IT project management problem looked like a nail, and they had the hammer. In other words, they had one solution, and it fit every problem. One of the major problems that TPM faced, and still faces, is the difference between *wants* and *needs*. If you remember anything from this introduction, remember that what the client wants is probably not what the client needs. If the project manager blindly accepts what the clients say they want and proceeds with the project on that basis, then the project manager is in for a rude awakening. Often in the process of building the solution, the client learns that what they need is not the same as what they requested. Here you have the basis for rolling deadlines, scope creep, and an endless trail of changes and reworks. It's no wonder that 70-plus percent of projects fail. That cycle has to stop. You need an approach that is built around change — one that embraces learning and discovery throughout the project life cycle. Moreover, it must have built-in processes to accommodate the changes that result from this learning and discovery.

I have talked with numerous project managers over the past several years about the problem of a lack of clarity and what they do about it. Most would say that they deliver according to the original requirements and then iterate one or more times before they satisfy the client's current requirements. I asked them why, if they knew that they were going to iterate, they didn't use an approach that has that feature built in. The silence in response to that question is deafening. All of the adaptive and agile approaches to project management that are currently coming into fashion are built on the assumption that changing requirements are a given as the client gains better focus on what they actually need. Sometimes those needs can be very different from the original wants.

Obviously, this is no longer your father's project management. The Internet and an ever-changing array of new and dazzling technologies have made a permanent mark on the business landscape. Technology has put most businesses in a state of confusion. How should a company proceed to utilize the Internet and extract the greatest business value? Even the more basic questions — "What business are we in?" "How do we reach and service our customers?" "What do our customers expect?" — had no answers in the face of ever-changing technology. The dot.com era flowered quickly with a great deal of hyperbole and faded just as quickly. A lot of companies came into existence on the shoulders of highly speculative venture capital in the 1990s and went belly-up by the end of the century. Only a few remain, and even their existence is tenuous. The current buzzwords *e-commerce* and *e-business* have replaced *B2B* and *B2C*, and businesses seem to be settling down, but we are still a long way from recovery.

The question on the table is this: "What impact should this have on your approach to project management?" The major impact should be that project management approaches must align with the business of the enterprise.

Project management needs to find its seat at the organization's strategy table. Project managers must first align to the needs of the organization, rather than their own home department. That is today's critical success factor.

Where Are We Going? — A New Mind-set

We are not in Kansas anymore! The discipline of project management has morphed to a new state, and as this book goes to press, that state is not yet a steady one. It may never be. What does all this mean to the struggling project manager?

To me the answer is obvious. You must open your minds to the basic principles on which project management is based in order to accommodate change and avoid wasted dollars and wasted time. For as long as I can remember, my colleagues and I have been preaching that one size does not fit all. The characteristics of the project suggest what subset of the traditional approach should be used on the project. This concept has to be extended to also encompass choosing the project management approach that you employ based on the characteristics of the project at hand. Interested readers can learn more about this new mind-set in my recent book *Effective Software Project Management* (Wiley, 2006). In that book I define a new discipline—one that fully integrates the project management life cycle with the software development life cycle. The result is an approach that aligns with the needs of the customer, the enterprise, and the project.

Introducing Extreme Project Management

Something new was needed, and along came *extreme project management (xPM)*. This approach embraced a high degree of change and highly complex situations in which speed was a critical success factor. B2B and B2C applications clearly fall into the extreme category. New product development and R&D projects are also typical extreme projects. More recently, the whole school of thought around these types of approaches to project management has been titled *agile project management*. Under the title of agile project management, you find extreme programming, SCRUM (named after a term used in rugby), Dynamic Systems Development Method (DSDM), Feature-Driven Development (FDD), Adaptive Systems Development (ASD), Crystal Light, and many others. These hybrids all focus on extreme software development projects, which are at the opposite end of the spectrum from traditional projects. Even with all of these hybrids, there is still something missing.

By suggesting, "one size does not fit all," I and other project management authors are, of course, talking about how the characteristics of the project should inform the project manager as to what pieces and parts of the traditional approach should be used on a given project. As projects went from high risk to low risk, from high cost to low cost, from critical mission to routine maintenance, and from groundbreaking technology to well-established technology, the project management approach appropriately went from the full methodology to a subset of the methodology. That was fine for making adjustments to the traditional approach, but now you have another factor to consider that has led to a very basic consideration of how a project should be managed. This factor can be posed as a question that goes to the very heart of project management: "What basic approach makes sense for this type of project?"

This new approach represents a radical shift away from trying to adapt TPM to fit the project toward one that is based on a very different set of assumptions and principles than obtained before.

I contend that the traditional world of project management belongs to yesterday. There will continue to be applications for which it is appropriate, but there is a whole new set of applications for which it is totally inappropriate. The paradigm must shift, and any company that doesn't make that shift is sure to be lost in the rush. "Change or die" was never a truer statement than it is today.

Introducing the Adaptive Project Framework

All of this discussion about traditional and new approaches is fine, but I see a wide gap between the traditional approach and these newer agile approaches; a gap occupied by a whole class of projects that cannot totally use the methodology of either approach and for which there is no acceptable project management methodology. To deal with projects that fall in the gap, a new approach is needed.

I call this new approach the *Adaptive Project Framework (APF)*. It is new. It is exciting. It works. I urge you to step outside the comfort zone of the traditional project management box and try the APF. Be assured that I have not abandoned TPM. There are many projects for which it is a good fit. It has several tools and processes that make sense even with the type of project for which APF was designed. Many of those tools and processes have been incorporated into the APF.

Developing a Taxonomy of Approaches

Why do you need yet another way of managing projects? Don't you have enough options already? There certainly are plenty of choices, but projects still fail at a high rate. I believe that part of the reason is because we haven't yet completely defined, at a practical and effective level, how to manage the types of projects that we are being asked to manage in today's business environment. Figure I-1 illustrates the point very effectively.

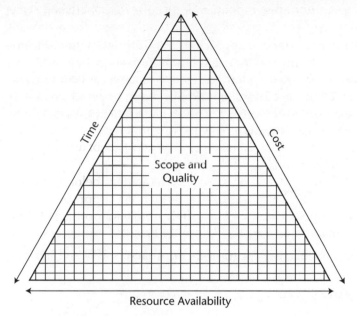

Figure I-1 Approaches to managing a project

We've had the traditional approach for almost 50 years now. It was developed for engineers and the construction industry during a time when what was needed and how to get it were clearly defined. Over the years, TPM has worked very well in that situation and still serves us well today when applied to those situations for which it was developed. Unfortunately, the world has not stood still. For the past several years project managers have been trying to contend with an entirely new environment. What do you do if what is needed is not clearly defined? What if it isn't defined at all? Many have tried to force fit the traditional approach into these situations, and it flat out doesn't work.

Moreover, what about those cases where what is needed is clearly defined but how to produce it isn't as obvious? These types of projects lie on a scale between the traditional and the extreme. Clearly, the traditional approach won't work. For the traditional approach to work, you need a detailed plan; and if you don't know how you will get what is needed, how can you generate a detailed plan? What about the extreme approach? I'm guessing that the *agilists* would argue that any one of the agile approaches would do just fine. I would agree that you could use one of them and probably do quite well. Unfortunately, you would be ignoring the fact that you know what is needed. It's a given, so why not use an approach that is designed around the fact that you know what is needed? Makes sense to me. Enter what I am calling the APF, an adaptive approach that spans the gap between TPM and xPM.

At the same time, it is important to appreciate the traditional and extreme approaches and know when and how to use them. If I am successful in developing an appreciation for all three methods, we will have a taxonomy of approaches that can meet any need for a sound approach to project management regardless of the nature of the project. The appropriate approach can be chosen once the type of project is known. Specifically:

- Figure I-1 shows that TPM works when the goal and the solution are clearly defined. If either the goal or the solution is not clearly defined, another approach is needed.

- When the solution is not clear, the appropriate approach is the APF. This is discussed in detail in Part II, "Adaptive Project Framework."

- When the goal is not clear, the appropriate approach is xPM, which is discussed in detail in Chapter 19.

Examples of all three approaches abound:

- A project to install an intranet system in a field office is clearly a traditional project. This project will have been done several times, and the steps to complete it are documented.

- A good example of an adaptive project is taken from history: John F. Kennedy's challenge to put a man on the moon and return him safely by the end of the decade. The goal statement could not be clearer. How it was to be accomplished was anybody's guess. There certainly were some ideas floating around NASA, but the detail was not there.

- There are hundreds of examples of extreme projects from the brief dot.com era of the late 1990s. Executives, in an attempt to maintain parity with their competition, got wrapped up in a feeding frenzy over the Internet. They challenged their technical staffs to build them a Web site ASAP on which they could conduct either B2B or B2C activities. They had no idea what it would look like or perhaps even what it would do, but they would know it when they saw it. The goal was very vague, and how it would be reached was anybody's guess.

One more concept differentiates these three approaches — the way the project converges on the solution. It is important to understand these differences, because they explain much of what is done in the course of using each approach. This concept is illustrated in Figure I-2 and the differences are as follows:

Project Management Process	Project Classification			
	A	B	C	D
Define				
Conditions of Satisfaction	R	R	O	O
Project Overview Statement	R	R	R	R
Approval of Request	R	R	R	R
Plan				
Conduct Planning Session	R	R	O	O
Prepare Project Proposal	R	R	R	R
Approval of Proposal	R	R	R	R
Launch				
Kick-off Meeting	R	R	O	O
Activity Schedule	R	R	R	R
Resource Assignments	R	R	R	O
Statements of Work	R	O	O	O
Monitor/Control				
Status Reporting	R	R	R	R
Project Team Meetings	R	R	O	O
Approval of Deliverables	R	R	R	R
Close				
Post-Implementation Audit	R	R	R	R
Project Notebook	R	R	O	O
	R = Required O = Optional			

Figure I-2 Plan-to-goal comparison

- TPM projects follow a very detailed plan that is built before any work is done on the project. The plan is based on the assumption that the goal (that is, the solution) is clearly specified at the outset. Apart from minor aberrations caused by change requests, the plan is followed and the goal achieved. The success of this approach is based on a correct specification of the goal during project definition and the initial scoping activities.

- APF projects follow a detailed plan, but the plan is not built at the beginning of the project. Instead, the plan is built in stages at the completion of each cycle that defines the APF project life cycle. The budget and the timebox (that is, the window of time within which the project must be completed) of the APF project are specified at the outset. At the completion of each cycle, the team and the client review what has been done and adjust the plan going forward. Using this approach the solution emerges piecemeal. Because planning has been done just-in-time and because little time and effort was spent on planning and scheduling solution components that never ended up in the final solution, an APF project finishes in less time and with less cost than a TPM project.

- xPM projects do not follow a plan in the sense of TPM or APF projects. Instead, an xPM project makes informed guesses as to what the final goal (or solution) will be. The guess is not very specific, as Figure I-2 conveys. A cycle of work is planned based on the assumption that the guess is reasonable. At the completion of the cycle, just as in the case of an APF project, a review of what was learned and discovered is factored into the specification of the goal, and a new goal definition is produced. This new definition is probably a little more accurate than the original guess. Figure I-2 would reflect this by having the ellipse shrink in volume and move up or down. The next cycle of work is planned based on the new goal. This process continues for some number of cycles and results in either an acceptable solution or the project being abandoned at the completion of some intermediate cycle. In most cases there is no specified timebox or budget for an xPM project. Instead, the project ends when a solution has been delivered or the client has killed the project because the cycle deliverables did not seem to be converging on an acceptable solution.

Why I Wrote This Book

I believe a number of professionals and practitioners are looking for some help. The information in this book can fulfill their needs. When scheduled training is not available or practical, my book can help. It is written to be studied. It is written to guide you as you learn project management. In addition, it is written to be a self-paced resource, one that will immerse you in managing a project for a simulated company. Let it work with you through the entire project life cycle.

On a more altruistic level, I have three reasons for writing this fourth edition:

- To come to the rescue of the discipline of project management. I believe that it is seriously out of alignment with the needs of our businesses. The high failure rates of projects are evidence of that misalignment. The problem is that project management is the hammer and all projects are seen as nails. This one-size-fits-all approach to project management simply doesn't work. The nature and characteristics of the project must dictate the type of management approach to be taken. Anything short of that will fail. As I mentioned previously, projects have fundamentally changed but our approach to managing them has not. We need a more robust approach to project management—one that recognizes the project environment and adapts accordingly.
- To introduce the APF. The APF is really a hybrid that takes the best from TPM and xPM. It closes the gap between projects with clearly

defined goals and solutions and projects without them. The work that I report here represents work in progress. By putting it before my colleagues, I expect that others will contribute to its further maturation.

- My continual challenge to offer a practical how-to guide for project managers in the management of their projects. My style is applications-oriented. While the book is based on sound concepts and principles of project management, it is by no means a theoretical treatise. It is written to be your companion.

How This Book Is Structured

The book consists of three parts organized into 21 chapters, an epilogue, and two appendixes. I have followed the Project Management Body of Knowledge (PMBOK) standards advocated by the Project Management Institute (PMI). As far as I am able to tell, what I present here is entirely compatible with PMBOK insofar as the approaches described do not contradict PMBOK. Once you have completed this book, you will have covered all nine knowledge areas of the PMBOK. The PMI recommends this book as one that every project manager should have in his or her library.

Part I: Traditional Project Management

Part I includes the entire previous edition with a few notable exceptions. After appearances by the O'Neill & Preigh Church Equipment Manufacturers and Jack Neift Trucking Company, I decided to retire both companies from active duty as case studies. The new cases are Pleasantown Playground Project and Pizza Delivered Quickly.

The new cases take on a much different flavor than the ones they replace. These new cases give me a chance to introduce and have you practice some of the contemporary nuances of projects. For the college and university faculty who are using my book in their courses, I have also added a few discussion questions at the end of each chapter. These are designed to actively engage the class in a sharing of ideas about how they would handle the situations presented.

Part II: Adaptive Project Framework

In Part II you leave the world of the traditional project manager behind. I have already introduced the idea that contemporary projects are very different from those that the engineering profession and construction industry used as their models for developing the traditional approach to project management. The world that you enter in this part of the book is the world of fast-paced, high-change, and complex projects. Traditionalists have tried unsuccessfully to adapt their ideas and processes to these types of projects. The failure rates that have been reported are testimony to their inability to adapt traditional thinking to a nontraditional environment. In this part I take the initial step toward defining the new approach.

The APF is the middle ground between TPM and xPM. In Chapter 19 I take the second step by considering projects whose goal is not or cannot be clearly stated. While the APF may work for some of these projects, they tend to be exploratory in nature and do not fit well with the types of projects for which the APF is best suited. In this chapter I introduce the extreme project and its management. The APF project is one in which requirements are reasonably well-known, whereas the extreme project's requirements become known as part of the discovery process that results from the iterative nature of the project. Another way of looking at the difference is that an APF project has a reasonably well-defined goal; an extreme project has a fuzzily defined goal at best.

Part III: Organizational Considerations

In Parts I and II, I develop the project management approaches that I feel span the entire landscape of project types. In this part I develop two topics that treat the environment in which project management takes place: the project portfolio and its management and the Project Support Office. Projects are thus viewed in the larger context of the organization that they support.

Chapter 20 discusses project portfolio management. The focus in many organizations is shifting away from the management and control of single projects to a focus on a portfolio of projects. Accompanying this shift in focus is a shift toward considering the portfolio from an investment perspective, just as the organization's investment portfolio has been considered for many years. At the time I was researching new materials for this book, the only published book on project portfolio management was a collection of journal articles assembled by Lowell D. Dye and James S. Pennypacker, *Project Portfolio Management* (Center for Business Practices, 1999). There were no how-to books on project portfolio management. Chapter 20 is the first attempt to begin to explore the topic. I am not giving you a tome on project portfolio management, only a starter kit. By institutionalizing the approach I give you, you will be able to enhance these basic concepts.

Chapter 21 discusses the Project Support Office (PSO). The PSO is a popular and fast-growing entity in organizations that wish to provide proactive project support.

Epilogue: Putting It All Together Finally

This was new with the third edition and is continued here in the fourth edition. As I suggest at the outset, project management is at a significant crossroads. The discipline has to adapt to the changing nature of projects. Some of the old has to give way to the new. I am using this epilogue to make my personal statements about where project management is as a discipline, where it needs to be, and how it might get there.

Appendixes

There are two appendixes:

- Appendix A tells you everything you need to know about the Web site (www.wiley.com/go/epm4e) that has been set up for this fourth edition. Among other information, the Web site contains reproducible versions of every figure and table in the book, which should be of particular interest to university and college faculty.

- Appendix B is an updated version of the bibliography from the third edition.

How to Use This Book

The original target audience for this book was the practicing project manager. However, as I discovered, many of the second and third edition sales were to university and college faculty. I certainly want to encourage their use of my book, so in this fourth edition I have further expanded the target market to include both practicing project managers and faculty. I have added discussion questions to each chapter; and to assist in lecture preparation, copies of all figures and tables are available on the Web site.

Using This Book as a Guide for Project Managers

This book adapts very well to whatever your current knowledge of or experience with project management might be:

- If you are unfamiliar with project management, you can learn the basics by simply reading and reflecting.

- If you wish to advance to the next level, I offer a wealth of practice opportunities through the case exercises.

■ If you are more experienced, I offer several advanced topics, including the APF and xPM in Parts II and III.

In all cases, the best way to read the book is from front to back. If you are an experienced project manager, feel free to skip around and read the sections as a refresher course.

The seasoned professional project manager will find value in the book as well. I have gathered a number of tools and techniques that appeared in the first edition of this book. The Joint Project Planning session, the use of Post-It notes and whiteboards for building the project network, the completeness criteria for generating the Work Breakdown Structure, the use of work packages for professional staff development, and milestone trend charts are a few of the more noteworthy and original contributions.

Using This Book as a Textbook for a Project Management Course

This book also works well as a text for a management course. The third edition has been adopted by over 60 colleges and universities. Programs at educational institutions ranging from community college through graduate school are using the book successfully. The general method of usage should be to assign specific reading from the book on topics to be discussed in class. In addition, use the case studies to tie the disparate range of topics together into a cohesive discussion. The case studies present an opportunity for discussion among the students and represent a platform from which to work that gives students a chance to discuss project management theories and techniques in a real-world setting. Discussion questions are already provided with each chapter, but it is suggested that instructors take their own topics and work them into the case.

Introducing the Case Studies

These cases are used throughout the book to give examples of various project management ideas and techniques. They are both project management cases and business cases and are constructed to give a view of possible scenarios that might exist in a real-world environment. The backgrounds for each case study follow.

CASE STUDY—PLEASANTOWN PLAYGROUND PROJECT BACKGROUND

Pleasantown is a southern California city of 80,000 residents located just outside Los Angeles. Playground space has been at a premium for many years, and many families have had no choice but to let their children play in the neighborhood streets. There have been minor accidents and, recently, one near miss of a catastrophe. The parents are concerned and ready to take action to rectify the situation.

There is a vacant parcel of city-owned land measuring 200' by 200'. It has been in disrepair for over 30 years, accumulating old tires, discarded appliances, broken bottles, and all sorts of trash. You have been informed that it is available to be turned into a playground. Due to significant pressure by various citizen groups, the city entertained proposals for converting the parcel into usable space for children. You and a group of six concerned neighbors submitted a proposal that was accepted by the city. According to the terms of the proposal, your group of seven will head up a fundraiser, recruit volunteers, and build the playground. The city expects the project to be finished by September 1. As part of the terms and conditions, your group has agreed that the city can dedicate the new facility with a gala event that they will plan and hold on City Founders Day on September 1. Because it is now April 1, you have a very tight schedule.

In addition to the time constraint, you have tentatively established the budget at $30,000 because that is about the most you can hope to raise through activities such as car washes, bake sales, etc. In addition, you hope to get local merchants to donate materials and other non-cash resources.

CASE STUDY—PIZZA DELIVERED QUICKLY (PDQ) BACKGROUND

Pizza Delivered Quickly (PDQ) is a family-owned local chain (four stores) of eat-in and home delivery pizza stores. Recently PDQ has lost 30 percent of sales revenue due mostly to a drop in their home delivery business. They attribute this solely to their major competitor, who recently promoted a program that guarantees 45-minute delivery service from order entry to home delivery. PDQ advertises one-hour delivery. PDQ currently uses computers for in-store operations and the usual business functions but otherwise is not heavily dependent upon software systems to help them receive, process, and home deliver their customers' orders. Dee Livery, their president, has decided to increase their penetration into the home delivery market by locating what she is calling "pizza factories" throughout their market. A pizza factory is not a retail establishment. It receives orders from a central order-taking facility and prepares the pizzas. A delivery truck picks up the baked pizzas and delivers them. Pepe Ronee, their Manager of Information Systems, has been charged with developing a software application to identify "pizza factory" locations and creating the software system needed to operate them. In commissioning this project, Dee Livery has said to pull out all the stops. She further stated that the future of PDQ depends on this project. She wants the team to investigate an option to deliver the pizza unbaked and "ready for the oven" in 30 minutes or less or deliver it pre-baked in 45 minutes or less.

(continued)

CASE STUDY—PIZZA DELIVERED QUICKLY (PDQ) BACKGROUND
(continued)

Two software development projects are identified here:

◆ The first is a software system to find pizza factory locations.

◆ The second is a software system to support factory operations.

Clearly, the first is a very complex application. It will require the heavy involvement of a number of PDQ managers. The goal can be clearly defined but even with that the solution will not be at all obvious. The second focuses on routine business functions and should be easily defined. Off-the-shelf commercial software may be a big part of the final solution to support factory operations.

These are obviously very different software development projects requiring very different approaches. The pizza factory location system will be a very sophisticated modeling tool. The requirements, functionality, and features are not at all obvious. Some of the solution can probably be envisioned, but clearly the whole solution is elusive at this early stage. Exactly how it will do modeling is not known at the outset. It will have to be discovered as the development project is under way. The operations system can utilize commercial off-the-shelf (COTS) order-entry software that will have to be enhanced at the front end to direct the order to the closest factory and provide driving directions for delivery, and to provide other fulfillment tasks on the back end. The requirements, functionality, and features of this system may be problematic.

NOTE The first case study, Pleasantown Playground Project, is used primarily in Part I and is therefore reintroduced in Chapter 1, the first chapter of Part I. The second case study, Pizza Delivered Quickly (PDQ), is used primarily in Part II and is therefore reintroduced in Chapter 13, the first chapter of Part II. The text and questions concerning the case studies are also available on the book's Web site at www.wiley.com/go/epm4e.

Who Should Read This Book

Even though my industry experience in information technology is clearly evident, I have tried to write this book to be industry-independent. Whether you are a seasoned project manager professional or a first-time project manager, you will find useful information in this book. I have incorporated a healthy mix of introductory and advanced topics. Much of what I have written comes from my own experiences as project manager, project management consultant, and trainer.

In all cases the material is presented in how-to mode. It was written with the expectation that you use my tools and processes, and I believe that this is the way to make that possible.

Putting It All Together

I have given you my assessment of the project management environment and how it has led me to propose a taxonomy of approaches — Traditional Project Management (TPM), Adaptive Project Framework (APF), and Extreme Project Management (xPM). Based on what I know about the types of projects that the project manager encounters, I believe that TPM, APF, and xPM represent a rich enough taxonomy to handle these very diverse project types.

Traditional Project Management

I think you will find my treatment of Traditional Project Management (TPM) a refreshing change from the usual fare you have been subjected to. In keeping with the format of the second and third editions, you will have plenty of opportunity to practice the tools and techniques that I have used successfully for many years and am now sharing with you. In all of the chapters throughout the book, I close with a "Discussion Questions" section. These questions are thought provoking and should give readers food for thought and offer instructors teaching from this book ample opportunity to engage the class in lively discussion. The questions often set up a situation and ask for a recommended action. There are no right answers. The short, practical exercises; thought-provoking discussion questions; and simulated problems reinforce your practice of newly acquired knowledge. You'll also find a rich source of practice-oriented materials, such as the use of Post-It notes and whiteboards for project planning, many of which are not to be found in other books on the subject.

For those who are familiar with the previous edition, you will note that Part I in this edition contains essentially the entire previous edition. In other words, I have not deleted any material on Traditional Project Management but have actually added new information. In Part I, you will find new or expanded discussions of the project management environment, risk management, procurement management, managing client expectation, estimating cost, organizing the project team, establishing team operating rules, communications management, change management, project status meetings, and critical chain project management.

New in this fourth edition is the addition of selected materials from my recently published book *Effective Software Project Management* (Wiley, 2006). My intention is to expand your thinking into some of the newer realms of project management. I believe that we are seeing a marriage of software development life cycles and project management life cycles. In this book I only want to give you a taste of that evolution. If you are interested in reading and studying more on this topic, consult *Effective Software Project Management*.

Good luck!

What Is a Project?

Things are not always what they seem.
— Phaedrus, Roman writer and fabulist

CHAPTER LEARNING OBJECTIVES

After reading this chapter, you will be able to:

- ◆ **Define a project**
- ◆ **List a project's characteristics**
- ◆ **Distinguish a project from a program, activity, and task**
- ◆ **Understand the three parameters that constrain a project**
- ◆ **Know the importance of defining and using a project classification rule**
- ◆ **Understand the issues around scope creep, hope creep, effort creep, and feature creep**
- ◆ **Be able to explain the project from the perspective of goal and solution clarity or lack of clarity**
- ◆ **Understand the characteristics of the complexity/uncertainty domain that define the project**

Defining a Project

To put projects into perspective, you need a definition — a common starting point. All too often people call any work they have to do a "project." Projects actually have a very specific definition. If a set of tasks or work to be done does not meet the strict definition, then it cannot be called a project. To use the project management techniques presented in this book, you must first have a project.

A *project* is a sequence of unique, complex, and connected activities having one goal or purpose and that must be completed by a specific time, within budget, and according to specification.

This definition tells you quite a bit about a project. To appreciate just what constitutes a project take a look at each part of the definition.

Sequence of Activities

A project comprises a number of activities that must be completed in some specified order, or *sequence*. An *activity* is a defined chunk of work.

CROSS-REF I expand on this informal definition of an activity later in Chapter 4.

The sequence of the activities is based on technical requirements, not on management prerogatives. To determine the sequence, it is helpful to think in terms of inputs and outputs.

- What is needed as input in order to begin working on this activity?
- What activities produce those as output?

The output of one activity or set of activities becomes the input to another activity or set of activities.

Specifying sequence based on resource constraints or statements such as "Pete will work on activity B as soon as he finishes working on activity A" should be avoided because they establish an artificial relationship between activities. What if Pete wasn't available at all? Resource constraints aren't ignored when you actually schedule activities. The decision of what resources to use and when to use them comes later in the project planning process.

Unique Activities

The activities in a project must be *unique*. A project has never happened before, and it will never happen again under the same conditions. Something is always different each time the activities of a project are repeated. Usually the variations are random in nature — for example, a part is delayed, someone is sick, a power failure occurs. These are random events that can happen, but you never are sure of when, how, and with what impact on the schedule. These random variations are the challenge for the project manager.

Complex Activities

The activities that make up the project are not simple, repetitive acts, such as mowing the lawn, painting the house, washing the car, or loading the delivery truck. They are *complex*. For example, designing an intuitive user interface to an application system is a complex activity.

Connected Activities

Connectedness implies that there is a logical or technical relationship between pairs of activities. There is an order to the sequence in which the activities that make up the project must be completed. They are considered connected because the output from one activity is the input to another. For example, you must design the computer program before you can program it.

You could have a list of unconnected activities that must all be complete in order to complete the project. For example, consider painting the interior rooms of a house. With some exceptions, the rooms can be painted in any order. The interior of a house is not completely painted until all its rooms have been painted, but they may be painted in any order. Painting the house is a collection of activities, but it is not considered a project according to the definition.

One Goal

Projects must have a single *goal*, for example, to design an inner-city play-ground for ADC (Aid to Dependent Children) families. However, very large or complex projects may be divided into several *subprojects*, each of which is a project in its own right. This division makes for better management control. For example, subprojects can be defined at the department, division, or geographic level. This artificial decomposition of a complex project into subprojects often simplifies the scheduling of resources and reduces the need for interdepartmental communications while a specific activity is worked on. The downside is that the projects are now interdependent. Even though interdependency adds another layer of complexity and communication, it can be handled.

Specified Time

Projects have a specified *completion date*. This date can be self-imposed by management or externally specified by a customer or government agency. The deadline is beyond the control of anyone working on the project. The project is over on the specified completion date whether or not the project work has been completed.

Within Budget

Projects also have *resource limits*, such as a limited amount of people, money, or machines that are dedicated to the project. While these resources can be adjusted up or down by management, they are considered fixed resources to the project manager. For example, suppose a company has only one Web designer at the moment. That is the fixed resource that is available to project managers. Senior management can change the number of resources, but that luxury is not available to the project manager. If the one Web designer is fully scheduled, the project manager has a resource conflict that he or she cannot resolve.

CROSS-REF I cover resource limits in more detail in Chapter 7.

According to Specification

The customer, or the recipient of the project's deliverables, expects a certain level of functionality and quality from the project. These expectations can be self-imposed, such as the specification of the project completion date, or customer-specified, such as producing the sales report on a weekly basis.

Although the project manager treats the specification as fixed, the reality of the situation is that any number of factors can cause the specification to change. For example, the customer may not have defined the requirements completely, or the business situation may have changed (this happens in long projects). It is unrealistic to expect the specification to remain fixed through the life of the project. Systems specification can and will change, thereby presenting special challenges to the project manager.

CROSS-REF I show you how to handle changing client requirements effectively in Chapter 10.

What Is a Program?

A *program* is a collection of projects. The projects must be completed in a specific order for the program to be considered complete. Because programs comprise multiple projects, they are larger in scope than a single project. For example, the United States government has a space program that includes several projects such as the Challenger project. A construction company contracts a program to build an industrial technology park with several separate projects.

Unlike projects, programs can have many goals. The NASA space program is such that every launch of a new mission includes several dozen projects in the form of scientific experiments. Except for the fact that they are all aboard the same spacecraft, the experiments are independent of one another and together define a program.

Establishing Temporary Program Offices

As the size of the project increases it becomes unwieldy from a management standpoint. A common practice is to establish a temporary program office to manage these large projects. One of my clients uses a team size of 30 as the cutoff point. Whenever the team size is greater than 30, a program office is established. That program office consists of nothing more than the management structure needed for the project. There will be a program director and one or more program administrators as support. The program administrators support the program manager as well as the teams. Even for teams of size 30 there will often be a subteam organization put in place to simplify the management of the team. Each subteam will be led by a subproject manager. When the project is completed, the program office disbands.

Establishing Permanent Program Offices

A permanent program office is established to manage an ongoing and changing portfolio of projects. The portfolio consists of projects that have something in common — for example, all might be funded from the same budget, might be linked to the same goal statement, or might use the same resource pool. The permanent program office, unlike the temporary program office, manages a continuously changing collection of projects.

Project Parameters

Five constraints operate on every project:

- Scope
- Quality
- Cost
- Time
- Resources

These constraints form an interdependent set; a change in one can require a change in another constraint in order to restore the equilibrium of the project.

In this context, the set of five parameters form a system that must remain in balance for the project to be in balance. Because they are so important to the success or failure of the project, I want to discuss them individually.

Scope

Scope is a statement that defines the boundaries of the project. It tells not only what will be done but also what will not be done. In the information systems industry, scope is often referred to as a *functional specification*. In the engineering profession, it is generally called a *statement of work*. Scope may also be referred to as a document of understanding, a scoping statement, a project initiation document, and a project request form. Whatever its name, this document is the foundation for all project work to follow. It is critical that scope be correct. I spend considerable time discussing exactly how that should happen in Chapter 3 where I talk about Conditions of Satisfaction.

Beginning a project on the right foot is important, and so is staying on the right foot. It is no secret that scope can change. You do not know how or when, but it will change. Detecting that change and deciding how to accommodate it in the project plan are major challenges for the project manager.

CROSS-REF Chapter 3 is devoted to defining project scope, and scope management is discussed in Chapter 10.

Quality

Two types of quality are part of every project:

- The first is *product quality*. This refers to the quality of the deliverable from the project. The traditional tools of quality control, discussed in Chapter 2, are used to ensure product quality.

- The second type of quality is *process quality*, which is the quality of the project management process itself. The focus is on how well the project management process works and how can it be improved. Continuous quality improvement and process quality management are the tools used to measure process quality. These are discussed in Chapter 5.

A sound quality management program with processes in place that monitor the work in a project is a good investment. Not only does it contribute to customer satisfaction, it helps organizations use their resources more effectively and efficiently by reducing waste and rework. Quality management is one area that should not be compromised. The payoff is a higher probability of successfully completing the project and satisfying the customer.

Cost

The dollar cost of doing the project is another variable that defines the project. It is best thought of as the budget that has been established for the project. This is particularly important for projects that create deliverables that are sold either commercially or to an external customer.

Cost is a major consideration throughout the project management life cycle. The first consideration occurs at an early and informal stage in the life of a project. The customer can simply offer a figure about equal to what he or she had in mind for the project. Depending on how much thought the customer put into it, the number could be fairly close to or wide of the actual cost for the project. Consultants often encounter situations in which the customer is willing to spend only a certain amount for the work. In these situations, you do what you can with what you have. In more formal situations, the project manager prepares a proposal for the projected work. That proposal includes an estimate (perhaps even a quote) of the total cost of the project. Even if a preliminary figure has been supplied by the project manager, the proposal allows the customer to base his or her go/no-go decision on better estimates.

Time

The customer specifies a time frame or deadline date within which the project must be completed. To a certain extent, cost and time are inversely related to one another. The time a project takes to be completed can be reduced, but costs increase as a result.

Time is an interesting resource. It can't be inventoried. It is consumed whether you use it or not. The objective for the project manager is to use the future time allotted to the project in the most effective and productive ways possible. Future time (time that has not yet occurred) can be a resource to be traded within a project or across projects. Once a project has begun, the prime resource available to the project manager to keep the project on schedule or get it back on schedule is time. A good project manager realizes this and protects the future time resource jealously.

CROSS-REF I cover this topic in more detail in Chapter 5, Chapter 7 (where I talk about scheduling project activities), and Chapter 9.

Resources

Resources are assets, such as people, equipment, physical facilities, or inventory, that have limited availabilities, can be scheduled, or can be leased from an outside party. Some are fixed; others are variable only in the long term. In any case, they are central to the scheduling of project activities and the orderly completion of the project.

For systems development projects, people are the major resource. Another valuable resource for systems projects is the availability of computer processing time (mostly for testing purposes), which can present significant problems to the project manager with regard to project scheduling.

The Scope Triangle

Projects are dynamic systems that must be kept in equilibrium. Not an easy task, as you shall see! Figure 1-1 illustrates the dynamics of the situation.

The geographic area inside the triangle represents the scope and quality of the project. Lines representing time, cost, and resource availability bound scope and quality. Time is the window of time within which the project must be completed. Cost is the dollar budget available to complete the project. Resources are any consumables used on the project. People, equipment availability, and facilities are examples.

> **NOTE** While the accountants will tell you that everything can be reduced to dollars, and they are right, you will separate resources as defined here. They are controllable by the project manager and need to be separately identified for that reason.

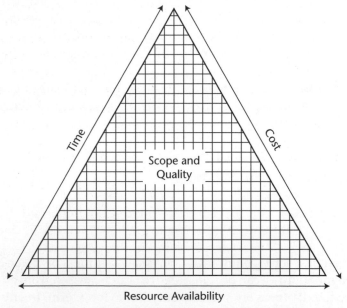

Figure 1-1 The scope triangle

The project plan will have identified the time, cost, and resource availability needed to deliver the scope and quality of a project. In other words, the project is in equilibrium at the completion of the project planning session and approval of the commitment of resources and dollars to the project. That will not last too long, however. Change is waiting around the corner.

The scope triangle offers a number of insights into the changes that can occur in the life of the project. For example, the triangle represents a system in balance before any project work has been done. The sides are long enough to encompass the area generated by the scope and quality statements. Not long after work begins, something is sure to change. Perhaps the customer calls with an additional requirement for a feature that was not envisioned during the planning sessions. Perhaps the market opportunities have changed, and it is necessary to reschedule the deliverables to an earlier date, or a key team member leaves the company and is difficult to replace. Any one of these changes throws the system out of balance.

The project manager controls resource utilization and work schedules. Management controls cost and resource level. The customer controls scope, quality, and delivery dates. These points suggest a hierarchy for the project manager as solutions to accommodate the changes are sought. I return to this topic in greater detail in Chapter 10.

Scope Creep

Scope creep is the term that has come to mean any change in the project that was not in the original plan. Change is constant. To expect otherwise is simply unrealistic. Changes occur for several reasons that have nothing to do with the ability or foresight of the customer or the project manager. Market conditions are dynamic. The competition can introduce or announce an upcoming new version of its product. Your management might decide that getting to the market before the competition is necessary.

Your job as project manager is to figure out how these changes can be accommodated. Tough job, but somebody has to do it! Regardless of how the scope change occurs, it is your job as project manager to figure out how, if at all, you can accommodate the change.

Hope Creep

Hope creep is the result of a project team member's getting behind schedule, reporting that he or she is on schedule, but hoping to get back on schedule by the next report date. Hope creep is a real problem for the project manager. There will be several activity managers within your project, team members who manage a hunk of work. They do not want to give you bad news, so they are prone to tell you that their work is proceeding according to schedule when, in fact, it is not. It is their hope that they will catch up by the next report period, so they mislead you into thinking that they are on schedule. The activity managers hope that they will catch up by completing some work ahead of schedule to make up the slippage. The project manager must be able to verify the accuracy of the status reports received from the team members. This does not mean that the project manager has to check into the details of every status report. Random checks can be used effectively.

Effort Creep

Effort creep is the result of the team member's working but not making progress proportionate to the work expended. Every one of us has worked on a project that always seems to be 95 percent complete no matter how much effort is expended to complete it. Each week the status report records progress, but the amount of work remaining doesn't seem to decrease proportionately. Other than random checks, the only effective thing that the project manager can do is to increase the frequency of status reporting by those team members who seem to suffer from effort creep.

Feature Creep

Closely related to scope creep is *feature creep*. Feature creep results when the team members arbitrarily add features and functions to the deliverable that they think the customer would want to have. The problem is that the customer didn't specify the feature, probably for good reason. If the team member has strong feelings about the need for this new feature, formal change management procedures can be employed.

CROSS-REF The change management process is discussed in Chapter 10.

An example illustrates the point. The programmer is busy coding a particular module in the system. He or she gets an idea that the customer might appreciate having another option included. The systems requirements document does not mention this option. It seems so trivial that the programmer decides to include it rather than go through the lengthy change process.

While this approach may seem rather innocent, look at some possible consequences. First of all, because the feature is not in the system requirements document, it is also not in the acceptance test procedure, the systems documentation, the user documentation, and the user training program. What will happen if something goes wrong with the new option? How will another programmer know what to do? What will happen when the user discovers the option and asks for some modification of it? You can see the consequences of such an innocent attempt to please. The message here is that a formal change request must be filed, and if it is approved, the project plan and all related activities will be appropriately modified.

Applications of the Scope Triangle

There are only a few graphics that I want you to burn into your brain because of their value throughout the entire project life cycle. The scope triangle is one such graphic. It will have at least two major applications for you: as a problem escalation strategy and as a reference for the project impact statement in the scope change process.

Problem Escalation

The scope triangle enables you to ask the question, "Who owns what?" The answer will give you an escalation pathway from project team, to resource manager, to customer. The project team owns how time, budget, and resources are used. Within the policies and practices of the enterprise any of these may be moved within the project to resolve problems that have arisen. In solving a problem the project manager should try to find a solution within the constraints of how the time, budget, and resources are used. They do not need to go outside of their sphere of control.

The next step in the escalation strategy would be for the project manager to appeal to the resource managers for problem resolution. The resource manager owns who gets assigned to a project and also owns any changes to that assignment that may arise.

The final step in the problem escalation strategy is to appeal to the customer. They control the amount of time that has been allocated to the project. They control the amount of money that has been allocated. Finally, they control the scope of the project. Whenever the project manager appeals to the customer, it will be to get an increase in time or budget and some relief from the scope by way of scope reduction or scope release.

Project Impact Statement

The second major application of the scope triangle is as an aid in the preparation of the Project Impact Statement. This is a statement of the alternative ways of accommodating a particular scope change request of the customer. The alternatives are identified by reviewing the scope triangle and proceeding much along the same lines as discussed in the previous paragraph. Chapter 10 has a detailed discussion of the scope change process and the use of the Project Impact Statement.

Project Classifications

In this section, I characterize projects in terms of a detailed set of variables. The value of these variables is used to determine which parts of the project management methodology must be used and which parts are left to the discretion of the project manager to use as he or she sees fit.

Classification by Project Characteristics

Many organizations choose to define a classification of projects based on such project characteristics as these:

- **Risk** — Establish levels of risk (high, medium, low)
- **Business value** — Establish levels (high, medium, low)
- **Length** — Establish several categories (e.g., 3 months, 3 to 6 months, 6 to 12 months, etc.)
- **Complexity** — Establish categories (high, medium, low)
- **Technology used** — Establish several categories (well-established, used somewhat, basic familiarity, unknown, etc.)
- **Number of departments affected** — Establish some categories (one, few, several, all)
- **Cost**

The project profile determines the classification of the project. The classification defines the extent to which the project management methodology is to be used.

I strongly advocate this approach because it adapts the methodology to the project. "One size fits all" does not work in project management. In the final analysis, I defer to the judgment of the project manager. Apart from the parts required by the organization, the project manager should adopt whatever parts of the methodology he or she feels improves his or her ability to help successfully manage the project. Period.

Project types are as follows:

Type A projects. Projects of Type A are the high-business-value, high-complexity projects. They are the most challenging projects the organization undertakes. Type A projects use the latest technology, which, when coupled with high complexity, causes risk to be high also. To maximize the probability of success, the organization requires that these projects utilize all the methods and tools available in their project management methodology. An example of a Type A project is the introduction of a new technology into an existing product that has been very profitable for the company.

Type B projects. Projects of Type B are shorter in length, yet they still are significant projects for the organization. All of the methods and tools in the project management process are probably required. The projects generally have good business value and are technologically challenging. Many product development projects fall in this category.

Type C projects. Projects of Type C are the projects occurring most frequently in an organization. They are short by comparison and use established technology. Many are projects that deal with the infrastructure of the organization. A typical project team consists of five people, the project lasts six months, and the project is based on a less-than-adequate scope statement. Many of the methods and tools are not required for these projects. The project manager uses those tools, which are optional, if he or she sees value in their use.

Type D projects. Projects of Type D just meet the definition of a project and may require only a scope statement and a few scheduling pieces of information. A typical Type D project involves making a minor change in an existing process or procedure or revising a course in the training curriculum.

Table 1-1 gives a hypothetical example of a classification rule.

These four types of projects might use the parts of the methodology shown in Figure 1-2. The figure lists the methods and tools that are either required or optional given the type of project.

Table 1-1 Example Project Classes and Definitions

CLASS	DURA-TION	RISK	COM-PLEXITY	TECH-NOLOGY	LIKELIHOOD OF PROBLEMS
Type A	> 18 months	High	High	Breakthrough	Certain
Type B	9–18 months	Medium	Medium	Current	Likely
Type C	3–9 months	Low	Low	Best of breed	Some
Type D	< 3 months	Very low	Very low	Practical	None

Project Management Process	Project Classification			
	A	B	C	D
Define				
Conditions of Satisfaction	R	R	O	O
Project Overview Statement	R	R	R	R
Approval of Request	R	R	R	R
Plan				
Conduct Planning Session	R	R	O	O
Prepare Project Proposal	R	R	R	R
Approval of Proposal	R	R	R	R
Launch				
Kick-off Meeting	R	R	O	O
Activity Schedule	R	R	R	R
Resource Assignments	R	R	R	O
Statements of Work	R	O	O	O
Monitor/Control				
Status Reporting	R	R	R	R
Project Team Meetings	R	R	O	O
Approval of Deliverables	R	R	R	R
Close				
Post-Implementation Audit	R	R	R	R
Project Notebook	R	R	O	O
	R = Required O = Optional			

Figure 1-2 The use of required and optional parts of the methodology by type of project

Classification by Project Type

There are many situations in which an organization repeats projects that are of the same type. Following are some examples of project types:

- Installing software
- Recruiting and hiring
- Setting up hardware in a field office
- Soliciting, evaluating, and selecting vendors
- Updating a corporate procedure
- Developing application systems

These projects may be repeated several times each year and probably will follow a similar set of steps each time they are done.

CROSS-REF You will look at the ramifications of that repetition when I discuss Work Breakdown Structure templates in Chapter 4.

It is important to note then that you can classify project by type of project. The value in doing this is that each type of project utilizes a specific subset of the project management methodology. For example, projects that involve updating a corporate procedure are far less risky than application systems development projects. Therefore, the risk management aspects of each are very different. Risk management processes will be less important in the corporate procedure project; conversely, they will be very important in the applications development project.

The Changing Face of Projects

NOTE This section is adapted from a similar work by the author, *Effective Software Project Management* (Wiley, 2006).

When I think of the project landscape, I think of it in very simple terms. I see it as a two-dimensional grid like the one shown in Figure 1-3.

The first dimension relates to the goal of the project. The goal is either clearly specified (therefore known) or it is not clearly specified (therefore not known). It's an all-or-nothing situation. The boundary between clear and not clear is more conceptual than actual. The same is true of the second dimension, which relates to the solution or how you expect to reach the goal. That also has two categories. The solution is either clearly specified (and therefore known) or it is not clearly specified (and therefore not known). If you intersect these two dimensions as shown in the figure, then you have defined a four-category classification of projects. This classification is simple but inclusive of every project. That is, every project that ever has been or ever will be must fall into one and only one of these four categories.

Figure 1-3 The project landscape

Why is this important? First and foremost, the characteristics of the deliverables or solution to be developed will play an important role in determining the model that will be used. Each of these quadrants presents the project team with a number of decisions regarding how to go forward. The next sections briefly examine each quadrant and the salient aspects of clarity or lack thereof with respect to goal and solution.

Quadrant 1: Goal and Solution Are Clearly Specified

How could it be any better than to clearly know the goal and the solution? This is the best of all possible worlds, but it is also the least likely to occur in today's fast-paced, continuously changing business world. Projects that fall into this quadrant are familiar to the organization. Perhaps similar projects have been done several times before. There are no surprises. The client has clearly specified the goal and how to reach that goal. Little change is expected. A variety of plan-driven approaches are in use for such projects. The limiting factors in these plan-driven approaches are that they are change-intolerant, are focused on delivering according to time and budget constraints, and rely more on compliance to plan than on delivering business value. The plan is sacred, and conformance to it is the hallmark of a successful project team.

Because of the times we live in, these approaches are rapidly becoming dinosaurs. At least the frequency of their application is diminishing rapidly. They are giving way to a whole new collection of approaches that are more customer-focused and deliver business value rather than adhere to a schedule and budget plan.

In addition to a clearly defined goal and solution, projects that correctly fall into this quadrant have several identifying characteristics as briefly identified below.

Low Complexity

Other than the fact that the project really is simple, this will often be attributable to the fact that the project rings of familiarity. It might be a straightforward application of established business rules and therefore take advantage of artifacts produced in previous projects. To the team it might look like a cut-and-paste exercise. In such cases integration and testing will be the most challenging phases of the project. You will still find situations where the project is complex but still well-defined. However, these are rare.

Well-Understood Technology Infrastructure

A well-understood technology infrastructure is one that is stable and has been the foundation for many projects in the past. That means that the accompanying skills and competencies to work with the technology infrastructure are well-grounded in the teams.

Low Risk

The total environment for projects in this quadrant is that it is known. All that could happen to put the project at risk has occurred in the past, and you have well-tested and well-used mitigation strategies in place. Experience has rooted out all of the mistakes that could be made. The customer is confident that they have done a great job identifying requirements, functions, and features, and they are not likely to change. Except for acts of nature and other unavoidable events, the project is protected from avoidable events. You find few unanticipated risks in development projects in this quadrant.

Experienced and Skilled Developer Teams

Past projects have been good training grounds for the teams. They have had opportunities to learn or to enhance their skills and competencies.

Quadrant 2: Goal Is Clearly Specified but Solution Is Not

You have a host of incremental, iterative, and adaptive approaches to project management that can be used when the goal is clearly defined but how to reach the goal — the solution — is not. As you give some thought to where your projects would fall in this landscape, consider the possibility that many if not most of them are these types of projects. If that is the case, shouldn't you also be considering using an approach to managing these projects that accommodates the goal and solution characteristics of the project rather than trying to force-fit some other approach that was designed for projects with much different characteristics?

I contend that the adaptive and iterative class of projects is continuously growing. I make it a practice at all "rubber chicken" dinner presentations to ask about the frequency with which the attendees encounter Quadrant 2 projects. With very small variance they say that at least 75 percent of all their projects are Quadrant 2 projects. Many of them try to adapt Quadrant 1 approaches to Quadrant 2 projects and meet with very little success. The results have ranged from mediocre success to outright failure. Quadrant 2 projects present a different challenge and need a different approach. For years I have advocated that the approach to the project must be driven by the characteristics of the project. To reverse the order is to court disaster.

Quadrant 3: Goal and Solution Are Not Clearly Specified

Quadrant 3 extends to the remotest boundaries of project types. Quadrant 3 projects are those projects whose goal and solution cannot be clearly defined. What little planning is done is done just in time, and the project proceeds through several iterations until it converges on an acceptable goal and solution. If instead there isn't any prospect of convergence, the customer might pull the plug and cancel the project at any time and look for alternative approaches.

Quadrant 4: Goal Is Not Clearly Specified but the Solution Is

The fourth category represents projects whose goal is not known but whose solution is. This is an impossible situation. It would be equivalent to solutions that go looking for problems. Nevertheless, we all have had experiences working with professional services organizations that practice such approaches. They advocate a one-size-fits-all approach, which has never shown to be very successful. I have always discouraged a one-size-fits-all approach with my clients. Most see the wisdom in adopting this position.

The Complexity/Uncertainty Domain of Projects

Each quadrant of the project landscape has different profiles when it comes to risk, team, communications, customer involvement, specification, change, business value, and documentation. This section examines the changing profile of each domain as you move from quadrant to quadrant.

Complexity and uncertainty are positively correlated with one another. As projects become more complex, they become more uncertain. That follows from at least four other relationships, as commented on in the next four sections.

In the Quadrant 1 model you know where you are going, and you know precisely how you are going to get there. It's all in the requirements, functionality, and features. Your plan reflects all of the work, the schedule, and the resources that will get you there. No complexity here. As soon as you move away from a clearly specified solution and are in Quadrant 2, the world is no longer as kind to you as it was while you were in Quadrant 1. The minute you have uncertainty anywhere in the project, complexity increases. You have to devise a plan to fill in the missing pieces. There will be some added risk — you might not find the missing piece, or when you do, you find that it doesn't fit in with what you already have built — go back two steps, undo some previous work, and do the required rework. The plan changes. The schedule changes. A lot of the effort spent earlier on developing a detailed plan has gone to waste. By circumstance it has become non-value-added work. If you had only known.

As less and less of the solution is known, the realities of non-value-added work becomes more and more a factor. Time has been wasted. Quadrant 2 models are better equipped to handle this uncertainty and the complexity that results from it. The models are built on the assumption that the solution has to be discovered. Planning becomes less of a one-time task done at the outset to a just-in-time task done as late as possible. You have less and less reliance on a plan and more reliance on the tacit knowledge of the team. That doesn't reduce the complexity, but it does accommodate it. So even though complexity increases as you move from Quadrant 1 to 2 to 3, you have a way to deal with it for the betterment of your customer and your sanity as a project manager.

Requirements

As project complexity increases, the likelihood of nailing requirements decreases. This follows logically from the fact that the human brain can retain in memory only about seven pieces of information at a time. The dimensions of complexity are likely to far exceed that constraint. In a complex product the extent of the number of requirements, functionality, and features can be staggering. Some will conflict with each other. Some will be redundant. Some will be missing. Many of these might not become obvious until well into the design, development, and even integration-testing tasks.

Flexibility

As project complexity increases so does the need for process flexibility. Increased complexity brings with it the need to be creative and adaptive. Neither is comfortable in the company of rigid processes. Quadrant 2 projects are easily compromised by being deluged with process, procedure, documentation, and meetings. Many of these are unrelated to a results-driven approach. They are the relics of plan-driven approaches. Along with the need for increased flexibility in Quadrant 2 and 3 projects is the need for increased adaptability. Companies that are undergoing a change of approach that recognizes the need to support not just Quadrant 1 projects but also Quadrant 2 projects are faced with a significant and different cultural and business change. For one, the business rules and rules of the project engagement will radically change. Expect resistance.

Flexibility here refers to the project management process. If you are using a one-size-fits-all approach, you have no flexibility. The process is the process is the process. Not a very comforting situation if the process gets in the way of common sense behaviors and compromises your ability to deliver value to your customer. Wouldn't you rather be following a strategy that allows you to adapt to the changing situations?

Quadrant 1 projects generally follow a traditional project management methodology. The plan is developed along with a schedule of deliverables and other milestone events. A formal change management process is part of the game plan. Progress against the planned schedule is tracked, and corrective actions are put in place to restore control over schedule and budget. A nice neat package isn't it? All is well until the process gets in the way of product development. For example, if the business situation and priorities change and result in a flurry of scope change requests to accommodate the new business climate, then an inordinate amount of time is then spent processing change requests at the expense of doing value-added work. The schedule slips beyond the point of recovery. The project plan, having changed several times, becomes a contrived mess. Whatever integrity there was in the initial plan and schedule is now lost among the changes.

Quadrant 2 is altogether different. Project management is really nothing more than organized common sense, so when the process you are using gets in the way, you adapt. The process is changed to maintain focus on doing what makes sense to protect the creation of business value. Unlike Quadrant 1 processes, Quadrant 2 processes expect and embrace change as a way to a better solution and as a way to maximize business value within time and budget constraints. That means choosing and continually changing the approach to increase the business value that will result from the project. Realize that to some extent scope is a variable in these types of approaches.

Quadrant 3 projects are even more dependent upon flexible approaches. Learning and discovery take place throughout the project, and the team and customer must adjust how they are approaching the project at a moment's notice.

Adaptability

The less certain you are of project requirements, functionality, and features, the more need you have to be adaptable with respect to process and procedure. Adaptability is directly related to the extent to which the team members are empowered to act. The ability of the team to adapt increases as empowerment becomes more pervasive. Remember to make it possible for the team members to be productive, and stay out of their way. Don't encumber the team members with the need to get sign-offs that have nothing to do with delivering business value. Pick them carefully and trust them to act in the best interest of the customer.

Change

As complexity increases so does the frequency and need to receive and process change requests. A plan-driven project is not designed to effectively respond to change. Change upsets the order of things as some or all of the project plan is affected. Resource schedules are compromised. The more that change has to be dealt with, the more time is spent processing and evaluating the changes. That time is lost to the project. It should have been spent on value-added work. Instead it was spent processing change requests.

You spend so much time developing your project plan for a Quadrant 1 project that the last thing you want is to have to change it, but that is the reality in Quadrant 1 projects. Scope change always seems to add more work. Did you ever receive a scope change request from your customer that asked you to take something out? Not too likely. The reality is that the customer discovers something else they should have asked for in the solution. They didn't realize that or know that at the time. That leads to more work, not less. The call to action is clear — choose Quadrant 1 models when specifications are as stable as can be. The architects of the Quadrant 2 and 3 models knew this and so designed approaches that expected change and were ready to accommodate it.

Risk

Risk increases as you move from Quadrant 1 to 2 to 3. In Quadrant 1 you clearly know the goal and the solution and can build a definitive plan for getting there. The exposure to risks associated with product failure is low. The focus can then shift to process failure. A list of candidate risk drivers would have been compiled over past similar projects. Their likelihood, impact, and the appropriate mitigations are known and documented. Like a good athlete, you have anticipated what might happen and know how to act if it does.

As the project takes on the characteristics of Quadrant 2, two forces come into play. First, the project management approach becomes more flexible and lighter. The process burden lessens as more attention is placed on delivering business value than on conformance to a plan. At the same time the product risk increases. Risk increases in relation to the extent to which the solution is not known. On balance that means more effort should be placed on risk management as the project moves through Quadrant 2 and looks more like a Quadrant 3 project. You will have less experience with these risks because they are specific to the product being developed. In Quadrant 3, risk is the highest because you are in a research and development environment. Process risk is almost nonexistent because the ultimate in flexibility has been reached in this quadrant, but product risk is extremely high. You will have numerous product failures because of the highly speculative nature of Quadrant 3 projects, but that is okay. Those failures are expected to occur. Each product failure gets you that much closer to a functional solution, if such solution can be found within the operative time and budget constraints. At worst those failures eliminate one or more paths of investigation and so narrow the range of possible solutions.

Team Cohesiveness

In Quadrant 1, the successful team doesn't really have to be a team at all. You assemble a group of specialists and assign each to their respective tasks at the appropriate times. Period. The plan is sacred, and the plan guides them through their task. It tells them what they need to do, when they need to do it, and how they know they have finished their task. They are a group of specialists. They each know their discipline and are brought to the team to apply their discipline to a set of specific tasks. When they have met their obligation, they often leave the team to return later if needed. Period.

The situation quickly changes when the project is a Quadrant 2 or 3 project. First of all, you have a gradual shift of the team make-up from a team of specialists to a team of generalists. The team takes on more of the characteristics of a self-directed team. They become self-sufficient and self-directing as the project moves from a Quadrant 2 to a Quadrant 3 project. Quadrant 1 teams are not co-located. They don't have to be. Quadrant 2 and 3 teams are co-located. Research has shown that co-location adds significantly to the successful completion of the project.

Communications

Lack of timely and clear people-to-people communications has been shown to be the single most frequent reason for project failure. In this discussion I include both written and verbal communications media in making that statement. As you move in the direction of increased complexity and heightened uncertainty, communication requirements increase and change. When complexity and uncertainty are low, the predominant form of communications is written. Status reports, change requests, meeting minutes, issues reporting, problem resolution, project plan updates, and other written reports are commonplace. As uncertainty and complexity increase, written communications give way to verbal communication. The burden of plan-driven approaches is lightened, and the communications requirements of value-driven approaches take over.

Value-driven communications approaches are the derivatives of meaningful customer involvement, where discussions generate status updates and plans going forward. Because projects that are high in complexity and uncertainty depend on frequent change, they have a low tolerance of written communications. In these project situations, the preparing, distributing, reading, and responding to written communications is viewed as non-value-added work. It is to be avoided, and the energy spent on value-added work.

Customer Involvement

Consider for a moment a project from your experience in which you were most certain of the goal and the solution. You would probably be willing to bet your first-born child that you had nailed requirements and that they would not change. Yes, that type of project might just be a pipe dream but give me the benefit of the doubt. For such a project you might ask: Why do I need to have my customer involved except for the ceremonial sign-offs at milestone events? A fair question, and ideally you wouldn't need their involvement. How about a project at the other extreme — where the goal is very elusive and no solution would seem to be in sight? In such cases the complete involvement of the customer, as a team member perhaps, would be indispensable. What I have painted here are the extreme cases in Quadrant 1 and Quadrant 3.

Quadrant 1 projects are team-driven projects. Customer involvement is usually limited to clarifying questions as they arise and giving sign-offs and approvals at the appropriate stages of the project life cycle. It would be accurate to say that customer involvement in Quadrant 1 projects is reactive and passive. But all that changes as you move into Quadrant 2 projects. Now the customer must take a more active role than they did in Quadrant 1 projects. For Quadrant 3 projects, meaningful customer involvement is essential. In fact, the customer should take on a proactive role. The project goes nowhere without that level of commitment from the customer.

Finding the solution to a project is not an individual effort. In Quadrant 1 the project team under the leadership of the project manager is charged with finding the missing parts of the solution. In some cases the customer is passively involved, but for the most part the team solves the problem. The willingness of the customer to even get passively involved depends on how you have dealt with them so far in the project. If you bothered to include them in the planning of the project, they might have some sympathy and help you out. But don't count on it. Beginning with Quadrant 2 and extending through Quadrant 3, you find more and more reliance on meaningful customer involvement. In your effort to maintain a customer focus and deliver business value you are dealing with a business problem, not a technology problem. You have to find a business solution. Who is better equipped to help than the customer? After all, you are dealing with their part of the business. Shouldn't they be the best source of help and partnership in finding the solution? This involvement is so critical that without it you have no chance of being successful with Quadrant 3 projects.

Meaningful customer involvement can be a daunting task for at least the three reasons cited below.

The Customer's Comfort Zone

The customer has been trained ever since the 1950s to take up a passive role and let the technical gurus do their job. That training went well, and now you have to retrain them. In many instances their role was more ceremonial than formal. They didn't understand what they were approving but had no recourse but to sign. The sign-off at milestone events was often a formality because the customer didn't understand the techie-talk, was afraid not to sign-off because of the threat of further delays, and didn't know enough about development to know when to ask questions and when to push back. Now you are asking them to step into a new interactive role and become meaningfully engaged in the project life cycle. Many are not poised to take up that responsibility, one that is ratcheted up a notch as the project moves further into Quadrant 2 toward Quadrant 3, with less and less known about the solution. The project team is faced with a critical success factor of gaining meaningful customer involvement throughout the project. In Quadrant 3 their involvement is even more proactive and engaging. Quadrant 3 projects require that the customer take a co-leadership role with the project manager to keep the project moving forward and adjusted in the direction of increasing business value.

At the same time, the customer's comfort zone is growing. They have become smarter. It is not unusual to find customers who were once more technically involved. They go to conferences where presentations often include technical aspects. They know how to push back. They know what it takes to build solutions. They've built some themselves using spreadsheet packages and other applications tools. That knowledge has two possible consequences: These customers can be supportive or they can be obstacles to progress.

Ownership by the Customer

Establishing ownership by the customer of the project product and process is critical. I often ensure that ownership by organizing the project team around co-managers — one from the provider side and one from the customer side. These two individuals are equally responsible for the success of the project. That places a vested interest squarely on the shoulders of the customer manager. This sounds really good, but it is not easily done. I can hear my customers saying, "This is a technology project, and I don't know anything about technology. How can I act in a managerial capacity?" The answer is simple, and it goes something like this, "True, you don't have a grasp of the technology involved, but that is a minor point. Your real value to this endeavor is keeping the business focus constantly in front of the team. You can bring that dimension to the team far better than any one of the technical people on the team. You will be an indispensable partner in every decision situation faced in this project."

This ownership is so important that I have postponed starting customer engagements because the customer can't send a spokesperson to the planning meeting. When they do, you have to be careful that they don't send you a weak representative who merely wasn't busy at the time or who doesn't really understand the business context of the project. Maybe there's a reason that person wasn't busy.

Customer Sign-Off

This is often the most anxiety-filled task that you ever ask of your customer. Some customers think that they are signing their lives away when they approve a document or a deliverable. You are going to have to dispel that perception. This world is one of constant change, high speed, and high risk. Given that, how could anyone reasonably expect that what works today will work tomorrow? Today's needs might not even appear on the radar screen next week. No matter how certain you are that you have nailed the requirements, you wouldn't expect them to remain static for the length of the project. It simply won't happen. That means that you had better anticipate change as a way of life in almost every project.

Specification

What does this mean? Simply put it advises you that the choice of project management approach should be based on an understanding of the confidence you have that the specifications have been completely and clearly defined and documented and that scope change requests will not arise from any shortcomings in the specifications documents. As that specification certainty diminishes, your best options lie in the iterative strategies that populate Quadrant 2 — those that allow the solution to become more specific and complete as the project commences or that allow you to discover the solution as the project commences. Finally, if you have very little confidence that you have clearly and completely documented the specifications, then your choice of a project management approach takes on the flavor of the research and development strategies that populate Quadrant 3.

The project management approaches that require a high level of specification certainty tend to be change intolerant. Consider the situation where a significant change request comes early in the project life cycle. That could render much of the planning work obsolete. A large part of it will have to be redone. That contributes to the non-value-added work expenditure of the approach you have chosen. If changes like that are to be expected, an approach that is more tolerant and supportive of change should be chosen. The non-value-added work could have been greatly diminished or removed all together.

If you look inside the specifications document, you can find more detailed information that might help you decide on the best project management approach. Specifications are composed of requirements, functions, and features. These array themselves in a hierarchical structure much like the one shown in Figure 1-4.

Uncertainty at the requirements level has more impact on choice of development approach than does uncertainty at the functionality level, which has more impact than that at the features level. Despite all of these efforts, you still have changes on any of those fronts that could significantly impact your best efforts. That's life.

Change

The less you know about requirements, functionality, and features, the more you have to expect change. In Quadrant 1 you know everything there is to know about requirements, functionality, and features for this project. The assumption is that there will be little or no internal forces for change during the project. Externally, however, that is not the case. Actions of competitors, market forces, and technological advances can cause change, but that is present in every project and can only be expected. The best the enterprise can do is maintain a position of flexibility in the face of such unpredictable but certain events.

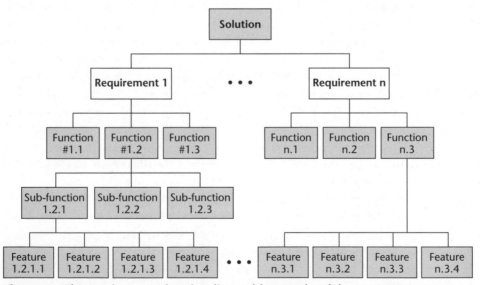

Figure 1-4 The requirements, functionality, and features breakdown structure

Quadrant 2 is a different story altogether. Any change in this quadrant comes about through the normal learning process that takes place in any Quadrant 2 project. When the customer has the opportunity to examine and experiment with a partial solution, they will invariably come back to the project team with suggestions for other requirements, functionality, and features that should be part of the solution. These suggestions can be put into one of two categories: "wants" or "needs."

Wants might be little more than the result of a steak appetite on a baloney budget. It is up to the project manager to help the customer defend their want as a true need and hence get it integrated into the solution. If they fail to do that, their suggestion should be relegated to a wish list. Wish lists are seldom revisited. If, conversely, they demonstrate its value and hence transfer it to a true need, it is up to the project manager to accommodate that new requirement, functionality, or feature into the solution set. It might have to be prioritized in the list of all needs.

In Quadrant 3 you have a further reliance on change to affect a good business-valued product. In fact, Quadrant 3 projects require change in order to have any chance of finding a successful solution. Change is the only vehicle that will lead to a solution.

Business Value

This domain would seem to be trivial. After all, aren't all projects designed to deliver business value? These projects were commissioned based on the business value they would return to the enterprise. This is all true. However, traditional project approaches focus on meeting the plan-driven parameters: time, cost, scope. When originally proposed, the business climate was such that the proposed solution was the best that could be had. In a static world that condition would hold. Unfortunately the business world is not static, and the needs of the customer aren't either. Bottom line: What will deliver business value is a moving target. Quadrant 1 development projects aren't equipped with the right stuff to deliver business value.

It follows then that Quadrant 1 projects deliver the least business value and that business value increases as you move from Quadrant 1 to Quadrant 2 to Quadrant 3. At the same time, however, as you move from quadrant to quadrant, risk increases, which means that higher-valued projects need to be commissioned as you move across the quadrants. Remember that the expected business value of a project is the product of (1-risk) and value. Risk here is expressed as the probability of failure, and the probability of success is therefore (1-risk).

**CASE STUDY — PLEASANTOWN PLAYGROUND
PROJECT BACKGROUND**

Pleasantown is a southern California city of 80,000 residents located just outside Los Angeles. Playground space has been at a premium for many years, and many families have had no choice but to let their children play in the neighborhood streets. Because of minor accidents and, recently, one near miss, concerned parents are ready to take action to rectify the situation.

There is a vacant parcel of city-owned land measuring 200' by 200'. It has been in disrepair for over 30 years, accumulating old tires, discarded appliances, broken bottles, and all sorts of trash. You have been informed that it is available to be turned into a playground. Because of significant pressure by various citizen groups, the city entertained proposals for converting the parcel into usable space for children. You and a group of six concerned neighbors submitted a proposal that was accepted by the city. According to the terms of the proposal, your group of seven will head up a fundraiser, recruit volunteers, and build the playground. The city expects the project to be finished by September 1. As part of the terms and conditions, your group has agreed that the city can dedicate the new facility with a gala event that they will plan and hold on City Founders Day on September 1. Because it is now April 1, you have a very tight schedule.

In addition to the time constraint, you have tentatively established the budget at $30,000 because that is approximately the most you can hope to raise through activities such as car washes, bake sales, and so on. In addition, you hope to get local merchants to donate materials and other non-cash resources.

What does this mean? Simple: Whatever project management approach you adopt for the project, it must be one that allows redirection as business conditions change. The more uncertainty present in the project, the more you need to be able to redirect to take advantage of changing conditions and opportunities.

As projects move through Quadrants 1 to 2 to 3, they become more customer-facing. The focus changes from conformance to plan to delivery of business value. The Quadrant 1 models focus on conformance to plan. If they also happen to deliver maximum business value it would be more the result of an accident than the result of a clairvoyant project plan. The focus on delivery of business value is apparent in all of the Quadrant 2 and 3 models. It is designed into the models.

Putting It All Together

You now should know that I advocate a very specific definition of a project. If a collection of work is to be called a project, it must meet the definition. Once you know that you have a project, it will be subjected to a specific set of requirements regarding its management. That is the topic of the next chapter.

Discussion Questions

1. Suppose the scope triangle were modified as follows: Resource Availability occupies the center. The three sides are Scope, Cost, and Schedule. Interpret this triangle as if it were a system in balance. What is likely to happen when a specific resource on your project is concurrently allocated to more and more projects? As project manager, how would you deal with these situations? Be specific.

2. Where would you be able to bring about cost savings as a program manager for a company? Discuss these using the standard project constraints.

3. Discuss ways in which scope creep occurred on projects with which you have been associated. Was the project manager able to reverse scope creep? Is it possible to reverse scope creep? Defend your yes or no answer.

4. Identify projects from your experiences that you would classify as Q1, Q2, and Q3 projects. Explain your choices.

Traditional, Adaptive, Extreme: A Dynamic Project Management Landscape

*A manager . . . sets objectives, . . . organizes, . . . motivates, . . .
communicates, . . . measures, . . . and develops people. Every manager
does these things — knowingly or not. A manager may do them
well or may do them wretchedly but always does them.*

— Peter Drucker

CHAPTER LEARNING OBJECTIVES

After reading this chapter, you will be able to:

◆ Understand the relationship between people management and project management

◆ Appreciate the importance of project planning

◆ Recognize the characteristics of projects that fail

◆ Understand the five phases of the traditional project management life cycle

◆ See how the project plan is a model

◆ Explain several variations to traditional project management

◆ Use the tools of quality management as they apply to improving the process of traditional project management

◆ Understand how risk management can be applied to the steps that describe the traditional project management process

◆ Use several methods to assess risk on a project

◆ Plan for and mitigate risk

◆ Understand the procurement process

(continued)

CHAPTER LEARNING OBJECTIVES

◆ Explain the relationship between traditional project management and the systems development life cycle

◆ Explain the relationship between traditional project management and the new product development life cycle

◆ Appreciate the significance of the project pain curve

◆ Understand risk and its relationship to project failure

Principles of Project Management

When you think of the principles of management, you usually associate them with the management of people. The management of people includes defining what the business unit will do, planning for the number and type of staff who will do it, organizing the staff, monitoring their performance of the tasks assigned them, and finally bringing a close to their efforts. Those same principles also apply to projects.

Project management is a method and a set of techniques based on the accepted principles of management used for planning, estimating, and controlling work activities to reach a desired end result on time — within budget and according to specification.

Over the years that I have consulted and offered training in Traditional Project Management (TPM), I have observed a number of project management methodologies that, on first look, seem to differ from one another. On closer examination, I actually found that a number of underlying principles are present in the more successful methodologies. From them, I fashioned a TPM life cycle that was first published by Weiss and Wysocki.[1]

Since that publication, I continue to compare this life cycle with client methodologies. The results confirm my assumptions that features reoccur in successful methodologies. More recently, the Project Management Institute published its Project Management Body of Knowledge (PMBOK), which has an underlying life cycle that is remarkably similar to the one I adopted in my consulting practice. The one I present in this book parallels PMBOK. If your organization has a methodology in place, compare it to the model given here. If you map your methodology to this life cycle, you may discover that you already do bits and pieces of TPM without realizing it. You may not be referring to each phase by the same names as I do, but the actions in that phase are probably what you've been doing all these years. Take comfort, for TPM can be

---

[1]Joseph W. Weiss and Robert K. Wysocki, *5-Phase Project Management: A Practical Planning and Implementation Guide* (Reading, Mass.: Perseus Books, 1992), ISBN 0-201-56316-9.

defined as nothing more than organized common sense. In fact, if it were not common sense, I would have a difficult time gaining any converts!

Figure 2-1 shows the TPM life cycle. The following sections walk you through its five phases. Please refer to this figure as you read the following sections.

Figure 2-1 The TPM life cycle

Defining

The first phase of the TPM life cycle is the Defining Phase. This phase is the one most often given the least attention. The Defining Phase scopes the project. In collaboration with the customer, the problem and solution are identified and documented. What will be produced (the deliverables) is also defined and clearly documented.

One of the first tasks for project managers is to define the work that needs to be done in their area of responsibility. Exactly the same task applies to people management. In project management, however, the Defining Phase is very formal, whereas in people management it can often be informal.

Every project has one goal: an agreement between the requestor and the project manager about the deliverable — what is to be accomplished in the project. The goal tells the project developers where they are going so that when the project is completed they know it. Ideally, the Defining Phase begins with an exchange of information between a requestor and a provider (usually the project manager). The information exchange usually involves a conversation between the two parties to assure one another that both the request and the response, in the form of deliverables, are clearly understood.

In the TPM life cycle, the goal is bounded by a number of objective statements. These objective statements clarify the fuzziness of the goal statement. Taken as a pair, the goal and objective statements define the project. They are the framework within which the entire project planning process can be successfully conducted.

After the scope is complete, it is documented in the form of the Project Overview Statement (POS). The POS is a brief document (usually one page) that provides, in the language of the business, a high-level description of the project.

The POS, or some form of it, is in wide use. I can trace the early history of the POS back to Texas Instruments in the early 1960s. TI used the POS to enable anyone in the organization to submit an idea for a project. It was the company's version of a project initiation form. The POS is also referred to as a document of understanding, a scope statement, an initial project definition, and a statement of work. In my consulting practice, I have encountered organizations that require risk analysis, cost/benefit analysis, return on investment calculations, internal rate of return estimates, and break-even analysis as attachments to the POS. This information is used to determine whether the project should go forward to the detailed planning phase. If the project, as described in the POS, is approved, it moves to the detailed planning phase.

The Defining Phase sets the scope of the project. It forms the basis for deciding whether a particular function or feature is within the scope of the project.

Remember that even the best of intentions to define project scope will fall short of the mark. The scope of the project can change for a variety of reasons, which are investigated in Chapter 10 — sometimes far more frequently than the project manager would prefer. As mentioned in the previous chapter, these changes are called scope creep; they are a way of life in today's organizations. Scope creep can be the bane of the project manager if it is not dealt with effectively. Scope creep occurs for a variety of reasons, from something the client forgot to include in the business requirements document to a change in business priorities that must be reflected in the project.

The project manager must respond to scope creep by documenting the alternative courses of action and their respective consequences on the project plan. A good project manager will have a formal change management process in place to address scope creep. I have much more to say on this topic in Chapter 10.

Defining the project includes the following artifacts, which are listed and briefly described in the following sections.

State the Problem/Opportunity

The project is initially bounded by either a problem that the enterprise recognizes as important to be solved or an untapped business opportunity that is on the enterprise's radar screen. The important thing to remember here is that this is not a statement that needs to be defended or explained. Everyone in the management chain will recognize it and accept it as fact.

Establish the Project Goal

This part answers the question regarding what this project will do in responding to the problem or opportunity statement. It may propose to resolve the entire problem or opportunity or only some part of it.

Define the Project Objectives

To further clarify the project boundaries of the goal, a number of objective statements should be proposed.

Identify the Success Criteria

These are quantitative metrics with specific values provided as a definition of success. They must be measurable and not subject to debate. Ultimately, the enterprise will clearly see that they have been met or not met.

List Assumptions, Risks, and Obstacles

These are high-level statements that will affect the success of the project. See Chapter 3 for a more detailed discussion of the Defining Phase and the Project Overview Statement.

Planning

The second phase of the TPM life cycle is to develop the project plan. In this phase, the details about the project are determined. This may be an exercise for one or two individuals, but it often takes place in a formal planning session attended by those who will have an affect on or be affected by the project.

Planning — or rather, effective planning — is painful. For many people, planning doesn't seem like real work. Because projects are always behind schedule, you are tempted to skip planning so that you can get down to the real work of the project. Experience has shown that good planning can actually decrease the time required to complete a project, even taking the planning time into account. Planning reduces risk, and in my experience it can increase productivity by as much as 50 percent. I find it interesting that project teams do not have time to plan, but they do have time to repeat work. What insanity!

Planning the project includes the artifacts listed and briefly described in the sections that follow. The details are found in Chapters 4–8.

Identify Project Activities

To identify the work of the project a hierarchical decomposition is created. It defines the work down to a sufficient level of detail so that estimates of time, cost, and resource requirements can be made. The artifact is called the Work Breakdown Structure (WBS). Chapter 4 provides a detailed discussion about how the WBS is created.

Estimate Activity Duration

Duration is the estimated amount of time that will elapse from the start to the end of the work needed to complete a given activity. Six estimation techniques are discussed in Chapter 5.

Determine Resource Requirements

You may be tempted to say something like "Harry is the best software developer we have. We need to get Harry to work on this activity." Sooner or later that may be an appropriate request, but for now identify the resource only by position title — Software Developer. How many of each position title will you need for each activity? Chapter 5 has more details on estimating resource requirements.

Construct/Analyze the Project Network

Now it's time to build the schedule. This includes dependency relationships between activities, and these have to be established first. Then the sequence of activities can be established and a schedule obtained. That schedule may not meet stated deadlines and will likely have to be adjusted. Chapter 6 provides the necessary details for building and analyzing the project network.

Prepare the Project Proposal

The deliverable from the planning session is the project proposal. This document includes the following:

- A detailed description of each work activity
- The resources required to complete the activity
- The scheduled start and end date of each activity
- The estimated cost and completion date of the project

In some organizations there can be any number of attachments, such as feasibility studies, environmental impact statements, or best-of-breed analysis. The project plan is a description of the events to come. In that sense, it is a model of the project. As events occur in the project, the model is affected and can change to describe how future events in the project are likely to occur. Because the project plan is a model, you can use it to test alternative strategies for redirecting future events. As project work begins, the nature of the project changes — sometimes radically. Activities can get behind or ahead of schedule, and team members can be reassigned, leave the company, or get sick. Market situations can change, rendering all or some of the project objectives obsolete. These events can occur one at a time or in clumps, and the project manager must be ready to analyze, decide, and act. You should already have an appreciation for the complexity of the project plan and work. There are, in fact, several dimensions to consider when trying to formulate a going-forward strategy. Here are just a few:

- If a project activity finishes earlier or later than the schedule date, can the resource schedule for later activities be adjusted accordingly?

- If one or more project activities finish late, can other resources assigned to the project be reallocated to restore the project to its original schedule?

- How can the project manager simultaneously compress the project schedule while avoiding unresolvable resource scheduling conflicts?

- What resources can be reallocated from one project to another without adversely affecting each project's schedule?

Any one of these situations requiring a decision involves a number of interdependent variables. It is unlikely that any project manager could process these variables and all of the possible variations without the aid of a computer-based project model and the supporting software, such as Microsoft Project, ABT Workbench, Open Plan, or any one of several other software packages.

Once the project proposal is approved, the project enters the Launch Phase of the TPM life cycle, in which the final details of the work schedule are completed and project work begins.

Launching

The third phase of the TPM life cycle is to launch the plan. In this phase, the project team is specified. It is important to eliminate the notion that an individual is solely responsible for the success (or failure) of the project. It is true that you can point to examples in which the efforts of an individual brought the project to successful completion, but these cases are rare. Although some specific team members could have been identified earlier in the life cycle, additional members are identified during this stage. In contemporary organizations, the project team is often cross-functional and can span other organizational boundaries.

Launching the project includes the artifacts listed and briefly described in the sections that follow. The details can be found in Chapter 8.

Recruit and Organize the Project Team

It's time to replace the position titles in the project plan with actual people. If it still makes sense to have Harry, the best software developer on your team, then go for it. There is no guarantee, of course, that Harry is available when you need him. There will probably be a number of negotiations between you and the resource managers before you have your team assembled.

Establish Team Operating Rules

Sometimes early in the Launch Phase you can bring your team together for the first time. They may not be a team but only a group of people who have been assigned to the project. It's your job as project manager to turn them into a team. The better the job you do at this the better will be your chances of success. The team will help draft the rules of the engagement. How will they function together? Such areas as meetings (frequency, length, when, and where are some of the meeting parameters), problem solving, conflict resolution, and the change process are some of the rules that need to be established and agreed to by everyone.

Level Project Resources

The project schedule that was built around position titles will probably not work now that real people are in those positions. Because they will have other commitments, the schedule must be adjusted to fit those commitments.

Document Work Packages

Several activities are critical to completing a project successfully. To protect the project against any adverse effects on these activities, the project manager must request that a work package be written for them. The work package is nothing more than a primitive project plan, written by the person in charge of completing the activity, that details how the activity will be done.

Monitoring and Controlling

As soon as project work commences, the project enters the Monitoring Phase. A number of project status reports will have been defined in the previous phase; these are now used to monitor the project's progress. Some of these reports are used only by the project team, while others are distributed to management and the customer.

Change management is a big part of this phase, and procedures will have been installed as part of the Launch Phase to process change requests. Change requests will always cause some amount of project replanning. When the requests are received, the feedback loop is activated, and the project manager revisits the project plan to identify ways to accommodate the change request. Problems also can occur as work finishes ahead of or behind schedule. A problem-escalation procedure will have been defined during the Launch Phase to handle these situations.

Monitoring and controlling the project includes the artifacts listed and briefly discussed in the sections that follow. The details can be found in Chapter 10.

Establish Progress Reporting System

Most reporting systems establish a weekly status update from the team members who have an activity open for work that week. Open for work means that the start date has been passed and the activity is not yet complete. The update documents what has been done, what remains to be done, and most important, how long it will take to complete the activity. This is the basic information that the project manager will use to determine the project schedule going forward. Any slippages are noted and the necessary corrective action put in place to restore the schedule to the plan.

Install Change Control Tools/Process

This ranges from a very informal to a very formal process as the size and complexity of the project increases. Basically, an intake function does a preliminary evaluation and determination of how to proceed with the request. The request is then analyzed and alternative fulfillment options are identified and perhaps prioritized. A decision must be made regarding how to go forward, and the necessary project plan changes are implemented.

Define Problem-Escalation Process

Problem escalation is inevitable. The hierarchy is to first look within the project team for a resolution. If such a resolution is not found, the problem is escalated to the resource manager level and an attempt at resolution is sought there. Failing that, the problem is escalated to the customer for resolution.

Monitor Project Progress Versus Plan

Using the input from the progress reporting system, the project manager can assess how the project is progressing against the plan. Variances and trends are noted and the appropriate corrective action plans put in place to correct the anomalies.

Revise Project Plans

This is linked to both the change control process and the problem escalation process. As a result of changes that are approved or problems that are solved, the project schedule and resource schedule will be affected. This is the purpose of the single feedback loop in the TPM project management approach.

> **CROSS-REF** Problem-escalation procedures and a formal change management process, discussed in Chapter 10, are essential to effective project control.

Closing

The final phase of the TPM life cycle begins when the customer says the project is finished. The "doneness criteria" will have been specified and agreed to by the customer as part of the project plan. A number of activities occur to close out the project. Closing the project includes the artifacts listed and briefly described in the following sections. The details can be found in Chapter 11.

Obtain Client Acceptance

This must be a formal process because it signals the end of the project work and the satisfaction of the client's needs. The validation of having satisfied the client's needs comes in the form of an acceptance test procedure. This is often nothing more than a checklist of required features and functions. When all of those items have been checked off as having been provided and attested to in the final testing phase, the project work is deemed completed. That document should be created during the Planning Phase and kept up to date as change requests arise and are approved.

Install Project Deliverables

This step puts the deliverables in production status. That may have already occurred as part of final acceptance testing, however. In either case the customer needs to verify that the solution is working as expected. That verification represents the formal transition from development to maintenance mode.

Complete Project Documentation

The project is not done until the paperwork is done and filed. A smart project manager will start this documentation at the very start of the project and keep it updated as the project commences. That minimizes an onerous task! It would be foolish not to do so.

Complete Post-Implementation Audit

The Closing Phase is very important to TPM, but unfortunately it is the part that is most often neglected or omitted by management. Rather than spend time in the Closing Phase of the current project, the project manager is under pressure to get started on the next project. Often the next project is already behind schedule and work hasn't yet begun. It is easy for management to skip the Closing Phase because it is perceived as an overhead expense, it is easily overlooked, and it delays getting the next project underway.

The Closing Phase evaluates what occurred during the project and provides historical information for use in planning and executing future projects. This historical information is best kept in a document called a *project notebook*. To be useful, the notebook should be in an electronic form so that it is easy to retrieve and summarize project information for use in projects currently being planned. Every good closing provides answers to the following questions:

- Do the project deliverables meet the expectations of the requestor?
- Do the project deliverables meet the expectations of the project manager?
- Did the project team complete the project according to plan?
- What information was collected that will help with future projects?
- How well did the project management methodology work and how well did the project team follow it?
- What lessons have you learned from this project?

Celebrate

This is very important to the general well-being and morale of the team members, but it is often forgotten because of the pressure to move on to the next project, which is already behind schedule. The celebration doesn't have to be an expensive five-star dinner. The public recognition of a job well done and the grateful thanks of senior management, the sponsor, and the customer go a long way. Inscribed coffee mugs or T-shirts are simple ways to give team members a nostalgic reminder of the project as they look at the items sitting in a visible spot in their cubicles and think back to their parts in the project.

Variations to Project Management Approaches

For several years now, I and other project management authors have suggested that "One size does not fit all." I am, of course, talking about how the characteristics of the project should inform the project manager as to what pieces and parts of the traditional approach should be used on a given project and what new or adapted pieces and parts should be used. As the project goes from high risk to low risk; from high cost to low cost; from critical mission to routine maintenance; from groundbreaking technology to well-established technology, the project management approach goes from the full methodology to a subset of the methodology and even to an adapted subset. That's fine for making adjustments to the traditional approach, but you have another factor to consider that has led to yet another basic consideration of how a project should be managed. This question goes to the very heart of project management: "What basic approach makes sense for this type of project?" Once an approach is chosen, the subtleties of adapting it to the project can be addressed.

NOTE It bears repeating: One size does not fit all.

I contend that the traditional world of project management belongs to yesterday. Although there will continue to be applications for which standard approaches are appropriate, there is a whole new set of applications for which the standard approaches are totally inappropriate. The paradigm must shift. Any company that doesn't accommodate that shift is sure to be lost in the rush. "Change or die" was never a truer statement than it is today.

Why do you need yet another way of managing projects? Don't you have enough options already? There certainly are plenty of options, but projects still fail at a high rate. I believe that part of the reason is because we haven't yet completely defined, at a practical and effective level, how to manage the types of projects that we are being asked to manage in today's business environment.

Traditional Project Management (TPM) practices require that the customer requirements be clearly and completely defined before any planning can take place. Most contemporary thinkers on the topic would suggest that it is impossible to completely and clearly document requirements at the beginning of any project. Whether you agree or not, that condition is likely to exist in the most contemporary projects, and there are many reasons for that. Here I will consider these situations as well as the inevitable scope change request and its impact on project management processes. In doing that you will learn alternative approaches to project management that handle these difficult situations, while maintaining a customer-facing focus throughout the entire project life cycle.

TPM practices were defined and have matured in the world of the engineer and construction professional, where the team expected (and got) a clear statement from customers as to what they wanted, when they wanted it, and how much they were willing to pay for it. All of this was delivered to the project manager wrapped in a neat package. The i's were all dotted and the t's were all crossed. All the correct forms were filed and all the boxes were filled in with the information requested. Everyone was satisfied that the request was well documented and that the deliverables were sure to arrive when and as requested. The project team clearly understood the solution they would be expected to provide and they could clearly plan for its delivery. That describes the world of the project manager until the mid-1950s. By then the computer was well on its way to becoming a viable commercial resource but it was still the province of the engineer. Project management continued as it had under the management of the engineers. The first sign that change was in the wind for the project manager arose in the early 1960s. Using computers to run businesses was now a reality, and we began to see position titles such as programmer, programmer analyst, systems analyst, and primitive types of database architects emerging. These professionals were really engineers in disguise, and somehow they were expected to interact with the business and management professionals (who were totally mystified by the computer and the mystics that had figured out how to communicate with it) to design and implement business systems to replace manual processes. This represented a total metamorphosis of both the business world and the project world, and we would never look back.

In the face of all the changes that were ushering in the information society, TPM wasn't showing any signs of change. To the engineer, every project management problem looked like a nail and they had the hammer. It seemed to be working, or at least no one was complaining that it wasn't.

Buried beneath the mysticism that surrounded the computer was another problem that would soon surface — that is, the inability of the businessperson to tell the difference between wants and needs. The confusion arose from the glamour surrounding the computer. It was touted as the silver bullet: All we needed to do was push a button and the rest would be automatic. The conduct of business was going to become simple. The wants got in the way of seeing the real needs.

That problem still persists to this day. If you remember anything from this introduction, remember that what the customer wants is probably not what the customer needs. Wants are more associated with a solution. Needs are more associated with the underlying problem. If the project manager blindly accepts what the customers say they want and proceeds with the project on that basis, the project manager is in for a rude awakening. Often in the process of building the solution, the customer learns that what they need is not the same as what they requested. Here we have the basis for rolling deadlines, scope creep, and an endless trail of changes and reworks. TPM has to strain to keep up with the realities of projects such as these. It's no wonder that 70+ percent of projects fail. That has to stop. We need an approach that is built around change — one that embraces learning and discovery throughout all of the project life cycle. It must have built-in processes to accommodate the changes that result from this learning and discovery.

When we think of the principles of management, we usually associate them with the management of people. The management of people includes defining what the business unit will do; planning for the number and type of staff who will do it; organizing the staff; monitoring their performance of the tasks assigned them; and finally bringing a close to their efforts. Those same management principles also apply to projects.

We are not in Kansas anymore! The discipline of project management has morphed to a new state; and as this monograph is being written, that state has not yet reached a steady one. It may never reach a steady state. What does this mean to the struggling project manager? Take courage; it's not as grim as it may seem.

> **WARNING** The discipline of project management has morphed to a new state and that state is not yet a steady one. It may never reach a steady state.

To me the answer is obvious. We must open our minds to the basic principles on which project management is based so as to accommodate change and avoid wasted dollars and wasted time. For as long as I can remember, I have been preaching that one size does not fit all. The characteristics of the project suggest what subset of the traditional approach should be used on it. This concept has to be extended. First you must choose the project management approach based on the characteristics of the project at hand. Then you can choose how that approach should be adapted to effectively manage the project.

In this edition of the book I introduce a number of ways to organize and manage complex projects in the face of uncertainty. The approaches discussed in this book were originally introduced in my recent book on software development project management, *Effective Software Project Management* (Wiley, 2006). In this book I redefine those approaches for the more general practice of project management. For the purposes of this book I am classifying these five approaches into three categories:

- Traditional (Linear, Incremental)
- Adaptive (Iterative, Adaptive)
- Extreme

These categories form a continuum that ranges from certainty (goal and solution are clearly defined and a Linear approach is appropriate) to some uncertainty (goal is clearly defined but solution is not clearly defined and some form of Adaptive approach is appropriate) to major uncertainty (goal and solution are not clearly defined and some form of extreme approach is appropriate). Table 2-1 provides more detail about the specifics of how project characteristics relate to choice of approach.

In Figure 2-2 certainty is measured with respect to requirements and solution. The less certain you are that you have clearly defined requirements, the more you should choose an approach at the high uncertainty end of the continuum. Once you understand the nature of the project to be undertaken you can confidently choose the approach that offers the best chance of a successful completion.

The first decision to be made on any project is what methodology is best for that type of project. The characteristics of the project suggest the project management approach best suited to those characteristics, as Table 2-1 illustrates.

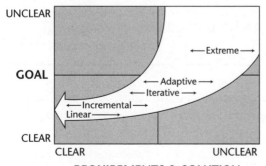

Figure 2-2 Project management life cycle approaches

Table 2-1 Project Characteristics as a Determinant of Which Project Management Approach to Use

Use **Linear** approaches when:	The solution and requirements are clearly defined
	You do not expect too many scope change requests
	The project is routine and repetitive
	You can use established templates
Use **Incremental** approaches when:	Same conditions as the Linear approach but the customer wants to deploy business value incrementally
	There may be some likelihood of scope change requests
Use **Iterative** approaches when:	You feel that requirements are not complete or may change
	You will learn about remaining requirements in the course of doing the project
	Some features of the solution are not yet identified
Use **Adaptive** approaches when:	The solution and requirements are only partially known
	There may be functionality that is not yet identified
	There will be a number of scope changes from the customer
	The project is oriented to new product development or process improvement
	The development schedule is tight and you can't afford rework or replanning
Use **Extreme** approaches when:	The goal and solution are not clearly known
	The project is an R&D type project

You'll explore each of these in more detail throughout the book. In Chapters 13–18 I discuss the Iterative and Adaptive approaches. In Chapter 19 I discuss the Extreme approach.

Traditional Project Management Approaches

For the purposes of this book I am collapsing the Linear and Incremental approaches into a single classification — traditional models. The specific models I will present are all subtle variations of the traditional approach, so there is little sacrifice of clarity.

Linear Project Management Approaches

We start with the simplest situation — the Linear model — as a foundation for the variations I will discuss. Figure 2-3 illustrates the Linear approach to project management.

The major weakness of this model is that knowledge gained from one phase, such as Launch, cannot be used to revise and improve the project plan. There is no going back to an earlier phase to improve its deliverables, even within a phase that linearity is enforced. For example, suppose the project involves the development of a software application. The Monitoring and Controlling Phase includes a systems development life cycle. Simply, it might consist of systems design, detailed design, build, test, and implement. That, too, is done without going back to an earlier part of the systems development life cycle, so an improved solution discovered during build cannot be reflected in a revised and improved design. There is no going back.

A scope change request from the customer giving rise to the feedback loop upsets the balance in the project schedule and perhaps the resource schedule as well. One or more of the team members must analyze the request and issue a Project Impact Statement. This takes the team members away from their scheduled project work, potentially putting the project behind schedule.

WARNING The Linear approach to project management is change intolerant.

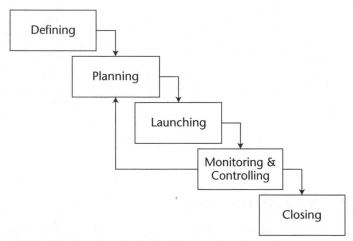

Figure 2-3 The Linear approach to project management

Incremental Project Management Approaches

On the surface, the only difference between the Linear and Incremental approaches is that the deliverables in the Incremental approach are released according to a schedule. That is, a partial solution is initially released, and then at some later point in time additional parts of the solution are added to the initial release to form a more complete solution. Subsequent releases add to the solution until the final increment releases the complete solution. All of this happens in a linear fashion, as shown in Figure 2-4, so that in the end the solution is the same as if a Linear approach had been followed.

A more in-depth investigation would show that there are significant differences between the Incremental approach and the Linear approach. Two are worth mentioning. The first has to do with scope change requests. In the Linear approach, these are not expected or encouraged. In the Incremental approach, change is actually encouraged. The initial release of a partial solution gives the customer an opportunity to experiment with it in a production scenario and find areas that could be improved. That encourages change requests.

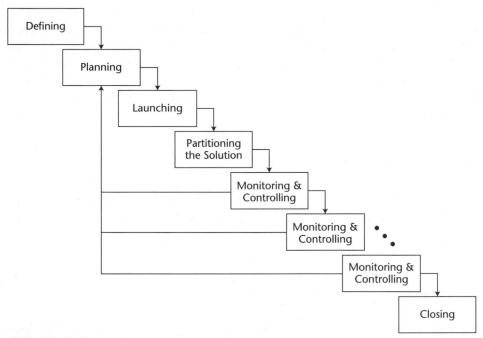

Figure 2-4 Incremental approach to project management

The second difference is related to how the full solution is decomposed into partial solutions whose development would then be planned in a sequential fashion and released in that same order. The release schedule needs to be consistent with the dependencies that exist between each partial solution. To be clear, what if a particular release depended upon the features and functions scheduled for development in a later release? There goes the integrity of the release schedule. Extensive replanning often follows — significantly changing the release schedule. I discuss the variations to Traditional Project Management more thoroughly later in the chapter in the section "Variations within the Traditional Project Management Approach."

Adaptive Project Management Approaches

What about those cases where what is needed is clearly defined but how to produce it isn't as obvious? These types of projects occupy a space in the landscape somewhere between traditional and extreme projects. Many managers have observed that the vast majority of their projects are a closer fit with Adaptive Project Management approaches than either TPM or Extreme Project Management (xPM). Clearly the traditional approach won't work when the solution is not known. For the traditional approach to work you need a detailed plan; and if you don't know how you will get what is needed, how can you generate a detailed plan? What about the extreme approach? I'm guessing that the "agilists" would argue that any one of the agile approaches would do just fine. I agree that you could use one of them and probably do quite well. Unfortunately, you would be ignoring the fact that you know what is needed. It's a given. Why not use an approach that incorporates the fact that you know what is needed?

Two approaches fall into this Adaptive category. The first is the Iterative Project Management approach. It is appropriate for those projects for which some of the features are missing or not clearly defined. When the solution is less clearly specified — functions as well as features are missing or not clearly defined — then the Adaptive Project Management approach, which I am calling the Adaptive Project Framework (APF), is appropriate. I developed APF in two concurrent but independent client engagements over three years ago.

Iterative Project Management Approach

As soon as some of the details of a solution are not clearly defined or perhaps are even missing, you should turn to an Iterative approach. I am aware of at least four: Evolutionary Development Waterfall, SCRUM, Rational Unified Process (RUP), and Dynamic Systems Development Method (DSDM). See the bibliography for references to all four approaches. The approach that I use is shown in Figure 2-5.

Figure 2-5 Iterative approach to project management

This is not unlike prototyping, which has been around for several years now. The objective is to show the customer an intermediate and perhaps incomplete solution and ask them for feedback on changes they would like to see. Those changes are integrated into the solution and another solution is presented. This process repeats itself until either the customer is satisfied and has no further changes to recommend or the budget/time runs out. This approach differs from the Incremental approach in that change is expected. In fact, change is a necessary part of this approach.

Iterative approaches definitely fall in the class of learn and discover. In Figure 2-5 the learning and discovering experience takes place inside the feedback loop. With each iteration more and more of the depth of the solution is revealed. That follows from the customer having an opportunity to play with the current solution and give feedback to the project team.

Adaptive Project Management Approach

The next step away from a complete solution is the Adaptive approaches. Here the missing pieces of the solution extend to functionality that is missing or not clearly defined. That is a more serious shortcoming than is found in the Iterative approach. I developed the Adaptive Project Framework (APF) for just such situations. APF is an approach that spans the gap between TPM and xPM. At the same time, however, you should appreciate the Traditional and Extreme approaches and know when and how to use them. If I am successful in demonstrating this, you will have at your disposal a taxonomy of approaches that will meet the need for a sound approach to project management regardless of the nature of the project. The appropriate approach can be chosen once the type of project is known.

So far, I have described cases where the solution was clearly defined and the model used depended upon other factors such as risk or the need for rapid development. In this section I am going to relax the requirement that the solution be clearly known. Many people have suggested that this is actually a more likely scenario than those covered by TPM. The stage is now set to take your first look at the APF. Figure 2-6 is a graphic portrayal of how the APF is structured. The five phases that define APF are called Version Scope, Cycle Plan, Cycle Build, Customer Checkpoint, and Post-Version Review. Chapters 13–19 cover APF in considerable detail.

Extreme Project Management Approach

The final model type arises in those projects whose solution and goal are not known or not clearly defined. Here you are in the world of pure research and development, new product development, and process improvement projects. These are high-risk, high-change projects. In many cases they are also high-speed projects.

When so little is known about the goal and solution one might be concerned about how to approach such projects. What tools, templates, and processes will work in these cases? Will any of them work? This can be a high anxiety time for all but the most courageous, risk-taking, flexible, and creative project teams.

Figure 2-6 Adaptive approach to project management

What do you do if what is needed is not clearly defined? What if it isn't defined at all? Many have tried to force fit the traditional approach into these situations and it flat out doesn't work. Extreme Project Management (xPM) is designed to handle projects whose goal can only be fuzzily defined or really not defined at all. Building a B2B Web site with no further specification is an excellent example. Much like the early stages of an R&D project, building the B2B Web site starts out with a guess, or maybe several guesses. As the project commences the customer reflects upon the alternatives chosen and gives some direction to the development team. This process repeats itself repeatedly. Either the partial solution converges on a satisfactory solution or it is killed along the way. In most cases, there is no fixed budget or timeline. Obviously, the customer wants it completed ASAP for as little as possible. Furthermore, the lack of a clear goal and solution exposes the project to a lot of change. Unfortunately, the nature of this project does not lend itself to fixed time and cost constraints.

This chapter defines the Extreme project and provides a high-level overview of the four phases that constitute the xPM approach. As such, it is a good starting point for the executive or manager who simply needs to become familiar with the xPM approach.

INSPIRE Project Management Approach

The model I am recommending is called INSPIRE. INSPIRE is an acronym that stands for **IN**itiate, **SP**eculate, **I**ncubate, and **Re**view, as shown in Figure 2-7. By its very nature, xPM is unstructured. It is designed to handle projects with "fuzzy goals" or goals that cannot be defined because of the exploratory nature of the extreme project. The theme here is that the learning and discovery take place between the customer and the project team in each iteration, moving the project forward. The idea is an adaptation of the Flexible Project Model introduced in 2000 by Doug DeCarlo in his eXtreme Project Management Workshop and recently published in book form. Recall that the difference between xPM and APF is that APF requires a clearly defined goal, whereas xPM does not.

xPM is an Iterative approach. It iterates in an unspecified number of short cycles (one- to four-week cycle lengths are typical) in search of the solution (in other words, the goal). It may find an acceptable solution, or it may be cancelled before any solution is reached. It is distinguished from APF in that the goal is unknown, or, at most, someone has a vague but unspecified notion of what the goal consists of. Such a customer might say, "I'll know it when I see it." That isn't a new revelation to experienced project managers; they have heard that many times before. Nevertheless, it is their job to find the solution (with the customer's help, of course).

Figure 2-7 Extreme approach to project management

APF is further distinguished from xPM in that xPM requires the customer to be more involved within and between cycles, whereas APF requires customer involvement between cycles. Drug research provides a good example of the Extreme project. Suppose, for example, that the goal is to find a natural food additive that will eliminate the common cold. This is a wide-open project. Constraining the project to a fixed budget or fixed timeline makes no sense whatsoever. More than likely, the project team will begin by choosing some investigative direction or directions and hope that intermediate findings and results will accomplish two things:

- The just finished cycle will point to a more informed and productive direction for the next and future cycles. In other words, xPM includes learning and discovery experiences just as APF does.

- Most important of all is that the funding agent will see this learning and discovery as potentially rewarding and will decide to continue the funding support.

There is no constrained scope triangle in xPM as there is in TPM and APF projects. Recall that those TPM and APF projects have time and funding constraints that were meaningful. "Put a man on the moon and return him safely by the end of the decade" is pretty specific. It has a built-in stopping rule. When the money or the time runs out, the project is over. xPM does have stopping rules, but they are very different. There are two stopping rules in xPM:

- One, the project is over when the solution is found. Success!

- Two, the project is over when the sponsor is not willing to continue the funding. The sponsor might withdraw the funding because the project is not making any meaningful progress. It is not converging on an acceptable solution. In other words, the project is killed. Failure!

CROSS-REF Chapter 19 discusses INSPIRE in more detail.

Variations within the Traditional Project Management Approach

As already indicated, over the years the nature of projects has changed, so it makes sense that the approaches to Traditional Project Management have also changed. Two approaches are discussed in this book: Rapid Development and Staged Delivery. The first is a variation of the Linear approach. The second is a variation of the Incremental approach.

Rapid Development Project Management Approach

This variation arises when business and/or market conditions require a rapid deployment of the complete solution. Rather than use a single swim lane of project phases and tasks, the Rapid Development variation uses a number of parallel swim lanes. Each swim lane is a linear succession of project phases and tasks that accomplish some of the deliverables of the solution. When all swim lanes are complete, their deliverables are integrated into the final, complete solution.

Choosing this variation involves several considerations. The first is risk. The work of the project is compressed into a shorter time frame than the single swim lane approach. That causes risk to increase because of such factors as scope change, resource contention, and problem resolution. There is less time to analyze and take action than in the single swim lane approach. In addition, the opportunities to recover are fewer and more difficult than in the single swim lane approach. The second consideration is accommodating scope change requests. The third is how to define the swim lanes. The fourth is resource management

A common variation of the standard Waterfall Model is one that allows the project schedule to be compressed. This is done by creating parallel "swim lanes" of development activity. The linearity of the process is still maintained with these parallel swim lanes. Figure 2-8 depicts such an approach. There are several things to consider in creating such a development schedule. The first is risk. By squeezing the work into a shorter time frame, the incidence of errors and staff scheduling conflicts increases.

Figure 2-8 Rapid Development project management approach

There are two major considerations regarding this model. The first is how to approach such a project — that is, how to decompose the development effort into separate swim lanes. The first objective would be to decompose the functionality into independent sets. The fewer dependencies there are across the swim lanes, the easier it will be to schedule resources and work. The second objective would be to make the functionality within a swim lane as cohesive as possible. Does the functionality fit together? The second consideration addresses the strengths and weaknesses of this model. Its major strength is that it enables the customer to get to market sooner rather than later. That is a major business value-add for the approach.

WARNING There is no such thing as a free lunch. The price you pay, or the weakness of this approach, is that it increases risk of project failure. The work is compressed into a much shorter time frame so there is less opportunity to recover from mistakes or resource scheduling problems.

Staged Delivery Project Management Approach

This variation arises when an early entry into the market with a partial solution is advised. The full solution is deployed in successive increments over time until the full solution is realized. Both the Rapid Development and Staged Delivery variations arrive at the same solution as the Traditional approach. They just get there by different routes.

In choosing this variation there are three considerations.

Member Reassignment

There will inevitably be some delay between the end of one stage and the beginning of the next. That delay can be dangerous because there will be a temptation to assign team members to other short-term tasks while waiting to start the next stage. The short term can extend to a longer term and compromise the next stage.

Loss of Priority

It's also possible that the completion of an interim stage exposes the project to reprioritization. Even though the solution is only partially deployed, the priority of the remaining stages may be overshadowed by some other project. The rationale may be that the later stages can be delayed. The current stage deliverables will get you by until you can reinstate this project's priority.

Encouraging Scope Change

The time between stages when the customer is working with a partial solution is just asking for scope change requests. Now that the customer sees how this part of the solution is working, they will have suggestions for change. It's just human nature.

Figure 2-9, adapted to a focus on project management and not software development, is from Steve McConnell's book *Software Project Survival Guide* (Microsoft Press, 1998).

This model works well in those situations where it is to your advantage to deliver business value early. If that is the case, you should prioritize the functionality to phases to deliver maximum business value. The stages could be long or short depending on the needs of the customer.

NOTE Another reason to adopt this model is to give you some breathing room in case the early releases give the customer a reason to suggest changes. In other words, you are protecting yourself against requirements not having been completely defined and agreed to.

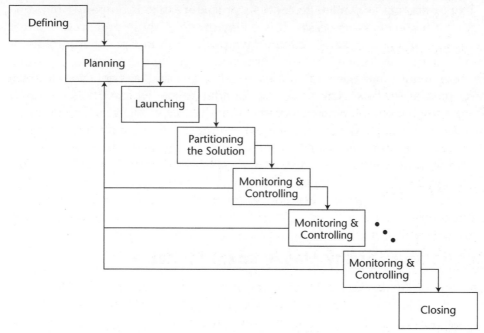

Figure 2-9 Staged Delivery project management approach

Quality Management

To meet customer requirements, and do so on time and within budget, the project manager must incorporate sound quality management practices. He or she will be concerned with the quality of the following:

- The product/service/process that is the deliverable from the project
- The project management process itself

Countless books have been written on the product side of quality; I will not repeat those presentations here, as others have done a far better job than I could hope to achieve in this book. The bibliography in Appendix B lists some publications that may be of interest to you.

In this section I focus on the process of TPM. Emphasis is on the two tools and techniques that I have successfully integrated and used in my consulting practice to improve the process of TPM: the Continuous Quality Management Model and the Process Quality Management Model.

Continuous quality management is a procedure that a company can use to improve its business processes. It is a way of life in those organizations that want to attain and sustain a competitive position in fast-paced information-age industries. A second tool is integrated after the definition steps. This tool, process quality management, is used to relate critical success factors to business processes. This establishes the foundation on which the Continuous Quality Management Model proceeds to conduct a gap analysis that identifies processes and steps within processes where improvement opportunities might be made. Any number of improvement projects can be undertaken, and the resulting improvements are checked against targeted improvements, with further projects commissioned. Because new improvement opportunities always present themselves, a series of feedback loops, shown in Figure 2-10, continues the process.

Continuous Quality Management Model

Continuous quality management is most evident in customer-driven organizations. Levi Strauss, Motorola, and Xerox are but a few. Companies that have applied for or won the coveted Baldridge Award, an award recognizing exemplary quality management within the company, are also on the list.

The Continuous Quality Management Model shown in Figure 2-10 is cyclical, as depicted by the feedback loops. Feedback loop A occurs when there have been significant process changes and the relationship between critical success factors (CSF) and a process may have changed. Feedback loop B occurs when a business process may have changed and affected the gap analysis. Feedback loop C simply continues the priority scheme defined earlier and selects another business process for improvement. Feedback loop D usually involves continued improvement efforts on the same business process. The results of the current project may not have been as expected, or new improvement ideas may have arisen while the current project was being conducted. That is, the TPM phase of the model is adaptive. Scope changes will often result from lessons learned during project execution.

Process Quality Management Model

Figure 2-11 is a schematic of the Process Quality Management Model (PQMM). I have used this model successfully in my project management engagements that involve quality improvement programs. The model is based on the assumption that the enterprise has documented its mission, vision, and CSFs. With these in place, the processes that drive the business are identified and related to the CSFs using a grading system in which each business process is assigned a grade of A (excellent) through E (embryonic).

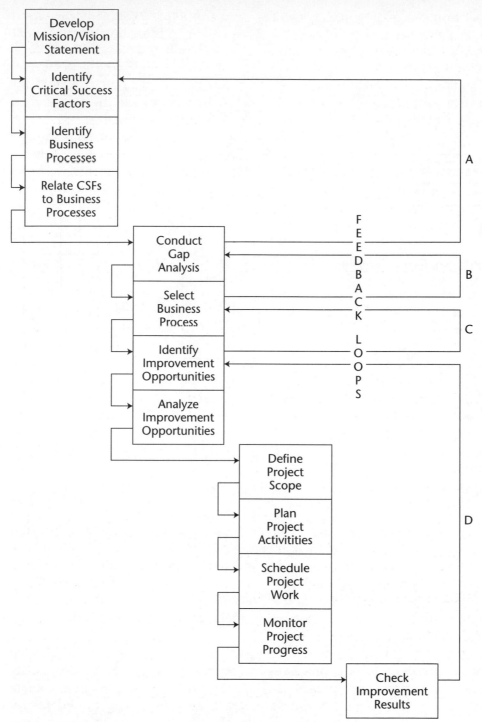

Figure 2-10 The Continuous Quality Management Model

Figure 2-11 The Process Quality Management Model

The next step is to identify which business processes affect which CSFs and mark each with an X, as shown in Figure 2-11. The number of CSFs that have been related to each business process is counted, and the results are tabulated into the zone map. For example, in Figure 2-11, two business processes (P7 and P14) were given a grade of C and are related to five CSFs, as reflected by the 2 in the cell that lies at the intersection of the column labeled C and the row labeled 5 in the zone map.

By taking into account the process grade and the number of CSFs affected by the process, business processes can be ranked according to the priority needs for improvement programs. Those cells that lie in Zone 1 will contain data points that identify business processes that are strong candidates for improvement. In this example, P2, P4, P5, P6, P12, and P16 are business processes whose combination of grade and number of related CSFs identify them as processes where improvement efforts should be focused. The results are analyzed to identify and prioritize improvement opportunities for a given process. A project idea emerges out of this analysis, and the TPM life cycle begins.

Risk Management

Many would say that the major responsibility of the project manager is to manage risk. For that reason and that reason alone you should place risk and its effective management at the top of your list. In this section I examine risk, its identification, its assessment, and its management through the life of the project.

In project management, a risk is some future event that results in a change, either positive or negative, to the project. For the most part, risk is associated with loss, at least in the traditional sense. Loss can be estimated. The estimate is the mathematical product of the probability that the event will occur and the severity of the loss if it does. This estimate will force a choice on the project manager's part as to what to do, if anything, to mitigate the risk and reduce the loss that will occur. In general, risk deals with entrepreneurial risk, where there is not only a probability of loss but also a possibility of gain. This is common in businesses where capital is put at risk in order to fund a new business venture. This type of risk is outside the scope of my treatment. Here I will deal with risk in the traditional sense, where risk involves the possibility of loss.

This estimate is the basis of a series of choices that the project manager has to make. First of all, should any action be taken? If the cost of the action exceeds the estimated loss, no action should be taken. Simply hope that the event doesn't occur. The second choice deals with the action to be taken. If action is called for, what form should it take? Some actions may simply reduce the probability that the event will occur. Other actions will reduce the loss that results from the occurrence of the event. It is usually not possible to reduce either the probability or the loss to zero. Whatever actions are taken will only tend to reduce the loss in the final analysis.

The business decision is to assess how the expected loss compares to the cost of defraying all or some of the loss and then taking the appropriate action. With project management, the risks that need to be managed are those that will hurt the project itself. While the project may affect the total business, the total business isn't the domain of the project manager.

NOTE Newer risk theories deal with entrepreneurial risk for which there is not only a probability of loss, but a possibility of gain. This is common in businesses where capital is put at risk in order to fund a new business venture. For the most part, in this book I deal with risk in the traditional sense, where risk is the possibility of loss.

Risk management is a broad and deep topic, and I am only able to brush the surface in this book. A number of reference books on the topic are available. The bibliography in Appendix B lists some specific titles you can use as a reference. The risk analysis and management process that I briefly describe answers the following questions:

- What are the risks?
- What is the probability of loss that results from them?
- How much are the losses likely to cost?
- What might the losses be if the worst happens?
- What are the alternatives?
- How can the losses be reduced or eliminated?
- Will the alternatives produce other risks?

To answer these questions I define risk management in four phases: identification of risk, assessment of risk, risk response planning, and monitoring and controlling.

Identifying Risk

To establish the risk management for the project, the project manager and project team must go through several processes. The first is identifying risk.

In this part of the process the entire team is brought together to discuss and identify the risks that are specific to the current project. I recommend that the meeting focus solely on risk. A meeting with such a single focus enables the entire project team to understand the importance of risk management, and it gets everyone thinking about the various risks involved in the project.

TIP Don't assume that you have identical risks on projects that look alike. Take some time to identify the risks specific to the current project so that any new risks can be identified and managed. While the experienced project manager certainly knows what general type of risks exist for each project, the professional project manager takes nothing for granted and always identifies risks for the project at the outset.

The list of risks can be cumulatively developed in parallel with other project planning activities. Once that list is built, the team can move to the second step in the risk management process.

Risk Categories

Risk arises from several different directions but it generally can be classified into one of four categories. The following sections itemize the risks that fall into each category.

Technical Risks

Includes:

- Quality and performance goals generally related to the technology used on the project
- Technology suitability, reliability, and the quality/performance standards
- Technology availability and complexity issues

Project Management Risks

Includes:

- Poor allocation of the project's resources
- Inadequate project management structure — proper planning processes to define critical deliverables for each project phase
- Inadequate planning resources, resource inexperience, poor use of management disciplines
- Cost and schedule risk due to the aforementioned project management risks

Organizational Risks

Includes:

- Supportability risks
- Lack of prioritization of projects
- Inadequacy or interrupted funding
- Inadequacy or interrupted resource assignments
- Conflicts with other competing projects
- Policies that do not support efficient management
- Policies and agendas that impede the project from accomplishing its objectives

External Risks

Includes:

- Shifting legal or regulatory requirements
- Supplier and contractor risks and contract issues with same
- Force *majeure* risks, economic collapse, work stoppages (strikes)
- Programmatic or supportability risks caused by external parties
- Deliverables from teams external to your own

Many of these will be true risks caused by nature and other uncontrollable factors.

Assessing Risk

As mentioned, there are two major factors in assessing risk. The first one is the probability that the risk event will occur. For instance, when a project involves migrating legacy systems to new systems, the interface points between the two are often where problems occur. The professional project manager will have a good sense of these types of risks and the chances that they will occur.

NOTE If you are certain that an event will occur, it's not a risk; it's a certainty. This type of event isn't handled by risk management. Because you are sure that it will occur, no probability is involved. No probability, no risk.

When the team puts together the risk identification list, nothing should be ruled out at first. Let the team brainstorm risk without being judgmental. The team will put up some risks with small probabilities. Those risks are so small that you can ignore them. For instance, the risk that a meteor will destroy the building in which you work is miniscule. If you're worrying about events like that, you won't be much of a project manager. It's the risks that actually might occur that you manage.

The second part of risk assessment is the impact the risk will have on the project. If a risk has a 50 percent probability of occurring, you need to assess what the impact will be, because a 50-50 chance of something happening is fairly high. If, however, the risk event has a low impact rating, you won't need to manage it. This information should also be discussed at the first risk meeting.

To assign a numerical score to a risk event, you simply multiply the probability of the risk occurring times the impact that the event's occurrence would have. While at first glance this seems to be a rigorous mathematical process, it's not. The probability of an occurrence is subjective to a great extent, as is the impact of the event. You should get advice from the team regarding both the probability of occurrence and the impact risks will have on the project, but in the end your experience and a good dose of common sense will give you a good start on handling the risk.

Qualitative Assessment

Rather than get hung up on numeric assessments, I recommend the risk matrix shown in Figure 2-12.

For each risk, evaluate the probability that it will occur on a low, medium, high scale and the expected loss on a low, medium, high scale. If the risk falls in a red cell, action is required and a mitigation plan must be put in place. If the risk falls in a yellow cell, further analysis is required. One consideration might be to compare the cost of the mitigation plan against the loss to determine whether the mitigation plan makes business sense. For example, if you are trying to solve a $100 problem with a $1,000 solution, it doesn't make business sense. The appropriate action is simply to hope that the event does not occur. Finally, if the risk falls in a green cell, it can be ignored for the time being. Later information might change the evaluation of that risk and some action might be advisable.

Dynamic Risk Assessment

The risk matrix approach is basically static. By that I mean an analysis is done during planning and a risk management plan put in place. Another approach that I have used with great success is a dynamic approach. In this approach, risk is continuously assessed at each phase of the project. An example will help explain how this approach is used.

Once the risk drivers have been identified, they must be ranked from most likely to have an impact on the project to least likely to have an impact on the project. Label them A (most likely) through J (least likely) and array the data as shown in Figure 2-13. The column entries are 1 = low risk, 2 = medium risk, and 3 = high risk. Actually, any metric can be used as long as the lower numbers are at the low-risk end and the higher numbers are at the high-risk end.

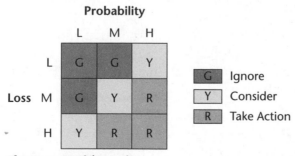

Figure 2-12 Risk matrix

Project Activity	A	B	C	D	E	F	G	H	I	J	Score
Rqmnts Anlys	2	3	3	2	3	3	2	2	1	1	22
Specifications	2	1	3	2	2	2	1	2	2	3	20
Prel Design	1	1	2	2	2	2	1	2	2	2	17
Design	2	1	2	2	2	3	1	2	2	1	18
Implement	1	2	2	3	3	2	1	2	2	1	19
Test	2	2	2	2	2	3	2	2	2	2	21
Integration	3	2	3	3	3	3	2	3	3	2	27
Checkout	1	2	2	3	3	3	2	3	2	2	23
Operation	2	2	3	3	3	3	3	3	1	1	24
Score	16	16	22	22	23	24	15	21	17	15	191

Maximum score is 270. Risk level for this project is 191/270 = 71%.

Figure 2-13 Risk assessment worksheet

The data given in the worksheet is from a hypothetical project. The columns are the top risk drivers that were identified from the candidate list, and the rows are steps in a process. For the sake of an example, I chose steps from a hypothetical systems development life cycle. Any collection of process steps may be used, so the tool has broad application for a variety of contexts. A score of 1 is given to those risk drivers that will not impact the process step if they should occur, 2 is for a medium relationship, and 3 is for a strong relationship. Actually, any numeric scale may be used. The row and column totals are evaluated relative to one another and to scores from similar projects. These totals tell the story. High column totals suggest a risk driver that is operative across a number of steps in the process. High row totals suggest a process step that is affected by several risk drivers. Finally, the total for the whole worksheet gives you a percentage figure that can be used to compare this project against similar completed projects. The percentage is relative, but it may suggest a rule that provides an early warning of projects that are high risk overall.

To analyze the resulting scores, first examine column totals that are large relative to other column totals. Because their column totals are high, they can potentially affect several process steps. The project team should identify strategies for either reducing the probability of the risk occurring or mitigating its impact, or both, should the event associated with that risk occur. The row totals can be analyzed in the same fashion.

Planning Risk Response

The next step in risk management is to plan, as much as possible, the responses that will be used in the event that the identified risks occur. For instance, you may want to include a clause in your hardware contract with the vendor that if the servers don't get to you by a certain date, then they will pay a penalty. This penalty gives the vendor an incentive to analyze and mitigate the risks involved in late delivery of key equipment. For all the risks listed in the risk identification that you choose to act upon, you should have some type of action in mind. It's not enough simply to list the risks; you need to plan to do something about the risk events should they occur.

Another example of risk planning is planning for key personnel. What will you do if one of the key developers leaves the company before finishing the coding? This risk will impact the project severely if it occurs. Having someone capture code as it is written and debriefing with the developer each day are two ways of dealing with the risk of key personnel loss. How many others can you come up with? Coming up with contingency plans such as these is risk response planning.

You should understand five different risk responses:

- **Accept** — Do nothing because the cost of the fix is more expensive than the expected loss.
- **Avoid** — Elect not to do the part of the project associated with the risk.
- **Contingency planning** — Frame plans to deal with the risk consequence and monitor risk regularly (identify contingency trigger points).
- **Mitigate** — Reduce either the probability of occurrence, the loss, or both.
- **Transfer** — Outsource

Risk Monitoring and Control

Once you've identified the risk, assessed the probability and impact of the risks, and planned what to do if the risk event occurs, you need to monitor and control the project risks. The process of writing down the risks and assessing them makes everyone on the project team aware of their existence and is a good place to start. Start by creating a risk log. This document lists all risks that you want to manage, identifies who is supposed to manage the risk, and specifies what should be done to manage the risk event. A risk log is a simple template that can be created in MS Word. A typical risk log will contain five fields:

- **ID number** — The ID number always remains the same, even if the risk event has occurred and been managed. If you take the risk off of the list and file it elsewhere, don't assign the old number to a new risk. Leave the number the same or there will be a great deal of confusion.
- **Risk description** — The risk description is a short statement of the risk event.

- **Risk owner** — The risk owner is the person who has to manage the listed risk.

- **Action to be taken** — The action to be taken lists what the owner is going to do to deal with the risk event.

- **Outcome** — The outcome tells you what happened.

Use the risk log to keep track of risk in the project and you'll have control over it. When you go to status meetings, you should always talk about risks and their management by the team. Keep the risks in front of the team so that each member will be aware of what risks are coming up and what is to be done about the risk event. It's good project management.

Procurement Management

As a project manager, you will always have projects for which you must obtain hardware, software, or services from outside sources. This process is known as *procurement,* and the professional project manager must have a basic understanding of the procedure so that he or she can ensure that the organization is getting the right materials at the best cost. To manage procurement, you need to go through a few processes, which are discussed in the next few sections.

Planning Procurement

Planning procurement involves both what you're going to procure and the time that you're going to procure it. Also included in this planning is addressing the make or buy decision. I'll talk about this decision first.

The standard IT organization usually has an opportunity to decide between building the needed software or buying the off-the-shelf variety:

Buying — If no software is available, the decision is easy. You make the software yourself. But most of the time, you're not doing something so unique that someone hasn't already done it before. If you buy the software off the shelf, you're getting software that has already been tested, and you can contact users to see how it has worked. Buying off the shelf mitigates the risk level, because you're not the first one using the application. While this sounds nice, there is another factor to consider. By buying already-written applications, you may not be getting something that exactly fits your needs. You have to weigh the benefit of getting an existing application with the disadvantage of not having something that fits exactly.

Making — The make decision for procurement means that you will be working with new code, testing it yourself, and then installing something completely new in the system. Actually, very few applications are completely new; rather, some parts of them are.

From a procurement standpoint, you have to factor in which strategy is the most efficient and cost-effective for the organization. Don't just take a short-term look. If you use an off-the-shelf application and everyone is unhappy with it, it's going to cost you in the long rbun. Consider everything carefully before making your decision to procure.

After you've gone through the make-versus-buy decision, you need to consider all the things you need to procure and when you need to procure them. What you need will be made clearer by going through requirements gathering. This process is a major part of the procurement process and can't be overemphasized. When you're gathering requirements, talk to all the potential users and get their requirements. Collate the list of requirements and circulate it to everyone who contributed. You may need to negotiate some of the requirements because they may add too much cost to the project. Almost certainly, the requirements you get the first day you ask for them will change by the time you're ready to solicit bids for the project.

WARNING Make sure that as the requirements list changes during this period, you keep the document containing the requirements under version control. Failure to do this will result in major confusion.

The "when" question is just as important as the "what." If you need servers four months from now, you don't want to tie up the organization's money today. Look through all your needs, whether services or materials, to determine why you need them. This information gives you a way to manage your budget, and good procurement helps keep the organization's cash under control. You will get much of this information after you've defined the work needed to complete the project. The sequence in which this work will be done will give you some idea of when you need various items. Timing is a big part of procurement control and needs to be closely managed.

Soliciting Requests for Proposals

After you've done your requirements gathering, you can begin to prepare procurement documents for solicitation. These documents, called Requests for Proposals (RFPs), are what vendors use to determine how they should respond to your needs. The clearer the RFP, the better off you and the vendor are, because you will be providing basic information about what you want. The more specific you are, the better the chance that the vendor will be able to respond to you quickly and efficiently.

Many organizations have a procurement office. In this case, you need to give them a document with your requirements and let them do their work. If you don't have a procurement office, you need to prepare a document to send to the vendors. You'll want to have a lead writer, probably not you, and someone from the legal department to ensure that what you've asked for in the document is clear and forms the basis for a contract between you and the vendor.

> **NOTE** Remember that a contract always implies some type of adversarial relationship. Both parties to the contract wish to get the best possible terms for their side, so as you put out an RFP, keep in mind that although you definitely want to get the best possible terms for your side, you must make sure the terms aren't so difficult that they prohibit many people from responding. You must encourage as much participation in your RFP as possible. Don't get into a draconian mode whereby the RFP almost punishes those people who are responding to it.

You need to state the time conditions for response, which means that you state how many days you will give people to respond, as well as how long you will need to review the responses before making a choice. By putting a timeline on both the vendor and your organization, the process goes faster, and expectations are clear at the beginning of the process.

Managing RFP Questions and Responses

You need to have some mechanism whereby you can answer questions concerning the RFP. There are a couple key ways to do this:

- You can call a vendor meeting at which you answer all questions posed by the vendors that are present. However, after the meeting, you must also publish, in some form, your responses to the questions so that all vendors, including those who were not present at the meeting, are given a fair chance to see your responses.

- A more modern approach is to put your RFP online and respond to questions online. This arrangement gives everyone interested in responding to your RFP a chance to see other organizations' questions and to have a permanent record of your responses to questions posed. This process works only if you have someone constantly monitoring the website for questions, and someone who is responsible for answering the questions. This process also eliminates the traveling burden on vendors that may be far away geographically. By going online, you level the playing field for all vendors.

Selecting Vendors

Before you even start reading the responses to your proposal, set the standards for choosing a given vendor. These criteria may be technically based, experience based, or cost based, but whatever basis you use for choosing a vendor, it must remain the same for all of the vendors. If you are a public company, every vendor you've turned down will ask for a copy of the winning bid. If they think they have a better bid, all sorts of nasty things may occur (read: legal action). If, however, you have a standards chart, you can point out that everyone was rated with the same criteria and that the winner had the best overall number. By determining your criteria for choice early in the process, it is easier to make a decision and then defend it if need be.

Managing Contracts

Specifically, in the case where the application is to be written solely by the vendor, the project manager's primary job is contract management. Contract management involves the following:

- The vendor must supply you with deliverable dates so that you can determine whether the project is on time.

- The vendor should also supply a Work Breakdown Structure detailing how the vendor breaks down the scope of the project and showing the tasks that make up the completion of a deliverable.

- Regular status meetings to track progress. This meeting should be formal and occur on specified dates. The status meetings should occur at least once a week, although in the early stages of the project, you may choose to have them more often. The weekly status meetings give you an idea of how the vendor is proceeding in fulfilling the contract, and by having them at the weekly intervals, you won't allow the project to get very far off course. This way, you can correct at most a week's worth of problems; anything longer than that leads to unmanageable problems.

In your contract, state who the contract manager will be for your organization. If you are project managing the project, it will probably be you, but in some organizations, contract management functions are handled by a specific department or team. I prefer contract management to be in the hands of the project manager, or at least to have the project manager as part of the contract management team.

> **NOTE** If the contract is run on a deliverable basis — that is, the vendor agrees to given deliverables on certain dates — it is extremely important to state the payment mechanism. The person who signs off on each deliverable is extremely important to the vendor and should be specifically assigned in the RFP.

Closing Out the Contract

Closing out the contract is often an overlooked function of the project manager. It both certifies what has been done and gives all parties a chance to deal with open issues and final payments. The professional project manager will be aware of all of the steps that must be followed in the procurement process even though he or she may not be the person directly responsible for managing them. This is just another part of being a project management professional. Consider the following as you bring a contract to a close:

- Lack of a clear understanding of when the project is finished is a plague that permeates IT. When you write your RFP, state clearly how the project finishes and what the final deliverable is. Failure to do this will almost always lead to cost overruns in the form of maintenance activities under the heading of project work. State what the final product of the project is to be, who is to determine if it has been delivered, and what is to be done with any open issues. Make this information as clear as possible and you will save the company thousands of dollars.

- After the contract is closed, make sure you file all of the materials used during the project. These materials include the original RFP, the project baseline, the scope statement, the WBS, the various plans used to manage the project, and all changes, including those that were requested but turned down. You also need to show all payments and make sure that any subcontractors on the project were paid. Confirming that subcontractors have been paid is done through the vendor, who must show that all payables to subcontracts have been made.

- Put all this information into a large file and keep it. How long? I have seen instances of disputes coming up years after a project is finished. Keep it as long as the project product is in use. Ideally, keep these records permanently.

Project Management Institute

The Project Management Institute (PMI), founded in 1970, has become the premier professional society for project managers. With a worldwide membership exceeding 250,000 the PMI has become an indispensable part of every serious project manager's professional and career development.

Project Management Body of Knowledge Standards

The Project Management Institute's Project Management Body of Knowledge (PMBOK) was first published in 1987. Now in its third iteration, PMBOK defines the detailed practices associated with 44 basic project management processes. These 44 processes naturally group themselves into five process groups and nine knowledge areas. Table 2-2 lists those processes by process group and knowledge area.

Table 2-2 Project Management Processes Arranged by Process Group and Knowledge Area

KNOWLEDGE AREA	INITIATING PROCESS GROUP	PLANNING PROCESS GROUP	EXECUTING PROCESS GROUP	MONITORING/ CONTROLLING PROCESS GROUP	CLOSING PROCESS GROUP
Project Management Integration	Develop Project Charter Develop Preliminary Project Scope Statement	Develop Project Management Plan	Direct and Manage Project Execution	Monitor and Control Project Risk – Integrated Change Control	Close Project
Project Scope Management		Scope Planning Scope Definition Create WBS		Scope Verification Scope Control	
Project Time Management		Activity Definition Activity Sequencing Activity Resource Estimating Activity Duration Estimating Schedule Development		Schedule Control	

(continued)

Table 2-2 (continued)

KNOWLEDGE AREA	INITIATING PROCESS GROUP	PLANNING PROCESS GROUP	EXECUTING PROCESS GROUP	MONITORING/ CONTROLLING PROCESS GROUP	CLOSING PROCESS GROUP
Project Cost Management		Cost Estimating Cost Budgeting		Cost Control	
Project Quality Management		Quality Planning	Perform Quality Assurance	Perform Quality Control	
Project Human Resources Management		Human Resource Planning	Acquire Project Team Develop Project Team	Manage Project Team	
Project Communications Management		Communications Planning	Information Distribution	Performance Reporting Manage Stakeholders	
Project Risk Management		Risk Management Planning Risk Identification Qualitative Risk Analysis Quantitative Risk Analysis Risk Response Planning		Risk Monitoring and Control	
Project Procurement Management		Plan Purchases and Acquisitions Plan Contracting	Request Seller Response Select Sellers	Contract Administration	Contract Close

OPM3 Standards

In 2003 the PMI introduced the Organizational Project Management Maturity Model (OPM3). OPM3 is designed to link the strategy of the enterprise with the successful outcome of its projects. OPM3 provides the content of the standard, a way for an organization to assess and compare its performance against the standard, and a platform for implementing organizational change. It is a descriptive tool, not a proscriptive tool. By using OPM3 the enterprise is free to decide if and how to improve its project management practices.

The framework that supports the assessment is a collection of over 600 best practices categorized according to their relationship to portfolio, program, or project. An enterprise's maturity level is measured by their compliance to the best practices. A discussion of that measure is beyond the scope of this book. Interested readers should contact the PMI for the appropriate publications.

Putting It All Together

You now have all of the fundamentals to begin a TPM project. In this chapter I presented a high-level overview of the TPM life cycle. In the ensuing chapters I dig deeper into the life cycle and show you, step by step, how to plan and execute a traditional project.

I introduced you to the life cycle of the project and discussed quality management and risk management as integral parts of TPM. Beginning with Chapter 3 and extending through Chapter 11, you will explore the five phases of the TPM methodology in great detail. My goal is to give you enough practical examples and case exercises to get you started on the road to world-class project management.

I would be remiss, however, if I did not warn you of what lies ahead. It is easy to talk about the benefits of practicing sound TPM, but difficult to actually do it. The pressures of the job and the seemingly unrealistic deadlines we all face tempt us to get on with the work and not spend the necessary time preparing for work.

"Pay me now or pay me later" applies equally well to project planning. When the team and your management are anxious for work to begin, it is difficult to focus on developing a solid plan of action before you are pressed into service. At times it may seem that the level of detail in the plan is overkill, but it is not. You will have to accept that on faith at this point. The project manager must resist the pressure to start project work and instead spend the necessary time up front generating a detailed project plan. It has been demonstrated that a poor planning effort takes its toll later in the project as schedules slip, quality suffers, and expectations are not met.

The pain curve (see Figure 2-14) demonstrates that proper planning is painful but pays off in less pain later in the project. To not plan is to expose yourself to significant pain as the project commences. In fact, that pain usually continues to increase. It would continue to increase indefinitely except that someone usually pulls the plug on the project once the pain reaches unbearable levels. The following chapters give you the skills you need to make project planning less painful.

Discussion Questions

1. Identify the points in the project management life cycle where client involvement is needed. What specific action would you take as project manager to ensure that involvement?

2. The post-implementation audit is vitally important in improving the practice of project management and the process of project management, yet it is always so difficult to get senior management and the client to allocate the time to authorize and participate in these audits. Knowing that, what would you as project manager do to help alleviate this problem?

3. Where in the five-phase life cycle of a project do you think the most failures occur? Defend your answer.

4. You are the project manager of a caveman group going out to hunt mastodons. Describe your efforts at risk mitigation.

5. For each of the project management approaches identify a project from your experience that seems to be a good fit. Explain your choices.

CASE STUDY – PIZZA DELIVERED QUICKLY (PDQ)

6. Referring to the PDQ Case Study, what project management approach or approaches would you use for each of the subsystems? Defend your choice.

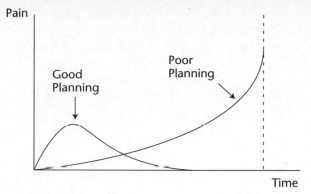

Figure 2-14 The project management life cycle pain curve

Defining the Project

Prediction is very difficult, especially about the future.
— Neils Bohr

Define the problem before you pursue a solution.
— John Williams, CEO, Spence Corp.

CHAPTER LEARNING OBJECTIVES

After reading this chapter, you will be able to:

- ◆ Understand what managing client expectations really means
- ◆ Explain the Conditions of Satisfaction development process
- ◆ Develop the Conditions of Satisfaction document
- ◆ Recognize the importance of maintaining the Conditions of Satisfaction throughout the entire project life cycle
- ◆ Define the basic parts and function of the Project Overview Statement
- ◆ Write a saleable Project Overview Statement for your project idea using the language of your business
- ◆ Understand the role of the Project Overview Statement in the project management life cycle
- ◆ Write clear goal and objective statements
- ◆ Establish measurable criteria for project success
- ◆ Identify relevant assumptions, risks, and obstacles
- ◆ Discuss attachments to the Project Overview Statement and their role in project approval

(continued)

> **CHAPTER LEARNING OBJECTIVES** *(continued)*
>
> ◆ Understand the approval process for the Project Overview Statement
>
> ◆ Know what constitutes a Project Scoping Meeting
>
> ◆ Create a Project Definition Statement
>
> ◆ Understand prototyping, business process diagramming, and use cases as tools for identifying and documenting requirements

If you don't know where you are going, how will you know when and if you ever get there? So many times I have seen projects get off to a terrible start simply because there never was a clear understanding of exactly what was to be done. A definition of completeness or doneness was never documented and agreed to. This chapter gets you started on the right foot with a series of activities that lead to a clearly defined and understood definition of what the project is all about. I begin with a communications tool called Conditions of Satisfaction (COS).

NOTE The traditional project management approach assumes you have a clear understanding of what is to be done. In Chapters 13–19 where we deal with Adaptive and Extreme project management, I relax that requirement and deal with situations where the goal is not clearly, or cannot be clearly, defined.

The deliverable from the Conditions of Satisfaction will be a one-page document (with attachments) called the Project Overview Statement (POS). The Project Overview Statement clearly states what is to be done. It is signed by the parties who completed the Conditions of Satisfaction exercise. Once the POS is approved, the scoping phase is complete.

NOTE The COS works well for smaller projects. It does not scale to large projects. For larger projects a more formal process for gathering requirements is needed. See the "Requirements Gathering" section later in this chapter.

Managing Client Expectations

Somehow clients always seem to expect more than we are prepared to deliver. This expectation gap is more the result of a failure to communicate than it is of anything else. This lack of communications starts at the beginning of a project and extends all the way to the end. I believe that it does not have to happen. In this section I share a tool that I have used successfully for many years.

Understand at the outset that the tool is easy to explain and understand, but difficult to put into practice.

Sorting Wants versus Needs

I believe that the root cause of many problems that come up in the course of a project originate in a disconnect between what the client says they want and what they really need. The disconnect may come about because the client is swept up in a euphoria over the technology and is so enamored with what they see on the Web, for example, that they have convinced themselves they have to have it without any further thought of exactly what it is they really need. The disconnect can also come about because the client does not really know what they need. TPM forces them to specify what they want. If there is any reason to believe that what the client says they want is different from what they need, the project manager has the responsibility of sifting and sorting this out ASAP. It would be a mistake to proceed without having the assurance that wants and needs are in alignment. You don't want to start the project not knowing that the solution is in fact what will satisfy the client. That is one of the reasons for the Conditions of Satisfaction, discussed in the next section.

Wants and needs are related to one another yet fundamentally different. Wants tend to be associated with a solution that the client envisions. Needs tend to be associated with the problem. If wants are derived from a clear understanding of needs, then it is safe to proceed based on what the client wants, but you cannot always know that this is the case. To be safe, I always ask the client why they want what they want. By continuing this practice of asking why, you will eventually get to the root of the problem. The solution to that problem will be what the client really needs.

Developing Conditions of Satisfaction

If I had to pick one area where a project runs into trouble, I would pick the very beginning. For some reason, people have a difficult time understanding what they are saying to one another. How often do you find yourself thinking about what you are going to say while the other party is talking? If you are going to be a successful project manager, you must stop that kind of behavior. An essential skill that project managers need to cultivate is good listening skills.

Good listening skills are important in the project planning phase for two different project situations:

- The first situation, and the ideal one, occurs when a client makes a request for a project. At this point, two parties are brought together to define exactly what the request is and what kind of response is appropriate. The deliverable from this conversation is a COS.

■ The second, and more likely, situation occurs when you inherit what I call the "water cooler project." As the name suggests, these are the projects that are assigned to you when you accidentally meet your manager at the water cooler. Up to that point, you probably had not heard of the project, but you now need to find out all about it ASAP. The COS document is the result of your investigation.

This section describes the process for developing the COS.

The conversations and negotiations that eventually lead to an agreed-on COS have several dimensions. The process of developing the COS involves four parts:

Request. A request is made.

Clarification. The provider explains what he or she heard as the request. This conversation continues until the requestor is satisfied that the provider clearly understands the request. Both parties have now established a clear understanding of the request.

Response. The provider states what he or she is capable of doing to satisfy the request.

Agreement. The requestor restates what he or she understands the provider will provide. The conversation continues until the provider is satisfied that the requestor clearly understands what is being provided. At this point both parties have established a clear understanding of what is being provided.

Let's walk through an example. Suppose you want a certain model of widgets in forest green to ship to your warehouse by December 1, 2007. You decide to visit the manufacturer to make this request. The conversation would go something like this:

Requestor: I would like you to build five prototypes of the new forest green widgets and ship them to my warehouse on December 1, 2007.

Provider: You are asking if we can get five green widget prototypes into your warehouse by December 1, 2007?

Requestor: Actually, if you can get them shipped by December 1, 2007, that will be acceptable. But remember they have to be forest green.

Provider: So if on December 1, 2007, I can ship five forest green widgets to your warehouse, you will be satisfied.

Requestor: Yes, but they must be the new model, not the old model.

Provider: The new model?

Requestor: The new model.

Provider: I believe I understand what you have asked for.

Requestor: Yes, I believe you do.

Provider: Because of my current production schedule and the fact that I have to change paint colors, I can ship two forest green widgets on November 25, 2007 and the remaining three on December 8, 2007.

Requestor: If I understand you correctly, I will get five prototypes of the new forest green widgets in two shipments — two prototypes on November 25 and three on December 8. Is that correct?

Provider: Not exactly. You won't receive them on those dates. I will ship them to your warehouse on those dates.

Requestor: So, let me summarize to make sure I understand what you are able to do for me. You will build a total of five forest green prototypes of the new widgets for me and ship two of them on November 25 and the remaining three on December 8?

Provider: That is correct.

Establishing Clarity of Purpose

By the time you leave, both you and the manufacturer have stated your positions and know that the other party understands your position. While the example is simple, it does establish a language between you and the provider, and both of you understand the situation. The seeds have been planted for a continuing dialog. As the project work progresses, any changes that come up can be dealt with effectively because the effort has been made up front to understand each other.

The next step in the COS process is to negotiate to closure on exactly what will be done to meet the request. Obviously, some type of compromise will be negotiated. The final agreement is documented in the POS.

Our example was fairly simple. More than likely, the parties will not come to an agreement on the first pass. This process repeats itself, as shown in Figure 3-1, until there is an agreed-to request that is satisfied by an agreed-to response. As part of this agreement there will be a statement, called *success criteria*, in the POS that specifies when and how the request will be satisfied. It is important that this statement be very specific. Do not leave whether or not the conditions have been met up to interpretation. An ideal statement will have only two possible results — the criteria were met or the criteria were not met. There can be no in-between answer here. The success criteria (aka doneness criteria) will become part of the POS. The result is documented as the COS and becomes input to the POS.

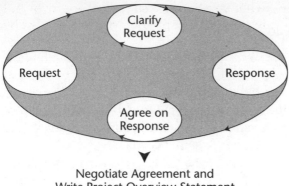

Figure 3-1 Establishing the Conditions of Satisfaction

This early step of establishing and agreeing to what will be done is very important to the success of the project. It is difficult to do a thorough job, especially when everyone is anxious to get to work on the project. It is also a painful process. People can be impatient; tempers may flare. You may be inclined to skip this step. Remember: pain me now or pain me later. You choose what you are willing to live with. Even if the request seems straightforward, do not assume that you understand what the requestor has asked or that the requestor understands what you will provide, even if the request seems straightforward. Always use the COS to ensure that you both understand what is expected.

Specifying Business Outcomes

As indicated in the previous section, it is a good idea to specify within the COS exactly what outcomes demonstrate that the COS has been met. The outcomes have been called success criteria, explicit business outcomes, and objectives, among other names. Whatever term you use, you are referring to a quantitative metric that signals success. I discuss that metric in more detail later in the chapter. For now just understand that it is a quantitative measure (profit, cost avoidance, improved service levels) that defines success.

Creating the Project Overview Statement

The Conditions of Satisfaction statement provides the input you need to generate the Project Overview Statement (POS). The POS is a short document (ideally one page) that concisely states what is to be done in the project, why it is to be done, and what business value it will provide to the enterprise when completed.

The main purpose of the POS is to secure senior management approval and the resources needed to develop a detailed project plan. It will be reviewed by the managers who are responsible for setting priorities and deciding what projects to support. It is also a general statement that can be read by any interested party in the enterprise. For this reason, the POS cannot contain any technical jargon that generally would not be used across the enterprise. Once approved, the POS becomes the foundation for future planning and execution of the project. It becomes the reference document for questions or conflicts regarding project scope and purpose.

My idea for the POS originated at Texas Instruments in the early 1960s. They used the POS as part of a process whereby anyone in the organization could suggest an idea for increasing efficiency, improving productivity, or seizing a business opportunity. One particular example has stayed with me over all these years. It involved a maintenance man whose only equipment was a Phillips head screwdriver. He walked those halls of an approximately 1,800,000 square foot building and tightened the screws that held the wall-mounted ashtrays in position. They became loose from people or equipment bumping into them. The maintenance man had an idea for replacing these screws with another fastening device that would not work loose and presented his idea with a POS. The project was funded and he was appointed project manager. The project was completed successfully and his job was thus eliminated. I hope he was able to move on to something a little more challenging and rewarding! Today several organizations use the POS or some adaptation of it.

Because the POS can be drafted rather quickly by one person, it serves to capture a brief statement of the nature of the idea. Senior management can react to the proposed idea without spending too much time. If the idea has merit, the proposer will be asked to provide a detailed plan. The idea may be conditionally accepted, pending a little more justification by the proposer. Again, the idea is pursued further if it has merit. Otherwise, it is rejected at this early stage, before too much time and too many resources are spent on needless planning.

The POS serves other purposes, as well, including use in the following situations:

Inherited project. Sometimes you inherit a project. In these instances, the project has been defined and scoped; a budget, staff resources, and a completion date also have been determined. In this scenario, do you write a POS? Yes!

There are at least two reasons to write a POS when you inherit a project. The first is to become familiar with and understand the project and the customer's and management's expectations. I can't stress enough how important it is for requestor and provider to ensure that what will be delivered is what the customer expects.

The second reason is that the POS will become the referent for the planning team. It is the foundation on which the project plan will be built. The project team can use the POS as the tiebreaker or referent to resolve any misunderstandings. In this case, the project scope has been determined, and it is up to the planning team to ensure that the resulting project plan is within the scope of the project, as defined in the POS.

A reference for the team. An equally important reason for writing a POS is to give your team briefing information on the project. Besides reaching a consensus with your customer on what will be done, the team members need to have an understanding of the project at their level of involvement. Think of this as a Conditions of Satisfaction for the team. Here the focus is on ensuring that the project manager and the team have a common understanding of the project. The POS serves as a good briefing tool for staff members who are added after the project commences. It helps them get up to speed with their understanding of the project.

Parts of the POS

The POS has five component parts:

- Problem/opportunity
- Project goal
- Project objectives
- Success criteria
- Assumptions, risks, obstacles

Its structure is designed to lead senior managers from a statement of fact (problem/opportunity) to a statement of what this project will address (project goal). Given that senior management is interested in the project goal and that it addresses a concern of sufficiently high priority, they will read in more detail on exactly what the project includes (project objectives). The business value is expressed as quantitative business outcomes (success criteria). Finally, a summary of conditions that may hinder project success are identified (assumptions, risks, obstacles). Let's take a look at each of these sections more closely. An example POS is shown in Figure 3-2.

Stating the Problem/Opportunity

The first part of the POS is a statement of the problem or opportunity that the project addresses. This statement is fact — it does not need to be defined or defended. Everyone in the organization will accept it as true. This is critical because it provides a basis for the rest of the document. The POS may not have the benefit of the project manager's being present to explain what is written or to defend the reason for proposing the project to management. A problem or opportunity statement that is known and accepted by the organization is the foundation on which to build a rationale for the project. It also sets the priority with which management will view what follows. If you are addressing a high-priority area or high-business-value area, your idea will get more attention and senior management will read on.

PROJECT OVERVIEW STATEMENT	Project Name	Project No.	Project Manager
Problem/Opportunity			
Goal			
Objectives			
Success Criteria			
Assumptions, Risks, Obstacles			
Prepared by	Date	Approved by	Date

Figure 3-2 An example POS

There are several examples of situations that will lead to a statement of the problem or opportunity that has given rise to this POS:

Known problem/opportunity area. Every organization has a collection of known problems. Several attempts to alleviate part of or the entire problem may have already been made. The POS gives proposers a way to relate their idea to a known problem and to offer a full or partial solution. If the problem is serious enough and if the proposed solution is feasible, further action will be taken. In this case, senior managers will request a more detailed solution plan from the requestor.

With the business world changing and redefining itself continuously, opportunities for new or enhanced products and services present themselves constantly. Organizations must be able to take advantage of them quickly because the window of opportunity is not wide and is itself constantly moving. The POS offers an easy way to seize these opportunities.

Customer request. Internal or external customers make requests for products or services, and their requests are represented in the COS. The POS is an excellent vehicle for capturing the request and forwarding it to senior management for resolution. More recently, with the empowerment of the worker, workers not only receive the request but also have the authority to act on the request. The POS, coupled with the COS, establishes an excellent and well-defined starting point for any project.

Corporate initiative. Proposals to address new corporate initiatives should begin with the POS. Several ideas will come from the employees, and the POS provides a standardized approach and document from which senior management can prioritize proposals and select those that merit further attention. A standard documentation method for corporate initiatives simplifies senior management's decision-making process for authorizing new projects.

Mandated requirements. In many cases a project must be undertaken because of a mandated requirement, arising from market changes, customer requirements, federal legislation, as well as other sources. The POS is a vehicle for establishing an agreement between the provider and the decision maker about the result of the project. The POS clarifies for all interested parties exactly how the organization has decided to respond to the mandate.

Establishing the Project Goal

The second section of the POS states the goal of the project — what you intend to do to address the problem or opportunity identified in the problem/opportunity section. The purpose of the goal statement is to get senior management to value the idea enough to read on. In other words, they should think enough of the idea to conclude that it warrants further attention and consideration. Several submissions may propose the same issue. Because yours will not be the only one submitted, you want it to stand out among the crowd.

A project has one goal. The goal gives purpose and direction to the project. It defines the final deliverable or outcome of the project so that everyone understands what is to be accomplished in clear terms. The goal statement will be used as a continual point of reference for any questions that arise regarding scope or purpose.

The goal statement must not contain any language or terminology that might not be understandable to anyone having occasion to read it. In other words, no techie talk allowed. It is written in the language of the business so that anyone who reads it will understand it without further explanation from the proposer. Under all circumstances avoid jargon.

Just like the problem or opportunity statement, the goal statement is short and to the point. Keep in mind that the more you write, the more you increase the risk that someone will find fault with something you have said. The goal statement does not include any information that might commit the project to dates or deliverables that are not practical. Remember that you do not have much detail about the project at this point.

The specification of a date deserves further discussion because it is of major interest to the client and to senior management. First, and most important, you do not control the start date and therefore you cannot possibly know the end date. For example, it might be that the most specific statement you could make at this point in time is that you could complete the project approximately 9 to 12 months after starting. Even such a broad statement as that is fraught with risk because you do not know the particulars of the project yet. Senior management will need some type of statement regarding completion before they will give authorization to continue the project to the planning stages. Your objective is to postpone giving any fixed duration or completion date until you have completed the project plan.

Unfortunately, most of us have a habit of accepting as cast in stone any number that we see in writing, regardless of the origin of the number. The goal statement should not include a specific completion date. (Easier said than done, I realize.) If you expect management to ask for a date, estimate the date to the nearest quarter, month, or week as appropriate, but with the caveat that the estimated delivery date will become more specific as you learn more about project specifics. It is important that management understand how some of the early numbers are estimated, and that a great deal of variability exists in those early estimates. Assure them that better estimates will be provided as the project plan is built and the project work is undertaken. Leave the specific dates for the detailed planning session, when a more informed decision can be made.

George Doran's S.M.A.R.T. characteristics provide the criteria for a goal statement:[1]

Specific. Be specific in targeting an objective.

Measurable. Establish a measurable indicator(s) of progress.

Assignable. Make the object assignable to one person for completion.

Realistic. State what can realistically be done with available resources.

Time-related. State when the objective can be achieved — that is, duration.

In practice I have incorporated the S.M.A.R.T. characteristics into both the POS and the project plan. The specific characteristic can be found in the problem/opportunity statement, the goal statement, and the objective statements discussed later in this chapter. The measurable characteristic is incorporated into the success criteria, discussed later in the chapter. The assignable, realistic, and time-related characteristics are part of the project plan and are discussed in Chapters 4 through 8.

Defining the Project Objectives

The third section of the POS describes the project objectives. Think of objective statements as a more detailed version of the goal statements. The purpose of objective statements is to clarify the exact boundaries of the goal statement and define the boundaries or the scope of your project. In fact, the objective statements you write for a specific goal statement are nothing more than a decomposition of the goal statement into a set of necessary and sufficient objective statements. That is, every objective must be accomplished in order to reach the goal, and no objective is superfluous.

A good exercise to test the validity of the objective statements is to ask if it is clear what is in and what is not in the project. Statements of objectives should specify a future state, rather than be activity based. I like to think of them as statements that clarify the goal by providing details about the goal. Think of them as subgoals and you will not be far off the mark.

It is also important to keep in mind that these are the *current* objective statements. They may change during the course of planning the project. This will happen as details of the project work are defined. We all have the tendency to put more on our plates than we need. The result is to include project activities and tasks that extend beyond the boundaries defined in the POS. When this occurs, stop the planning session and ask whether the activity is outside the scope of the project; and, if so, whether you should adjust the scope to include the new activity or delete the new activity from the project plan.

---

[1]George T. Doran, "There's a S.M.A.R.T. Way to Write Management Goals and Objectives," *Management Review* (November 1981): 35–36.

TIP You will find that throughout the project planning activities discussed in this book, there will be occasions to stop and reaffirm project boundaries. Boundary clarification questions will continually come up. Adopting this questioning approach is sound TPM.

An objective statement should contain four parts:

An outcome. A statement of what is to be accomplished.

A time frame. A preliminary estimate of duration.

A measure. Metrics that will measure success.

An action. How the objective will be met.

In many cases the complete objective statement will be spread across the POS rather than collected under the heading of "Objectives." This is especially true for the time frame and measures of success.

Identifying Success Criteria

The fourth section of the POS answers the question "Why do we want to do this project?" It is the measurable business value that will result from doing this project. It sells the project to senior management.

Whatever criteria are used, they must answer the question "What must happen for us and the customer to say the project was a success?" The Conditions of Satisfaction will contain the beginnings of a statement of success criteria. Phrased another way, success criteria form a statement of doneness. It is also a statement of the business value to be achieved; therefore, it provides a basis for senior management to authorize the resources to do detailed planning. It is essential that the criteria be quantifiable and measurable, and, if possible, expressed in terms of business value. Remember that you are trying to sell your idea to the decision makers.

No matter how you define success criteria, they all reduce to one of three types:

Increased revenue. As a part of the success criteria, that increase should be measured in hard dollars or as a percentage of a specific revenue number.

Reduced costs. Again, this criterion can be stated as a hard-dollar amount or a percentage of some specific cost. Be careful here because oftentimes a cost reduction means staff reductions. Staff reductions do not mean the shifting of resources to other places in the organization. Moving staff from one area to another is not a cost reduction.

Improved service. Here the metric is more difficult to define. It's usually some percentage of improvement in customer satisfaction or a reduction in the frequency or type of customer complaints.

In some cases, it can take some creativity to identify the success criteria. For example, customer satisfaction may have to be measured by some pre- and post-surveys. In other cases, a surrogate might be acceptable if directly measuring the business value of the project is impossible. Be careful, however, and make sure that the decision maker buys into your surrogate measure. Also be careful of traps such as this one: "We haven't been getting any customer complaint calls; therefore, the customer must be satisfied." Did you ever consider the possibility that the lack of complaint calls may be the direct result of your lack of action responding to complaints? Customers may feel that it does no good to complain because nothing happens to settle their complaint.

The best choice for success criteria is to state clearly the bottom-line impact of the project. This is expressed in terms such as increased margins, higher net revenues, reduced turnaround time, improved productivity, reduced cost of manufacture or sales, and so on. Because you want senior management approval of your proposal, you should express the benefits in the terms with which they routinely work.

While you recognize bottom-line impact as the best success criteria, that may not be possible. As an alternative, consider quantifiable statements about the impact your project will have on efficiency and effectiveness, error rates, reduced turnaround time to service a customer request, reduced cost of providing service, quality, or improved customer satisfaction. Management deals in deliverables, so always try to express your success criteria in quantitative terms. By doing this, you avoid any possibility of disagreement as to whether the success criteria were met and the project was successful.

Senior management also will look at your success criteria and assign business value to your project. In the absence of other criteria, this will be the basis for their decision whether to commit resources to complete the detailed plan. The success criteria are another place to sell the value of your project. For example, one success criteria can be as follows:

This reengineering project is expected to reduce order entry to order fulfillment cycle time by 6 percent.

Management may conclude from this number:

If that is all you expect to gain from this project, we cannot finance the venture.

Alternatively, they may respond:

If you can get 6 percent improvement from our current process, that will be a remarkable feat — so remarkable, in fact, that we would like more detail on how you expect to get that result. Can you provide an analysis to substantiate your claim?

Subjective measures of success will not do the job. You must speak quantitatively about tangible business benefits. This may require some creativity on your part. For example, when proposing a project that will have an impact on customer satisfaction, you will need to be particularly creative. There may be some surrogates for customer satisfaction. A popular approach to such situations is to construct a pre- and post-survey. The change will measure the value of the project.

Listing Assumptions, Risks, and Obstacles

The fifth section of the POS identifies any factors that can affect the outcome of the project and that you want to bring to the attention of senior management. These factors can affect deliverables, the realization of the success criteria, the ability of the project team to complete the project as planned, or any other environmental or organizational conditions that are relevant to the project. You want to record anything that can go wrong.

> **WARNING** Be careful, however, to put in the POS only those items that you want senior management to know about and in which they will be interested. Save for the Project Definition Statement (PDS) those items that are quite specific and too detailed to be of interest to senior managers. (I discuss the PDS in more detail later in the chapter.) The PDS list may be extensive. It will generate good input for the risk analysis discussed in Chapter 2.

The project manager uses the assumptions, risks, and obstacles section to alert management to any factors that may interfere with the project work or compromise the contribution that the project can make to the organization. Management may be able to neutralize their impact. Conversely, the project manager will include in the project plan whatever contingencies can help reduce the probable impact and its effect on project success.

Do not assume that everyone knows what the risks and perils to the project will be. Planning is a process of discovery — discovery about the project and those hidden perils that cause embarrassment for the team. Document them and discuss them.

Note several areas where the project can be exposed to factors that may inhibit project success:

Technological. The company may not have much or any experience with new technology, whether it is new to the company or new to the industry. The same can be said for rapidly changing technology. Who can say whether the present design and technology will still be current in three months or six months?

Environmental. The environment in which the project work is to be done can also be an important determinant. An unstable or changing management structure can change a high-priority project to a low-priority project overnight. If your project sponsor leaves, will there be a new sponsor?

And if so, how will he or she view the project? Will the project's priority be affected? High staff turnover will also present problems. The project team cannot get up on the learning curve if turnover is high. A related problem stems from the skill requirements of the project. The higher the skill level required, the higher the risk associated with the project.

Interpersonal. Relationships between project team members are critical to project success. You don't have to be friends, but you do have to be coworkers and team players. If sound working relationships are not present among the project team or stakeholders, there will be problems. These interpersonal problems should be called to the attention of senior management.

Cultural. How does the project fit with the enterprise? Is it consistent with the way the enterprise functions, or will it require a significant change to be successful? For example, if the deliverable from the project is a new process that takes away decision-making authority from staff who are used to making more of their own decisions, you can expect development, implementation, and support problems to occur.

Causal relationships. We all like to think that what we are proposing will correct the situation addressed. Assumptions about cause-and-effect relationships are inevitable. The proposer assumes that the solution will, in fact, solve the problem. If this is the case, these assumptions need to be clearly stated in the POS. Remember that the rest of the world does not stand still waiting for your solution. Things continue to change, and it is a fair question to ask whether your solution depends on all other things remaining equal.

Attachments

Even though I strongly recommend a one-page POS, there will be instances in which a longer document is necessary. As part of their initial approval of the resources to do detailed project planning, senior management may want some measure of the economic value of the proposed project. They recognize that many of the estimates are little more than a guess, but they will nevertheless ask for this information. In my experience, I have seen two types of analyses requested frequently:

- Risk analysis
- Financial analysis

The following sections briefly discuss these types of analysis. Check the bibliography in Appendix B for sources where you can find more information about these topics.

Risk Analysis

In my experience, risk analysis is the most frequently used attachment to the POS. In some cases, this analysis is a very cursory treatment. In others, it is a mathematically rigorous exercise. Many business-decision models depend on quantifying risks, expected loss if the risk materializes, and the probability that the risk will occur. All of these are quantified, and the resulting analysis guides management in its project approval decisions.

In high-technology industries, risk analysis is becoming the rule rather than the exception. Formal procedures are established as part of the initial definition of a project and continue through the life of the project. These analyses typically contain the identification of risk factors, the likelihood of their occurrence, the damage they will cause, and containment actions to reduce their likelihood or their potential damage. The cost of the containment program is compared with the expected loss as a basis for deciding which containment strategies to put in place.

Financial Analyses

Some organizations require a preliminary financial analysis of the project before granting approval to perform the detailed planning. Although such analyses are very rough because not enough information is known about the project at this time, they will offer a tripwire for project-planning approval. In some instances, they also offer criteria for prioritizing all of the POSs senior management will be reviewing. Some of the possible analyses are as follows:

Feasibility studies. The methodology to conduct a feasibility study is remarkably similar to the problem-solving method (or scientific method, if you prefer):

1. Clearly define the problem.

2. Describe the boundary of the problem — that is, what is in the problem scope and what is outside the problem scope.

3. Define the features and functions of a good solution.

4. Identify alternative solutions.

5. Rank alternative solutions.

6. State the recommendations along with the rationale for the choice.

7. Provide a rough estimate of the timetable and expected costs.

The project manager will be asked to provide the feasibility study when senior management wants to review the thinking that led to the proposed solution. A thoroughly researched solution can help build credibility for the project manager.

Cost/benefit analysis. These analyses are always difficult to do because you need to include intangible benefits in the decision process. As mentioned earlier in the chapter, things such as improved customer satisfaction cannot be easily quantified. You could argue that improved customer satisfaction reduces customer turnover, which in turn increases revenues, but how do you put a number on that? In many cases, senior management will take these inferences into account, but they still want to see hard-dollar comparisons. Opt for the direct and measurable benefits to compare against the cost of doing the project and the cost of operating the new process. If the benefits outweigh the costs over the expected life of the project deliverables, senior management may be willing to support the project.

Break-even analysis. This is a timeline that shows the cumulative cost of the project against the cumulative revenue or savings from the project. Wherever the cumulative revenue or savings line crosses the cumulative cost line is that point where the project recoups its costs. Usually senior management looks for an elapsed time less than some threshold number. If the project meets that deadline date, it may be worthy of support. Targeted break-even dates are getting shorter and shorter because of more frequent changes in the business and its markets.

Return on investment. This section analyzes the total costs as compared with the increased revenue that will accrue over the life of the project deliverables. Here senior management finds a common basis for comparing one project against another. They look for the high ROI projects or the projects that at least meet some minimum ROI.

CROSS-REF Many books provide more detailed explanations of each of these analyses. The bibliography in Appendix B contains some suggested titles.

Using the Joint Project Planning Session to Develop the POS

The Joint Project Planning (JPP) session is the tool I recommend for developing the project plan. I do not discuss the full project planning exercise until Chapter 8. However, this section briefly describes how it could be used to draft the POS. In fact, there will be situations where you will want to convene a planning session to draft the POS.

Whenever a COS exercise has not been completed and the project manager is given the project assignment (remember the water cooler example?), the first step that project manager should take is to convene a preplanning session to draft a POS. This session should involve the customer or his or her representative, the project manager, and, if they have been identified, key members of the project team.

Drafting the POS is the first part of the JPP. It may have to be completed in two parts. The first part drafts the POS; the second part completes the detailed plan after having received approval of the POS.

The first order of business is to agree on the request and the response to the request. These are the Conditions of Satisfaction, and they become the problem/opportunity, goal, objectives, and success criteria parts of the POS.

Next, you conduct a sanity check with those who were not party to developing the COS. Discussion should follow until all parties are satisfied with the request and the response. Expect to add to the COS in reaching consensus.

The last item is to complete the assumptions, risks, and obstacles portion. Here the planning participants will be able to offer a number of points to consider.

Beginning with the POS, the planning team will often begin the planning session by spending some time discussing the POS in greater detail. This will deepen the team's understanding of the scope of the project. That additional information should be documented in the Project Definition Statement (PDS). The PDS is a document for the exclusive use of the project team. It is discussed later in this chapter.

Submitting a Project for Approval

After the POS is complete, it is submitted to management for approval. The approval process is far from a formality. It is a deliberate decision on the part of senior management that the project as presented does indeed have business value and that it is worth proceeding to the detailed planning phase. As part of the approval process, senior management asks several questions regarding the information presented. Remember, they are trying to make good business decisions and need to test your thinking along the way. My best advice is to remember that the document must stand on its own. You will not be present to explain what you meant. Write in the language of the business, and anticipate questions as you review the content of the POS.

During this process, expect several iterations. Despite your best efforts to make the POS stand on its own, you will not be successful at first. Senior management always has questions. For example, they can question the scope of the project and may ask you to consider expanding or contracting it. They may ask for documentation showing how you arrived at the results that you claim in your success criteria. If financial analyses are attached, you may have to provide additional justification or explanation of the attachments.

The approved POS serves three audiences:

Senior management. Their approval is their statement that the project makes enough business sense to move to the detailed planning stage.

The customer. The customer's approval is his or her concurrence that the project has been correctly described and that he or she is in agreement with the solution being offered.

The team. The approved POS is their message from senior management and the customer that the project has been clearly defined at this high level of detail.

Approval of the POS commits the resources required to complete a detailed plan for the project. It is not the approval to do the project. Approval to proceed with the project is the result of an approval of the detailed plan. At this early stage, not too much is known about the project. Rough estimates of time or cost variables (or WAGs, for "wild a** guesses," if you prefer; SWAGs are the scientific version) are often requested from the project manager and the project team, as well as what will be done and of what value it is to the enterprise. More meaningful estimates of time and cost are part of the detailed plan.

Gaining management approval of the POS is a significant event in the life of a project. The approving manager questions the project manager, and the answers are scrutinized very carefully. While the POS does not have a lot of detailed analysis supporting it, it is still valuable to test the thinking of the proposer and the validity of the proposed project. It is not unusual to have the project manager return to the drawing board several times for more analysis and thought as a prerequisite to management approval. As senior managers review the POS, you can anticipate the following review questions:

- How important is the problem or opportunity to the enterprise?
- How is the project related to our critical success factors (CSFs)?
- Does the goal statement relate directly to the problem or opportunity?
- Are the objectives clear representations of the goal statement?
- Is there sufficient business value as measured by the success criteria to warrant further expenditures on this project?
- Is the relationship between the project objectives and the success criteria clearly established?
- Are the risks too high and the business value too low?
- Can senior management mitigate the identified risks?

The approval of the POS is not a perfunctory or ceremonial approval. By approving the document, professionals and managers are saying that, based on what they understand the project to involve and its business value, it demonstrates good business sense to go to the next level — that is, to commit the resources needed to develop a detailed project plan.

Participants in the Approval Process

Several managers and professionals participate in the approval process:

Core project team. At the preliminary stages of the project, a core project team may have been identified. These will be the managers, the professionals, and perhaps the customer who will remain on the project team from the beginning to the very end of the project. They may participate in developing the POS and reach consensus on what it contains.

Project team. Some potential members of the project team are usually known beforehand. Their subject matter expertise and ideas should be considered as the POS is developed. At the least, you should have them review the POS before submission.

Project manager. Ideally, the project manager will have been identified at the start and can participate in drafting the POS. Because he or she will manage the project, this person should have a major role to play in its definition and its approval.

Resource managers. Those who will be asked to provide the skills needed at the times when they will be needed are certainly important in the initial definition of the project and later during its detailed planning. There is little point in proposing a project if the resources are not or cannot be made available to the project.

Function/process managers. Project deliverables don't exist in a vacuum. Several units will provide input to or receive output from the project products or services. Their advice should be sought. Give them an early chance to buy into your project.

Customer. Our project management methodology includes a significant role for the customer. I have discussed the COS as a prerequisite to, or a concurrent exercise in developing, the POS. Many professionals are not skilled in interpersonal communications. Developing the COS is a difficult task.

In some situations the customer is the project manager — for example, if the development of a product or service affects only one department or in projects where the customer is very comfortable with project management practices. In these situations, I encourage the customer to be the project manager. The benefits to the organization are several: buy-in, lower risk of failure, better implementation success, and deliverables more likely to meet the needs of the customer, to name a few. Commitment and buy-in are always difficult to get. Having the customer as project manager solves that problem. For this approach to work, the technical members of the project team take on the role of advisor and consultant. It is their job to keep the feasible alternatives, and only the feasible alternatives, in front of the project manager. Decision making will be a little more difficult and time-consuming. By engaging the customer as project manager, the customer not only appreciates the problems that are encountered but also gains some skill in resolving them. I have seen marvelous learning-curve effects that have their payoff in later projects with the same customer.

Senior management. Senior management support is a critical factor in successful projects and successful implementation of the deliverables. Their approval says, "Go and do detailed planning; we are authorizing the needed resources."

Approval Criteria

The approval criteria at this stage of the project life cycle are not as demanding as they will be when it's time to approve the project for execution or addition to the organization's project portfolio. All that senior management is looking for at this point is a rough estimate of the value of the project to the organization. Their approval at this stage extends only to an approval to plan the project. That detailed project plan will give them a more specific estimate of the cost of the project. Knowing the actual costs, senior management can calculate the return that they can expect from the project.

Project Approval Status

In the absence of approval to plan the project, senior management might take one of several courses of action:

- They may reject the proposal out of hand. That decision will often be based on a comparison of expected benefits versus total cost coupled with a time frame as to when the benefits will be realized.

- They may request a recalibration of the goal and scope of the project followed by a resubmission to seek approval to plan the project.

- They might decide that a later resubmission is in order. In other words, they are not ready to commit to the project at this time.

Finally, the approval may be associated with a consideration to add the project to the organization's project portfolio. I defer discussion of that topic to Part III of this book, which discusses project portfolio management.

Conducting COS Milestone Reviews

The COS is not a static agreement. It is a dynamic agreement that becomes part of the continual project monitoring process. Situations change throughout the project life cycle and so will the needs of the customer. That means that COS will change. At every major project status review and project milestone, review the COS. Do they still make sense? If not, change them and adjust the project plan accordingly.

Requirements Gathering

As I indicated earlier in the chapter, the COS approach does not scale very well, so for large or complex projects you should opt for a requirements gathering approach. This is a more formal and structured approach to defining the project.

Requirements gathering is the first and very challenging task that the project manager and core team will face in the life of the project. To do this effectively is as much an art as it is a science. On the art side of the equation the project manager will have to read the customer and approach the gathering tasks appropriately. Some customers will be open and proactive in participating, others will not. Some will be sure of their needs, whereas others will be expressing their wants, which may be very different from their needs. The project team should be searching for needs. Wants often turn out to be an attempt by the customer to define a solution. On the science side of the equation are the many techniques that have been used successfully to gather and document requirements. I have had good success using an adaptation of the Volere Process, prototyping, business process diagramming, and use cases. Those are the four approaches discussed in this chapter.

What Are Requirements?

Requirements are the things that we should discover before starting to fully design, build, or execute a project. Discovering the requirements during execution/construction is so inefficient and detrimental that we will assume that no competent and right-thinking person would do so. A requirement exists because either the type of product demands certain functions or qualities, or the client wants the requirements to be part of the product/project delivery.

Project requirements start with what the customer really needs and end when those needs are satisfied. In the end-to-end chain of specifications, there is an ongoing danger of misunderstanding and ambiguity. This often leads to non-essential or over-specified requirements. Figure 3-3 illustrates the point.

Figure 3-3 Different perspectives on requirements

The Requirements Breakdown Structure

For the purposes of this book, I want you to envision a Requirements Breakdown Structure (RBS) much like the one shown in Figure 3-4.

The structure is useful as an aid in helping decide which project management approach is best for the project. For example, Linear and Incremental approaches would be appropriate for those projects in which all of the features for all sub-functions and functions are defined as part of the Defining Phase. If some features are thought to be missing, an Iterative approach may be appropriate. If some of the features and some of the functions are not known, then an Adaptive approach would be appropriate. Finally, if not only the functions are not known but also the project goal and solution are not known, then an Extreme approach would be best.

Figure 3-4 The Requirements Breakdown Structure

Types of Requirements

Requirements define the product or service that constitutes the deliverable of the project. These requirements are the basis for changes that a customer is seeking. At this stage, after stakeholder assessment, the project manager and the project team are now tasked with going through the steps to establish the requirements baseline. This process is a systematic, step-by-step effort that requires diligence. It is these requirements that will be used for estimating the cost and time for the project. Ultimately, these requirements drive acceptance of the product or service by the customer. Requirements are separated into four categories, not just considered as one large bucket of information.

Functional Requirements

Functional requirements specify what the product or service must do. They are actions that the product or service must take, such as check, calculate, record, retrieve. For example, *the service shall accept a scheduled time and place for delivery*.

Non-Functional Requirements

Non-functional requirements demonstrate the properties that the product or service should have in order to do what it must do. These requirements are the characteristics or qualities that make the product or service attractive, or usable, or fast, or reliable. Most non-functional requirements are associated with performance criteria and are usually those requirements that will establish the product or service boundary. Non-functional requirements can sometimes be generated by the refinement of a global requirement. Non-functional requirements are usually associated with performance criteria that set the parameters for how a system is to function. For example, *the product shall have a home-made appearance,* or *the product shall be packaged so as to be attractive to senior citizens.*

Global Requirements

Global requirements describe the highest level of requirements within the system or project. Global requirements describe properties of the system as a whole. During the initial stages of a project, many requirements end up being global requirements. They require the project manager and the team to refine them through the methods of requirement generation. Global requirements is a relatively new term. In the past, these have been called general requirements or product constraints or constraining requirements. The caution with global requirements is that in most cases they can be turned into non-functional requirements simply by asking the questions associated with what, why, or how. In fact, it is wise to move a global requirement to a non-functional requirement in order to gain a better focus on what the requirement really is. For example, *the system shall run on the existing network,* or *the system must be scalable.*

Product/Project Constraints

Product/project constraints are those requirements that, on the surface, resemble design constraints or project constraints. Design constraints are those preexisting design decisions that mandate how the final product must look or how it must comply technologically. Project constraints cover the areas of budget and schedule along with deadlines and so on. One important note here is that product constraints can be listed as global requirements, but project constraints *cannot.* For example, *the maximum system response time for any customer-based transaction must not exceed 4 milliseconds* or *the total out-of-pocket cost plus five-year maintenance must not exceed $35 million.*

   It is very important to realize that requirements identification and categorization is critical to understanding the direction of the project. It is now that the framework for the project begins to take shape.

Volere Requirements Process

This section is based on a modified Volere Requirements Process and its associated Specification Template. I have found this to be a best practice. Originally designed for use in Systems Application Development, the process is a generic requirements gathering and specification process whose principles can be applied to small and large projects across varied industries.

A graphic of the complete Volere Requirements Process (see Figure 3-5) shows the activities and how they are linked by their deliverables. The deliverables are shown as moving from one activity to the next. This represents the concept that the output from one activity is input to the next. This is not a hard-and-fast rule, as it is usually necessary for activities to iterate and overlap before the final product of the process is achieved.

Project Start

This is the same as the Scoping Meeting discussed later in the chapter. The project start is a joint planning meeting(s) where the project principals work together to define the project's overall objectives. Their goal is to gather enough facts and information to document the project scope and gain commitment for the project from the proper stakeholders.

Trawl for Knowledge

Once the kickoff is completed, the project manager and team (where applicable) start mining for knowledge and data. The initial scope of work and objectives must be broken down into specific types of work (disciplines and technology areas) for further detailed study. The team must query the users of the product, system, or facility in order to achieve the correct balance of functionality, constructability, compliance, operability, reliability, and maintainability.

To get started on the right foot in the requirements identification part of the baselining process, the project manager and the project team must have a stakeholder analysis along with considerable source documentation. The process of requirements identification should be just that — identification and only identification. Once a list of requirements is created, the team can assess what category to put them in. This must be done in order to prepare for effective requirements generation.

Figure 3-5 A modified Volere Requirements Process

The start of requirements identification — the systematic approach used to develop the details associated with each of the requirements — is prefaced by a discussion that focuses on the readiness of the requirements for the next step. These questions center on the next stakeholder. It is important here to double-check that nothing (as far is known at this point) is missing. A key question is "Is there sufficient detail to move on?" If the answer is yes, then it is on to generation; if no, then it is back to the stakeholders and the source documents for more discovery.

The steps to generate requirements begin by looking at the business function as a whole. This is quickly followed by the selection of a method or methods for generation. This effort must be planned. While in the generation session, be prepared with the appropriate documentation method to ensure that each requirement is documented.

There are several approaches to requirements gathering that can be imbedded within the Volere Process:

- Facilitated Group Session
- Interviews
- Observation
- Requirements Reuse
- Business Process Diagramming
- Prototyping
- User Stories
- Use Cases

As I have already indicated, from among these options I single out business process diagramming, prototyping, and use cases as the three that I have had the most success with. Typically, more than one method is chosen to generate the requirements on a project. Selecting the best methods to generate potential requirements for the project is the responsibility of the project manager, who must evaluate each method for costs, ease of implementation, and risks. Further, selection of a particular method should be based on specific product and project needs, as well as proven effectiveness. Certain methods have been proven effective for specific industries and products. An example of this would be using physical, three-dimensional modeling in product development and construction. We'll come back to a more detailed discussion of these three methods after this section.

Table 3-1 briefly describes the strengths and risks associated with each method.

Table 3-1 Methods for Requirements Gathering

METHOD	STRENGTHS	RISKS
Facilitated Group Sessions	Excellent for cross-functional processes	Use of untrained facilitators can lead to a negative response from users
	Detailed requirements can be documented and verified immediately	Time and cost of planning/executing session can be high
	Resolves issues with an impartial facilitator	
Prototypes	Innovative ideas can be generated	Customer may want to implement prototype
	Users clarify what they want	Difficult to know when to stop
	Users identify requirements that may be missed	Specialized skills required
	Customer focused	Absence of documentation
	Early proof of concept	
	Stimulates thought process	
Interviews	End user participation	Descriptions may differ from actual detailed activities
	High-level description of functions and processes provided	Without structure, stakeholders may not know what information to provide
		Real needs ignored if analyst is prejudiced
Observation	Specific/complete descriptions of actions provided	Documenting and videotaping may be time-consuming, expensive, and have legal overtones
	Effective when routine activities are difficult to describe	Confusing/conflicting information must be clarified
		Misinterpretation of what is observed

(continued)

Table 3-1 (*continued*)

METHOD	STRENGTHS	RISKS
Requirements Reuse	Requirements quickly generated/refined	Significant investment for developing archives, maintenance, and library functions
	Redundant efforts reduced	May violate intellectual rights of previous owner
	Customer satisfaction enhanced by previous proof	Similarity may be misunderstood
	Quality increase	
	Reinventing the wheel minimized	
Business Process Analysis	Excellent for cross-functional processes	Implementation of improvement is dependent on an organization open to changes
	Visual communication	Good facilitation, data gathering, and interpretation required
	Verification of "what is/what is not"	Time-consuming
Use Case Scenarios	State of system described before entering the system	Newness has resulted in some inconsistencies
	Completed scenarios used to describe state of system	Information may still be missing from scenario description
	Normal flow of event/exceptions revealed	Long interaction required
	Improved customer satisfaction and design	Training expensive

Write the Specification

At this stage of the requirements process, I would refer to all requirements as "potential requirements." The reason for this designation is that so far the requirements have not been fully scrutinized and/or have not passed the tests that would clear the quality gateway. Prior to inspection at a quality gateway, they need to be documented in a consistent format.

I recommend that you create a template on which to record the vital information regarding each requirement. That template should contain the following kinds of information.

Requirement Number

For traceability reasons each requirement must be uniquely identified. The reason is straightforward — requirements must be traceable throughout the development of the product, so it is convenient and logical to give each requirement a unique number. I use 'number' to mean any unique identifier, although it can be any kind of identifier you wish. To keep this from being an onerous clerical task, I suggest you use a simple sequential number. It is not important how you uniquely identify the requirement as long as you identify it.

Requirement Type

This will be one of the four requirement types identified earlier in this chapter. Attaching the type to the requirement is useful in several ways:

- The requirements can be sorted into type. By comparing all requirements of one type, you can more readily discover requirements that conflict with one another.

- It is easier to write an appropriate fit criterion when the type of requirement is established.

- By grouping all the known requirements of one type, it becomes more apparent if some of them are missing or duplicated.

Event/Use Case Number

The context of the work is broken into smaller pieces using the business events as the partitioning tool. For each business event, you decide which part of the response to that event will be carried out by the product. It is this part of the response — the part being done by the product — that is referred to as a use case. When you identify each use case, you identify the user or users who will interface with that part of the product. Each business event is given a number for convenient referencing. Similarly, each use case is numbered. For traceability and change control purposes, it is useful to keep track of all requirements that are generated by a business event. Each of your product use cases corresponds to a business event and the product use case. If, however, you choose to cluster your requirements into sub-use cases, then you will need a separate numbering system for your use cases. Whatever your preference, tag each requirement so that you can identify to which parts of the business it relates (business events) and to which parts of the product it relates (use cases).

During later analysis, you will analyze each business event and use case separately. Thus, it is convenient to be able to collect all the requirements for that part of the work. This will help you to find missing requirements, and to confirm the actions of a use case with its users.

Description

The description is the intent of the requirement. It is an English (or whatever natural language you use) statement in the user's words as to what is required. Do not be too concerned that it may contain ambiguities (but neither should you be sloppy with your language), as the Fit Criterion will eliminate any failings in the language. The objective when you first write the requirement is to capture the user's, or the client's, wishes, so for the moment a clear statement of the user's intentions suffices.

Rationale

The rationale is the reason behind the requirement's existence. It tells why the requirement is important, and what contribution it makes to the product's purpose. Adding a rationale to a requirement helps you to clarify and understand it. Having this justification of the requirement helps you to assess its importance when you are testing for gold plating in the quality gateway activity.

Source

The source is the nature of the person who raised the requirement in the first instance, or the person to whom it can be attributed. You should attach the source to your requirements so that you have a referral point if questions arise about the requirement, or if the requirement is rejected by the quality gateway. The person who raises the requirement must have the knowledge and authority that is appropriate for the type of requirement.

Fit Criteria

The fit criteria are quantified goals that the solution has to meet — they are acceptance criteria. While the description of the requirements is written in the language of the users, the fit criterion is written in a precise quantified manner so that solutions can be tested against the requirement.

The fit criteria set the standard to which the builder constructs the product. While they do not say how the implementation will be tested, they do provide the goals that the tests will use when they determine whether each requirement has been met.

Customer Satisfaction and Customer Dissatisfaction

The satisfaction ranking is a measure of how happy the client will be if you successfully deliver an implementation of the requirement. The scale ranges from 1 to 5, where 1 means that the client is unconcerned about the outcome and 5 means that the client will be extremely happy if you successfully deliver a product that contains the requirement.

The dissatisfaction rating is also on a scale of 1 to 5. In this context it measures the amount of unhappiness the client will feel if you do not successfully deliver this requirement. A 1 means that the client will be unconcerned if the product appears without this requirement, and the scale progresses through to 5, meaning that your client will be extremely angry if you do not successfully deliver this requirement.

Naturally, your client is expecting the product to be able to record the road network so that it can tell the engineers which roads have to be treated. The client is unlikely to get excited over this requirement, so the satisfaction rating may be anything from 3 to 5. However, if the product cannot record changes to roads, you would expect the client to be rather angry, and thus would give a dissatisfaction rating of 5.

This is a feature of the product that would be useful and nice to have. Your client may give this a satisfaction rating of 5. However, the requirement is not crucial to the correct operation of the product — the engineers would eventually notice if readings failed to turn up from one of the weather stations. In this case, the client may well rate the dissatisfaction at 2 or 3.

The satisfaction/dissatisfaction ratings are used to place a value against each of the requirements. The purpose of asking your client to rate the satisfaction or dissatisfaction level is that he or she will consider the requirement more seriously. It also provides an opportunity for the customer to let you know how they feel about each of the requirements. Later, these ratings will be weighed against the cost of the requirement.

The ratings are set either by your client or by a panel made up of the significant stakeholders. If the product is for sale to external customers, then these ratings should be done by a panel that represents the potential customers.

In one complex case I came across, portable telephones were being developed for sale in different countries. The marketing team had identified that customer priorities differed from country to country. Thus, the value ratings had to be separately assessed for each target country.

Dependencies

Dependencies are other requirements that have an impact on the given one. For example, there may be another requirement that will have to be changed if this one changes, or one whose data is linked very closely to the data that this one uses. Alternatively, there may be other requirements whose continued existence depends on the existence of this one.

Conflicts

Conflicts are other requirements that contradict this one, or make this one less feasible. For example, there may be a requirement that the product has to calculate the shortest route to a destination. There may be another that requires the product to calculate the quickest route to the destination. There could well be a conflict between these two if they are both considered to be the preferred route and if conditions dictated that the shortest route was not always the quickest route.

Similarly, you may discover a conflict between two or more requirements when you design the product and begin to look at solutions. It may be that the solution to one requirement means that the solution to the other is impossible, or severely restricted.

Conflicting requirements are a normal part of development. Don't be concerned when conflicts between requirements appear — as long as you can identify that the conflict exists you can work toward solving it.

History

This is the place to record the date when the requirement was first raised, dates of changes, date of deletion, date of passing through the quality gateway, and so on. Add the names of people responsible for these actions if you think it will help later.

> **NOTE** At this point the requirements are potential requirements. They must pass scrutiny in order to be part of the functional specification.

Quality Gateway

This is a single gateway that every requirement must pass through before it can become a part of the specification or scope. Every requirement must be checked for completeness, relevance, coherency, traceability, and several other qualities before it can be added to the specification or scope.

Requirements must be completely unambiguous and must be able to be measured against the client's expectation. If it can't be measured, then you can't be sure that the project/product will meet the client's expectations. This measurement is the fit criterion, and the gateway process ensures that a fit criterion is attached to each requirement. This also prohibits "requirements creep." The technology or readiness review is a form of the quality gateway. A peer review serves as a quality gateway for the definitive project scope, schedule, and budget.

Requirements Reuse

Prior to developing new requirements, you would review the specifications written for previous projects to determine potentially reusable material and standards. Sometimes you may be able to use these requirements in their entirety, although most times a bit of revision and customization will be necessary.

Take Stock of the Specification

The quality gateway exists to keep inaccurate requirements out of the specification or scope; however, it deals with one requirement at a time. At the point where you think the specification is complete (or close to being so), you would conduct a specification review to uncover missing requirements, consistency issues, and any unresolved conflicts between requirements (conflicting requirements).

This is also an opportunity to reassess the cost, schedule, and risk parameters of the product/project. This should continue iteratively until all elements of the specification or scope have been completely reviewed and approved.

At this point, there is confidence that the requirements specification (as written) can now become the requirements baseline. The most important reason for baselining is so that the project can proceed with the knowledge that the baselined requirements are essentially complete and reasonably stable. When the requirements are baselined, iterations of requirements generation have ceased adding significant value to the product. It is an indication that, with minor exceptions handled through change management, all requirements have been identified. It is now that the project manager can direct the project team to proceed toward finalization of cost and schedule estimates.

As a major precursor to the decision to baseline, it is essential to run the preliminary specification through a thorough analysis. This is a formal review accompanied by a detailed analysis that focuses on the attributes. In a "motherhood-type" statement, good requirements have certain attributes that make them good. An absence of attributes that can be verified and validated can render the product or service useless, or at least render it to the point where it cannot be baselined and the project cannot go forward.

In the requirements analysis, the attributes are verified through adequate measuring and testing. This is accomplished as a step-by-step process addressing each attribute. The process is a bit time-consuming, but the value is tremendous.

Table 3-2 is a list of attributes and the respective question(s) to ask about each one.

Table 3-2 Requirements Attributes

ATTRIBUTE	QUESTION(S) TO ASK
Completeness	Are the requirements essentially complete? Are some requirements missing?
Clarity	Are the requirements clear? Are they ambiguous or imprecise?
Validity	Do the requirements reflect the customer's intentions?
Measurability	Does the requirement have a fit criterion [measurement]?
Testability	Can the criterion be used to test whether the requirement provides the solution?
Maintainability	Will the implementation be difficult or easy to understand or maintain?
Reliability	Can reliability and availability requirements be met?
Look and Feel	Have all human factors been met (GUI, ergonomics, etc.)?
Feasibility	Can the requirements be implemented?
Precedent	Has a requirement similar to this been implemented before?
Scale	Are the requirements large and/or complex?
Stability	How often and to what degree might the requirements change?
Performance	Can the performance be met on a consistent basis?
Safety	Can the safety requirements be fully demonstrated?
Specifications	Is the documentation adequate to design, implement, and test the system?

The actual writing of the specification should use a combination of text and graphics. This provides those who will be the next-in-line users of the requirements with the documentation needed to go into design through to development and testing and finally to implementation. Once written, the specification must go through a review before final approval. There are three suggested methods for reviewing requirements:

- **Internal Review** — The Internal Review is conducted prior to formal evaluation and is aimed at identifying and correcting problems with potential requirements. This is usually led by a review facilitator with support from project team members and focuses on the material found in the preliminary specification — the goal is to find what may be missing or incomplete.

- **Walkthrough** — A walkthrough with the customer provides a good understanding of their needs. This method is used periodically and informally during the requirements generation process and involves some form of prototyping. This is a good method for obtaining customer feedback and, overall, getting user involvement.

- **Negotiation** — Negotiation is the process of resolving conflicts in requirements and reaching agreement with the stakeholders. This is an essential step in refining requirements. It is important to conduct these types of negotiations before the requirements baseline is approved. Too often, requirements generation teams avoid surfacing conflicts with customers and end users, allowing requirements errors to slip into design and development. This over-the-wall technique of requirements is both time-consuming and costly.

All requirements need to be approved by the critical stakeholders — for example, senior management, the customer, and the sponsor — before they become a part of the requirements baseline. The project team prepares the official copy of the specification for sign-off. The project manager must use his or her skills to sell the baseline and get approval. It is imperative to move to the next phase.

Analyze, Design, and Build

After the specification/scope has been completely reviewed and approved, the project team then begins the task of developing detailed and definitive estimates for time, cost, risk, and resources required.

Product Use and Evolution

This step is out of scope for the present project. It becomes input to further repetitions of the project to improve the product. The project or product is put to use for its intended function. Part of this phase is the transition from design to build to transfer care, custody, and control. This transition should include a detailed "lessons learned" session (post-mortem). For long projects, it should be conducted after each successive phase. This session should document breakthroughs in technology, approach, design, testing, commissioning, validation, and so on. The information will be used to facilitate a more streamlined process for successive similar projects.

Project Scoping Meeting

There are a variety of ways to scope the project. At one extreme is a formal multiple-day meeting and at the other extreme is scoping by walking around and conducting one-on-one interviews with sponsors, stakeholders, and customers. Both extremes and all of the variants in between are valid. It all depends. This section suggests the best way from my experiences. You will most likely throttle that way back to what is realistic for your environment, and that's okay.

The Project Scoping Meeting is your first substantive encounter with the customer. You may have had a Conditions of Satisfaction session and agreed on a high-level scope for the project. Typically that is a one-on-one meeting between the project manager and the customer. The Project Scoping Meeting takes the COS deliverable to the next level of detail. In this meeting, the core project team will be present, as will several key managers, staff, and end users of the project deliverables.

Purpose

There are two purposes in holding a Scoping Meeting. The first, which I talked about earlier in the chapter, is to draft the Project Overview Statement (POS). This is a one-page document that describes the project at a very high level. It is the document that will be submitted for consideration of planning the project. The second is to draft the requirements document. This document will be used as input to decide which project management approach is the best fit for this type of project.

Attendees

A meeting of about 15–20 people is manageable. If that is not adequate, you might think about having more than one scoping meeting. Three groups need to be represented:

- **The customer group.** Decision makers as well as operations-level staff should be represented. Among them should be the individual(s) who suggested the project.

- **The core members of the project team.** The core members are those experienced professionals who will be with the project from beginning to end. They are likely to be project- and subproject-level people.

- **The facilitator group.** There will typically be two or three such individuals. They are experienced in planning and facilitating the tasks that will be done during the Scoping Meeting.

Agenda

The agenda of this meeting should be as follows:

- Introductions
- Purpose of the meeting (led by the facilitator)
- Conditions of Satisfaction (conduct or review if done earlier)
- Description of current state (by customer representative)
- Description of end state (by customer representative)
- Requirements definition and documentation (led by facilitator)
- Discussion of the gap between current and end state
- Choose the "best fit" project management approach to close the gap
- Draft and approve the Project Overview Statement (whole group)
- Adjourn

For very small projects, the agenda can be accomplished in one or two days. It would not be unusual for larger, more complex projects to require a full work week to cover the agenda.

Deliverables

The optional deliverables that should come out of this meeting could include the following:

- Conditions of Satisfaction
- Requirements Document
- Project Overview Statement

The Project Definition Statement

As an optional deliverable from the Scoping Meeting, the core project team will often draft a more detailed POS that I call the Project Definition Statement (PDS). Just as the customer and the project manager benefit from the POS, the project manager and the project team can benefit from the PDS. The PDS uses the same form as the POS but incorporates considerably more detail. The project manager and the project team use the detailed information provided in the PDS for the following:

- As a basis for detailed project planning
- To merge the requirements document into a POS-like format
- To clarify the project for management

- As a reference that keeps the team focused in the right direction
- As an orientation for new team members
- As a method for discovery by the team

In most cases the PDS expands on two sections of the POS:

Project objectives. In the POS, the project objectives are written so that they can be understood by anyone who might have reason to read them. In the PDS, the situation is somewhat different. The PDS is not circulated outside the project team; therefore, the language can be technical and the development more detailed. Project objectives take on more of the look of a functional requirements or functional specification document. The purpose is to provide a description that the project team can relate to.

Assumptions, risks, and obstacles. The POS contains statements of assumptions, risks, and obstacles that will be of interest to senior management. For the PDS, the list will be of interest to the project team. For that reason, it will be much longer and more detailed. In my experience, this list is built during the Joint Project Planning session, whereas the POS list is built as part of the scoping activity of the project.

The PDS document was discussed for the first time in the second edition of this book. Since then, my consulting engagements have verified that the PDS can be used by the team to help them understand the project at their level of detail. The POS did not satisfy this need, so I developed the PDS. It is simply a variant of the POS designed specifically for the team. In implementing the PDS, I did feel that it could further clarify the communications problems that often arise in the project as team members come and go. In the several cases where I have used it, it has proven to be of value to the team.

At this point, you have documented the project through the POS and received approval from senior management to go forward with detailed project planning. The next four chapters are devoted to the second phase of the project management life cycle (which was discussed in Chapter 2): developing the detailed project plan.

Business Process Diagramming

NOTE This section is adapted from Appendix K of *Effective Software Project Management* by Robert K. Wysocki (Wiley, 2006).

Often, you will choose to start identifying requirements for the project by mapping the current ("As Is" process) business process or processes that are going to be affected. You might also want to map the business process after the solution is installed ("To Be" process). Both of these are excellent artifacts to use as input to the requirements gathering process.

From the systems development perspective, the process of gathering requirements often begins with knowledge of the current or "As Is" business process and ends with the "To Be" business process. That gap is filled with new or enhanced project deliverables. Having the "As Is" and the "To Be" business process flow diagrams is an invaluable aid in the ensuing solutions development effort.

It is an ongoing dictum of today's business that you must continuously improve your business processes. The old saying "If it ain't broke, don't fix it" no longer applies. If you aren't improving your processes and the way that they support your customers, you run the risk of losing market share. Your customer should also be taking the lead in approaching your teams to demand process improvement. Conversely, they are your customers, and you should be ever watchful for ways to improve the service they deliver to their customers.

All organizations are under pressure to improve. The pressure can come from the customer, the competition, environmental change, or a combination of the three. The improvements can be in their products or their processes. It is all too often the case that the customer doesn't give their business to the company with the best product. When customers find that a business is too difficult to deal with, they will decide to use second best, a supplier who is easier to deal with.

This also applies to internal organizations. One reason for outsourcing is a belief (frequently inaccurate) that other groups will be easier, faster, or cheaper to deal with. Internal organizations need to counter this belief by clearly demonstrating that they are continuously improving what they can deliver and their methods of delivery.

What Is a Business Process?

A business process is a collection of activities that takes one or more kinds of input from one or more different sources and produces value for the customer (see Figure 3-6). The focus of the business must be to ensure that the effort of dealing with the process does not outweigh the value received from completing the process.

Figure 3-6 What is a business process?

For example, order entry/fulfillment is a clear example of a business process. From the customer's viewpoint, the process starts when the customer places an order; it ends when the customer receives the goods requested. There are numerous activities in between. Credit checks may be run to confirm that the customer can pay for the order. Inventory is accessed to confirm you have what the customer is requesting. A typical list of activities would include the following:

- Receiving the order
- Logging the order
- Verification of completeness
- Customer credit check
- Determining the price
- Inventory checking
- Production request
- Order picking
- Order packaging
- Shipment

You will notice that the activity in a high-level business process might be regarded as a process itself by the performing organization. Processes can be decomposed into other processes until you reach the task level where some interim component is produced. The key is to start with the customer as the focus of the original process and define the subprocesses by their contribution to added value.

Characteristics of Business Processes

The more you understand business processes, the more you can improve them. To do that, you must clearly understand several characteristics of business processes:

- Flow — The method for transforming input into output
- Effectiveness — How well customer expectations are met
- Efficiency — How well resources are used to produce an output
- Cycle time — The time taken for transformation from input to final output
- Cost — The expenses of the entire process
- Non-value-added time — The time between process steps when no work is done on the product/service

Except for effectiveness and efficiency, these items are self-explanatory.

Process Effectiveness

Process effectiveness is how well the process meets the requirements of the end customer. It measures the quality of the process. Effectiveness is also how well the output of the process meets the input requirements of internal customers and how well the inputs from the suppliers meet the requirements of the process.

The effectiveness of every process can be improved. The direct result of increased effectiveness is happier customers, improved sales, and an increase in market share.

The first step in bringing about an improvement in process effectiveness is to identify the most important effectiveness characteristics. Effectiveness characteristics are indicators of how well the process is functioning. The goal is to be sure that the output meets the customer requirements.

Typical lack of effectiveness indicators are as follows:

- Unacceptable product and/or service
- Customer complaints
- High warranty costs
- Decreased market share
- Backlog
- Redoing completed work
- Rejected output
- Late output
- Incomplete output

During the walkthrough, the team should be constantly looking for and identifying effectiveness characteristics.

Process Efficiency

The achievement of process efficiency is for the primary benefit of the customer. Typical efficiency characteristics are as follows:

- Cycle time per unit of transaction
- Resources per unit of output
- True-value-added cost percentage of total process cost
- Poor quality cost per unit of output
- Wait time per unit of transaction

During the walkthrough, the team should be looking for ways to measure efficiency.

> **NOTE** Cost is an extremely important aspect of the process. Every organization should be looking for ways to control costs within their operations. The cost of a process is an accountability issue that should be analyzed. By controlling costs you will be able to increase your bottom line.

Streamlining Tools

Streamlining is the trimming of waste and excess in order to improve performance and quality. There are 11 tools for streamlining:

Bureaucracy Elimination

Removing unnecessary administration tasks, approvals, and paperwork.

Duplication Elimination

Removing identical activities that are performed at different parts of the process.

Value-Added Assessment

Evaluating every activity in the business process to determine its contribution to meeting customer requirements. Real-value added activities are the ones that the customers would pay you to do.

Simplification

Reducing the complexity of the project.

Process Cycle-Time Reduction

Determining ways to compress cycle time to meet or exceed customer expectations. Typical ways to reduce cycle time are as follows:

- Serial versus parallel activities
- Change activity sequence
- Reduce interruption
- Improve timing
- Reduce output movement
- Location analysis

Error Proofing

Making it difficult to do the activity incorrectly. Error proofing is the process of eliminating the opportunity to create errors. This can be accomplished in many ways. For example, you can automate a data entry process to remove the human error factor. Everyone has a tendency to make errors; therefore, the more you can automate a process the greater likelihood that a careless error will not occur.

Upgrading

Making effective use of capital equipment and the working environment to improve overall performance. Upgrading refers not only to improving your technology or office equipment, but also to your personnel. Continuous learning is the norm in today's business world. Organizations that provide training and educational incentives will reap large dividends in the long run due to increased profit and higher employee morale.

Simple Language

Reducing the complexity of the way you write and talk, making your documents easy to comprehend by all who use them. Simplifying the language of your documentation and training manuals will increase effectiveness. Some organizations become burdened by wordy reports and memos. Documentation should be written in simple language for a particular audience.

Standardization

Selecting a single way of doing an activity and having all employees do the activity that way all the time. Standardization of work procedures is important to ensure that all current and future employees use the best way to perform activities related to the process. When each person is doing the activity differently, it is difficult, if not impossible, to make major improvements in the process. Standardization is one of the first steps in improving any process, and is accomplished by the use of procedures. These standardization procedures should

- Be realistic, based on careful analysis
- Clarify responsibilities
- Establish limits of authority
- Cover emergency situations
- Not be open to different interpretations

- Be easy to understand
- Explain each document, its purpose, and its use
- Define training requirements
- Define minimum performance standards

Supplier Partnership

The output of the process is highly dependent on the quality of the inputs the process receives. The overall performance of any process improves when its suppliers' input improves.

All outputs require inputs, and in many cases these inputs come from outside suppliers. The first step in this streamlining process is to analyze the inputs to determine their necessity in the process. An organization can lower costs and increase efficiency by eliminating inputs that are not needed. The next step is to work with suppliers to make sure that the inputs are being delivered on time and are of the highest quality.

Big Picture Improvement

This technique is used when the first ten streamlining tools have not provided the desired results. It is designed to help the process improvement team look for creative ways to drastically change the process. There comes a point in time when you have to be willing to step back and look at the big picture of the process. By looking at the big picture, you examine the process from the perspective of what you would do if you abandoned the old way of doing things and started from scratch.

Defining a Business Process Improvement Project

The continuous improvement of business processes should be a high priority for every contemporary organization. Every time a process is executed a wealth of data and information is produced as a by-product. This data and information has great value in helping the process managers identify and isolate areas where improvement can be made. A business process improvement (BPI) project uses that data and information as input to programs designed to improve the process under consideration. This is represented graphically in Figure 3-7.

The goal of a BPI project is to eliminate or at least reduce the effect resulting from one or more process activities that are preventing the process from performing up to its potential.

There is a recurring backlog
at this process activity

Business Process

Figure 3-7 A business process improvement project

Figure 3-7 shows that a backlog exists at a process activity. From the diagram you might conclude that the backlog is the result of two upstream process activities both delivering output to the single process activity, and that process activity is not staffed to handle the volume. What seems like a simple solution — namely, add staff — might solve the backlog problem at that process activity but create another backlog at the following step. The backlog is just transferred, and the efficiency of the total process is not changed at all. This illustrates a common problem — subprocess maximization that may or may not positively affect the total process. In fact, it could reduce the efficiency of the total process. Obviously each of the activities in a business process could make the overall process cumbersome to deal with. The goal of business process improvement is to eliminate (or at least reduce) the pain coming from the activities that are doing the most damage, and this also implies that there may be one or more precursor projects that have determined the sources of pain, confusion, and/or chaos.

Beyond a single process improvement project, there is a continuous process improvement program. These by definition do not end. They focus on a complete process or process of processes. Their improvement goal is often of the form of an ideal end state and for all practical purposes will never be reached, but is a worthy goal nevertheless.

Watching Indicators of Needed Improvement

You need to define and track several metrics in order to discover process improvement opportunities. Some of the situations you will want to detect are as follows:

- Excessive wait time between process steps
- Backlog at a process step
- Idle workstations in the business process
- Frequent rework

- Excessive non-value-added work
- Errors and mistakes
- Frequent exception situations

For example, an order placement process might have a number of disconnects such as the following:

- Sales reps take too long to enter orders
- Too many entry and logging steps
- The same level of credit checking is done for existing and new customers
- Credit checking is done before order picking

Any of the preceding is a possible process improvement project.

Creating a Business Process Diagram

How do you diagrammatically represent a business process? You can use the standard flowchart symbols to keep it simple and couched in symbols you are already familiar with. Figure 3-8 lists the more commonly used symbols, and the following bulleted list explains them.

- **Operation** — This box denotes that a change has taken place. The input is somehow changed as a result of having gone through this process.
- **Movement** — This symbol denotes the movement of output from one process step to become the input to the next process step.

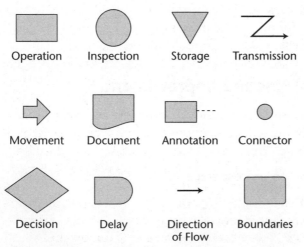

Figure 3-8 Standard flow chart symbols

- **Decision** — This is a decision step. A question needs to be answered. The two flows that emanate from a decision box are either Yes/True or No/False.

- **Inspection** — Someone other than the person producing the output must inspect it for quality, conformance, or some other tangible characteristic. Often an approval is included as a successful inspection.

- **Document** — This denotes a paper document.

- **Delay** — This symbol denotes a wait state in a process. It's usually associated with something joining a queue and waiting for the next process step to occur.

- **Storage** — Indicates that an item has been placed in storage and must wait for a release before moving to the next process step. These usually represent wasted time that must be removed from a process.

- **Annotation** — Provides added detail about some process, which is needed for clarification. It might also include the position title of the person responsible for the process.

- **Direction of Flow** — Denotes the order of process steps.

- **Transmission** — The interrupted arrow indicates when information is to be transmitted from one physical or virtual location to another.

- **Connector** — Used to connect flow between two separate locations; often used as an off-page connector.

- **Boundaries** — Denotes the initiating and closing process of a flow diagram. Usually the words START or BEGIN are associated with the initiating process, and STOP or END with the closing process.

Business Process Diagram Formats

Three common formats are used to render business process diagrams. The first (see Figure 3-9) is the top-down and left-to-right format. It is commonly used in program and system flow charts. The second is the "swim-lane" format (see Figure 3-10). It identifies the actors who participate in the business process.

Figure 3-9 is the format software developers will be most familiar with. It harkens back to the early days of programming and is the standard they adopted several decades ago. It follows the logical thought patterns of the software developer and is therefore their popular choice.

Figure 3-10 is the format I prefer when diagramming business processes. For one, it is a customer-facing format. By that I mean it is intuitive to the customer and represents their processes in a way that they can easily understand.

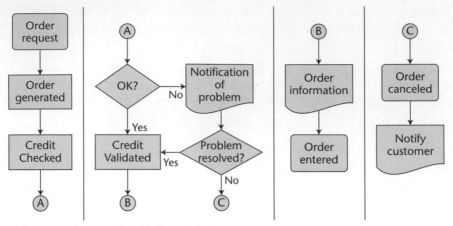

Figure 3-9 The top-down left-to-right format

Figure 3-10 The swim-lane format

Context Diagrams

One way to describe your process at a very high level is the context diagram. It is a good starting point. A context diagram describes a rough process or a set of processes. It generally has only a few components:

- A stick figure representing the external entity that is triggering the process

- A large circle representing the organization responding to the request
- A text block showing each organization or process acting to fulfill the request
- Arrows showing the rough flow between text blocks

The context diagramming process (see Figure 3-11) requires that the group identify one or more candidate processes. For example, a process might start with a customer request/action and end with a fulfillment. The modeling activity starts by identifying those two points. You show the process start by using an arrow from the customer to the organization. You show the process end by using an arrow from the organization to the customer. That provides an initial bounding of the process, and the group can decide whether that particular process has enough issues to warrant more time diagramming. If the process merits more discussion, the diagramming process continues by identifying the first group to receive the request and the action sequence that the organization performs to fulfill the request. Simply put, the group uses Post-it notes and arrows to show what goes on in the organization to fulfill the request. This should be done at a high level, and the constrained area of the circle helps maintain this high-level perspective.

Frequently the group will make refinements as they go. The most common refinement is a clearer identification of the customer being focused upon or the transaction being performed. For example, "customer" might become "existing customer" if the process is different (or should be different) for an existing customer versus a new customer. The group can then annotate the process with success criteria, issues, and so on.

Figure 3-11 Context diagramming process

Business Process Work Flow Diagrams

When you need to identify the actual and ideal path that any product or service follows in order to map process quality and identify deviations and improvement opportunities, the flow chart is another tool that can be beneficial in mapping process quality and performance. It is a picture of steps in a process, and can be used to examine the relation and sequence of steps; to identify redundancy, unnecessary complexity, and inefficiency in a process; and to create common understanding of the flow of the process.

Considered one of the simplest tools, the flow chart can be as basic or technically intricate as the process it is used to illustrate. Each type of process step is traditionally identified on the chart by a standardized geometric shape. A flow chart illustrates a process from start to finish and should include every step in between. By studying these charts you can often uncover loopholes, which are potential sources of trouble. Flow charts can be applied to anything from the travels of an invoice and the flow of materials to the steps in making a sale or servicing a product.

In process improvement, flow charts are often used to clarify how a process is being performed or to agree upon how it should be performed. When a process is improved, the changes should be noted on the flow chart in order to standardize the revised flow.

Follow these steps to create a flow chart:

1. Decide on the process to be diagrammed.
2. Define the beginning and ending steps of the process, also known as boundaries.
3. Describe the beginning step using the Boundaries symbol.
4. Keep asking "What happens next?" and writing each of the subsequent steps in Operations symbols below the Boundaries symbol.
5. When a decision step is reached, write a yes/no question in a diamond and develop each path.
6. Make sure that each decision loop reenters the process or is pursued to a conclusion.
7. Describe the ending step using the Boundaries symbol. Sometimes a process may have more than one ending boundary.

Documenting the "As Is" Business Process

One approach to identifying those goals is to develop a clear understanding of how the process is currently functioning (As Is) and how the process could work in the future (To Be). Knowing the gap between the present and the future is input to a plan to change the process (that is, to remove the gap).

The As Is is nothing more than a picture of how things are currently working. If you were talking about a hotel, you could build a model of the workflow associated with a guest obtaining a room, using hotel facilities, and checking out of the hotel.

For an old hotel with no automated systems, the steps would be manual and highly dependent upon the accuracy of individuals. Having this set of data alone can make some areas prime candidates for improvement.

There is a tremendous temptation to skip the As Is. People will say they know the process and what needs to be changed. If you skip this step, the team doesn't gain an increased understanding of how the process really works. Without that understanding, you have a very real chance of negatively impacting the customer.

Envisioning the "To Be" State

This model is a picture of how the process *could* work. The same work may be done, but the flow might be very different. In some cases tasks in the As Is state might be eliminated entirely. The intent of this model is to get people to talk about how it could be. This is sometimes done by having the subject matter experts explain how they would do things if they were building a brand-new process unconstrained by the way you have always done things. This is frequently referred to as the "green field" approach. Another approach is to have people identify those areas where they would like to change the current system to do things differently.

Defining the "As Is" to "To Be" Gap

The difference or "delta" between the As Is and the To Be shows the opportunities for improvement. It involves building a comparison of the two so that the differences can be categorized. Some tasks might be eliminated entirely. Some tasks might be done faster than they were before. Some tasks that had been sequential might be done in parallel. Others might be done to a higher level of quality. Some opportunities for eliminating the gap might include the following:

- Eliminate some tasks
- Speed up some tasks
- Introduce parallelism
- Increase quality

Prototyping

Many customers cannot relate to a narrative description of a system but they can relate to a visual representation of that system. For requirements gathering purposes, the idea of a prototype was conceived several decades ago. Its original purpose was to help customers define what they wanted. By showing them a mock-up of a solution they could comment on it and give the developers more insight into what constitutes an acceptable solution. Originally these prototypes were storyboard versions, not production versions. (Later prototypes did become production versions of the solution but that is another story for another time.)

Use Cases

Use cases are an excellent forum for working with the customer to define the functions and features of the solution. They tell the story of how the solution will operate in the mind of the customer and are documented following a specific graphic and textual format. They are rendered in the language of the customer and for that reason have found favor with most developers. In this section, I describe use cases in sufficient detail to get you started. The bibliography in Appendix B has several additional references for those who would like to explore use cases in more detail. Figure 3-12 depicts the position of use cases in the overall project scoping exercise.

Project scoping can be part of the Definition Phase or part of the Planning Phase. It is a matter of procedure and protocol in the organization. In the figure I show project scoping as lying between the Definition Phase, which has the POS as output, and the Planning Phase. It will be the same regardless of where you position it in your project management process. Requirements gathering consists of several different approaches of which use cases is but one. Once the use cases have been defined and documented, a single requirements document is assembled and the project can move to the approval stage or, if the approval stage has already been reached, to the Planning Phase.

There are two artifacts in use cases: use case diagrams and use case flow of events, both of which are described in the following sections.

Use Case Diagrams

A use case diagram is a simple way to describe how an individual interacts with a business process. It consists of one of more stick figures (the actors), ovals (the process steps), and connecting arrows (the interactions), as shown in Figure 3-13.

Figure 3-12 Use cases in the scoping phase

Actor: Someone or something outside the
system that interacts with the system

The System

Use Case: A sequence of steps performed
by the system to produce value for the actor

Figure 3-13 Use case diagram

An actor initiates the use case by interacting directly with the system. The
system gathers information from the actor, processes it, and returns a result to

the actor. In the simple example of Figure 3-13, the system asks the actor a question, the answer is processed by the system, and a result (money in this case) is delivered to the actor. This is the so-called "happy path." Several scenarios may spin off of this simple example. For example, in one scenario the actor may provide the wrong answer, and the system aborts the request. Alternatively, the system may give the actor a second opportunity to provide the correct answer. If this were an ATM scenario, it may be that the customer wishes to withdraw more than is in the account, and the system will return the appropriate message without the money, of course. The actor I have referred to is called the *primary actor*. There may be secondary actors as well. For example, if the online bank transaction requires another actor to verify account status, that actor is called a *secondary actor*. Again, the secondary actor may be someone or something, such as another system.

Use Case Flow of Events

This document reads like the script in a play. It is initiated with an action by the primary actor, the system responds, the actor takes another action, and this back and forth exchange continues until the use case ends. Consider the example of an order entry transaction with PDQ and a few of the scenarios that could follow. In this use case the actor is a customer who has direct access to the system. If a person were taking the order from the customer, they would be the actor and not the customer.

CASE STUDY – PIZZA DELIVERED QUICKLY (PDQ)

Here is an example of an order entry use case for PDQ.

BASIC FLOW OF PLACING AN ORDER

1. This use case begins when the actor indicates they want to place an order
2. The system requests order information (coupon information)
3. Actor provides valid order information
4. Actor indicates order information is complete
5. System validates address (additional detail)
6. System prices order
7. System displays the completed order with price
8. Actor confirms order
9. System assigns order to appropriate preparation location
10. System prioritizes order

CASE STUDY – PIZZA DELIVERED QUICKLY (PDQ) *(continued)*

The use case ends when the system prioritizes the store orders.

Again, this use case is the so-called "happy path." There are several alternatives that could fall under this use case. They are called *scenarios*. One scenario might be that the actor changes his or her mind and cancels the order after finding out the price. Another scenario might be that the system cannot validate the address and terminates the order.

Putting It All Together

In TPM, a clear understanding of the scope of the project is critical to the planning and execution phases of the project. I have described the Conditions of Satisfaction and the Project Overview Statements as the two basic tools for developing a joint agreement and a joint statement of scope in collaboration with the client. As you will see in later chapters, these documents are the foundation of the TPM approach.

Discussion Questions

1. Traditional project management depends heavily on being able to clearly define what the client needs. You cannot create a detailed project plan without that information. Within the framework of the TPM, what could you do if it were not possible to get that clear definition?

2. You have run the Conditions of Satisfaction by the book, and your gut tells you that the client's wants may be a bit too far-reaching. In fact, you have a strong suspicion that what they need is not what they have told you they want. Within the framework of TPM, what could you do?

3. Identify a business process in your organization with which you are familiar and can envision the need for change. Create the As Is and To Be business process flow. In describing the To Be business process be as creative and imaginative as you like.

CASE STUDY – PIZZA DELIVERED QUICKLY (PDQ)

4. Define the As Is and To Be business process flow diagrams for PDQ. You will have to make some assumptions. Just state them in your response.

Building the Work Breakdown Structure

Let all things be done decently and in order.

— I Corinthians 14:40

CHAPTER LEARNING OBJECTIVES

After reading this chapter, you will be able to:

◆ Recognize the difference between activities and tasks

◆ Understand the importance of the completeness criteria to your ability to manage the work of the project

◆ Explain the approaches to building the Work Breakdown Structure

◆ Determine which approach to use for generating the Work Breakdown Structure for a given project

◆ Generate a complete Work Breakdown Structure

◆ Use a Joint Project Planning session to generate a Work Breakdown Structure

◆ Understand top-down versus bottom-up processes for building the Work Breakdown Structure in the Joint Project Planning session

◆ Use the Work Breakdown Structure as a planning tool

◆ Use the Work Breakdown Structure as a reporting tool

The Work Breakdown Structure

The Work Breakdown Structure (WBS) is a hierarchical description of the work that must be done to complete the project as defined in the Project Overview Statement (POS). Several processes can be used to create this hierarchy, which I discuss in this chapter.

The requirements document is the input to the WBS construction process. If it is complete, then a traditional approach to project management can be taken. In most cases it will not be complete and some other project management approach will have to be taken. I leave that discussion for later and concentrate in this chapter on how to build a complete WBS.

An example of the WBS is shown in Figure 4-1.

To begin the discussion of the WBS, you need to be familiar with the terms introduced in Figure 4-1. The first term is *activity*. An activity is simply a chunk of work. Later in this chapter, in the section "Six Criteria to Test for Completeness in the WBS," I expand on this definition. The second term is *task*. Note that in Figure 4-1, activities turn to tasks at some level in the hierarchy. A task is a smaller chunk of work. While these definitions seem a bit informal, the difference between an activity and a task will become clearer shortly.

The terms "activity" and "task" have been used interchangeably among project managers and project management software packages. Some would use the convention that activities are made up of tasks, while others would say that tasks are made up of activities, and still others would use one term to represent both concepts. In this book, I refer to higher-level work as activities. An activity is composed of two or more tasks. When the tasks that make up an activity are complete, the activity is complete.

Another term is *work package*. A work package is a complete description of how the tasks that make up an activity will actually be done. It includes a description of the what, who, when, and how of the work. I describe work packages in more detail later in this chapter.

Breaking down work into a hierarchy of activities, tasks, and work packages is called *decomposition*. For example, take a look at the top of the WBS in Figure 4-1. Notice that the goal statement from the POS is defined as a *Level 0* activity in the WBS. The next level, Level 1, is a decomposition of the Level 0 activity into a set of activities defined as *Level 1* activities. These Level 1 activities are major chunks of work. When the work associated with each Level 1 activity is complete, the Level 0 activity is complete. For this example, that means the project is complete. As a general rule, when an activity at Level *n* is decomposed into a set of activities at Level *n* + 1 and the work associated with those activities is complete, the activity at Level n, from which they were defined, is complete.

Figure 4-1 Hierarchical visualization of the Work Breakdown Structure

Decomposition is important to the overall project plan because it enables you to estimate the duration of the project, determine the required resources, and schedule the work. The complete decomposition is developed by using the completeness criteria discussed later in this chapter. By following those criteria, activities at the lowest levels of decomposition will possess known properties that enable you to meet planning and scheduling needs.

This process of decomposition is analogous to the process many of us used in school to prepare a detailed outline of a research paper we were going to write. Despite the teacher's extolling the value of preparing the outline before we wrote the paper, we chose to do it the other way around — writing the paper first and extracting the outline from it. That won't work in project planning. We have to define the work before we set out to do it.

Those who have experience in systems development should see the similarity between hierarchical decomposition and functional decomposition. In principle, there is no difference between a WBS and a functional decomposition of a system. My approach to generating a WBS departs from the generation of a functional decomposition in that I follow a specific process with a stopping rule for completing the WBS. I am not aware of a similar process for generating the functional decomposition of a system. Veterans of systems development might even see some similarity to older techniques such as stepwise refinement or pseudo-code. These tools do, in fact, have a great deal in common with the techniques I use to generate the WBS.

Uses for the WBS

The WBS has four uses:

Thought process tool. First, and maybe foremost, the WBS is a thought process. As a thought process, it is a design and planning tool. It helps the project manager and the project team visualize exactly how the work of the project can be defined and managed effectively. It would not be unusual to consider alternative ways of decomposing the work until an alternative is found with which the project manager is comfortable.

Architectural design tool. When all is said and done, the WBS is a picture of the work of the project and how the items of work are related to one another. It must make sense. In that context, it is a design tool.

Planning tool. In the planning phase, the WBS gives the project team a detailed representation of the project as a collection of activities that must be completed in order for the project to be completed. It is at the lowest activity level of the WBS that we will estimate effort, elapsed time, and resource requirements; build a schedule of when the work will be completed; and estimate deliverable dates and project completion.

Project status reporting tool. The WBS is used as a structure for reporting project status. The project activities are consolidated (that is, rolled up) from the bottom as lower-level activities are completed. As work is completed, activities will be completed. Completion of lower-level activities causes higher-level activities to be partially complete. Some of these higher-level activities may represent significant progress whose completion will be milestone events in the course of the project. Thus, the WBS defines milestone events that can be reported to senior management and the customer.

NOTE Trying to find a happy compromise between a WBS architecture that lends itself well to the planning thought process and the rolling up of information for summary reporting can be difficult. It is best to have input from all the parties that may be using the WBS before settling on a design. There is no one right way to do it; it's subjective. You will get better with practice.

In the final analysis, it is the project manager who decides on the architecture of the WBS and the level of detail required. This detail is important because the project manager is accountable for the success of the project. The WBS must be defined so that the project manager can manage the project. That means that the approach and detail in the WBS might not be the way others would have approached it. Apart from any senior management requirements for reporting or organizational requirements for documentation or process, the project manager is free to develop the WBS according to his or her needs and those of management. Because of this requirement, the WBS is not unique. That should not bother you because all that is required is a WBS that defines the project work so that you, the project manager, can manage it. "Beauty is in the eyes of the beholder" applies equally well to the WBS.

Generating the WBS

The best way to generate the WBS is as part of the Joint Project Planning (JPP) session. I describe the steps as we look at two different approaches to building the WBS. Before I discuss those approaches, I want to recall where we are in the planning process and then offer a few general comments about procedures I have followed in my practice regardless of the approach taken.

One of two simple decomposition processes is used to identify the activities that must be performed from the beginning to the completion of the project. These activities are the lowest level of managed work for the project manager. At this point in the planning process, you should have completed the Project Overview Statement. You may have to go back and reconsider the POS as a result of further planning activities, but for now assume the POS is complete. My technique for generating the WBS will reduce even the most complex project to a set of clearly defined activities. The WBS will be the document that guides the remainder of the planning activities.

As many as 10 to 20 participants may be involved in building the WBS, so gathering around a computer screen won't do the job. Neither will projecting the screen on an overhead LCD projector. The only way I have found that works consistently is to use Post-It notes, marking pens, and plenty of whiteboard space. In the absence of whiteboard space, you might wallpaper the planning room with flip-chart or butcher paper. You cannot have too much writing space. Using butcher paper, I have even filled the four walls of the planning room and several feet of hallway outside the planning room. It is sloppy, but it gets the job done.

Two approaches can be used to identify the project activities. The first is the top-down approach; the second is the bottom-up approach.

Top-Down Approach

The top-down approach begins at the goal level and successively partitions work down to lower levels of definition until the participants are satisfied that the work has been sufficiently defined. The completion criteria discussed later in this chapter structure the partitioning exercise for this approach.

Once the project activities have been defined using the top-down approach, they are defined at a sufficient level of detail to enable you to estimate time, cost, and resource requirements first at the activity level and then aggregate to the project level. Because the activities are defined to this level of detail, project time, cost, and resource requirements are estimated much more accurately.

Once the activities are described, you can sequence the project work so that as many activities as possible are performed in parallel, rather than in sequence. In other words, the list of activities can be sequenced so that the project duration (clock time needed to complete all project work) will be much shorter than the sum of all the times needed to complete each activity.

I recommend two variations of the top-down approach. I have used both in my consulting practice.

Team Approach

The team approach, while it requires more time to complete than the subteam approach discussed next, is the better of the two. In this approach the entire team works on all parts of the WBS. For each Level 1 activity, appoint the most knowledgeable member of the planning team to facilitate the further decomposition of that part of the WBS. Continue with similar appointments until the WBS is complete. This approach enables all members of the planning team to pay particular attention to the WBS as it is developed, noting discrepancies and commenting on them in real time.

Subteam Approach

When time is at a premium, the planning facilitator will prefer the subteam approach. The first step is to divide the planning team into as many subteams as there are activities at Level 1 of the WBS. Then follow these steps:

1. The planning team agrees on the approach to building the first level of the Work Breakdown Structure.

2. The planning team creates the Level 1 activities.

3. A subject matter expert leads the team in further decomposition of the WBS for his or her area of expertise.

4. The team suggests decomposition ideas for the expert until each activity within the Level 1 activities meets the WBS completion criteria.

Note that the entire planning team decides on the approach for the first-level breakdown. After that the group is partitioned into subteams, with each subteam having some expertise for that part of the WBS. It is hoped that they will have all the expertise they need to develop their part of the WBS. If not, outside help may be brought in as needed. Be careful not to clutter the team with too many people.

It is important to pay close attention to each presentation and ask yourself these questions: Is there something in the WBS that I did not expect to see? Or is there something not there that I expected to see? The focus here is to strive for a complete WBS. In cases where the WBS will be used for reporting purposes, the project manager must be careful to attach lower-level activities to higher-level activities to preserve the integrity of the status reports that will be generated.

As the discussion continues and activities are added and deleted from the WBS, questions about agreement between the WBS and the POS will occur. Throughout the exercise, the POS should be posted on flip-chart paper and hung on the walls of the planning room. Each participant should compare the scope of the project as described in the POS with the scope as presented in the WBS. If something in the WBS appears out of scope, challenge it. Either redefine the scope or discard the appropriate WBS activities. Similarly, look for complete coverage of the scope as described in the WBS with the POS. This is the time to be critical and carefully define the scope and work to accomplish it. Mistakes found now, before any work is done, are far less costly and disruptive than they will be if found late in the project.

The dynamic at work here is one of changing project boundaries. Despite all efforts to the contrary, the boundaries of the project are never clearly defined at the outset. There will always be reasons to question what is in and what is not in the project. That is fine. Just remember that the project boundaries have not yet been formally set. That will happen once the project has been approved to begin. Until then, you are still in the planning mode, and nothing is set in concrete.

Bottom-Up Approach

Another method for identifying the activities in the project is to take a bottom-up approach. This approach is more like a brainstorming session than an organized approach to building the WBS.

The bottom-up approach works as follows: The first steps are the same as those for the top-down approach. Namely, the entire planning team agrees to the first-level breakdown. The planning team is then divided into as many groups as there are first-level activities. Each group then makes a list of the activities that must be completed in order to complete the first-level activity. To do this, they proceed as follows:

1. Someone in the group identifies an activity and announces it to the group. If the group agrees, then the activity is written on a slip of paper and put in the middle of the table. The process repeats itself until no new ideas are forthcoming.

2. The group then sorts the slips into activities that seem to be related to one another. This grouping activity should help the planning team add missing activities or remove redundant ones.

3. Once the team is satisfied it has completed the activity list for the first-level breakdown, the members are finished. Each group then reports to the entire planning team the results of its work.

4. Final critiques are given, missing activities are added, and redundant activities are removed.

WARNING While this approach has worked well in many cases, there is the danger of not defining all activities or defining activities at too high or low a level of granularity. The completeness criteria that I define later in the chapter are not ensured through this process. My caution, then, is that you may not have as manageable a project as you would if you followed the top-down approach. Obviously, risk is associated with the bottom-up approach; if you do not have to take the risk, why expose yourself to it voluntarily? Unless there is a compelling reason to the contrary, I recommend the top-down approach. In my experience there is less danger of missing part of the project work using the top-down approach.

WBS for Small Projects

While I have advocated a whiteboard-and-marker approach to building the WBS, I would be remiss if I did not make you aware of some automated tools that you might want to consider for small projects. Small projects are those in which the team might be you or you and only one or two others. While the approaches described previously could certainly be used, you might want to consider modifying the approach taken to incorporate some help from available software. I have used a technique called *mindmapping*.

Mindmapping has been popularized by Joyce Wycoff[1] and Tony Buzan.[2] The technique is best described as a graphic dump of your brain. It is a nonsequential approach to recording your thoughts about things that must be done or considered in completing a certain task. Figure 4-2 is an example output from a software package called MindManager, which was developed and is sold through the Buzan Centre.[3]

[1]Joyce Wycoff, *Mindmapping* (New York: Berkley Books, 1991).

[2]Tony Buzan, *The Mind Map* (New York: Penguin Group, 1996).

[3]The Buzan Centre's U.S. distribution center can be contacted at (561) 881-0188 or BuzanCentres@Buzan.co.uk.

Figure 4-2 A typical mindmap generated by MindManager

Intermediate WBS for Large Projects

For very large projects, you may be tempted to modify the top-down approach. While I prefer to avoid modification, difficulty in scheduling people for the planning meeting may necessitate some modification. I offer here not another approach but rather a modification to the top-down approach.

As project size increases, it becomes unwieldy to build the entire WBS with the entire planning team assembled. When the size of the project forces you into this situation, begin by decomposing the WBS down to Level 3. At that point, develop intermediate estimates of time, resources, and dependencies for all Level 3 activities. The planning session is adjourned, and the Level 3 activity managers are charged with completing the WBS for their part of the project. They will convene a JPP session to complete that work. The JPP facilitator may choose to consolidate these Level 3 WBSs into the WBS for the entire project. Then the full JPP team can be reassembled and the planning process continues from that point.

In many large projects, the project manager may manage only down to the Level 3 activities and leave it to the Level 3 activity managers to manage their part of the project according to the schedule developed at Level 3.

Iterative Development of the WBS

Once the Requirements Breakdown Structure (RBS) has been built, the best fit project management approach will become obvious. Depending on the degree of completeness of the RBS, you will choose one of the five approaches (Linear, Incremental, Iterative, Adaptive, or Extreme). As discussed earlier in the chapter, the less you know about the RBS and the less certain you are that the customer has been able to define the solution, the more likely you are to choose an approach toward the Adaptive and Extreme part of the landscape. The Linear and Incremental approaches require a complete WBS. The Iterative approaches can work in those cases where all of the functionality has been defined and only a few features have not. These features will be described at the lower levels of decomposition of the WBS, but they will not be completely defined. When there are missing or incomplete functions, an Adaptive approach should be used, and the WBS will have large gaps that need to be defined through iteration. Finally, when even the goal is not clearly defined, very little of the WBS can be built at the beginning of the project. Both the goal and solution (functions and features) must be defined through iteration.

Six Criteria to Test for Completeness in the WBS

Developing the WBS is the most critical part of the JPP. If you do this part right, the rest is comparatively easy. How do you know that you've done this right? Each activity must possess the following six characteristics in order to be considered complete — that is, completely decomposed. Once an activity has reached that status its name changes from activity to task. The six characteristics that an activity must possess to be called a task are as follows:

- Status/completion is measurable.
- The activity is bounded.
- The activity has a deliverable.
- Time and cost are easily estimated.
- Activity duration is within acceptable limits.
- Work assignments are independent.

If the activity does not possess all six of these characteristics, decompose the activity and check again at that next lower level of decomposition. As soon as an activity possesses the six characteristics, there is no need to further decompose it. As soon as every activity in the WBS possesses these six characteristics, the WBS is defined as complete. Earlier, a four-criteria version of this completion test was introduced by Weiss and Wysocki (1991).[4] I have continued to refine the criteria and present an updated version here. The following sections look at each of these characteristics in more detail.

Status and Completion Are Measurable

The project manager can question the status of an activity at any point in time during the project. If the activity has been defined properly, that question is answered easily. For example, if a system's documentation is estimated to be about 300 pages long and requires approximately four months of full-time work to write, here are some possible reports that your activity manager could provide regarding the status:

- The activity is supposed to take four months of full-time work. I've been working on it for two months full-time. I guess I must be 50 percent complete.

- I've written 150 pages, so I guess I am 50 percent complete.

- I've written and had approved 150 pages and estimate that the remaining work will require two more months. I am 50 percent complete.

No one would buy the first answer, but how many times is that the information we get? Even worse, how many times do we accept it as a valid statement of progress? Although the second answer is a little better, it doesn't say anything about the quality of the 150 pages that have been written, nor does it say anything about the re-estimate of the remaining work. You can see that an acceptable answer must state what has been actually completed (approved, not just written, in this example) and what remains to be done, along with an estimate to completion. Remember that you always know more tomorrow than you do today. After working through about half of the activity, the activity manager should be able to give a very accurate estimate of the time required to complete the remaining work.

A simple metric that has met with some success is to compute the proportion of tasks completed as a percentage of all the tasks that make up the activity. For example, suppose the activity has six tasks associated with it and four of the tasks are complete; the ratio of tasks completed to total tasks is 4/6 — that is, the activity is 66 percent complete. Even if work were done on the fifth task in this activity, because the task is not complete on the report date it cannot be counted in the ratio. This metric certainly represents a very objective measure. Although it isn't completely accurate, it is a good technique. Best of all, it is quick. A project manager and activity manager do not have to sit

---

[4]Joseph W. Weiss and Robert K. Wysocki, *5-Phase Project Management: A Practical Planning and Implementation Guide* (Reading, MA: Perseus Publishing Company, 1991).

around mired in detail about the percentage complete. You can use this same approach to measure the earned value of an activity.

CROSS-REF I define and discuss earned value in Chapter 10.

The Activity Is Bounded

Each activity should have a clearly defined start and end event. Once the start event has occurred, work can begin on the activity. The deliverable is most likely associated with the end event that signals work is closed on the activity. For example, using the systems documentation example, the start event might be notifying the team member who will manage the creation of the systems documentation that the final acceptance tests of the system are complete. The end event would be notifying the project manager that the customer has approved the systems documentation.

The Activity Has a Deliverable

The result of completing the work that makes up the activity is the production of a deliverable. The deliverable is a visible sign that the activity is complete. This sign could be an approving manager's signature, a physical product or document, the authorization to proceed to the next activity, or some other sign of completion. The deliverable(s) from an activity is output from that activity, which then becomes input to one or more other activities that follow its completion.

Time and Cost Are Easily Estimated

Each activity should have an estimated time and cost of completion. Being able to do this at the lowest level of decomposition in the WBS enables you to aggregate to higher levels and estimate the total project cost and the completion date. By successively decomposing activities to finer levels of granularity, you are likely to encounter primitive activities that you have performed before. This experience at lower levels of definition gives you a stronger base on which to estimate activity cost and duration for similar activities.

CROSS-REF Chapter 5 covers activity duration estimation in more detail.

Activity Duration Is Within Acceptable Limits

While there is no fixed rule for the duration of an activity, I recommend that activities have a duration of less than two calendar weeks. This seems to be a common practice in many organizations. Even for long projects in which contractors may be responsible for major pieces of work, they will generate plans that decompose their work to activities having this activity duration. Exceptions will occur when the activity defines process work, such as in many manufacturing situations. In addition, there will be exceptions for those activities whose work is repetitive and simple. For example, if you are going to build 500 widgets and it takes 10 weeks to complete this activity, you need not decompose the activity into five activities with each one building 100 widgets. This type of activity requires no further breakdown. If you can estimate the time to check one document, then it does not make much difference if the activity requires two months to check 400 documents or four two-week periods to check 100 documents per period. The danger you avoid is longer-duration activities whose delay can create a serious project-scheduling problem.

Work Assignments Are Independent

It is important that each activity be independent. Once work has begun on the activity, it should continue reasonably well without interruption and without the need for additional input or information until the activity is complete. The work effort could be contiguous, but it can be scheduled otherwise for a variety of reasons. You can choose to schedule it in parts because of resource availability, but you could have scheduled it as one continuous stream of work.

Related to activity independence is the temptation to micromanage an activity. Best practices suggest that you manage an individual's work down to units of one week. For example, Harry is going to work on an activity that will require 10 hours of effort. The activity is scheduled to begin on Monday morning and be completed by Friday afternoon. Harry has agreed that he can accommodate the 10 hours within the week, given his other commitments that same week. Harry's manager (or the project manager) could ask Harry to report exactly when during the week he will be working on this 10-hour activity and then hold him to that plan, but what a waste of everyone's time that would be! Why not give Harry credit for enough intelligence to manage his commitments at the one-week level? No need to drill down into the workweek and burden Harry with a micro-plan and his manager with the task of managing that micro-plan. Such a scenario may in fact increase the time to complete the activity because it has been burdened with unnecessary management overhead.

The Seventh Criteria for Judging Completeness

I've separated this from the preceding six criteria because it is not a criterion in the same sense as those six. The seventh is pure judgment on the part of the project manager. A WBS could be defined as complete based on the preceding six criteria, yet the project manager might have a lingering doubt simply because of the way the client conducted themselves during the WBS decomposition process. Something might alert the project manager that things may not be what they seem to be. For example, perhaps the client never seemed to be fully engaged or never bought into the decomposition process. They simply went along with the exercise but never really contributed to it. That might give you reason to suspect that scope change requests may be just around the corner and that you had better have chosen a project management approach that accommodates change, rather than one that incorrectly assumes the WBS to be complete. Better to be safe than sorry. If there is any doubt in your mind about the completeness of the WBS, choose some type of Iterative approach so that you will be in a position to accept scope change requests.

Exceptions to the Completion Criteria Rule

In some cases the completion criteria do not have to be satisfied in order for the WBS to be considered complete. Two common scenarios are discussed in the sections that follow.

Stopping Before Completion Criteria Are Met

A common situation where this occurs is duration related. Suppose the activity calls for building 100 widgets, and it takes one day per widget. The maximum duration for a task has been set at 10 days. If you follow that rule, you would decompose the activity to build 100 widgets into 10 activities. That doesn't add any value to the WBS; it only adds management time. Leave the activity at 100 days and simply ask for status at the appropriate intervals. Adding activities that simply increase management time and not value to the project are a waste of time.

Decomposing Beyond Completion of the Criteria

For projects of a shorter duration, say four weeks, it would be poor management to set that acceptable duration at 10 days. That would create a situation with too few management checkpoints and hence create a project that would be poorly managed. For these situations the acceptable duration limit might be set at three days, for example. Even shorter duration limits might be imposed for projects that contain surgical procedures or other processes of very short duration. If the entire surgical procedure lasts only a few hours, the acceptable duration limit might be set at a few minutes. These will always be judgment calls on your part. Do what makes sense, rather than conform to a rule that might not be appropriate given the situation.

NOTE Always remember that project management is not much more than organized common sense.

One other situation often arises when decomposition beyond satisfaction of the completion criteria makes sense. That is with activities that are considered high risk or have a high estimated duration variance. An activity with an eight-day duration and five-day variance should raise your concern. Even though the activity has met the duration limit of 10 days, you should further decompose it in an attempt to isolate high-risk parts or the high variance parts of the activity. Again, do what makes sense.

Using a Joint Project Planning Session to Build the WBS

The best way to build a WBS is as a group activity. To create the WBS, assemble a facilitator, the project manager, the core members of the project team, and all other managers who might be affected by the project or who will affect the project. The important thing to have present in this part of the planning session is the expertise and the decision makers who can provide input into the WBS. This exercise should be continuous; you do not want to interrupt it while you go looking for input from people who should already be in the session. The exercise is easy to explain and understand, as you will see in the following section, but it is difficult to execute, as I will explain in the text that follows. The tools are low-tech (Post-It notes, marking pens, and whiteboards), but they greatly facilitate the orderly completion of the task.

Linear or Incremental Approaches

The following steps are followed when the RBS has been completely and clearly defined and you have decided to use a Linear or Incremental approach to the project:

1. The entire planning team should decide on the first-level decomposition of the goal statement. One obvious approach would be to use the objective statements from the POS as the first-level decomposition. Objectives are generally of great interest to senior managers, and this fact might be a major consideration in the team's choice. For a software development project, the systems development phases will often be a good first-level decomposition.

2. After the first-level decomposition is developed, the team has two options regarding how to proceed:

■ Without a doubt, the best way (from a WBS completion point of view) is to have the entire planning team remain intact and complete the WBS together. Often this will not work because it takes more of everybody's time. In particular, it ties up the time of several high-level managers more than the second option.

■ The second option is to divide the planning team into groups and let each group take one or more of the first-level activities and complete the WBS for that part only.

Whichever approach is used, it is essential that the entire group have the opportunity to review the final WBS and offer critiques of it. It is important that these efforts be made, because the WBS must be complete, and every member of the team will see the final result of the JPP.

Iterative, Adaptive, or Extreme Approaches

While these three approaches are quite different regarding the way the project is managed, they are quite similar regarding the way a partial WBS is built. In all three cases as much of the WBS will be built as can be at the outset of the project. The remaining parts of the WBS will be built as a result of the knowledge gained about the solution through iteration. Before you even begin to build the WBS, you will know (from the degree to which the RBS is complete) that one of the Iterative, Adaptive, or Extreme approaches will be used. Knowing this ahead of time will prepare you for building whatever parts of the WBS can be built at the outset.

Decomposition should include the planning team and especially the customer stating that they clearly understand what each activity includes as part of the functions and features of the solution. If there is any doubt, mark that activity as not completely and clearly defined. Further specification of those functions or features will result through iteration. This is not the time to speculate on what that further definition might be. If it appears in the WBS it is there because you know for certain that it is part of the solution. As part of the solution either it will be completely and clearly defined or it will be missing some degree of specificity. Completing that specificity is part of the work of the project.

Approaches to Building the WBS

There are many ways to build the WBS. Even though we might like the choice to be a personal one that the project manager makes (after all, he or she is charged with managing the project, so why not allow that person to choose the architecture that makes that task the easiest?), unfortunately that will not work in many cases. The choice of approach must take into consideration the uses to which the WBS will be put. What may be the best choice for defining the work to be done may not be the best choice for status reporting.

There is no one correct way to create the WBS. Hypothetically, if we put each member of the JPP session in a different room and ask them all to develop the project WBS, they might all come back with different renditions. That's all right — there is no single best answer. The choice is subjective and based more on the project manager's preference than on any other requirements. In practice, I have sometimes tried to follow one approach only to find that it was making the project work more confusing, rather than simpler. In such cases, my advice is simply to throw away the work you have done and start all over again with a fresh approach.

There are three general approaches to building the WBS:

Noun-type approaches. Noun-type approaches define the deliverable of the project work in terms of the components (physical or functional) that make up the deliverable. This approach is the one currently recommended by PMI.

Verb-type approaches. Verb-type approaches define the deliverable of the project work in terms of the actions that must be done to produce the deliverable. Verb-type approaches include the design-build-test-implement and project objectives approaches. This approach was recommended by PMI prior to the current release of PMBOK.

Organizational approaches. Organizational approaches define the deliverable of the project work in terms of the organizational units that will work on the project. This type of approach includes the department, process, and geographic location approaches.

You have seen these approaches used in practice to create the WBS. The following sections take a look at each of these approaches in more detail.

Noun-Type Approaches

There are two noun-type approaches:

Physical decomposition. In projects that involve building products, it is tempting to follow the physical decomposition approach. Consider a mountain bike, for example. Its physical components include a frame, wheels, suspension, gears, and brakes. If each component is to be manufactured, this approach might produce a simple WBS. As mentioned previously, though, you have to keep in mind the concern of summary reporting.

For example, consider rolling up all the tasks related to gears. If you were to create a Gantt chart for reporting at the summary level, the bar for the gears' summary activity would start at the project start date. A Gantt chart is a simple graphical representation of the work to be done and the schedule for completing it. The Gantt chart consists of a number of rectangular bars — each one representing an activity in the project. The length of each bar corresponds to the estimated time it will take to complete the activity. These bars are arranged across a horizontal time scale, with the left edge of the bar lined up with the scheduled start of the activity. The bars are arranged vertically in the order of scheduled start date. The resulting picture forms a descending stair-step pattern. That is, after all, where the detail tasks of doing design work would occur. The finish of the bar would occur at about the project completion date. That is where testing and documentation for the gears occurs. Using the summary Gantt chart as a status reporting tool for the gears doesn't have much use. The bar extends from the beginning to the end of the timeline. The same is true of all the other nouns mentioned. Showing all of them on a summary Gantt chart would simply look like the stripes on a prison uniform.

This type of WBS is initially attractive because it looks similar to, and in fact could be identical to, a company's financial Chart of Accounts (CoA). CoAs are noun-oriented because they account for the cost of developing things such as gears and brakes. A CoA should not be confused with the WBS. The WBS is a breakdown of work; the CoA is a breakdown of costs. Most popular project management software products provide code fields that can be used to link project task costs with accounting CoA categories.

Functional decomposition. Using the bicycle example, we can build the WBS using the functional components of the bicycle. The functional components include the steering system, gear-shifting system, braking system, and pedaling system. The same cautions that apply to the physical decomposition approach apply here as well.

Verb-Type Approaches

There are two verb-type approaches:

Design-build-test-implement. The design-build-test-implement approach is commonly used in those projects that involve a methodology. Application systems development is an obvious example. Using the bicycle example again, a variation on the classic waterfall categories could be used. The categories are design, build, test, and implement. If you were to use this architecture for your WBS, then the bars on the Gantt chart would all have lengths that correspond to the duration of each of the design, build, test, and implement activities, and hence would be shorter than the bar representing the entire project. Most, if not all, would have differing start and end dates. Arranged on the chart, they would cascade in a stair-step manner; hence, the name "waterfall." These are just representative categories; yours may be different. The point is that when the detail-level activity schedules are summarized up to them, they present a display of meaningful information to the recipient of the report.

Remember, the WBS activities at the lowest levels of granularity must always be expressed in verb form. After all, we are talking about work, and that implies action, which, in turn, implies verbs.

Objectives. The objectives approach is similar to the design-build-test-implement approach and is used when progress reports at various stages of project completion are prepared for senior management. Reporting project completion by objectives provides a good indication of the deliverables that have been produced by the project team. Objectives are almost always related to business value and will be well received by senior management and the customer as well. There is a caveat, however. This approach can cause some difficulty because objectives often overlap. Their boundaries can be fuzzy. Using this approach, you'll have to give more attention to eliminating redundancies and discovering gaps in the defined work.

Organizational Approaches

The deployment of project work across geographic or organizational boundaries often suggests a WBS that parallels the organization. The project manager would not choose to use this approach but rather would use it out of necessity. In other words, the project manager has no other reasonable choice. These approaches offer no real advantages and tend to create more problems than they solve. I list them here only because they are additional approaches to building the WBS.

Geographic. If project work is geographically dispersed (our space program, for example), it may make sense from a coordination and communications perspective to partition the project work first by geographic location and then by some other approach at each location.

Departmental. Departmental boundaries and politics being what they are, you might benefit from partitioning the project first by department and then within department by whatever approach makes sense. You benefit from this structure in that a major portion of the project work is under the organizational control of a single manager. Resource allocation is simplified this way. Conversely, you add increased needs for communication and coordination across organizational boundaries using this approach.

Business process. The final approach involves breaking the project down first by business process and then by some other method for each process to may make sense. This has the same advantages and disadvantages as the departmental approach but the added complication that integration of the deliverables from each process can be more difficult than in the former case.

Again, no single approach can be judged to be best for a given project. My advice is to consider each approach at the outset of the JPP session and pick the one that seems to bring the most clarity to defining the project work.

Representing the WBS

Whatever approach you use, the WBS can be generically represented, as shown in Figure 4-3. The goal statement represents the reason for doing the project. The Level 1 partitioning into some number of activities (also known as chunks of work) is a necessary and sufficient set of activities. That is, when all of these first-level activities are complete, the project is complete. For any activity that does not possess the six characteristics, partition it into a set of necessary and sufficient activities at Level 2. The process continues until all activities have met the six criteria. The lowest level of decomposition in the WBS defines a set of activities that will each have an activity manager, someone who is responsible for completing the activity.

The lowest-level activities are defined by a work package. A work package is simply the list of things to do to complete the activity. The work package may be very simple, such as getting management to sign off on a deliverable, or it may be a mini project and consist of all the properties of any other project, except that the activity defining this project possesses the six criteria and need not be further partitioned. I return to the work package in Chapter 7.

Some examples will help clarify this idea. Figure 4-3 is a partial WBS for building a house, and Figure 4-4 is the indented outline version (for those of you who prefer an outline format to a hierarchical graph). Both convey exactly the same information.

Figure 4-5 shows the WBS for the traditional waterfall systems development methodology. For my systems readers, this format could become a template for all your systems development projects. It is a good way to introduce standardization into your systems development methodology.

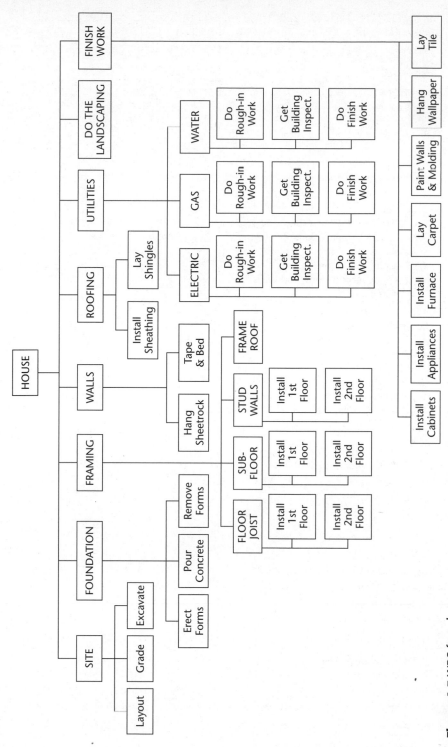

Figure 4-3 WBS for a house

1. SITE PREPARATION
   1.1 Layout
   1.2 Grading
   1.3 Excavation
2. FOUNDATION
   2.1 Erect Forms
   2.2 Pour Concrete
   2.3 Remove Forms
3. FRAMING
   3.1 Floor Joists
        3.1.1. Install First-Floor Joists
        3.1.2. Install Second-Floor Joists
   3.2 Subflooring
        3.2.1. Install First-Floor Subflooring
        3.2.2. Install Second-Floor Subflooring
   3.3 Stud Walls
        3.3.1. Erect First-Floor Stud Walls
        3.3.2. Erect Second-Floor Stud Walls
   3.4 Frame the Roof
4. UTILITIES
   4.1 Electrical
        4.1.1. Do Rough-in Work
        4.1.2. Get Building Inspection
        4.1.3. Do Finish Work
   4.2 Gas
        4.2.1. Do Rough-in Work
        4.2.2. Get Building Inspection
        4.2.3. Do Finish Work
   4.3 Water
        4.3.1. Do Rough-in Work
        4.3.2. Get Building Inspection
        4.3.3. Do Finish Work
5. WALLS
   5.1 Hang Sheetrock
   5.2 Tape and Bed
6. ROOFING
   6.1 Install Sheathing
   6.2 Lay Shingles
7. FINISH WORK
   7.1 Install Cabinets
   7.2 Install Appliances
   7.3 Install Furnace
   7.4 Lay Carpet
   7.5 Paint Walls and Molding
   7.6 Hang Wallpaper
   7.7 Lay Tile
8. LANDSCAPING

Figure 4-4 Indented outline WBS for a house

Figure 4-5 WBS for a waterfall systems development methodology

Putting It All Together

Getting the WBS correct and complete is the only way a traditional project is going to succeed. In this chapter I have discussed several ways to build a WBS and how to test for its completeness.

Discussion Questions

1. The WBS identifies all of the work that must be done to complete the project. What would you do if the answer to a question posed as part of the work determined which of two alternatives you should pursue?

2. Under what conditions might you choose to decompose an activity that met all of the six completeness criteria? Give specific examples.

3. Can you think of any activities that would not meet all six completeness criteria and yet need not be further decomposed? Give specific examples.

CASE STUDY – PLEASANTOWN PLAYGROUND PROJECT

The Level 1 WBS for the Pleasantown Case Study consists of the following:

1.0 Set up administration

2.0 Promote playground

3.0 Recruit volunteers

4.0 Raise funds

5.0 Design playground

6.0 Acquire materials

7.0 Prepare site

8.0 Open playground

Given that Level 1 WBS, answer the following:

4. Pick any three of the Level 1 activities and decompose them down to the level at which the six completion criteria are met for all of your lowest-level activities.

CASE STUDY – PIZZA DELIVERED QUICKLY (PDQ)

The PDQ System consists of four subsystems:

- ◆ Pizza Factory Locator System
- ◆ Order Entry System
- ◆ Routing and Scheduling System
- ◆ Inventory Control System

Given those subsystems, answer the following:

5. Pick one of these subsystems and build a complete WBS. You may have to make assumptions in order to complete this exercise. If so, state them clearly.

Estimating Duration, Resource Requirements, and Cost

Round numbers are always false.
— Samuel Johnson, English critic

Figures are not always facts.
— Aesop, Greek fabulist

You get more control over estimation by learning from evolutionary, early, and frequent result deliveries than you will if you try to estimate in advance for a whole large project.
— Tom Gilb, Principles of Software Engineering Management

CHAPTER LEARNING OBJECTIVES

After reading this chapter, you will be able to:

- ◆ Understand the difference between effort and duration
- ◆ Explain the relationship between resource loading and task duration
- ◆ List and explain the causes of variation in task duration
- ◆ Use any one of six task duration estimation methods
- ◆ Use a particular estimation technique
- ◆ Assign resources to meet project schedules
- ◆ Understand the process of creating cost estimates at the task level
- ◆ Schedule people to project activities using a skill matrix
- ◆ Understand the process of determining resource requirements at the task level

Estimating Duration

Before you can estimate duration, you need to make sure everyone is working from a common definition. The duration of a project is the elapsed time in business working days, not including weekends, holidays, or other non-work days. Work effort is labor required to complete a task. That labor can be consecutive or nonconsecutive hours.

NOTE Beginning with this chapter and continuing through Chapter 11, I drop the use of the term "activity" and replace it with "task." At this point in the planning process all of the lowest-level activities in the WBS have met the completion criteria and are therefore called tasks.

Duration and work effort are not the same thing. For example, I had a client pose the following situation: The client had a task that required him to send a document to his attorney, where it would be reviewed, marked up, and then returned. He had done this on several previous occasions, and it normally took about 10 business days before the document was back in his office. He knew the attorney took only about 30 minutes to review and mark up the document. His question was, what's the duration? The answer is 10 days. The work effort on the part of the attorney is 30 minutes.

It is important to understand the difference between labor time and duration time. They are not the same. Suppose an estimate has been provided that a certain task requires 10 hours of focused and uninterrupted labor to complete. Under normal working conditions, how many hours do you think it will really take? Something more than 10 for sure. To see why this is so, consider the data shown in Figure 5-1.

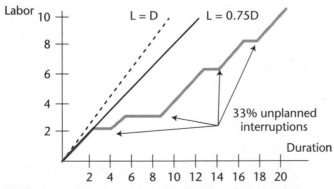

Figure 5-1 Elapsed time versus work time

If a person could be focused 100 percent of the time on a task, he or she could accomplish 10 hours of work in 10 hours. Such a person would indeed be unique, for it is more likely that his or her work will be interrupted by e-mail, beepers, meetings, coffee breaks, and socializing. Several estimates have been made regarding the percentage of a person's day that he or she can devote to project work. Past data that I have collected from information technology professionals indicates a range of 66 to 75 percent. More recently, among the same client base, I have seen a downward trend in this percentage to 50 to 65 percent. Using the 75 percent estimate means that a 10-hour task will require about 13 hours and 20 minutes to complete. That is *without* interruptions, which, of course, always happen.

For some professionals, interruptions are frequent (technical support, for example); for others, interruptions are infrequent (mountain climbers, for example). I polled the 17-person technical support unit of a midsize information services department and found that about one-third of their time was spent on unplanned interruptions. Unplanned interruptions might include a phone call with a question to be answered, a systems crash, power interrupts, random events of nature, the boss stopping in to visit on an unrelated matter, or a personal call from your golfing buddies. Using the 75 percent focus figure and the 33 percent on unplanned interruptions figure means that a 10-hour task will take approximately 20 hours to complete.

It is this elapsed time that you are interested in when estimating for each task in the project. It is the true duration of the task. For costing purposes, you are interested in the labor time (work) actually spent on a task.

NOTE When estimating task duration, you have a choice to make: Do you want to estimate hours of billable labor to complete the task, or do you want to estimate the clock time required to complete the task? Probably both. The labor hours are needed in order to bill the client. The elapsed clock time is needed to estimate the project completion date. Some project managers will estimate labor and convert it to duration by dividing labor time by an established efficiency factor, typically ranging from 0.6 to 0.75.

Resource Loading versus Task Duration

The duration of a task is influenced by the amount of resources scheduled to work on it. I say influenced because there is not necessarily a direct linear relationship between the amount of resource assigned to a task and its duration.

Adding more resources to hold a task's duration within the planning limits can be effective. This is called "crashing the task." For example, suppose you are in a room where an ordinary-size, four-legged chair is in the way. The door to the room is closed. You are asked to pick up the chair and take it out of the room into the hallway. You might try to do it without any help, in which case you would perform the following steps:

1. Pick up the chair.
2. Carry it to the door.
3. Set the chair down.
4. Open the door.
5. Hold the door open with your foot as you pick up the chair.
6. Carry the chair through the door.
7. Set the chair down in the hallway.

Suppose you double the resources. You'll get someone to help you by opening the door and holding it open while you pick up the chair and carry it out to the hallway. With two people working on the task, you'd probably be willing to say it would reduce the time needed to move the chair out of the room and into the hallway.

Doubling the resources sounds like a technology breakthrough in shortening duration. Now double them again and see what happens. Now you've got four resources assigned to the task. It would go something like this: First, you hold a committee meeting to decide roles and responsibilities. Each person would like to get equal credit, so each one grabs a leg of the chair and tries to go through the door, but they all get stuck. (By the way, there's nobody left to open the door because each of the four resources is dedicated to one leg of the chair.)

The point of this silly example is to demonstrate that there are diminishing returns for adding more resources. You would probably agree that there is a maximum loading of resources on a task to minimize the task duration, and that by adding another resource you will actually begin to increase the duration. You have reached the crashpoint of the task. The *crashpoint* is that point where adding more resources will increase task duration. The project manager will frequently have to consider the optimum loading of a resource on a task.

A second consideration for the project manager is the amount of reduction in duration that results from adding resources. The relationship is not linear. Consider the chair example again. Does doubling the resource cut the duration in half? Can two people dig a hole twice as fast as one? Probably not. The explanation is simple. By adding the nth person to a task, you create the need for n more communication links. Who is going to do what? How can the work of several persons be coordinated? There may be other considerations that actually add work. To assume that the amount of work remains constant as you add resources is simply not correct. New kinds of work will emerge from the addition of a resource to a task. For example, adding another person adds the need to communicate with more people, which increases the duration of the task.

A third consideration for the project manager is the impact on risk that results from adding another resource. If you limit the resource to people, you must consider the possibility that two people will prefer to approach the task in different ways, with different work habits and different levels of commitment. The more people working on a task, the more likely one will be absent, the higher the likelihood of a mistake being made, and the more likely they will get in each other's way.

The fourth consideration has to do with partitioning the task so that more than one resource can work on it simultaneously. For some tasks this will be easy; for others it may be impossible. For example, painting a house is an example of a task that is partitionable. Rooms can be done by different painters, and even walls can be done by different painters. The point of diminishing returns is not an issue here. A different kind of example may be the writing of a computer program. That may not be partitionable at all. Adding a second programmer creates all kinds of work that wasn't present with a single programmer — for example, choosing a language to use, naming conventions, integration testing, and so on.

Variation in Task Duration

Task duration is a random variable. Because you cannot know what factors will be operative when work is underway on a task, you cannot know exactly how long it will take. There will, of course, be varying estimates with varying precision for each task. One of your goals in estimating task duration is to define the task to a level of granularity such that your estimates have a narrow variance — that is, the estimate is as good as you can get it at the planning stages of the project. As project work is completed, you will be able to improve the earlier estimates of activities scheduled later in the project.

There are several causes of variation in the actual task duration:

Varying skill levels. Your strategy is to estimate task duration based on using people of average skills assigned to work on the task. In actuality, this may not happen. You may get a higher- or lower-skilled person assigned to the task, causing the actual duration to vary from planned duration. These varying skill levels will be both a help and a hindrance to you.

Unexpected events. Murphy lives in the next cubicle and will surely make his presence known, but in what way and at what time you do not know. Random acts of nature, vendor delays, incorrect shipments of materials, traffic jams, power failures, and sabotage are but a few of the possibilities.

Efficiency of work time. Every time a worker is interrupted, it takes additional time to get to the level of productivity attained prior to the interruption. You cannot control the frequency or time of interruptions, but you do know that they will happen. As to their effect on staff productivity, you can only guess. Some will be more affected than others.

Mistakes and misunderstandings. Despite all of your efforts to be complete and clear in describing the work to be performed, you simply will miss a few times. This will take its toll in rework or scrapping semi-completed work.

Common cause variation. Apart from all of these factors that can influence task duration, the reality is that durations will vary for no reason other than the statistical variation that arises because the duration is in fact a random variable. It has a natural variation, and nothing you do can really decrease that variation. It is there and must be accepted.

Six Methods for Estimating Task Duration

Estimating task duration is challenging. You can be on familiar ground for some activities and on totally unfamiliar ground for others. Whatever the case, you must produce an estimate. It is important that senior management understand that the estimate can be little more than a WAG (wild a** guess). In many projects the estimate will improve as you learn more about the deliverables after having completed some of the project work. Re-estimation and replanning are common. In my consulting practice, I have found six techniques to be quite suitable for initial planning estimates:

- Similarity to other activities
- Historical data
- Expert advice
- Delphi technique
- Three-point technique
- Wide-band Delphi technique

The following sections take a look at each of these techniques in more detail.

Extrapolating Based on Similarity to Other Activities

Some of the activities in your WBS may be similar to activities completed in other projects. Your or others' recollections of those activities and their duration can be used to estimate the present task's duration. In some cases, this process may require extrapolating from the other task to this one, but in any case it does provide an estimate. In most cases, using the estimates from those activities provides estimates that are good enough.

Studying Historical Data

Every good project management methodology includes a project notebook that records the estimated and actual task duration. This historical record can be used on other projects. The recorded data becomes your knowledge base for estimating task duration. This technique differs from the previous technique in that it uses a record, rather than depending on memory. To estimate the duration of a task, simply extract similar tasks from the database and compute an average. That is a simple application of the database.

The historical data can be used in a more sophisticated way, too. One of my clients has built an extensive database of task duration history. They have recorded not only estimated and actual duration but also the characteristics of the task, the skill set of the people working on it, and other variables that they found useful. When a task duration estimate is needed, they go to their database with a complete definition of the task and, with some rather sophisticated regression models, estimate the task duration. They build product for market, and it is very important to them to be able to estimate as accurately as possible. Again, my advice is that if there is value added for a particular tool or technique, use it.

Seeking Expert Advice

When the project involves a breakthrough technology or a technology that is being used for the first time in the organization, there may not be any local experience or even professionals skilled in the technology within the organization. In these cases, you will have to appeal to outside authorities. Vendors may be a good source, as are non-competitors who use that technology.

Applying the Delphi Technique

The Delphi technique can produce good estimates in the absence of expert advice. This is a group technique that extracts and summarizes the knowledge of the group to arrive at an estimate. After the group is briefed on the project and the nature of the task, each individual in the group is asked to make his or her best guess of the task duration. The results are tabulated and presented, as shown in Figure 5-2, to the group in a histogram labeled First Pass. Those participants whose estimates fall in the outer quartiles are asked to share the reason for their guess. After listening to the arguments, each group member is asked to guess again. The results are presented as a histogram labeled Second Pass, and again the outer quartile estimates are defended. A third guess is made, and the histogram plotted is labeled Third Pass. Final adjustments are allowed. The average of the third guess is used as the group's estimate. Even though the technique seems rather simplistic, it has been shown to be effective in the absence of expert advice.

Figure 5-2 The Delphi technique

I attended an IBM business partners' meeting several years ago. One of the sessions dealt with estimating software development time, and the presenter demonstrated the use of the Delphi technique with a rather intriguing example. She asked if anyone in the group had ever worked in a carnival as a weight-guessing expert. None had, so she informed the group that they were going to use the Delphi technique to estimate the average weight of the 20 people who were in the room. She asked everyone to write his or her best guess as to his or her weight on a slip of paper. These were averaged by the facilitator and put aside. Each person took an initial guess as to the average weight, wrote it down, and passed it to the facilitator. She displayed the initial pass histogram and asked the individuals with the five highest and five lowest guesses to share their thinking with the group; a second guess was taken and then a third. The average of the third guess became the group's estimate of the average body weight. Surprisingly, the estimate was just two pounds off the reported average.

The approach the presenter used is actually a variation of the original Delphi technique. The original version used a small panel of experts (say, five or six) who were asked for their estimate independently of one another. The results were tabulated and shared with the panel, who were then asked for a second estimate. A third estimate was solicited in the same manner. The average of the third estimate was the one chosen. Note that the original approach does not involve any discussion or collaboration between the panel members. In fact, they weren't even aware of who the other members were.

Applying the Three-Point Technique

Task duration is a random variable. If it were possible to repeat the task several times under identical circumstances, duration times would vary. That variation may be tightly grouped around a central value, or it might be widely dispersed. In the first case, you would have a considerable amount of information on that task's duration as compared to the latter case, where you would have very little or none. In any given instance of the task, you would not know at which extreme the duration would likely fall, but you could make probabilistic statements about their likelihood in any case. Figure 5-3 illustrates the point.

The three-point technique gives you a framework for doing just that. To use the method, you need three estimates of task duration:

Optimistic. The optimistic time is defined as the shortest duration one has had or might expect to experience given that everything happens as expected.

Pessimistic. The pessimistic time is that duration that would be experienced (or has been experienced) if everything that could go wrong did go wrong, yet the task was completed.

Most likely. The most likely time is that time usually experienced.

For this method you are calling on the collective memory of professionals who have worked on similar activities but for which there is no recorded history. Obviously, Figure 5-3 is a graphical representation of the three-point method.

Applying the Wide-Band Delphi Technique

Combining the Delphi and three-point methods results in the wide-band Delphi technique. It involves a panel, as in the Delphi technique. In place of a single estimate, the panel members are asked, at each iteration, to give their optimistic, pessimistic, and most likely estimates for the duration of the chosen task. The results are compiled, and any extreme estimates are removed. Averages are computed for each of the three estimates, and the averages are used as the optimistic, pessimistic, and most likely estimates of task duration.

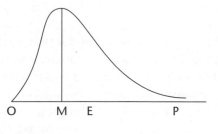

O: Optimistic
P: Pessimistic
M: Most Likely

$$E = \frac{O + 4M + P}{6}$$

Figure 5-3 The three-point method

Estimation Life Cycles

A word of advice on estimating is in order. Early estimates of task duration will not be as good as later estimates. It's a simple fact that you get smarter as the project work commences. Estimates will always be subject to the vagaries of nature and other unforeseen events. You can only hope that you gain some knowledge through the project to improve your estimates.

In the top-down project planning model, you start out with "roughly right" estimates, with the intention of improving the precision of these estimates later in the project. Management and the customer must be aware of this approach. Most of us have the habit of assuming that a number, once written, is inviolate and absolutely correct regardless of the circumstances under which the number was determined. This is unrealistic in the contemporary world of project management. It may have once been appropriate for the engineer, but that is not the case with the businessperson. Figure 5-4 illustrates the estimation life cycle concept.

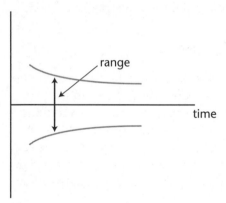

Figure 5-4 The estimation life cycle

During project planning most task estimates are not much better than a dart throw. Of course, if the task is one that has been done several times before under similar situations, then the estimate will have a narrower variance than it would had the task never been done before under any circumstances. As project work commences, the team will gain in knowledge and understanding of the project and the work needed to deliver. That includes improved estimates of future tasks in the project. Once the task has begun, even more information will come to light and the estimate (or better estimate to completion) will be quite accurate.

CASE STUDY – PLEASANTOWN PLAYGROUND PROJECT

Oftentimes the calendar of the resources who will be working on your project is not the usual work-week calendar. That is certainly the case here. Almost all of the resources will be either retired folks who live in the immediate vicinity of the playground, or they will be volunteers who are only available evenings and weekends. Estimation is therefore a bit complicated because of these work schedules.

You should still use the normal workday as the basis of your estimates, but when the resource availability is plugged in, the durations will stretch out over several weeks because much of the work will be done only on weekends or after normal business hours. For example, if a task takes four days to complete, it may take two weeks to schedule the four work days. In situations where work calendars are as mixed as in this case, the best approach is to estimate labor, not duration. Duration will come about as part of the process of assigning volunteers and accommodating their calendars.

Estimating Resource Requirements

By defining project activities according to the completion criteria, you should have reached a point of granularity with each task so that it is familiar. You may have done the task or something very similar to it in a past project. That recollection, or historical information, gives you the basis for estimating the resources you will need to complete the activities in the current project. In some cases, it is a straightforward recollection. In others, it is the result of keeping a historical file of similar activities. In still others, it may be the advice of experts.

The importance of resources varies from project to project. You can use the six estimation techniques discussed in the previous section to estimate the resource requirements for any project.

Types of resources include the following:

People. In most cases the resources you will have to schedule are human resources. This is also the most difficult type of resource to schedule.

Facilities. Project work takes place in locations. Planning rooms, conference rooms, presentation rooms, and auditoriums are but a few examples of facilities that projects require. The exact specifications as well as the precise time at which they are needed are some of the variables that must be taken into account. The project plan can provide the detail required. The facility specification will also drive the project schedule based on availability.

Equipment. Equipment is treated exactly the same as facilities. What is needed and when drive the task schedule based on availability.

Money. Accountants would tell you that everything is eventually reduced to dollars, and that is true. Project expenses typically include travel, rooms and meals, and supplies.

Materials. Parts to be used in the fabrication of products and other physical deliverables are often part of the project work, too. For example, the materials needed to build a bicycle might include nuts, bolts, washers, and spacers.

People as Resources

People are the most difficult type of resource to schedule because you plan the project by specifying the types of skills you need, when you need them, and in what amounts. Note that you do not specify the resource by name (that is, the individual) you need; this is where problems arise.

There are a few tools you can use to help you schedule people.

Skills Matrices

I find that an increasing number of my clients are developing skills inventory matrices for staff, and skill needs matrices for activities. The two matrices are used to assign staff to activities. The assignment could be based on task characteristics such as risk, business value, criticality, or skill development. Figure 5-5 illustrates how the process can work.

This process involves gathering inventory data for two inventories:

▪ An inventory of the demand for skills needed to perform the tasks associated with specific activities. This is represented as a matrix whose rows are the activities and whose columns are the skills. These include both current and long-term needs.

▪ An inventory of the current skills among the professional staff. This is represented as a matrix whose rows identify the staff and whose columns represent the skills.

Figure 5-5 Assigning staff to activities

The columns of both matrices define the same set of skills. This gives you a way to link the two matrices and assign staff to activities. This approach can be used for on-the-job staff development. As an on-the-job development strategy, the manager would have previously met with the staff member, helped him or her define career goals, and translated those goals into skill development needs. That information can now be used to assign staff to activities so that the work they will do on the task gives them that on-the-job development.

Skill Categories

This part of the skill matrix is developed by looking at each task that the unit must perform and describing the skills needed to perform the task. Because skills may appear in unrelated activities, the list of possible skills must be standardized across the enterprise.

Skill Levels

A binary assessment — that is, one either has the skill or doesn't — is certainly easier to administer, but it isn't sufficient for project management. Skills must be qualified with a statement about how much of the skill the person possesses. Various methods are available, and companies often develop their own skill-level system.

Resource Breakdown Structure

Just as there is a Work Breakdown Structure, so also is there a Resource Breakdown Structure. Figure 5-6 gives a simple example.

The Resource Breakdown Structure is used to assist in not only resource estimation but also cost estimation. The Resource Breakdown Structure is determined by the job families, which are defined by the human resources department. That definition is simply put into this hierarchical framework and used as the basis for identifying the positions and levels that are needed to staff the project, constructing the staffing budget from that.

Figure 5-6 Example of a Resource Breakdown Structure

Estimating Duration as a Function of Resource Availability

Three variables influence the duration estimate of a task, and all of them influence each other:

- The duration itself
- The total amount of work, as in person hours/days, that will be done on the task by a resource
- The percent per day of an individual's time that the resource can devote to working on it

Many project management software products today enable you to enter any two of these three variables, calculating the third for you. There is no one right way; it's a matter of what works best and is most consistent with the way you mentally approach estimating. There are four ways to approach the calculation of duration, total effort, and percent/day. Remember that two of them are specified and the third is calculated. The methods are listed here and described in the sections that follow:

- Assign as a total work and constant percent/day
- Assign as a duration and total work effort

- Assign as a duration and percent/day
- Assign as a profile

Assign as a Total Work and a Constant Percent/Day

If you know that the total "head down, focused" work effort required to do the task is 40 hours but that the resource can devote only 50 percent of his or her typical day to doing project task work, then the resulting duration is going to bc 80 hours, or 10 business days. The formula is simply as follows:

```
40 hours/0.50 = 80 hours
```

The duration becomes a calculated value based on the percent per day and the work. This is the method that most software products use as their default method. It's tempting to use a percent-per-day resource allocation value that's higher than it actually will be. We can be a bit squeamish about telling it like it really is. If that is done, the duration is shortened accordingly. The project completion date is then invalid because it is calculated using an overly optimistic duration.

Assign as a Duration and Total Work Effort

Alternatively, you could use your or someone else's experience and estimate the duration based on history. Then the total work could be averaged over that duration, yielding the percent per day value. Using the same values as before, the formula would look like this:

```
5 person days / 10 days = 0.5
```

Here again I'm making the assumption of an eight-hour day. In this case, the percent is calculated. Approaching the estimate from this direction (I'm just running the numbers a different way) seems in practice to avoid the problem of squeamishness. You still need to do a sanity check on the resulting value; don't just blindly accept it. In my consulting, I've found that this usually results in an estimated duration that comes closer to matching the actual duration when all is said and done.

Assign as a Duration and Percent/Day

The third method is to estimate the duration as previously described and assign the percent per day. This method will calculate the total work effort. The formula works like this:

```
10 days x 0.50 = 5 person days
```

Of the three methods, this is the least used.

Assign as a Profile

The three duration estimating and resource assignment methods discussed here all presume that the resource is going to work at about the same percent per day for each day of the task. In other words, they are flat-loaded at a constant rate. In reality, there will be times when a person cannot work at a constant rate because of other commitments. In such cases, the duration is estimated first and then the work is assigned at different percents over the 40-hour window. For example, you might assign the worker 75 percent for 20 hours and 50 percent for 20 hours. If you find yourself having to use this profiling of resource assignments capability on activities more than two or three times in a project, you may need to take your WBS to a lower level of detail. In doing that, the duration will be shorter and the resources can work in a contiguous manner for the entire task.

Estimating Cost

Now that you have estimated task duration and resource requirements, you have the data you need to establish the cost of the project. This is your first look at the dollars involved in doing the project. You know the resources that will be required and the number of hours or volume of resources needed. Unit cost data can be applied to the amount of resource required to estimate cost.

Resource Planning

You need to consider several questions concerning the resources for your project. As I have pointed out, adding resources doesn't necessarily mean that you will shorten the time needed for various activities. Adding too many people can actually add time to the project. Another factor to consider deals with the skill level of the resources.

Suppose that you are going to have a team of developers work on an application. When you are planning resources, you have to know the skill level of the potential resources. You may have to trade money for time. That means you may be able to get a lower cost by using a junior developer, but it's likely that you will also find the process takes longer. Knowing the skill sets of the available people and taking that into account when doing scheduling are a major part of resource planning.

Another issue to consider is that of using part-time people. At first glance, using part-time people looks like a good idea. It appears you can make good decisions concerning their schedules and that you are getting extremely efficient use of their time. However, this isn't reality, particularly if the part-time people are coders. Development is a mental task; you're working with knowledge workers. You can't turn a mental process on and off at will.

Similarly, scheduling people on two projects the same day won't be an efficient use of resources. It takes some time for a developer to get up to writing speed, so when you're scheduling, don't think you can schedule different projects for the same knowledge worker on the same day. That kind of schedule may look good on paper, but it doesn't work. Give your resources a chance to get into the flow of work and you'll be much more successful.

Cost Estimating

When doing an estimate, you need to consider a few concepts. The first is that no matter how well you estimate cost, it is always an estimate. One of the reasons that so many projects come in over budget is that people actually believe that they have done perfect estimating and that their baseline estimate is set in stone. Remember that it is always an estimate. Anytime you are forecasting the future, as you are when you plan a project, you are dealing with some amount of uncertainty. Because projects are unique by definition, you are doing an estimate. Projects are so often over budget because the budget is an estimate, not an exact mathematical calculation. Even experienced cost estimators miss the mark.

Having given you that warning, you still need to do your best to come up with a working budget for the project. Estimating can be done several ways. One is to find an analogous project, one that looks a great deal like the one you're currently planning. By using it as a guideline, you'll have a reference point for the costs. The caveat that you must keep in mind is that each project is unique, which means you will have a slightly different budget for your estimate than the one from the previous project. Don't use the exact same figures when you estimate; it will come back to haunt you sometime in the project.

Another good practice in estimating is to invite subject matter experts (SMEs) to help you prepare your estimate. Ideally, these SMEs will be able to discuss their areas of expertise and give you a better handle on the estimating for your current projects.

Three types of estimates are common in project management:

Order of magnitude estimate. This type means that the number given for the estimate is somewhere between 25 percent above and 75 percent below the number. Order of magnitude estimates are often used at the very beginning of the estimation process when very little detail is known about the project work and a rough estimate is all that management calls for. It is understood that this estimate will be improved over time.

Budget estimate. This type has a range of 10 percent over and 25 percent below the stated estimate. These estimates are generated during project planning time and are based on knowing some detail about the project activities.

Definitive estimate. This type is generally the one that is used for the rest of the project. It has a range of 5 percent over and 10 percent below the stated estimate. These estimates are most useful during project execution when new information helps further improve the estimates generated during project planning time.

When giving an estimate for a project, it's a good idea to have these three ranges in mind. Remember that even if you tell a sponsor that your estimate is an order of magnitude estimate, the sponsor will remember it for the rest of the project. Protect yourself in this case by writing "order of magnitude" on the estimate. Doing so will at least give you something with which to defend yourself if it comes to that.

Cost Budgeting

After you've done an estimate, you enter the cost budgeting phase. This is the phase when you assign costs to tasks on the WBS. Cost budgeting is actually very formulaic. You take the needed resources and multiply the costs times the number of hours they are to be used. In the case of a one-time cost, such as hardware, you simply state that cost.

Cost budgeting gives the sponsor a final check on the costs of the project. The underlying assumption is that you've got all the numbers right. Usually you'll have the cost of a resource right, but often it's tough to be exact on the total number of hours the resource is to be used. Remember that no matter what, you are still doing an estimate. Cost budgeting is different than estimating in that it is more detailed. However, the final output is still a best effort at expressing the cost of the project.

Cost Control

Cost control represents two major issues for the project manager:

- The first is how often you need to get reports of the costs. Certainly, it would be good if you could account for everything occurring on the project in real time. However, that is generally way too expensive and time-intensive. More likely, you'll get figures once a week. Getting cost status figures once a week gives you a good snapshot of the costs that are occurring. If you wait longer than a week to get cost figures, you may find that the project has spun out of control.

▪ The second issue deals with how you look at the numbers you're receiving. If you've done a cost baseline, then you'll have some figures against which you can measure your costs. What you're looking for is a variance from the original costs. The two costs you have at this point are your baseline and the actual costs that have occurred on the project. The baseline was the final estimate of the costs on the project. Your job is to look at the two and determine whether management action must be taken.

TIP How far off do the numbers need to be between the final estimate and your actual costs before you take some action? Usually 10 percent is the most allowed. However, if you see a trend appearing — usually meaning a trend of being over budget — you should take a look at the reasons behind the variance before it reaches 10 percent.

A word of advice: Keep in mind that for some projects time is the most important constraint. Remember Y2K? In cases like those, you must balance your need for cost control with the need for a definitive project ending time. There may be a trade-off in cost control for time constraints. As a project manager, you must be aware of these trade-offs and be ready to justify changes in costs to the sponsor based on other considerations such as time and quality.

Using a JPP Session to Estimate Duration, Resource Requirements, and Cost

You have assembled the SMEs on your planning team, so you have all the information you need to estimate task duration in the JPP session. The methodology is simple. During the WBS exercise, ask each subteam to provide task duration estimates as part of their presentation. The subteam's presentation will then include the task duration estimates they determined. Any disagreement can be resolved during the presentation.

Having conducted many JPP sessions, I can offer some advice for estimating task duration during the JPP session:

Get it roughly right. Do not waste time deciding whether the duration is nine days or 10 days. By the time the task is open for work, the team will have a lot more knowledge about the task and will be able to provide an improved estimate — rendering the debate a waste of time. After some frustration with getting the planning team to move ahead quickly with estimates, someone once remarked, "Are you 70 percent sure you are 80 percent right? Good, let's move on."

Spend more effort on front-end activities than on back-end activities. As project work commences, back-end activities may undergo change. In fact, some may be removed from the project altogether.

Consensus is all that is needed. If you have no serious objections to the estimate, let it stand. It is easy to get bogged down in minutia. The JPP session is trying enough on the participants. Don't make it any more painful than necessary. Save your energy for the really important parts of the plan — like the WBS.

Determining Resource Requirements

The planning team includes resource managers or their representatives. At the time the planning team is defining the WBS and estimating task duration, they also estimate resource requirements.

I have found the following practice effective:

1. Create a list of all the resources required for the project. For human resources, list only position title or skill level. Do not name specific people even if there is only one person with the requisite skills. Envision a person with the typical skill set and loading on the project task. Task duration estimates are based on workers of average skill level, and so should be resource requirements. You can worry about changing this relationship later in the planning session.

2. When the WBS is presented, resource requirements can be reported, too.

You now have estimated the parameters needed to begin constructing the project schedule. The task duration estimates provide input to planning the order and sequence of completing the work defined by the activities. After the initial schedule is built, you can use the resource requirements and availability data to further modify the schedule.

Determining Cost

The team should have access to a standard costing table. This table will list all resources, unit of measure, and cost per unit. It is then just a simple exercise in calculating the cost per resource based on the number of units required and the cost per unit. Many organizations have a spreadsheet template that will facilitate the exercise. These calculated figures can be transferred to the WBS and aggregated up the WBS hierarchy to provide a total cost for each task level in the WBS.

WHAT IF THE SPECIFIC RESOURCE IS KNOWN?

Knowing the specific resource will occur quite often, and you are faced with the question: Should you put that person in the plan? If you do and that person is not available when you need him or her, how will that affect your project plan? If he or she is very highly skilled and you used that information to estimate the duration of the task that person was to work on, you may have a problem. If you cannot replace him or her with an equally skilled individual, will that create a slippage that dominoes through the project schedule? Take your choice.

Putting It All Together

You now have all of the task-level data that you need to build the project plan. What remains is the intertask data in the form of dependencies and relationships. You can then build an initial project plan. In the next chapter, I discuss dependencies and relationships between activities and then explain how to display the project graphically in the form of a project network diagram.

Discussion Questions

1. You have used the three-point method to estimate the duration of a task that you know will be critical to the project. The estimate produces a very large difference between the optimistic and pessimistic estimates. What actions might you take, if any, regarding this task?

2. Discuss a project on which you've worked where time was the major factor in determining the success or failure of the project. What did you do about cost considerations? Did the sponsor(s) agree with the added cost? Was the project successful?

3. Prepare a simple budget showing an order of magnitude estimate, a budget estimate, and a definitive estimate. What did you have to do to make each successive budget closer to the final working budget?

CASE STUDY – PLEASANTOWN PLAYGROUND PROJECT

4. You completed part of the WBS in the last chapter. Try your hand at estimating duration, cost, and resource requirements for that part of the WBS. Please state any assumptions you have to make in order to complete this assignment.

Constructing and Analyzing the Project Network Diagram

Structure is not organization.
— Robert H. Waterman, Management consultant

The man who goes alone can start today, but he who travels with another must wait 'til that other is ready.
— Henry David Thoreau, American naturalist

In every affair consider what precedes and what follows, and then undertake it.
— Epictetus, Greek philosopher

Every moment spent planning saves three or four in execution.
— Crawford Greenwalt, President, DuPont

CHAPTER LEARNING OBJECTIVES

After reading this chapter, you will be able to:

◆ Construct a network representation of the project tasks

◆ Understand the four types of task dependencies and when they are used

◆ Recognize the types of constraints that create task sequences

◆ Compute the earliest start (ES), earliest finish (EF), latest start (LS), and latest finish (LF) times for every task in the network

◆ Understand lag variables and their uses

◆ Identify the critical path in the project

(continued)

CHAPTER LEARNING OBJECTIVES *(continued)*

◆ Define free slack and total slack and know their significance

◆ Analyze the network for possible schedule compression

◆ Use advanced network dependency relationships for improving the project schedule

◆ Understand and apply management reserve

◆ Use the critical path for planning, implementation, and control of the project tasks

The Project Network Diagram

At this point in the TPM life cycle, you have identified the set of tasks in the project as output from the WBS-building exercise and the task duration for the project. The next task for the planning team is to determine the order in which these tasks are to be performed.

The tasks and the task duration are the basic building blocks needed to construct a graphic picture of the project. This graphic picture provides you with two additional pieces of schedule information about the project:

▪ The earliest time at which work can begin on every task that makes up the project

▪ The earliest expected completion date of the project

This is critical information for the project manager. Ideally, the required resources must be available at the times established in this plan. This is not very likely. Chapter 7 discusses how to deal with that problem. In this chapter, I focus on the first part of the problem — creating an initial project network diagram and the associated project schedule.

Envisioning a Complex Project Network Diagram

A *project network diagram* is a pictorial representation of the sequence in which the project work can be done. You need to follow a few simple rules to build the project network diagram.

Recall from Chapter 1 that a project is defined as a sequence of interconnected tasks. You could simply perform the tasks one at a time until they are all complete, but in all but the most trivial projects this approach would not result in an acceptable completion date. In fact, it results in the longest time to complete the project. Any ordering that allows even one pair of tasks to be worked on concurrently results in a shorter project completion date.

Another approach is to establish a network of relationships between the tasks. You can do this by looking forward through the project. What tasks must be complete before another task can begin? Conversely, you can take a set of tasks and look backward through the project: Now that a set of tasks is complete, what task or tasks could come next? Both ways are valid. The one you use is a matter of personal preference. Are you more comfortable looking backward in time or forward? Our advice is to look at the tasks from both angles. One can be a check of the completeness of the other.

The relationships between the tasks in the project are represented in a flow diagram called a *network diagram* or *logic diagram*.

Benefits to Network-Based Scheduling

There are two ways to build a project schedule:

- Gantt chart
- Network diagram

The Gantt chart is the oldest of the two and is used effectively in simple, short-duration types of projects. As mentioned in Chapter 4, to build a Gantt chart the project manager begins by associating a rectangular bar with every task. The length of the bar corresponds to the duration of the task. He or she then places the bars horizontally along a timeline in the order in which the tasks should be completed. In some instances tasks are located on the timeline such that they are worked on concurrently with other tasks. The sequencing is often driven more by resource availability than any other consideration.

There are two drawbacks to using the Gantt chart:

- Because of its simplicity, the Gantt chart does not contain detailed information. It reflects only the order imposed by the manager and, in fact, hides much of that information. You see, the Gantt chart does not contain all of the sequencing information that exists. Unless you are intimately familiar with the project tasks, you cannot tell from the Gantt chart what must come before and after what.

- The Gantt chart does not tell the project manager whether the schedule that results from the Gantt chart completes the project in the shortest possible time or even uses the resources most effectively. The Gantt chart reflects only when the manager would like to have the work done.

Although a Gantt chart is easier to build and does not require the use of an automated tool, I recommend using the network diagram. The network diagram provides a visual layout of the sequence in which project work flows. It includes detailed information and serves as an analytical tool for project scheduling and resource management problems as they arise during the life of the project. In addition, the network diagram enables you to compute the earliest time at which the project can be completed. That information does not follow from a Gantt chart.

Network diagrams can be used for detailed project planning, during implementation as a tool for analyzing scheduling alternatives, and as a control tool:

Planning. Even for large projects, the project network diagram gives a clear graphical picture of the relationship between project tasks. It is, at the same time, a high-level and detailed-level view of the project. I have found that displaying the network diagram on the whiteboard or flip charts during the planning phase is beneficial. This way, all members of the planning team can use it for scheduling decisions.

CROSS-REF I explore using the network diagram in the JPP later in this chapter.

Implementation. For those project managers who use automated project management software tools, update the project file with task status and estimate-to-completion data. The network diagram is then automatically updated and can be printed or viewed. The need for rescheduling and resource reallocation decisions can be determined from the network diagram, although some argue that this method is too cumbersome because of project size. Even a project of modest size, say, 100 tasks, produces a network diagram that is too large and awkward to be of much use. I cannot disagree, but I place the onus on software manufacturers to market products that do a better job of displaying network diagrams.

Control. While the updated network diagram retains the status of all tasks, the best graphical report for monitoring and controlling project work will be the Gantt chart view of the network diagram. This Gantt chart cannot be used for control purposes unless you have done network scheduling or incorporated the logic into the Gantt chart. Comparing the planned schedule with the actual schedule, the project manager can discover variances and, depending on their severity, be able to put a get-well plan in place.

CROSS-REF Chapter 10 examines monitoring and controlling progress in more detail and provides additional reporting tools for analyzing project status.

Building the Network Diagram Using the Precedence Diagramming Method

One early method for representing project tasks as a network dates back to the early 1950s and the Polaris Missile Program. It is called the *task-on-the-arrow (TOA) method*. As Figure 6-1 shows, an arrow represents each task. The node at the left edge of the arrow is the event "begin the task," while the node at the right edge of the arrow is the event "end the task." Every task is represented by this configuration. Nodes are numbered sequentially, and the sequential ordering had to be preserved, at least in the early versions. Because of the limitations of the TOA method, ghost tasks had to be added to preserve network integrity. Only the simplest of dependency relationships could be used. This technique proved to be quite cumbersome as networking techniques progressed. One seldom sees this approach used today.

With the advent of the computer, the TOA method lost its appeal, and a new method replaced it. Figure 6-2 shows the *task-on-the-node (TON) method*. The term more commonly used to describe this approach is *precedence diagramming method (PDM)*.

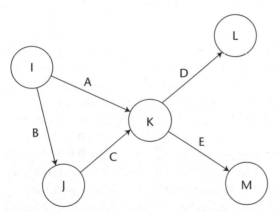

Figure 6-1 The task-on-the-arrow method

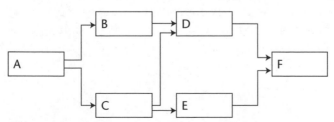

Figure 6-2 PDM format of a project network diagram

The basic *unit of analysis* in a network diagram is the task. Each task in the network diagram is represented by a rectangle called a task *node*. Arrows represent the predecessor/successor relationships between tasks. Figure 6-2 shows an example network diagram. You will take a more detailed look at how the PDM works later in this chapter.

Every task in the project will have its own task node (see Figure 6-3). The entries in the task node describe the time-related properties of the task. Some of the entries describe characteristics of the task, such as its expected duration (E), while others describe calculated values (ES, EF, LS, LF) associated with that task. I will define these terms shortly and give an example of their use.

In order to create the network diagram using the PDM, you need to determine the predecessors and successors for each task. To do this you ask, "What tasks must be complete before I can begin this task?" Here, you are looking for the technical dependencies between tasks. Once a task is complete, it will have produced an output, a deliverable, which becomes input to its successor tasks. Work on the successor tasks requires only the output from its predecessor tasks.

NOTE Later I incorporate management constraints that may alter these dependency relationships. For now I prefer to delay consideration of the management constraints; they will only complicate the planning at this point.

What is the next step? While the list of predecessors and successors to each task contains all the information you need to proceed with the project, it does not represent the information in a format that tells the story of your project. Your goal is to provide a graphical picture of the project. To do that, I need to spell out a few rules first. Once you know the rules, you can create the graphical image of the project. In this section, I teach you the few simple rules for constructing a project network diagram.

The network diagram is logically sequenced to be read from left to right. Every task in the network, except the start and end tasks, must have at least one task that comes before it (its immediate predecessor) and one task that comes after it (its immediate successor). A task begins when its predecessors have been completed. The start task has no predecessor, and the end task has no successor. These networks are called *connected*. In this book I have adopted the practice of using connected networks. Figure 6-4 gives examples of how the variety of relationships that might exist between two or more tasks can be diagrammed.

Figure 6-3 Task node

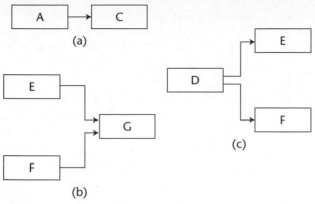

Figure 6-4 Diagramming conventions

Dependencies

A *dependency* is simply a relationship that exists between pairs of tasks. To say that task B depends on task A means that task A produces a deliverable that is needed in order to do the work associated with task B. There are four types of task dependencies, as illustrated in Figure 6-5.

　　Finish-to-start. The finish-to-start (FS) dependency says that task A must be complete before task B can begin. It is the simplest and most risk averse of the four types. For example, task A can represent the collection of data, and task B can represent entry of the data into the computer. To say that the dependency between A and B is finish-to-start means that once you have finished collecting the data, you may begin entering the data. I recommend using FS dependency in the initial project planning session. The finish-to-start dependency is displayed with an arrow emanating from the right edge of the predecessor task and leading to the left edge of the successor task.

　　Start-to-start. The start-to-start (SS) dependency says that task B may begin once task A has begun. Note that there is a no-sooner-than relationship between task A and task B. Task B may begin no sooner than task A begins. In fact, they could both start at the same time. For example, you could alter the data collection and data entry dependency: As soon as you begin collecting data (task A), you may begin entering data (task B). In this case there is an SS dependency between task A and B. The start-to-start dependency is displayed with an arrow emanating from the left edge of the predecessor (A) and leading to the left edge of the successor (B). I use this dependency relationship in the "Compressing the Schedule" section later in the chapter.

Figure 6-5 Dependency relationships

Start-to-finish. The start-to-finish (SF) dependency is a little more complex than the FS and SS dependencies. Here task B cannot be finished sooner than task A has started. For example, suppose you have built a new information system. You don't want to eliminate the legacy system until the new system is operable. When the new system starts to work (task A), the old system can be discontinued (task B). The start-to-finish dependency is displayed with an arrow emanating from the left edge of task A to the right edge of task B. SF dependencies can be used for just-in-time scheduling between two tasks, but they rarely occur in practice.

Finish-to-finish. The finish-to-finish (FF) dependency states that task B cannot finish sooner than task A. For example, refer back to our data collection and entry example. Data entry (task B) cannot finish until data collection (task A) has finished. In this case, task A and B have a finish-to-finish dependency. The finish-to-finish dependency is displayed with an arrow emanating from the right edge of task A to the right edge of task B. To preserve the connectedness property of the network diagram, the SS dependency on the front end of two tasks should have an accompanying FF dependency on the back end.

Constraints

The type of dependency that describes the relationship between tasks is determined as the result of *constraints* that exist between those tasks. Each type of constraint can generate any one of the four dependency relationships. Four types of constraints will affect the sequencing of project tasks and, hence, the dependency relations between tasks:

- Technical constraints
- Management constraints
- Interproject constraints
- Date constraints

The next sections take a look at each of these in more detail.

Technical Constraints

Technical dependencies between tasks are those that arise because one task (the successor) requires output from another (the predecessor) before work can begin on it. In the simplest case, the predecessor must be completed before the successor can begin. I advise using FS relationships in the initial construction of the network diagram because they are the least complex and risk-prone dependencies. If the project can be completed by the requested date using only FS dependencies, there is no need to complicate the plan by introducing other, more complex and risk-prone dependency relationships. SS and FF dependencies will be used later when you analyze the network diagram for schedule improvements.

Within the category of technical constraints, four related situations should be accounted for:

Discretionary constraints. Discretionary constraints are judgment calls by the project manager that result in the introduction of dependencies. These judgment calls may be merely a hunch or a risk-aversion strategy taken by the project manager. Through the sequencing tasks the project manager gains a modicum of comfort with the project work. For example, revisit the data collection and data entry example used earlier in the chapter. The project manager knows that a team of recent hires will be collecting the data and that the usual practice is to have them enter the data as they collect it (SS dependency). The project manager knows that this introduces some risk to the process; and because new hires will be doing the data collection and data entry, the project manager decides to use an FS, rather than SS, dependency between data collection and data entry.

Best-practices constraints. Best practices are past experiences that have worked well for the project manager or are known to the project manager based on the experiences of others in similar situations. The practices in place in an industry can be powerful influences here, especially in dealing with bleeding-edge technologies. In some cases, the dependencies that result from best-practices constraints, which are added by the project manager, might be part of a risk-aversion strategy following the experiences of others. For example, consider the dependency between software design and software build tasks. The safe approach has always been to complete design before beginning build. The current business environment, however, is one in which getting to the market faster has become the strategy for survival.

In an effort to get to market faster, many companies have introduced concurrency into the design-build scenario by changing the FS dependency between design and build to an SS dependency as follows. At some point in the design phase, enough is known about the final configuration of the software to begin limited programming work. By introducing this concurrency between designing and building, the project manager can reduce the time to market for the new software. While the project manager knows that this SS dependency introduces risk (design changes made after programming has started may render the programming useless), the project manager will adopt this best-practices approach.

Logical constraints. Logical constraints are like discretionary constraints that arise from the project manager's way of thinking about the logical way to sequence a pair of tasks. It's important for the project manager to be comfortable with the sequencing of work. After all, the project manager has to manage it. Based on past practices and common sense, we prefer to sequence tasks in a certain way. That's acceptable, but do not use this as an excuse to manufacture a sequence out of convenience. As long as there is a good, logical reason, that is sufficient justification. For example, in the design-build scenario, certainly several aspects of the software design lend themselves to some concurrency with the build task. Part of the software design work, however, involves the use of a recently introduced technology with which the company has no experience. For that reason, the project manager decides that the part of the design that involves this new technology must be complete before any of the associated build tasks can start.

Unique requirements. These constraints occur in situations where a critical resource — say, an irreplaceable expert or a one-of-a kind piece of equipment — is involved on several project tasks. For example, suppose a new piece of test equipment will be used on a software development project. There is only one piece of this equipment, and it can be used on only one part of the software at a time. It will be used to test several different parts of the software. To ensure that no scheduling conflicts arise with the new equipment, the project manager creates FS dependencies between every part of the software that will use this test equipment. Apart from any technical constraints, the project manager may impose such dependencies to ensure that no scheduling conflicts will arise from the use of scarce resources.

Management Constraints

A second type of dependency arises as the result of a management-imposed constraint. For example, suppose the product manager on a software development project is aware that a competitor will soon introduce a new product with similar features to their own. Rather than follow the concurrent design-build strategy, the product manager wants to ensure that the design of the new software will yield a product that can compete with the competitor's new product. He or she expects design changes in response to the competitor's new product and, rather than risk wasting the programmers' time, imposes the FS dependency between the design and build tasks.

You'll see management constraints at work when you analyze the network diagram and as part of the scheduling decisions you make as project manager. They differ from technical dependencies in that they can be reversed, whereas technical dependencies cannot. For example, suppose the product manager finds out that the competitor has discovered a fatal flaw as a result of beta testing and has decided to indefinitely delay the new product introduction pending resolution of the flaw. The decision to follow the FS dependency between design and build now can be reversed, and the concurrent design-build strategy can be reinstituted. That is, management will have the project manager change the design-build dependency from FS to SS.

Interproject Constraints

Interproject constraints result when deliverables from one project are needed by another project. Such constraints result in dependencies between the tasks that produce the deliverable in one project and the tasks in the other project that require the use of those deliverables. For example, suppose a new piece of test equipment is being manufactured by the same company that is developing the software that will use the test equipment. In this case, the start of the testing tasks in the software development project depends on the delivery of the manufactured test equipment from the other project. The dependencies that result are technical but exist between tasks in two or more projects, rather than within a single project.

Interproject constraints arise when a very large project is decomposed into smaller, more manageable projects. For example, the construction of the Boeing 777 took place in a variety of geographically dispersed manufacturing facilities. Each manufacturing facility defined a project to produce its part. To assemble the final aircraft, the delivery of the parts from separate projects had to be coordinated with the final assembly project plan. Thus, there were tasks in the final assembly project that depended on deliverables from other subassembly projects.

NOTE These interproject constraints are common. Occasionally, large projects are decomposed into smaller projects or divided into a number of projects that are defined along organizational or geographic boundaries. In all of these examples, projects are decomposed into smaller projects that are related to one another. This approach creates interproject constraints. Although I prefer to avoid such decomposition because it creates additional risk, it may be necessary at times.

Date Constraints

At the outset, I want to make it clear that I do not approve of using date constraints. I avoid them in any way I can. In other words, "just say no" to typing dates into your project management software. If you have been in the habit of using date constraints, read on.

Date constraints impose start or finish dates on a task, forcing it to occur according to a particular schedule. In our date-driven world, it is tempting to use the requested date as the required delivery date. These constraints generally conflict with the schedule that is calculated and driven by the dependency relationships between tasks. In other words, date constraints create unnecessary complication in interpreting the project schedule.

Date constraints come in three types:

No earlier than. This date constraint specifies the earliest date on which a task can be completed.

No later than. This date constraint specifies a date by which a task must be completed.

On this date. This date constraint specifies the exact date on which a task must be completed.

All of these date constraints can be used on the start or finish side of a task. The most troublesome application is the on-this-date constraint. It firmly sets a date and affects all tasks that follow it. The result is the creation of a needless complication in the project schedule and later in reporting the status of the project. The next most troublesome is the no-later-than constraint. It will not allow a task to occur beyond the specified date. Again, you are introducing complexity for no good reason. Both types can result in negative slack. If at all possible, do not use them. There are alternatives, which I discuss in the next chapter. The least troublesome is the no-earlier-than constraint. At worst, it simply delays a task's schedule and by itself cannot cause negative float.

Using the Lag Variable

Pauses or delays between tasks are indicated in the network diagram through the use of *lag variables*. Lag variables are best defined by way of an example. Suppose that data is being collected by mailing out a survey, and is entered as the surveys are returned. Imposing an SS dependency between mailing out the surveys and entering the data would not be feasible unless you introduced some delay between mailing surveys and getting back the responses that could be entered. For the sake of the example, suppose that you wait 10 days from the date you mail the surveys until you schedule entering the data from the surveys. Ten days is the time you think it will take for the surveys to arrive, for the recipients to answer the survey questions, and for them to get the surveys back to you in the mail. In this case, you have defined an SS dependency with a lag of 10 days. To put it another way, task B (data entry) can start 10 days after task A (mail the survey) has started.

Creating an Initial Project Network Schedule

As mentioned, all tasks in the network diagram have at least one predecessor and one successor task, with the exception of the start and end tasks. If this convention is followed, the sequence is relatively straightforward to identify. If, however, the convention is not followed, or if date constraints are imposed on some tasks, or if the resources follow different calendars, understanding the sequence of tasks that result from this initial scheduling exercise can be rather complex.

To establish the project schedule, you need to compute two schedules: the early schedule, which you calculate using the forward pass, and the late schedule, which you calculate using the backward pass.

The early schedule consists of the earliest times at which a task can start and finish. These are calculated numbers derived from the dependencies between all the tasks in the project. The late schedule consists of the latest times at which a task can start and finish without delaying the completion date of the project. These are also calculated numbers that are derived from the dependencies between all of the tasks in the project.

The combination of these two schedules gives you two additional pieces of information about the project schedule:

- The window of time within which each task must be started and finished in order for the project to complete on schedule
- The sequence of tasks that determine the project completion date

The sequence of tasks that determine the project completion date is called the *critical path*. The critical path can be defined in several ways:

- The longest duration path in the network diagram
- The sequence of tasks whose early schedule and late schedule are the same
- The sequence of tasks with zero slack or float (these terms are defined later in this chapter)

All of these definitions say the same thing: The critical path is the sequence of tasks that must be completed on schedule in order for the project to be completed on schedule.

The tasks that define the critical path are called *critical path tasks*. Any delay in a critical path task will delay the completion of the project by the amount of delay in that task. Critical path tasks represent sequences of tasks that warrant the project manager's special attention.

The *earliest start (ES)* time for a task is the earliest time at which all of its predecessor tasks have been completed and the subject task can begin. The ES time of a task with no predecessor tasks is arbitrarily set to 1, the first day on which the project is open for work. The ES time of tasks with one predecessor task is determined from the *earliest finish (EF)* time of the predecessor task. The ES time of tasks having two or more predecessor tasks is determined from the latest of the EF times of the predecessor tasks. The earliest finish (EF) time of a task is calculated as ((ES + Duration) – One Time Unit). The reason for subtracting the one time unit is to account for the fact that a task starts at the beginning of a time unit (hour, day, and so forth) and finishes at the end of a time unit. In other words, a one-day task, starting at the beginning of a day, begins and ends on the same day. For example, in Figure 6-6 note that task E has only one predecessor, task C. The EF for task C is the end of day 3. Because it is the only predecessor of task E, the ES of task E is the beginning of day 4. Conversely, task D has two predecessors, task B and task C. When there are two or more predecessors, the ES of the successor, task D in this case, is calculated based on the maximum of the EF dates of the predecessor tasks. The EF dates of the predecessors are the end of day 4 and the end of day 3. The maximum of these is 4; therefore, the ES of task D is the morning of day 5. The complete calculations of the early schedule are shown in Figure 6-6.

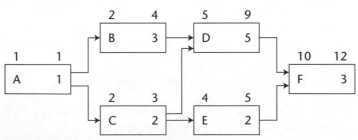

Figure 6-6 Forward pass calculations

The *latest start (LS)* and *latest finish (LF)* times of a task are the latest times at which the task can start or finish without causing a delay in the completion of the project. Knowing these times is valuable for the project manager, who must make decisions regarding resource scheduling that can affect completion dates. The window of time between the ES and LF of a task is the window within which the resource for the work must be scheduled or the project completion date will be delayed. To calculate these times, you work backward in the network diagram. First set the LF time of the last task on the network to its calculated EF time. Its LS is calculated as ((LF – Duration) + One Time Unit). Again, you add the one time unit to adjust for the start and finish of a task within the same day. The LF time of all immediate predecessor tasks is determined by the minimum of the LS, minus one time unit, times all tasks for which it is the predecessor.

For example, calculate the late schedule for task E in Figure 6-7. Its only successor, task F, has an LS date of day 10. The LF date for its only predecessor, task E, will therefore be the end of day 9. In other words, task E must finish no later than the end of day 9 or it will delay the start of task F and hence delay the completion date of the project. Using the formula, the LS date for task E will be 9 – 2 + 1, or the beginning of day 7. Conversely, consider task C. It has two successor tasks, task D and task E. The LS dates for them are day 5 and day 7, respectively. The minimum of those dates, day 5, is used to calculate the LF of task C — namely, the end of day 4. The complete calculations for the late schedule are shown in Figure 6-7.

Critical Path

As mentioned, the critical path is the longest path or sequence of tasks (in terms of task duration) through the network diagram. The critical path drives the completion date of the project. Any delay in the completion of any one of the tasks in the sequence will delay the completion of the project. The project manager pays particular attention to critical path tasks. The critical path for the example problem you used to calculate the early schedule and the late schedule is shown in Figure 6-8.

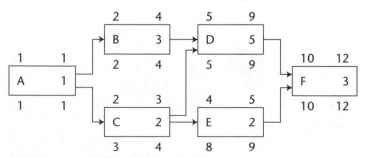

Figure 6-7 Backward pass calculations

Figure 6-8 Critical path

Calculating Critical Path

One way to identify the critical path in the network diagram is to identify all possible paths through the diagram and add up the durations of the tasks that lie along those paths. The path with the longest duration time is the critical path. For projects of any size, this method is not feasible, and you have to resort to the second method of finding the critical path — computing the slack time of a task.

Computing Slack

The second method of finding the critical path requires you to compute a quantity known as the task *slack time*. Slack time (also called *float*) is the amount of delay expressed in units of time that could be tolerated in the starting time or completion time of a task without causing a delay in the completion of the project. Slack time is a calculated number. It is the difference between the late finish and the early finish (LF – EF). If the result is greater than zero, the task has a range of time in which it can start and finish without delaying the project completion date, as shown in Figure 6-9.

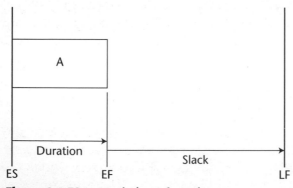

Figure 6-9 ES to LF window of a task

Because weekends, holidays, and other nonwork periods are not conventionally considered part of the slack, these must be subtracted from the period of slack.

There are two types of slack:

Free slack. This is the range of dates in which a task can finish without causing a delay in the early schedule of any tasks that are its immediate successors. Notice in Figure 6-8 that task C has an ES of the beginning of day 2 and an LF of the end of day 4. Its duration is two days, and it has a day 3 window within which it must be completed without affecting the ES of any of its successor tasks (task D and task E). Therefore, it has free slack of one day. Free slack can be equal to but never greater than total slack. When you choose to delay the start of a task, possibly for resource scheduling reasons, first consider tasks that have free slack associated with them. By definition, if a task's completion stays within the free slack range, it can never delay the early start date of any other task in the project.

Total slack. This is the range of dates in which a task can finish without delaying the project completion date. Consider task E in Figure 6-8. Task E has a free slack (or float) of four days, as well as a total slack (or float) of four days. In other words, if task E were to be completed more than three days later than its EF date, it would delay completion of the project. You know that if a task has zero slack, then it determines the project completion date. In other words, all the tasks on the critical path must be done on their earliest schedule or the project completion date will suffer. If a task with total slack greater than zero were to be delayed beyond its late finish date, it would become a critical path task and cause the completion date to be delayed.

Based on the method you used to compute the early and late schedules, the sequence of tasks having zero slack is defined as the critical path. If a task has been date constrained using the on-this-date type of constraint, it will also have zero slack. However, this constraint usually gives a false indicator that a task is on the critical path. Finally, in the general case, the critical path is the path that has minimum slack.

Near-Critical Path

Even though project managers are tempted to rivet their attention on critical path tasks, other tasks also require their attention. These make up what is called a *near-critical path*. The full treatment of near-critical tasks is beyond the scope of this book. I introduce the concept here so that you are aware that paths other than critical paths are worthy of attention. By way of a general example, suppose the critical path tasks are tasks with which the project team has considerable experience; duration estimates are based on historical data and are quite accurate in that the estimated duration will be very close to the actual duration.

Conversely, suppose there is also a sequence of tasks not on the critical path with which the team has little experience. Duration estimates have large estimation variances. Suppose further that such tasks lie on a path that has little total slack. It is very likely that this near-critical path may actually drive the project completion date even though the total path length is less than that of the critical path. This situation will happen if larger-than-estimated durations occur. Because of the large duration variances, such a case is very likely. Obviously, this path cannot be ignored.

Analyzing the Initial Project Network Diagram

After you have created the initial project network diagram, one of two situations will be present:

- The initial project completion date meets the requested completion date. Usually this is not the case, but it does sometimes happen.
- The more likely situation is that the initial project completion date is later than the requested completion date. In other words, you have to find a way to squeeze some time out of the project schedule.

You eventually need to address two considerations: the project completion date and resource availability under the revised project schedule. In this section, I proceed under the assumption that resources will be available to meet this compressed schedule. The next chapter covers the resource-scheduling problem. The two are quite dependent on one another, but they must be treated separately.

Compressing the Schedule

Almost without exception, the initial project calculations will result in a project completion date beyond the required completion date. That means the project team must find ways to reduce the total duration of the project to meet the required date.

To address this problem, you analyze the network diagram to identify areas where you can compress project duration. Look for pairs of tasks that allow you to convert tasks that are currently worked on in series into more parallel patterns of work. Work on the successor task might begin once the predecessor task has reached a certain stage of completion. In many cases, some of the deliverables from the predecessor can be made available to the successor so that work might begin on it.

WARNING Note that project risk increases because you have created a potential rework situation if changes are made in the predecessor after work has started on the successor. Schedule compressions affect only the time frame in which work will be done; they do not reduce the amount of work to be done. The result is the need for more coordination and communication, especially between the tasks affected by the dependency changes.

You first need to identify strategies for locating potential dependency changes. Focus your attention on critical path tasks because these are the tasks that determine the completion date of the project, the very thing you want to have an impact on. You might be tempted to look at critical path tasks that come early in the life of the project, thinking that you can get a jump on the scheduling problem, but this usually is not a good strategy for this reason: At the early stages of a project, the project team is little more than a group of people who have not worked together before (we'll refer to them as a herd of cats). Because you are going to make dependency changes (FS to SS), you are going to introduce risk into the project. Your herd of cats is not ready to assume risk early in the project. You should give them some time to become a real team before intentionally increasing the risk they will have to contend with. That means you should look downstream on the critical path for those compression opportunities.

A second factor to consider is focusing on tasks that are partitionable. A *partitionable* task is one whose work can be assigned to more than one individual working in parallel. For example, painting a room is partitionable. One person can be assigned to each wall. When one wall is finished, a successor task, such as picture hanging, can be done on the completed wall. That way, you don't have to wait until the room is entirely painted before you can begin decorating the walls with pictures.

Writing a computer program may or may not be partitionable. If it is partitionable, you could begin a successor task like testing the completed parts before the entire program is complete. Whether a program is partitionable depends on many factors, such as how the program is designed, whether the program is single-function or multifunction, and other considerations. If a task is partitionable, it is a candidate for consideration. You might be able to partition it so that when some of it is finished, you can begin working on successor tasks that depend on the part that is complete. Once you have identified a candidate set of partitionable tasks, you need to assess the extent to which the schedule might be compressed by starting the task's successor task earlier. There is not much to gain by considering tasks with short duration times. I hope I have given you enough hints at a strategy that you will be able to find those opportunities. If you can't, don't worry. I have other suggestions for compressing the schedule in the next chapter.

Assume you have found one or more candidate tasks to work with. See what happens to the network diagram and the critical path as dependencies are adjusted. As you begin to replace series (SF dependencies) with parallel sequences of tasks (SS dependencies), the critical path may change to a new sequence of tasks. This change will happen if the length of the initial critical path, because of your compression decisions, is reduced to a duration less than that of some other path. The result is a new critical path. Figure 6-10 shows two iterations of the analysis. The top diagram is the original critical path that results from constructing the initial network diagram using only FS dependencies. The critical path tasks are identified with a filled dot.

The middle diagram in Figure 6-10 is the result of changing the dependency between tasks A and B from FS to SS. Now, the critical path has changed to a new sequence of tasks. The new critical path is shown in the middle diagram of Figure 6-10 by the tasks with filled triangles. If you change the FS dependency between tasks C and D, the critical path again moves to the sequence of tasks identified by the filled squares.

Occasionally, some tasks always remain on the critical path. For example, notice in Figure 6-10 the set of tasks that have a filled circle, triangle, and square. They have remained on the critical path through both changes. I label this set of tasks a bottleneck. While further compression may result in this set of tasks changing, it does identify a set of tasks deserving of particular attention as the project commences. Because all critical paths generated to this point pass through this bottleneck, you might want to take steps to ensure that these tasks do not fall behind schedule.

Management Reserve

Management reserve is a topic associated with task duration estimates, but it more appropriately belongs in this chapter because it should be a property of the project network more so than of the individual tasks.

At the individual task level, you might be tempted to pad your estimates to have a better chance of finishing a task on schedule. For example, you know that a particular task will require three days of your time to complete, but you submit an estimate of four days just to make sure you can get the three days of work done in the four-day schedule you hope to get for the task. The one day that you add is padding. First, let's agree that you will not do this. Parkinson's Law (which states that work will expand to the time allotted to complete it) will surely strike you down, and the task will, in fact, require the four days you estimated it would take. Stick with the three-day estimate and work to make it happen. That is a better strategy. Now that you know padding is bad at the task level, you are going to apparently contradict yourself by saying that it is all right at the project level. There are some very good reasons for this.

Original Critical Path

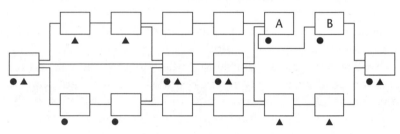

Critical Path after Changing AB from FS to SS

Critical Path after Changing CD from FS to SS

Figure 6-10 Schedule compression iterations

Management reserve is nothing more than a contingency budget of time. The size of that contingency budget can be in the range of 5 to 10 percent of the total of all the task durations in your project. The size might be closer to 5 percent for projects having few unknowns; it could range to 10 percent for projects using breakthrough technologies or that are otherwise very complex. Once you have determined the size of your management reserve, you create a task whose duration is the size of management reserve and put that task at the end of the project. It will be the last task, and its completion will signal the end of the project. This management reserve task becomes the last one in your project plan, succeeded only by the project completion milestone.

What is this management reserve used for? First, the project team should manage the project so that the reserve task is not needed; in reality, though, this is rarely possible. The date promised to the customer is the one calculated by the completion of the reserve task. The reserve task's duration can be shortened as necessary. For example, if the critical path slips by two days, the reserve task's duration will be reduced by two days. This holds the project completion date constant.

This technique keeps the management reserve task visible and enables you to manage the rate at which it's being used. If 35 percent of the overall project time line has elapsed and 50 percent of the reserve task has been used, you know you're heading for trouble.

Second, management reserve can be used as incentive for the project team. For example, many contracts include penalties for completing milestones later than planned, as well as rewards for completing milestones ahead of schedule. Think of management reserve as a contingency fund that you do not want to spend. Every day that is left in the contingency fund at the completion of the project is a day ahead of schedule for which the customer should reward you. Conversely, if you spend that contingency fund and still require more time to complete the project, this means that the project was completed later than planned. For every day that the project is late, you should expect to pay a penalty.

Using the JPP Session to Construct and Analyze the Network

I believe in using the appropriate technology, and nowhere is that more obvious than in your approach to constructing and analyzing the project network. If you have tried to use automated tools for this planning exercise, you have probably experienced nothing short of complete frustration. Automated tools will do the job for small projects or one-person project teams, but for large projects, they just get in the way.

For example, say your project has 100 tasks (which is not a large project). You can see only about six to eight task nodes on your computer screen at any time, so any attempt to analyze the network diagram using the automated tool will do nothing but add confusion. What you need is a tool that enables the planning team to see all the data at one time. How many people can you crowd around the computer screen and hope to get any meaningful work done? Even if you display the computer screen on a larger monitor you are still limited to six to eight nodes per view.

The best way to explain our approach for generating the project network diagram, which is foolproof by the way, is to discuss it step by step:

1. **Enter tasks and their durations in the software tool.** Print the network diagram. Because no dependencies have been entered, the network diagram for most software tools will be a columnar report with one task node per row — not a very informative network diagram, but it serves our purposes. Some software tools might display these nodes in formats other than columnar, and that will work just fine, too.

2. **Cut out each task node and tape it to a Post-It note.** (Don't forget to create start and end node milestones.) I recommend 3" by 3" Post-It notes because they enable you to put the node at the top and write in large numbers the task ID number on the bottom. This technique makes it possible for the project planning team to see the task ID from any-place in the planning room.

3. **Affix each Post-It note to the whiteboard in order.** I recommend placing them at the rightmost edge of the whiteboard space so that you have enough room to work. Ordering them by task ID number or WBS major category (or both) makes it easier to find them later.

4. **Place the start node at the left edge of the whiteboard.** Ask the planning group to identify all tasks that have no predecessors. As each task is called out, the planning group should listen to and voice any objections, such as they believe that one of the identified tasks does, in fact, have a predecessor. Once the objection is settled, the exercise continues. When no objections remain, place these tasks on the left side of the whiteboard and connect them to the start node with a black erasable marker pen. Continue this process until all the remaining tasks have predecessors.

   For each major part of the WBS, there will be a corresponding set of tasks that must be incorporated into the nodes already connected from the previous step. The most expert person on the planning team will facilitate the task sequencing exercise for the tasks that are in his or her area of expertise. This person will build his or her part of the network using a left-to-right build. That is, once a task has been posted on the left side of the whiteboard, what other task or tasks may now be worked on? The other members of the planning team are responsible for critiquing and commenting as the expert completes his or her part of the task sequencing. One expert at a time facilitates completing part of the task sequencing until the network diagram is complete. The conclusion of this exercise is a great time for a break. The team has reached a significant milestone in the project plan, and they deserve a rest.

5. **Input the network diagram into the software tool.** While the planning team is on break, the network diagram is input into the software tool by the planning facilitator and his or her assistant, whom I call a

technographer. As part of that exercise, this person can input the network sketch into the software tool and review the predecessor and successor data to ensure that the network is fully connected, noting and correcting any discrepancies. If a task does not have a logical successor task, it should be connected to the end task. Remember that fully connected means that every task (except the start and end tasks) has at least one predecessor and one successor task.

6. **Reassemble the planning team.** It is now time to determine whether the first draft of the network meets the project delivery dates. If it does, consider yourself fortunate. Usually it does not meet the expected completion date, and you need to analyze the network diagram. You can use the automated tool to find tasks on the critical path. Place a large red dot on the sequence of tasks that identify the critical path. The real value of the whiteboard-and-Post-It-note approach is that it facilitates using the planning group to identify ways to reduce the critical path time. To compress the project schedule, look for opportunities to change FS relationships to SS relationships, with perhaps some lag time introduced. Be careful not to get carried away with schedule compression, because it will aggravate the resource-scheduling problem. Remember that you are cramming the project work into a shorter window of time, which tends to increase the probability of creating scheduling conflicts. At each iteration, use the automated tool to check whether the critical path has moved to a new sequence of tasks. If it has, there may be other compression opportunities on the new critical path. When all of these types of schedule compression possibilities are exhausted, this part of the compression exercise is finished. Further improvements are discussed in the next chapter.

Now you've established a project schedule that meets the requested project completion date. The final step is to schedule the resources to complete the work according to the revised schedule.

Putting It All Together

You now know how to represent your project in the form of a precedence diagram from which you can calculate the initial schedule of the project. The missing ingredients are the resources and their availability. After that is factored into the schedule, the schedule could change. That is the topic covered in the next chapter.

Discussion Questions

1. The project network diagram has been constructed, and the project completion date is beyond the management-imposed deadline. You have compressed the schedule as much as possible by introducing parallel work through changes from FS to SS dependencies, and you still do not meet the schedule deadline. What would you do? (Hint: Use the scope triangle, discussed in Chapter 1.)

2. Even though all of your tasks have met the WBS completion criteria, what scheduling problems might prompt you to further decompose one or more of them, and how will that resolve the problems?

CASE STUDY – PLEASANTOWN

3. Complete the Pleasantown WBS started in Chapter 4 and construct the project network diagram. Calculate the ES, LF, and critical path. If the project is not completed by the Labor Day deadline, compress the schedule using the tools defined in this chapter.

Finalizing the Schedule and Cost Based on Resource Availability

The hammer must be swung in cadence, when more than one is hammering the iron.
— **Giordano Bruno, Italian philosopher**

Behind an able man there are always other able men.
— **Chinese proverb**

Work smarter, not harder.
— **Anonymous**

CHAPTER LEARNING OBJECTIVES

After reading this chapter, you will be able to:

◆ **Understand why resources should be leveled**

◆ **Utilize various approaches to leveling resources**

◆ **Determine the appropriate use of substitute resources**

◆ **Define a work package and its purposes**

◆ **Describe the format and explain the contents of a work package**

◆ **Know when to require a work package description**

Considering Resource Availability

The final step to putting together the project plan is to assign the resources according to the schedule developed in Chapter 6. Up to this point, you have identified the tasks in the project and developed a schedule that meets the expected end date of the project. Now you need to determine if you can accomplish this schedule with the resources available. This chapter looks at tools and methods available to help you answer this question.

There could be cases where the resources are not available according to the project schedule. In those situations, the project manager has to revert to the original project definition, budget, time, and resource allocations to resolve the scheduling problem, which may require additional time, budget, and resource allocation in order to comply with the requested deliverables and deliverable schedule.

Leveling Resources

Resource leveling is part of the broader topic of resource management. This is an area that has always created problems for organizations. Following are some of the situations that organizations have to deal with:

- Committing people to more than they can reasonably handle in the given time frame, reasoning that they will find a way to get it done but putting each of their projects in harm's way in so doing

- Changing project priorities and not considering the impact on existing resource schedules

- The absence of a resource management function that can measure and monitor the capacity of the resource pool and the extent to which it is already committed to projects

- Employee turnover and promotions that are not reflected in the resource schedule

Any organization that does not have a way of effectively handling these situations will find itself in a situation analogous to the flow through a funnel, as depicted in Figure 7-1.

Figure 7-1 is a graphic portrayal of the resource-scheduling problem. The diameter of the funnel represents the total of all resources available for the project. Tasks can pass through the funnel at a rate that is limited by the amount of work that can be completed by the available resources according to the schedule of the tasks. You can try to force more into the funnel than it can accommodate, but doing so only results in turbulence in the funnel. You are no doubt familiar with situations where managers try to force more work onto your already fully loaded schedule. The result is either schedule slippage or less than acceptable output. In the funnel example, it results in rupture due to overload (weekend time and long hours are the root cause of the rupture).

The core teamwork takes place at the center of the pipeline. This center, where the tasks flow through the funnel, is the smoothest because it is based on a well-executed schedule. The work assigned to the contract team takes place along the edge of the funnel. According to the laws of flow in a pipeline, there is more turbulence at the walls of the structure. The deliverables are the completed task work. Because the diameter of the funnel is fixed, only so much completed work can flow from it.

Too many organizations believe that by simply adding more into the top of the funnel, more will come out of the bottom. Their rationale is that people will work harder and more efficiently if they know that more is expected. While this may be true in a limited sense, it is not in the best interest of the project because it results in mistakes and compromised quality. Mistakes will be made as a direct result of the pressure from the overly ambitious schedule forced on people. In this chapter, I provide resource-leveling strategies that the project manager can adopt to avoid the situation depicted in the funnel example.

Take a step back for a moment. When you were creating the project network diagram, the critical path was the principal focal point for trying to finish the project by a specified date. Resource over- or under-allocation was not a consideration. You do this for a reason. It is important to focus your attention on planning one portion of the project at a time. If you can't reach the desired finish date based strictly on the logical order in which tasks must be completed, why worry about whether resources are over- or under-allocated? You've got another problem to solve first. After the finish date has been accepted, you can address the problem of over-allocation, and, in some cases, under-allocation.

Figure 7-1 The resource scheduling problem

Resource leveling is a process that the project manager follows to schedule how each resource is allocated to tasks in order to accomplish the work within the scheduled start and finish dates of the task. Recall that the scheduled start and finish dates of every task are constrained by the project plan to lie entirely within their ES-LF window. Were that not the case, the project would be delayed beyond its scheduled completion date. As resources are leveled, they must be constrained to the ES-LF window of the tasks to which they are assigned, or the project manager must seek other alternatives to resolve the conflict between resource availability and project schedule.

The resource schedule needs to be leveled for two reasons:

- To ensure that no resource is over-allocated. That is, you do not schedule a resource to more than 100 percent of its available time.

- The project manager wants the number of resources (people, in most cases) to follow a logical pattern throughout the life of the project. You would not want the number of people working on the project to fluctuate wildly from day to day or from week to week. That would impose too many management and coordination problems. Resource leveling avoids this by ensuring that the number of resources working on a project at any time is fairly constant. The ideal project would have the number of people resources relatively level over the planning phases, building gradually to a maximum during the project work phases, and decreasing through the closing phases. Such increases and decreases are manageable and expected in the life of a well-planned project.

Acceptably Leveled Schedule

As I begin this discussion of leveling resources, I want to be clear on one point. It is very unlikely, perhaps impossible, that you will develop a resource schedule that simultaneously possesses all the desirable characteristics I discuss. Of course, you will do the best you can and hope for a resource schedule that is acceptable to management and to those who manage the resources employed on your project. When a resource schedule is leveled, the leveling process is done within the availability of the resource to that project. When I discussed task estimating and resource assignments in Chapter 5, I said that resources are not available to work on a task 100 percent of any given day. Based on my clients' experiences, this number ranges from 50 to 75 percent. This value, for a typical average day, is the resource's maximum availability. Project management software products may also refer to it as max availability or max units. Some software applications allow this value to be varied by time period; others do not.

Ideally, you want to have a project in which all resource schedules can be accommodated within the resources' maximum availability. On occasion this may not be possible, especially when project completion dates are paramount, which means that some overtime may be necessary. We're all familiar with this. Overtime should be your final fallback option, however. Use it with discretion and only for short periods of time. If at all possible, don't start your project off with overtime as the norm. You'll probably need it somewhere along the line, so keep it as part of your management reserve.

CROSS-REF Chapter 6 contains an in-depth discussion of management reserve.

Resource-Leveling Strategies

You can use three approaches to level project resources:

- Utilizing available slack
- Shifting the project finish date
- Smoothing

Take a look at each of these strategies in more detail.

Utilizing Available Slack

Slack was defined in Chapter 6 as the amount of delay expressed in units of time that could be tolerated in the starting time or completion time of a task without causing a delay in the completion of the project. Recall that slack is the difference between the ES-LF window of a task and its duration. For example, if the ES-LF window is four days and the duration of the task is three days, its slack is 4 − 3, or one day.

Slack can be used to alleviate the over-allocation of resources. With this approach, one or more of the project tasks are postponed to a date that is later than their early start date but no later than their late finish date. In other words, the tasks are rescheduled but remain within their ES-LF window.

When you are seeking to level resources, having free slack can come in handy. Free slack, as mentioned in Chapter 6, is the amount of delay that can be tolerated in a task without affecting the ES date of any of its successor tasks. When you need to resolve the "stack-up" of tasks on the schedule, first determine whether any of the tasks has free slack. If any of them do, and if rescheduling the task to that later start date will solve the resource over-allocation problem, you are done. If moving the start date of the task does not resolve the over-allocation, you have to use total slack, and at least one other task will have its early start date delayed.

Shifting the Project Finish Date

Not all projects are driven by the completion date. For some, resource availability is their most severe constraint. On these projects, the critical path may have to be extended to achieve an acceptably resource-leveled schedule. This case could very well mean that the parallel scheduling on the task network diagram that moved the original finish date to an earlier one needs to be reversed. The start-to-start and finish-to-finish dependencies might need to be set back to the linear finish-to-start type.

In some cases, a project is of a low enough priority within the organization that it is used mostly for fill-in work. In that case, the completion date is not significant and doesn't have the urgency that it does in a time-to-market project. For most projects, however, moving the finish date to beyond a desired date is the least attractive alternative.

If you find yourself caught between over-allocated resources on a schedule that cannot be acceptably leveled and a firm, fixed completion date, you may have to consider reducing the scope of the project. Consider delaying some of the features to the next release as one way of resolving the issue. In saying this, I'm referring to the concepts introduced in the discussion of the scope triangle in Chapter 1.

Smoothing

Occasionally, limited overtime is required to accomplish the work within the scheduled start and finish dates of the task. Overtime can help alleviate some resource over-allocation because it allows more work to be done within the same scheduled start and finish dates. I call this *smoothing*, and through its use you eliminate resource over-allocations, which appear as spikes in the resource loading graphs. In effect, what you do is move some of the work from normal workdays to days that otherwise are not available for work. To the person doing the work, it is overtime.

Alternative Methods of Scheduling Tasks

Rather than treating the task list as fixed and within that constraint leveling resources, you could resolve the leveling problem by considering further decomposition of one or more tasks. One of the six characteristics of a complete WBS mentioned in Chapter 4 is task independence. Task independence means that once work has begun on a task, work can continue without interruption until the task is complete. Usually, you do not schedule the work to be continuous for a number of reasons, such as resource availability, but you could if you wanted. Other than for resource availability issues, the decision to do that may simply be a preference of the project manager.

Further Decomposition of Tasks

Resource availability, or rather the lack of it, can require some creative task scheduling on the part of the project manager. For example, suppose that a task requires one person for three days within a five-day window. There are two days of slack in the schedule for that task. In other words, the ES-LF window of the task is five days, and the task duration is three days. The project manager would prefer to have the task scheduled for its early start date, but the unavailability of the resource for three consecutive days beginning on the ES date will require scheduling the task work to a longer period of time. One solution would be to have the resource work for three nonconsecutive days as early as possible in the five-day window. Continuing with the example, suppose that the resource is available for the first two days in the five-day window and for the last day in the five-day window. To simplify the scheduling of the resource, the project manager could decompose the five-day task into two tasks — one two-day task and one one-day task. The two-day task would then have an FS dependency on the one-day task. The scheduled start and finish dates of the two tasks would be set so that they fit the availability of the resource. Other solutions to this scheduling problem are possible but I do not discuss them here. The one I have presented is the best approach to situations similar to the example.

Stretching Tasks

Another alternative that preserves the continuity of the task work is to stretch the work over a longer period of time by having the resource work on the task at a percent per day lower than was originally planned.

We can modify the previous example to illustrate this by stretching the task. Suppose the resource is available 80 percent of each day in the five-day window, and you need four days of work. The resource is therefore available for 0.80 times five days, or four days of work, over the five-day window. You need only four days of work from the resource, so how do you schedule the work in the five-day window to accomplish the four days of work you need? The solution is to stretch the task from four days to five and schedule the resource to work on the task for those five days. Because the resource can only work 80 percent of the time on the task, the resource will accomplish four days of work over a five-day period.

In this simple example, the percentage was constant over the five days, but it might also follow some profile. For example, suppose you needed the resource for three days and the resource was available full-time for the first and second days but only half-time for the remaining three days of the five-day window. You could first split the task into two tasks — a two-day task and a one-day task. The two-day task would fully use the resource and get two days of work completed. The second task would be stretched to two days, and the resource would be assigned half-time for two days to complete the remaining day of work on the task. In other words, you got the three days of work in four days — the first two days at full-time and the next two days at half-time. Resource availability can be the determining factor for how the task can be stretched within its ES-LF window and still get the required amount of work from the resource.

Assigning Substitute Resources

Our estimate of task duration was based on the assumption that a typically skilled resource will be available to work on the task. That may not be possible, however, because of the unavailability of the resource. This unavailability will be especially likely in the case of scarce resources such as some of the newer technologies. In this case, the project manager needs to use another strategy. One approach would be to use less-skilled resources and add to the total number of hours requested. Here, the thinking is that a less-skilled resource would require a longer period of time to complete the task work.

WARNING Be careful in using this tactic, however, because there is additional risk in using a less-skilled person, and it is not clear exactly what increase in task duration is needed to account for the person with fewer skills. This strategy works only for noncritical path tasks. Using it for a critical path task would extend the completion date of the project.

Cost Impact of Resource Leveling

It should be obvious to you that resource leveling almost always stretches the schedule. The case where it doesn't stretch the schedule may occur when slack is available in the right places in the schedule. Scheduling the work of a resource over a longer period of time not only removes scheduling conflicts, but also removes any over-allocations of that resource. To do all that, the project completion date is extended, which can have the following results:

▪ If the resources are billable based on the labor expended, project costs do not increase.

- If there are resources that are charged on a calendar basis, project costs will increase. Such expenses would be attributable to equipment and space on a rental agreement. In some cases, there may be increased people costs as well.

- If there are incentives for early completion and penalties for late completion of a project, a cost impact will be felt as well.

Implementing Micro-Level Project Planning

Micro-level planning is another step in the decomposition of the tasks that are assigned to an individual. It involves a decomposition to what I will call *subtasks*. In some cases, these subtasks may be a very simple to-do list or, in more complex situations, might appear as a very small project network. Remember that you are dealing with tasks that have met the six WBS completion criteria and are therefore relatively simple tasks of short duration.

Micro-level project planning begins with the lowest-level task defined in the WBS. Because it appears in the WBS, it will have management oversight by the project manager. The responsibility for completing this task within a defined window of time will be assigned to a task manager (or team leader, if you prefer). The task may be simple enough that all of the work of completing it is done by the task manager. In more complex situations, a small team assigned to the task manager will actually complete the work of the task. I'll use the word *subteam* in the discussion that follows, but recognize that the team may be only one person, the task manager.

The first thing the subteam must do is to continue the decomposition that was done in building the WBS, but this decomposition will be below the task level. As indicated previously, the subtasks might be nothing more than a simple to-do list that is executed in a linear fashion. More complex tasks will actually generate a task network diagram composed of tasks and their dependency relationships. Recall that the task must meet the completeness criteria discussed in Chapter 4. These tasks will each be less than two weeks' duration, so the subtasks that make them up will be of shorter duration. The decomposition should be fairly simple and result in tasks of one to three days' duration. I would be surprised if it took more than 10 subtasks to define the work of the task.

Using a project management software package to create the micro-level plan and its accompanying schedule is overkill. My suggestion is that you define the tasks and their dependency relationships, and schedule them on a whiteboard using Post-It notes and marking pens. Figure 7-2 is an example of what that whiteboard display might look like. The task consists of seven subtasks that are shown in the upper portion of the figure along with their dependencies. The lower portion of the figure shows the time-scaled schedule for the three members of the subteam. The shaded areas of the schedule are non-workdays and days when a resource is not available. Half-day time segments are the lowest level of granularity used.

> **TIP** You might adjust to a finer timescale as the project tasks would suggest. However, I have found that to be helpful in only a very few situations.

This task is typical of others in the project plan. It is simple enough that all of the work can be done at the whiteboard. Updating is very simple. There is no need for software support, which simply adds management overhead with little return on the investment of time expended to capture and manage it.

In the next section, I make the transition to work packages. What you have done so far is decompose a task into subtasks. In other words, you have a list of things that have to be done in order to complete the task. The work package describes exactly how you are going to accomplish the task through the identified subtasks. In other words, it is a mini-plan for your task.

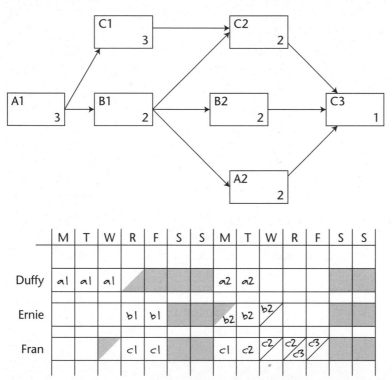

Figure 7-2 Example of a task dependency diagram and time-scaled resource schedule

> ### CASE STUDY — PLEASANTOWN PLAYGROUND PROJECT
>
> The calendar for this project will be very different from most situations you will encounter. Your team comprises volunteers, and they are only available on weekends and perhaps in the early evening after work. Figure 7-2 can be adapted to support even that unusual type of project calendar. You also should anticipate no-shows among your volunteers. They have other obligations and your project is not a high priority for many of them. Leadership and motivation are key. Ask yourself if there are comparable situations in your workplace. Do you depend on volunteers on any of your projects? How about trading favors with your colleagues?

Work Packages

At this point, you have essentially completed all JPP session tasks. The project work has been defined as a list of tasks; task duration and resource requirements are specified, the project network is built, the task schedule is done, and resources have been scheduled. The JPP session attendees have reached a consensus. Whew, that's a lot — and you probably wondered if it would ever be finished. There is one more step to go before project work can commence — that is, to define the work to be done in each task but at the task level. Recall from Chapter 4 that tasks are themselves made up of tasks. The work to be done within a task is called a *work package*.

This is really the final test of the feasibility of the schedule and resource-leveling decisions. The work package is a statement by each task manager as to how he or she plans to complete the task within the scheduled start and finish dates. It is like an insurance policy. For the project manager, the work package is a document that describes the work at a level of detail such that if the task manager or anyone working on the task were not available (if he or she were fired, hit by a bus on the way to work, or otherwise not available), someone else could use the work package to figure out how to continue the work of the task with minimal lost time. This safeguard is especially important for critical path tasks for which schedule delays are to be avoided.

A work package can consist of one or several tasks. On the one hand, this may be nothing more than a to-do list, which can be completed in any order. On the other hand, the work package can consist of tasks that take the form of a mini-project, with a network diagram that describes it. In this case, work packages are assigned to a single individual, called a task manager or work package manager. This manager is responsible for completing the task on time, within budget, and according to specification. Sounds like a project manager, doesn't it? That person has the authority and the access to the resources needed to complete the assignment.

Purpose of a Work Package

The work package becomes the bedrock for all project work. It describes in detail the tasks that need to be done to complete the work for a task. In addition to the task descriptions, the package includes start and end dates for the task.

The work package manager (or task manager) may decide to include the start and end dates for each task in the package so that anyone who has occasion to use the work package will have a sense of how the plan to complete the work will be accomplished.

WARNING Be careful if you adopt this approach because you encourage micromanagement on the part of the project manager. The more you say, the more you encourage objections. The trade-off, however, is protecting the project schedule. There is always a trade-off between the need for detail and the need to spend work time accomplishing work, not shuffling papers.

The work package also can be adapted to status reporting. Tasks constitute the work to be done. Checking off completed tasks enables you to measure what percent of the task is complete. Some organizations use the percent of tasks completed as the percent of task completion, which is a simple yet effective metric that serves as the basis for earned value calculations. Earned value is discussed in detail in Chapter 10.

Format of a Work Package

I recommend two work package documents:

Work package assignment sheet. This is a very special type of telephone directory used as a ready reference for the project manager. It contains some basic information about each work package and its manager.

Work package description report. This is a detailed description of the task plan. It contains much of the same information that is found in a project plan, but it focuses on tasks, not projects. It is therefore a much simpler document than a project plan, even though it contains the same type of information as the project plan.

Work Package Assignment Sheet

The work package assignment sheet, shown in Figure 7-3, is a report for the project manager only. It includes the earliest start and latest end dates for each task. This sheet is one of the few resources available to the project manager, and it should not be made available to anyone other than the project manager. The project manager is unlikely to tell a task manager that a given task is scheduled for completion on July 15, for example, when the task manager really has until August 15 because of slack. Task managers should be given only the scheduled start and end dates for their tasks.

The work package assignment sheet has limited value in smaller projects but can be invaluable in larger ones. For example, my business was once involved in a project that consisted of more than 4,000 tasks. Over the seven-year life of the project, more than 10,000 task managers were involved. This report became a phone directory that needed constant updating as team members came and went. Because of the complexity and personnel changes that accompany these large projects, the project manager needs an effective and efficient way of staying current with the project team membership, who is assigned to what, and how they will accomplish their work.

Work Package Description Report

A work package description report is a document prepared by the task manager in which he or she describes the details of how he or she will accomplish the work of the task. A very simple example of a work package, or statement of work, is shown in Figure 7-4.

WORK PACKAGE ASSIGNMENT SHEET		Project Name		Project No.		Project Manager	
Work Package		Schedule					
Number	Name	Early Start	Late Finish	Work Package Manager	Contact Information		
A	DESIGN	03/01/00	04/01/00	ANNA LYST			
B	PROD. EVAL	04/02/00	07/02/00	HY ROWLER			
C1	PLACE.LOCATE.PT1	04/02/00	03/04/01	SY YONARA			
C2	PLACE.LOCATE.PT2	07/03/00	03/04/01	HY ROWLER			
D	PROD.FCAST	07/03/00	03/04/01	SY YONARA			
E	PROD.DELETE	03/05/01	06/02/01	HY ROWLER			
F	PROMO.REGION	03/05/01	07/06/01	TERRI TORY			
H	PRICE	08/04/01	02/05/02	HY ROWLER			
I	PLACE.DESIGN	06/05/01	08/03/02	HY ROWLER			
J	PROMO.SALES.LEAD	07/07/01	11/05/01	TERRI TORY			
G	PROMO.MEDIA	07/07/01	02/05/02	SY YONARA			
K	PROMO.SALES.RPT	10/07/01	02/05/02	TERRI TORY			
L	SYSTEM.TEST	02/08/02	05/10/02	ANNA LYST			
M	SYSTEM.ACCEPT	05/10/02	06/10/02	ANNA LYST			
Prepared by		Date		Approved by		Date	Sheet 1 of 1

Figure 7-3 Work package assignment sheet

WORK PACKAGE DESCRIPTION

Project Name	Project No.			Project Manager	
Work Package Name	Work Package No.		Work Package Manager	Contact Info.	Date
Start Date	End Date	Critical Path Y N	Predecessor Work Package(s)	Successor Work Package(s)	

TASK

No.	Name	Description	Time (days)	Responsibility	Contact Info.

Prepared by	Date	Approved by	Date	Sheet 1 of 1

Figure 7-4 Work package description report

Once the project plan has been approved, it is the task manager's responsibility to generate the work package documentation. Not all tasks will require or should require work package documentation. The documentation can be limited to critical path tasks, near-critical path tasks, high-risk tasks, and tasks that use very scarce or highly skilled staff. It is the project managers who will decide which tasks need a work package description report.

The descriptions must be complete so that anyone could pick them up, read them, and understand what has to be done to complete the task. Each task must be described so that the status of the work package can be determined easily. Ideally, the task list is a check-off list. Once all the tasks have been checked off as being completed, the task is completed. Each task will also have a duration estimate attached to it. In some project planning sessions, these estimates may have been supplied as a bottom-up method of estimating task duration.

Putting It All Together

The work of planning the project is now complete. All that remains is to document the plan in the form of a project proposal and forward it to the appropriate manager(s) for approval. Approval at this stage is approval to do the project as defined in the project plan. In the next chapter, I bring together all the discussions from earlier chapters on the Joint Project Planning session. While I have discussed various parts of project planning, I have not yet given you a complete picture of exactly how a project planning session is planned and organized, who should attend, and how one is conducted.

Discussion Questions

1. Discuss the concept of the work package as an insurance policy. How is it an insurance policy, and what might it contain that would make it an insurance policy?

2. You have two options for a resource to work on a programming task:

   ▪ One choice is Harry. He is the most skilled programmer in the company and is therefore in constant demand. As a result, he is usually assigned to several projects at the same time. He is available to your project on a half-time basis. He currently has commitments to two other projects for the remaining half of his time.

   ▪ Your other choice is actually a team of two programmers, both of whom have average skills. They are recent hires into the company and have never worked together before. They could each be assigned to your project quarter-time. This would be the only project they would be working on. The remainder of their time will be spent in training.

   Which choice would you make and why? Are there conditions under which one choice would be preferred over the other? Be specific.

CASE STUDY – PLEASANTOWN PLAYGROUND PROJECT

3. You have already done a WBS and built the project schedule. As the project manager on this project, what assumptions have you made about resources that will give you a good chance to bring this project in on time? Is over-staffing a possibility in anticipation of no-shows? How would you plan for overstaffing? Give your costs for your resources and show when they will be used based on the current WBS. If you have access to MS Project and know how to use it, use it to complete this exercise.

CHAPTER

8

The Need to Plan: Conducting the Joint Project Planning Session

This report, by its very length, defends itself against the risk of being read.
— Winston Churchill, English Prime Minister

Learn to write well, or not to write at all.
— John Dryden, English poet

If you don't get the reader's attention in the first paragraph,
the rest of your message is lost.
— Public relations maxim

CHAPTER LEARNING OBJECTIVES

After reading this chapter, you will be able to:

◆ Understand the importance of planning to a TPM project

◆ Understand the purpose of the Joint Project Planning session

◆ Know how to plan a Joint Project Planning session

◆ Decide who should attend the Joint Project Planning session

◆ Understand all of the deliverables from the Joint Project Planning session

◆ Explain the purpose of the project proposal

◆ Know the contents of the project proposal

How often have you heard it said that planning is a waste of time? No sooner is the plan completed than someone comes along to change it. These same naysayers would also argue that the plan, once completed, is disregarded and merely put on the shelf so the team can get down to doing some real work. In people management, the planning activity involves deciding on the types of people resources that will be needed to discharge the responsibilities of the department. That means identifying the types of skills needed and the number of people possessing those skills.

The Importance of Planning

In TPM the project plan is indispensable. Not only is it a road map to how the work will be performed, it is also a tool for decision-making. The plan suggests alternative approaches, schedules, and resource requirements from which the project manager can select the best alternative.

> **NOTE** Understand that a project plan is dynamic. You *expect* it to change. A complete plan will clearly state the tasks that need to be done, why they are necessary, who will do what, when it will be completed, what resources will be needed, and what criteria must be met in order for the project to be declared complete and successful. However, TPM is not designed for change, even though it is expected. In Part II of this book, I discuss project management approaches that are designed for change. One of the many advantages of these approaches is that change is accommodated within the process itself. Change in the TPM world is something the project manager would rather not deal with. To the project manager who is using the approaches discussed in Part II, change is a necessary ingredient of a successful project.

There are three benefits to developing a project plan, and the sections that follow discuss each in turn.

Planning Reduces Uncertainty

Even though you would never expect the project work to occur exactly as planned, planning the work enables you to consider the likely outcomes and to put the necessary corrective measures in place.

Planning Increases Understanding

The mere act of planning gives you a better understanding of the goals and objectives of the project. Even if you were to discard the plan, you would still benefit from having done the exercise.

Planning Improves Efficiency

Once you have defined the project plan and the necessary resources to carry out the plan, you can schedule the work to take advantage of resource availability. You also can schedule work in parallel; that is, you can do tasks concurrently, rather than in series. By doing tasks concurrently, you can shorten the total duration of the project. You can maximize your use of resources and complete the project work in less time than by taking other approaches.

Just as Alice needed to know where in Wonderland she was going, so does the project manager. Not knowing the parameters of a project prevents measurement of progress and results in never knowing when the project is complete. The plan also provides a basis for measuring work planned against work performed.

Joint Project Planning Sessions

Chapters 4 to 7 have all included a brief discussion of how the Joint Project Planning (JPP) session relates to the chapter topics. In this chapter, I bring all of that information together, along with a treatment of the logistics of planning projects using the Joint Project Planning session.

All of the planning activities I've discussed so far to create the detailed project plan take place in a JPP session. I advocate and use a group process for generating the detailed project plan. The JPP is a group session in which all of the people who are involved in the project meet to develop the detailed plan. The session can last from one to three days, and it can be work-intensive. Conflict is common between session attendees, but the final result of this meeting is an agreement about how the project can be accomplished within a specified time frame, budget, resource availabilities, and customer specification.

NOTE My planning process shares many of the same features as Joint Requirements Planning (JRP) and Joint Applications Design (JAD) sessions. The JRP session is commonly used to design computer applications. My JPP is robust — that is, it can be used for any type of project, including the design and development of computer applications.

The objective of a JPP session is very simple: Develop a project plan that meets the Conditions of Satisfaction (COS) as negotiated between the requestor and the provider, and as described in the Project Overview Statement. Sounds simple, doesn't it?

Unfortunately, it doesn't happen with any regularity, for many reasons. People are generally impatient to get on with the work of the project. After all, there are deadlines to meet and other projects demanding your attention. You don't have time for planning; you have too much work to do and too many customers to satisfy. Regrettably, at the project's eleventh hour, when it is too late to recover from a poor plan, you bow in defeat. Next time, you promise yourself, you will pay more attention to the planning details. Somehow that next time never seems to come. It's time for change!

Planning the JPP Session

Team planning has always been viewed as advantageous over other forms of project planning, such as the project manager planning the project by walking around gathering data for the plan. In my experience, the synergy of the group provides far more accurate activity duration estimates, and more complete information input to the planning process itself. Perhaps the best advantage of all is that it creates a much stronger commitment to the project for all those who lived through the pain of generating and agreeing to the complete project plan. If all else fails, it is more fun than doing planning in isolation.

I know you sometimes feel that planning is a necessary evil. It is something you do because you have to and because you can then say that you have thought about where you want to go and how you are going to get there. Once written, plans are often bound in nice notebooks and become bookends gathering dust on someone's shelf.

Make up your mind right now to change that! Planning is essential to good project management. The plan that you generate is a dynamic document. It changes as the project commences. It will be a reference work for you and the team members when questions of scope and change arise. Make no bones about it: To do good planning is painful, but to do poor planning is even more painful. Take your choice.

The first document considered in the JPP session is the Project Overview Statement (POS). One may already exist and therefore will be the starting point for the JPP. If one doesn't exist, it must be developed as the initial part of or prerequisite to starting the JPP. The situation will dictate how best to proceed. The POS can be developed in a number of ways. If it is an idea for consideration, it will probably be developed by one individual — typically the person who will be the project manager. It can be departmentally based or cross-departmentally based. The broader the impact on the enterprise, the more likely it will be developed as the first phase of a JPP session. Finally, the POS may have been developed through a COS exercise. In any case, the JPP session begins by discussing and clarifying exactly what is intended by the POS. The project team might also use this opportunity to write the Project Definition Statement (PDS) — their understanding of the project.

The JPP session must be planned down to the last detail if it is to be successful. Time is a scarce resource for all of us, and the last thing you want to do is waste it. Recognize before you start that the JPP session will be very intense. Participants often get emotional and will even dig their heels in to make a point.

Before I discuss how the session is planned and conducted, I want to talk about who should attend.

Attendees

The JPP participants are invited from among those who might be affected by or have input into the project. If the project involves deliverables or is a new process or procedure, anyone who has input to the process, receives output from the process, or handles the deliverables should be invited to participate in the JPP. The customer falls into one or more of these categories and must be present at the JPP. Any manager of resources that may be required by the project team also will attend the JPP session. In many organizations, the project has a project champion (not necessarily the project manager or customer manager) who may wish to participate at least at the start.

Facilitator. A successful JPP session requires an experienced facilitator. This person is responsible for conducting the JPP. It is important that the facilitator not have a vested interest or bring biases to the session, because that would diminish the effectiveness of the plan. It must be developed with an open mind, not with a biased mind. For this reason, I strongly suggest that the project manager not facilitate the session. If using an outside consultant is not possible, I recommend a neutral party for facilitator, such as another project manager.

Project manager. Because the project manager is not leading the planning session, he or she can concentrate on the plan itself; that is the project manager's major role in the JPP. When that person is known, having the proposed project manager facilitate the JPP session may seem to be an excellent option, but it can be the wrong choice if the project is politically charged or has customers from more than one function, process, or resource pool. The project manager must be comfortable with the project plan. After all, the project manager is the one who has final responsibility when it comes to getting the project done on time, within budget, and according to specification.

Another project manager. Skilled JPP facilitators are hard to find. If the project manager is not a good choice for facilitator, then maybe another project manager — presumably unbiased — would be a good choice, especially if he or she has JPP experience.

JPP consultant. Project management consultants will often serve as another source of qualified JPP facilitators. Their broad experience in project management and project management consulting will be invaluable. This is especially true in organizations that have recently completed project management training and are in the process of implementing their own project management methodology. Having an outside consultant facilitate the JPP session is as much a learning experience as it is an opportunity to get off to a good start with a successful JPP session.

Technographer. The JPP facilitator is supported by a technographer, a professional who not only knows project management but also is an expert in the software tools used to support the project. While the JPP facilitator is coordinating the planning activities, the JPP technographer is recording planning decisions on the computer as they occur in real time. At any point in time — and there will be several — the technographer can print out or display the plan for all to see and critique.

Core project team. Commitment is so important that to exclude the core team from the JPP session would be foolish. Estimating activity duration and resource requirements will be much easier with the professional expertise these people can bring to the planning session. The core project team is made up of those individuals who will stay with the project from the first day to the last day. This does not mean that they are with the project full-time. In today's organization that is not to be expected unless the organization is totally projectized or uses self-directed teams.

Customer representative. This attendee is always a bit tricky. Face it: Some customers really don't want to be bothered. It is up to the project manager or champion to convince customers of the importance of their participation in the JPP session. I don't claim that this will be easy, but it is nevertheless important. The customer must buy in to the project plan. The customer won't get that if the project manager simply mails a copy of the plan. The customer must be involved in the planning session. To proceed without the customer's involvement is to court disaster. Changes to the project plan will occur, and problems will arise. If the customer is involved in preparing the plan, he or she can contribute to resolution of change requests and problem situations.

Resource managers. These managers control resources that the project will require. Putting a schedule together without input and participation from these managers would be a waste of time. They may have some suggestions that will make the plan all that more realistic, too. In some cases, they may send a representative who might also be part of the project team. The important factor here is that someone from each resource area is empowered to commit resources to the project plan.

Project champion. The project champion drives the project and sells it to senior management. In many cases, the champion can be the customer — an ideal situation because commitment is already there. In other cases, the project champion can be the senior managers of the division, department, or process that will be the beneficiary of the project deliverables.

Functional managers. Because functional managers manage areas that can either provide input to or receive output from the project deliverables, they or a representative should participate in the planning session. They will ensure that the project deliverables can be smoothly integrated into existing functions or that the functions will have to be modified as part of the project plan.

Process owner. For the same reasons that functional managers should be present, so should process owners. If the project deliverables do not smoothly integrate into their processes, either the project plan or the affected processes will have to be altered.

A formal invitation, announcing the project, its general direction and purpose, and the planning schedule, should be issued to all these individuals.

NOTE RSVPs are a must! Full attendance is so important that I have canceled JPP sessions because certain key participants were not able to attend. On one occasion, I acted as the project manager for a client and cancelled the JPP session because the customer did not think his attendance was important enough. My feedback to the customer was that as soon as it was a high enough priority for him to attend, I would schedule the JPP session. Pushback like this is tough, but the JPP is so critically important to the ultimate success of the project that I was willing to take this strong position with the customer.

Facilities

Because the planning team may spend as many as three consecutive days in planning, it is important that the physical facility is comfortable and away from the daily interruptions. To minimize distractions, you might be tempted to have the planning session off-site. However, while off-site seems preferable, I prefer on-site planning sessions. On-site planning sessions have both advantages and disadvantages, but with proper planning, they can be controlled. Easy access to information is a major advantage to on-site planning sessions in my experience; interruptions due to the daily flow of work are the major disadvantage. With easy access to the office made possible by cell phones and e-mail, the potential for distraction and interruptions has increased. These need to be minimized in whatever way makes sense.

Allocate enough space so that groups of four or five planning members each have separate work areas with tables, chairs, and flip charts. All work should be done in one room. In my experience, I have found that breakout rooms tend to be dysfunctional. To the extent possible, everybody needs to be present for everything that takes place in the planning session. The room should have plenty of whiteboard space or blank walls. In many cases, I have taped flip-chart paper or butcher paper to the walls. You can never have enough writing space in the planning room.

Equipment

You will need an ample supply of Post-It notes, tape, scissors, and colored marking pens. For more high-tech equipment, an LCD projector and a PC are all you need for everyone in the room to see the details as they come together.

The Complete Planning Agenda

The agenda for the JPP session is straightforward. It can be completed in one, two, or three sessions. For example, an early meeting with the requestor can be scheduled, at which time the COS are drafted. These will be input to the second session in which the POS is drafted. In those cases where the POS must be approved before detailed planning can commence, there will be an interruption until approval can be granted. Once approval is obtained, the third session can be scheduled. At this session (usually two or three days long), the detailed project plan can be drafted for approval.

Here's a sample agenda for the JPP session:

Session 1

1. Negotiate the Conditions of Satisfaction.

Session 2

1. Write the Project Overview Statement.

Session 3 (JPP session)

1. The entire planning team creates the first-level WBS.
2. Subject matter experts develop further decomposition, with the entire planning team observing and commenting.
3. Estimate activity durations and resource requirements.
4. Construct a project network diagram.
5. Determine the critical path.
6. Revise and approve the project completion date.
7. Finalize the resource schedule.
8. Gain consensus on the project plan.

Deliverables

The deliverables from the JPP session are provided in the project management life cycle and have already been discussed in detail in the appropriate chapters. They are repeated here:

Work Breakdown Structure. Recall that the Work Breakdown Structure (WBS) is a graphical or indented outline list of the work (expressed as activities) to be done to complete the project. It is used as a planning tool, as well as a reporting structure.

Activity duration estimates. The schedule, which is also a major deliverable, is developed from estimates of the duration of each work activity in the project. Activity duration estimates may be single-point estimates or three-point estimates, as discussed in Chapter 5.

Resource requirements. For each activity in the project, an estimate of the resources to perform the work is required. In most cases, the resources will be the technical and people skills, although they can also include such things as physical facilities, equipment, and computer cycles.

Project network schedule. Using the WBS, the planning team will define the sequence in which the project activities should be performed. Initially, this sequence is determined only by the technical relationships between activities, not by management prerogatives. That is, the deliverables from one or more activities are needed to begin work on the next activity. You can understand this sequence most easily by displaying it graphically. The definition of the network activities and the details of the graphical representation were covered in Chapter 6.

Activity schedule. With the sequence determined, the planning team will schedule the start date and end date for each activity. The availability of resources will largely determine that schedule.

Resource assignments. The output of the activity schedule will be the assignment of specific resources (such as skill sets) to the project activities.

Project notebook. Documentation of any type is always a chore to produce. Not so in the five-phase project management life cycle that I have used in this book. Project documentation happens as a natural by-product of the project work. All that is needed is to appoint a project team member to be responsible. His or her responsibilities include gathering information that is already available, putting it in a standard format, and electronically archiving it. This responsibility begins with the project planning session and ends when the project is formally closed.

CASE STUDY — PLEASANTOWN PLAYGROUND PROJECT

I remember a friend calling me. He was having a great deal of difficulty managing a project for his church group. His team were all volunteers and just weren't getting with the program. He reviewed how he had approached the project from a planning perspective. He did everything by the book except he forgot that his team were volunteers — just normal folk who wanted to help their pastor and the congregation as well. I told my friend to assume that the volunteers were not the least bit familiar with project management or the terminology. Therefore, if it were introduced, it would overwhelm them and lose them to the project. My friend did not follow this advice. He chased them away with his approach. More recently I had the opportunity to help my church plan and run a barrio fiesta. I never used a project management term, yet followed the life cycle exactly. The project was a success!

CASE STUDY — PLEASANTOWN PLAYGROUND PROJECT

This project is staffed mostly by volunteers. They will be neighborhood residents whose knowledge of project management processes will be weak at best. For the project manager this presents a particularly challenging situation. I've had one notable experience with such projects. I was the project manager for a barrio fiesta being sponsored by my church. I learned some valuable lessons from that experience which I now pass on to you.

- ◆ Jargon should be avoided at all costs.
- ◆ The schedule should be presented in tabular form.
- ◆ Let the team members have their say even if it costs precious time.
- ◆ Don't be too demanding of status reports — verbal reports should suffice
- ◆ Overstaff each task — there is a lot of attrition.
- ◆ Make tasks very simple and easy to complete.
- ◆ Break tasks down to as fine a level of detail as possible.

Project Proposal

The culmination of all the planning is the project proposal. The project proposal is the deliverable from the JPP session and is forwarded to the senior management team for approval to do the project. It states the complete business case for the project. This includes expected business value, as well as cost and time estimates. In addition to this information, the proposal details what is to be done, who is going to do it, when it is going to be done, and how it is going to be done. It is the road map for the project.

NOTE Expect feedback and several revisions before approval is granted. It is not the purpose of this section to spell out in detail what a project proposal should look like. The organization will have a prescribed format to follow. Rather, it is my intention to outline the contents you will be expected to submit.

Contents of the Project Proposal

Each organization will have a prescribed format for its project proposal, but most proposals have sections similar to the ones in the list that follows. You will see a remarkable resemblance to the topics covered in Chapters 3 through 7. Rightly so, for the project proposal is a restatement of all the planning work that has been done so far:

Background. This brief description details the situation that led to the project proposal. It often states the business conditions, opportunities, and any problems giving rise to the project. It sets the stage for later sections and puts the project in the context of the business.

Objective. This is another short section that gives a very general statement of what you hope to accomplish through this project. Avoid jargon because you don't know who might have reason to read this section. Use the language of the business, not the technical language of your department. The objective should be clearly stated so that there is no doubt as to what is to be done and what constitutes attainment of the objective.

Overview of the approach to be taken. For those who might not be interested in the details of how you are going to reach your objective, this section provides a high-level outline of your approach. Again, avoid jargon whenever possible. Give a brief statement of each step and a few sentences of supporting narrative. Brevity and clarity are important.

Detailed statement of the work. Here is where you provide the details of your approach. Include what will be done, when it will be done, who will do it, how much time will be required of them, and what criteria will be used to measure completeness. This is the road map of all the project work. I have found Gantt charts useful for presentations of schedule data. They are easily understood and generally intuitive even for people who are seeing them for the first time.

Time and cost summary. It is my practice to include a summary page of time and cost data. This usually works best if done as a Gantt chart. Often the data will have been stated over several pages, and it is brought together here for easy review and comment by the customer.

Appendices. I reserve the appendix for all supporting data and details that are not germane to the body of the proposal. Anticipate questions your customer might have, and include answers here. Remember that this is detail beyond the basic description of the project work. Supporting information is generally found here.

There are no hard-and-fast rules as to format. You will surely be able to find examples of successful proposals in your department to be used as guides. Once you have your ideas sketched out, share the proposal with a trusted colleague. His or her feedback may be the most valuable advice you can get.

Putting It All Together

In this chapter, I provided a structure for you to follow as you organize and conduct the planning session that will produce a detailed description of the project. Most books on project management devote very little space to the mechanics of producing a project plan. In my experience, poor planning is one of the major obstacles to successful project execution, and so I have given you my best advice on planning a project garnered from my many years of experience in planning projects with my clients.

This chapter also completes all of the planning discussion. The next two chapters cover implementation, beginning with a chapter on team organization (Chapter 9) and one on monitoring and controlling the project work (Chapter 10). Finally, Chapter 11 covers the closing activities that take place once the project work has been completed.

Discussion Questions

1. What are the advantages and disadvantages of holding a JPP session on-site versus off-site?

2. Your planning session seems to have reached an impasse. The planning team is divided between two ways to approach a particularly difficult part of the project. Approximately two-thirds of them want to use a well-tested and well-understood approach. The remaining third (of which you are a member) wants to use a new approach that holds the promise of significantly reducing the time to complete this part of the project. You are the project manager and feel very strongly about using the new approach. Should you impose your authority as project manager and take the new approach, or should you go with the majority? Why or why not? Be specific. Is there anything else you might do to resolve the impasse?

CASE STUDY – PLEASANTOWN PLAYGROUND PROJECT

3. Using the framework established in this chapter, set up the agenda and details for the Joint Project Planning Session for the Pleasantown Playground Project.

Building and Managing an Effective Project Team

The productivity of a workgroup seems to depend on how the group members see their own goals in relation to the goals of the organization.
— Paul Hersey and Kenneth H. Blanchard

When the best leader's work is done the people say, 'We did it ourselves.'
— Lao-Tzu, Chinese philosopher

When a team outgrows individual performance and learns team confidence, excellence becomes reality.
— Joe Paterno, football coach, Penn State University

CHAPTER LEARNING OBJECTIVES

After reading this chapter, you will be able to:

- ◆ Explain the relationship between the project manager and the functional manager
- ◆ Use projects for motivation and development
- ◆ Understand the concept of job design and how it relates to project management
- ◆ Define the three components of a project team
- ◆ Describe the characteristics of an effective project manager
- ◆ Describe the characteristics of an effective project team member

(continued)

CHAPTER LEARNING OBJECTIVES *(continued)*

◆ Understand the different roles and responsibilities of core versus contracted team members

◆ Help contracted team members become part of the team

◆ Establish team operating rules for problem solving, decision making, and conflict resolution

◆ Know the types of team meetings and when to use each type

◆ Establish and use a team war room

◆ Know project communications requirements and use

◆ Organize the project team

◆ Understand the complexities and challenges of managing multiple team projects

◆ Understand the various requirements gathering processes

◆ Define scope change processes and change management processes

◆ Understand and use the Project Office, Core Team, and Super Team structures to manage a multiple team project

◆ Know how to select the best-fit project organizational structure for a multiple team project

The project plan has been approved, and it's time to get on with the work of the project. Before you turn the team loose, you must attend to a few housekeeping chores.

Project Manager vis-à-vis the Functional Manager

I first want to juxtapose the roles of the project manager with those of the functional manager. The distinction is an important foundation to the material presented in this chapter:

▪ The objective of the project manager is clear: Complete the project on time, within budget, and according to the customer's Conditions of Satisfaction — in other words, according to specification. Staff development is not on the list. The only cases when staff development is an objective of the project manager occur when the project manager also has line responsibility for the project team, in self-managed teams or in project forms of organizational structures. In these cases, staff development is definitely part of the project manager's objectives. The project manager must develop the skills on his or her project team to handle whatever assignments come along.

- Conversely, the functional (or resource) manager's objectives include development of staff skills to meet project requirements and deployment of staff to projects. These objectives pertain regardless of the organizational structure.

The project manager's objectives and the functional (or resource) manager's objectives will often conflict. Part of the program for developing staff skills will occur through on-the-job training. Functional (or resource) managers will look for opportunities to deploy staff to project assignments that provide opportunities to learn new skills. The project manager, conversely, would rather have experienced staff assigned to project tasks, especially tasks that are critical to the completion of the project according to plan. The project manager will not be interested in being the training ground for professional staff.

A further complication arises in those situations where the functional (or resource) manager is also a project manager. In matrix organizations, this situation occurs frequently. Here the functional (or resource) manager is torn between assigning the best professionals to the task and assigning professionals who can learn new skills or enhance current skills.

The last conflict arises when the choice between assigning a skilled professional to a project not in his or her area of responsibility or assigning the professional to a project in his or her area of responsibility emerges. In matrix organizations, this situation can occur with regularity. The primary issues arise when the manager must assign staff to projects. He or she not only has to staff projects internal to functional responsibilities, but also assign staff to projects outside the functional area. The project manager must address such questions as these: What projects have priority? Should I assign my best staff to my projects? After all, I do have to take care of my needs, although that stance may be hard to explain to the other project managers. Or do I assign the best staff to outside projects? Am I shooting myself in the foot? After all, I do have responsibilities to meet and want to succeed in doing them.

TIP Always assigning the best professionals to projects within their area of responsibility will cause senior managers to wonder whether the functional (or resource) manager has the proper corporate focus.

I don't want you to think that the project manager is totally insensitive to staff development and motivation. He or she needs the commitment of each project team member and must therefore provide opportunities for development, but only with the goal of the project in mind. To the extent that the two are compatible, development will be an objective of the project manager.

Projects as Motivation and Development Tools

Not everyone can be motivated. In fact, in most cases all the manager can do is create an environment in which the subordinate might be motivated and then hope that he or she is. It's really like farming. All the farmer can do is pick the crop to plant, the acreage to plant it on, and the fertilizer to use, and then hope that nature supplies the right amounts of rain, wind, and sunshine. The same scenario applies to the project manager. He or she must create a working environment that is conducive to and encourages the development of the team member, leaving it up to them to respond positively.

Fortunately, you do have some information on what professional staff perceive as *motivators* and *hygiene factors* on the job. Motivators are those behaviors or situations that have a positive impact on the worker — they motivate the worker to better performance. Hygiene factors, on the other hand, are those things that, by their absence, have a negative impact on performance, but don't necessarily motivate the worker if they are present. To put it another way, workers have certain expectations, and to not fulfill them is to demotivate the workers. These are hygiene factors. For example, workers expect a reasonable vacation policy; to not have one acts as a demotivator. Conversely, having a good vacation policy does motivate the worker. The following list of motivators was created as a result of a 1959 survey of professionals by Frederick Herzberg,[1] a professor known for his research in motivational theory. Although the survey was conducted over 40 years ago, it has become a classic study and still applies today.

Motivators

Herzberg identified the following motivators:

- Achievement
- Recognition
- Advancement and growth
- Responsibility
- Work itself

[1]Both the Herzberg and Couger studies are reported in Toledo Mata and Elizabeth A. Unger, "Another Look at Motivating Data Processing Professionals," Department of Computer Science, Kansas State University, Manhattan, Kansas, 1988, p. 4.

Hygiene Factors

Herzberg identified the following hygiene factors:

- Company policy
- Administrative practices
- Working conditions
- Technical supervision
- Interpersonal relations
- Job security
- Salary

Note that the motivators are related to the job, specifically to its intrinsic characteristics; the hygiene factors are related to the environment in which the job is performed. This list offers both good news and bad news for the manager. The good news is that the manager has some amount of control over the motivators relating to the job. The bad news is that the hygiene factors, being environmental, are usually beyond the control of the manager. Managers can bring them to the attention of their senior management but are otherwise powerless to change them.

Daniel Couger, a professor of Computer Science at Colorado State, conducted a similar survey in 1988. Here the respondents were analysts and programmers. The responses were grouped by those areas that the respondents considered motivators and those that they considered demotivators. The combined list represents the areas ordered from highest motivator to lowest motivator:

- The work itself
- Opportunity for achievement
- Opportunity for advancement
- Pay and benefits
- Recognition
- Increased responsibility
- Technical supervision
- Interpersonal relations
- Job security
- Working conditions
- Company policy

The motivators that are high on the list tend to be intrinsic to the job, such as providing opportunities for advancement and for recognition, while the demotivators, which are lower on the list, tend to be environmental factors, such as working conditions (e.g., parking areas) and company policy (e.g., sick leave and vacation time).

Several of the motivators are directly controlled or influenced by actions and behaviors of the project manager regarding the work that the team member will be asked to do. They are as follows:

Challenge. Professionals respond to a challenge. In general, if you tell a professional that something cannot be done, his or her creative juices begin to flow. The result: a solution. Professionals dread nothing more than practicing skills, long since mastered, over and over again. Boredom can lead to daydreaming and lack of attention to detail, which results in errors. Challenging the professional does not mean that every moment of every day should be spent solving previously unsolved problems. Usually, an hour or two on a new and challenging task per day is sufficient to keep a professional motivated throughout the day.

Recognition. Professionals want to know that they are progressing toward a professional goal. Publicly and personally recognizing their achievements and following them with additional challenges tells the professional that his or her contribution is valued. Recognition, therefore, does not necessarily mean dollars, promotions, or titles.

Job design. Because the job itself is such an important part of the motivators, take a look at job design for just a moment. Five dimensions define a job:

Skill variety. Jobs that do not offer much task variety or the opportunity to learn and practice new skills become boring for most people. In designing jobs, it is important to consider building in some task variety. The variety, at the least, provides a diversion from what otherwise would be a tedious and boring workday. On the other hand, it also can provide a break during which the person can learn a new skill. With a little bit of forethought, the manager can find opportunities for cross-training by introducing some task variety for new skills development.

WARNING The manager should consider the risk involved in such actions. The person may not rise to the challenge of the new task or might not have the native ability to master the skills needed to perform the new task.

Task identity. People need to know what they are working on. This idea is especially true for contracted team members. The project manager should help them understand their work in relation to the entire project. Knowing that their task is on the critical path will affect their attitude and the quality of their work.

Task significance. In assessing a task's significance, workers ask themselves questions such as these: Does it make any difference if I am successful? Will anybody notice? Just how important is my work to the overall success of the project? Am I just doing busywork to pass the day? Team members need to know whether their effort and success make any difference to the success of the project.

Autonomy. Professionals want to know what is expected from them — what are the deliverables? They don't want to hear every detail of how they will accomplish their work. Systems people are rugged individualists. They want to exercise their creativity. They want freedom, independence, and discretion in scheduling their work and determining the procedures they will follow to carry it out.

Feedback. Good, bad, or indifferent, professionals want to know how effective they are in their work. Paying attention to a professional is motivating in itself. Having something good to say is even better. When performance is below expectations, tell them. If you can convince them that they own the problem, then ask them for an action plan to correct their marginal performance.

Recruiting the Project Team

Project plans and their execution are only as successful as the manager and team who implement them. Building effective teams is as much an art as a science.

When recruiting and building an effective team, you must consider not only the technical skills of each person but also the critical roles and chemistry that must exist between and among the project manager and the team members. The selection of project manager and team members will not be perfect — there are always risks with any personnel decision.

A project team has three separate components:

- Project manager
- Core team
- Contracted team

Be aware of the characteristics that should be part of an effective project manager and project team. The following sections describe the responsibilities of each of the three components to a project team. Also provided is a checklist that should assist you in your selection process, and guidelines for organizing the project in an organization.

The Project Manager

Project managers are the leaders of the projects. They are responsible for completing the project on time, within budget, and according to specification. They have the authority to get the job done. The project manager represents the project to the organization and to external groups. In many cases, the project manager has responsibility for more than one project simultaneously.

When to Select the Project Manager

The timing in selecting a project manager varies. Ideally, you want the project manager in the chair at the very beginning of the project. In some cases, the project manager might not be identified until the project has been approved for implementation. For example, in some organizations, senior management assigns project managers to projects after the project proposal has been approved. In those instances, the project manager will not have participated in the scoping and definition phases. This leads to a number of significant problems, one of which is short schedules. Short schedules arise in projects that are defined generally between the account representative and the customer (whether internal or external). These agreements usually constrain all sides of the triangle, as well as the scope. All too often, the project manager is put in a no-win situation. One rule that I learned a long time ago is this: *The sooner the project manager and team are involved in planning the project, the more committed they will be to its implementation.* (This is also true for other members in the organization whose expertise and resources are required to implement the project.)

Another problem with assigning the project manager after the project has been approved for implementation is buy-in by the project manager. Even when placed in situations that are not to his or her liking, the project manager must outwardly display enthusiasm and support for the project.

Selection Criteria

Harold Kerzner,[2] a pioneer in project management and one of the leading authorities in the field, states that because the roles and responsibilities of the

---

[2]Harold Kerzner, *Project Management: A Systems Approach to Planning, Scheduling, and Controlling* (New York: Van Nostrand Reinhold, 1984).

project manager are so important, his or her selection should be general management's responsibility. If you are working in a large organization, a group or committee is usually assigned to help screen project manager candidates.

A project manager must be experienced, capable, and competent in getting the project done on time, within budget, and according to specifications. Easier said than done. The potential project manager should have the following general skills:

Background and experience. Background and experience in good project management practices are difficult to find in many organizations. The problem is that the demand for experienced project managers outstrips the supply. The solution for many organizations is to create a learning laboratory for wannabe project managers, those who are acquiring project management skills and competencies. To help develop a cadre of project managers of varying backgrounds and experiences, a hierarchy of project management assignments is commonly put in place. That hierarchy might start at team member and then progress to task manager, project manager, and finally program manager. (These assignments have a one-to-one correspondence to projects ranging from Type D to Type A, as discussed in Chapter 1.) Project managers progress through this hierarchy as a result of training and experience in the skill areas needed to take on projects of increasing scope and complexity

In addition to on-the-job experience training, several alternatives to "build your own" project managers are available. The most common training method is to learn the project management skills through reviewing project documentation, attending and later supporting JPP sessions, observing project status meetings, maintaining project documentation, and playing the role of technographer in JPP sessions. By participating in whatever way is practical, an individual can gain the skills through on-the-job experiences.

Leadership and strategic expertise. The project manager is generally not the line manager of the team members. The project manager's job is to manage the work of the project. That puts him or her in relationships with the team members that are very different from the relationship that would evolve if the team members reported directly to the project manager. The project manager must get the team members' cooperation and support without having direct authority over them. It simply means that the project manager's skills as a leader are more important to his or her role. The project manager's success as a leader is also related to his or her ability to link the project to the strategy of the business. Often that will be at the heart of his or her relationship and any leverage he or she might have with the project team.

Technical expertise. There are two schools of thought regarding the level of technical expertise that a project manager should have. One school suggests that managing one project is like managing any other project. These are the same pundits who would say that if you can manage one department you can manage any department. I'll ignore the comment on managing departments, but I do take issue with the statement that project management is independent of the project being managed. Despite all that has been written and said about project management, the discipline is primitive. There is a lot we do not know about the successful management of projects. If that were not the case, how would you explain the high project failure rates as reported by the Standish Group and discussed in Chapter 2? While I would agree that the project manager does not need to be highly skilled in or have an intimate knowledge of the technology involved, he or she does need to have sufficient knowledge to know what questions to ask, how to interpret the answers, and whether he or she is being given the technical information needed to make a management decision.

Interpersonal competence. Sooner or later, the job of the project manager reduces to his or her ability to interact successfully with another individual. In the course of the project, the project manager will interact with the team, other project managers, business managers, functional managers, senior managers, the customer, outside contractors, and suppliers. These interactions will challenge all of the project manager's interpersonal skills as they relate to such areas as negotiations, conflict resolution, and problem resolution.

Managerial ability. Certain managerial skills are a superset of project management skills. By superset I mean that they apply to project management but are more appropriate on a larger scale to the business. These tend to be strategic and tactical in nature and include skills such as strategic planning, budget planning, staff planning, quality management, business process reengineering, and personnel development.

Core Team Members

Core team members are with the project from cradle to grave. They typically have a major role to play in the project and bring a skill set that has broad applicability across the range of work undertaken in the project. They might also have responsibility for key tasks or sets of tasks in the project.

Similar to the project manager's assignment, this assignment is usually not full-time. In matrix organizations, professional staff can be assigned to more than one project at a time. This case is especially true when a staff member possesses a skill not commonly found in the staff. A core team member will have some percentage of his or her time allocated to the project — perhaps one-quarter of the time of a full-time equivalent person.

When to Select the Core Team

Because the core team will be needed for the JPP session, its members should be identified as early as possible. The core team is usually identified at the beginning of the scoping phase. This means that the members can participate in the early definition and planning of the project.

Selection Criteria

Because of the downsizing, rightsizing, and capsizing going on in corporate America, much of the responsibility for choosing core team members has been designated to the project manager. While the situation differs from organization to organization, the project manager may have little or no latitude in picking core team members, even though he or she may have been given that responsibility. The problem stems from several causes:

- Most organizations have a very aggressive portfolio of projects with constantly changing priorities and requirements.
- The workload on the individual is so large that the thought of joining another team is not in his or her mind.
- Staff turnover, especially among highly technical and scarce professionals, is out of control in many organizations.

All of these situations make it difficult for the project manager to select the core dream team. For example, suppose a project manager has a choice between the A Team and the B Team. The A Team is the most skilled in a particular technology. Its members are the company's experts. The B Team, conversely, is made up of those individuals who would like to be on the A team but just don't have the experience and skills to justify A Team membership. The project manager would like to have all A Team members on the core team but realizes that this is just not going to happen. Even suggesting such a core team would be rejected out of hand by the managers of such highly skilled professionals. The politically savvy project manager would determine the project work that must have an A Team member and the project work that could get done with a B Team member and negotiate accordingly with the managers of these potential team members.

The project manager will have to pick his or her battles carefully, because he or she may want to consider the A Team for critical-path tasks, high-risk tasks, and high-business-value projects and accept the B Team for tasks and projects of lesser criticality. Be ready to horse trade between projects, too. Give the resource managers an opportunity to use noncritical path tasks as on-the-job training for their staff. Remember that they have as many staff development and deployment problems as you have project planning and scheduling problems. Trading a favor of staff development for an A Team member may be a good strategy.

In my project management consulting work, I identified a list of characteristics that many project managers have offered as successful characteristics in their core teams. For the most part, these characteristics are observed in individuals based on their experiences and the testimony of those who have worked with them. Typically, these are not characteristics whose presence or absence in an individual are determined through interviews.

In many cases, the project manager must take a calculated risk that the team member possesses these characteristics even though the individual has not previously demonstrated that he or she has them. It will become obvious very quickly whether or not the individual possesses these characteristics. If not, and if those characteristics are critical to the team member's role in the project, the project manager or the team member's line manager will have to correct the team member's behavior.

The characteristics that I consider important for the core team members are as follows:

Commitment. Commitment to the project by the core team is critical to the success of the project. The project manager must know that each core team member places a high priority on fulfilling his or her roles and responsibilities in the project. The core team must be proactive in fulfilling those responsibilities and not need the constant reminders of schedule and deliverables from the project manager.

Shared responsibility. Shared responsibility means that success and failure are equally the reward and blame of each team member. Having shared responsibility means that you will never hear one team member taking individual credit for a success on the project, or blaming another team member for a failure on the project. All share equally in success and failure. Furthermore, when a problem situation arises, all will pitch in to help in any way. If one team member is having a problem, another will voluntarily be there to help.

Flexibility. Team members must be willing to adapt to the situation. "That is not my responsibility" doesn't go very far in project work. Schedules may have to change at the last minute to accommodate an unexpected situation. It is the success of the project that has priority, not the schedule of any one individual on the project team.

Task-orientedness. In the final analysis it is the team members' ability to get their assigned work done according to the project plan that counts. In other words, they must be results-oriented.

Ability to work within schedules and constraints. Part of being results-oriented means being able to complete assignments within the time frame planned instead of offering excuses for failing to do so. It is easy to blame your delay on the delay of others — that is the easy way out. Team members will encounter a number of obstacles, such as delays caused by others, but they will have to find a way around those obstacles. The team depends on its members to complete their work according to plan.

Willingness for trust and mutual support. Trust and mutual support are the hallmarks of an effective team. That means that every member must convey these qualities. Team members must be trusting and trustworthy. Are they empathetic and do they readily offer help when it is clear that help is needed? Their interaction with other team members will clearly indicate whether they possess these characteristics. Individuals who do not will have a difficult time working effectively on a project team.

Team-orientedness. To be team-oriented means to put the welfare of the team ahead of your own. Behaviors as simple as the individual's use of "I" versus "we" in team meetings and conversations with other team members are strong indicators of team orientation.

Open-mindedness. The open-minded team member will welcome and encourage other points of view and other solutions to problem situations. His or her objective is clearly to do what is best for the team and not look for individual kudos.

Ability to work across structure and authorities. In contemporary organizations, projects tend to cross organizational lines. Cross-departmental teams are common. Projects such as these require the team member to work with people from a variety of business disciplines. Many of these people will have a different value system and a different approach than the team member might be used to working with. Adaptability, flexibility, and openness are desirable assets.

Ability to use project management tools. The team member must be able to leverage technology in carrying out his or her project responsibilities. Projects are planned using a variety of software tools, and the team member must have some familiarity with these tools. Many project managers will require the team member to input task status and other project progress data directly into the project management software tool.

CASE STUDY – PLEASANTOWN PLAYGROUND PROJECT

Recruiting a team of volunteers can be the most challenging recruiting experience you will ever face. Usually it is hard to get people to volunteer, so when you get a volunteer you want to use them in some capacity. They will probably have some idea as to what they would like to do, and you should honor that if at all possible. If they don't have any preference, consider yourself fortunate. They will fill positions for which others have not volunteered.

Contracted Team Members

The business-to-business environment is changing, and many changes are permanent. Organizations are routinely outsourcing processes that are not part of their core business or core expertise. There are two reasons to use contract team members instead of the company's own employees:

- Shortage of staff
- Shortage of skills

Those shortages have made it possible for a whole new type of business to grow — *tech-temps* is the name I associate with this new business opportunity. The day of the small contractor and niche market player is here to stay. To the project manager, this creates the need to effectively manage a team whose membership will probably include outside contractors. Some may be with the project for only a short time. Others may be no different from core teams except that they are not company employees.

Typically, contracted team members are available for only short periods of time on the project. They possess a skill that is needed for just a brief time. They are assigned to the project when it is time for them to contribute their skills. As soon as they have completed their assigned task, they leave the project.

Implications of Adding Contract Team Members

Contracted team members present the project manager with a number of challenges. In most systems development efforts, it is unlikely that professionals would be assigned full-time to the project team. Rather, people will join the project team only for the period of time during which their particular expertise is needed. The project manager must be aware of the implications to the project when contracted professionals are used, which may include the following:

- There may be little or no variance in the time contracted team members are available, so the tasks on which they work must remain on schedule.

- They must be briefed on their role in the project and how their task relates to other tasks in the project.

- Commitment of contracted members is typically a problem because their priorities probably lie elsewhere.

- Quality of work may be an issue because of poor levels of commitment. They just want to get the job done and get on with their next assignment. Often anything will do.

- Contracted team members will often require more supervision than core team members.

Selection Criteria

If the project manager (PM) has made the decision to buy rather than build a project team, the PM must determine who will get the business. Contracted team members are usually employed or represented by agencies that cater to technical professionals who prefer freelancing to full-time employment. These professionals are available for short-term assignments in their area of specialization. To employ these professionals, the project manager must make several decisions: what process to follow, who should be invited to submit information, and how to evaluate the information received. The evaluation often takes the form of a score sheet. The score sheet contains questions grouped by major features and functions, with weights attached to each answer. A single numeric score is often calculated to rank vendor responses. Nonquantitative data such as customer relations and customer service are also collected from reference accounts provided by the vendor.

The steps the project manager follows to engage the services of a contracted team member might look something like the following:

1. Identify the types of skills needed, the number of personnel, and the time frame within which they will be needed.

2. Identify a list of companies that will be invited to submit a proposal.

3. Write the request for proposal.

4. Establish the criteria for evaluating responses and selecting the vendor(s).

5. Distribute the request for proposal.

6. Evaluate the responses.

7. Reduce the list of vendors to a few who will be invited on site to make a formal presentation.

8. Conduct the on-site presentations.

9. Choose the final vendor(s), and write and sign the contract.

Types of Proposals

A project manager might consider three types of proposals as he or she looks for a vendor or agency to provide contracted team members: Request for Information, Request for Proposal, and Request for Quote.

Request for Information. A Request for Information (RFI) is used when an organization is looking for information relevant to a particular process or product. It usually does not have a written specification. The purpose of an RFI is to discover vendors and products that the organization will investigate further with one of the other two types of proposals.

Request for Proposal. A Request for Proposal (RFP) is used to find the vendor or vendors that can provide the best solution and price. The RFP always includes a specification that identifies the features, functions, physical specifications, performance requirements, and environment in which the requested deliverable must operate. Generally, descriptions of steps to be followed to select the vendor and the method of evaluation are included. In some cases, more than one vendor will be chosen. Each vendor will provide a piece of the final solution. Using several vendors presents special challenges to the project manager.

Request for Quote. The Request for Quote (RFQ) is used to find the best price-to-performance ratio for a given solution. In this case, the company knows exactly what it wants; it is only a matter of finding the vendor that best meets the Conditions of Satisfaction. The definition of what the company wants will often include the exact hardware, software, and more. This approach offers the PM a more easily managed situation than the multivendor alternative.

Types of Contracts

There are four types of contracts:

Retainer. These arrangements pay the contractor a fixed fee per period (usually monthly). Often no end date is specified. At some point, the organization will decide that the arrangement can terminate because the contractor's services are no longer needed. The retainer will state how many days per period are expected of the contractor, and the deliverables the contractor will provide. The deliverables are often only vaguely described, because such arrangements are usually investigative or design-related.

Time and materials. In these cases, a little more specificity exists, but a detailed specification is not available or cannot be provided. The company is willing to accept the risk of high costs in the face of unknowns.

Time and materials — not to exceed. Here the vendor assumes more of the risk. A detailed specification may not exist, but enough is known such that the contractor will meet the customer's requirements at a cost not to exceed a specified figure and within a specified time frame.

Fixed bid. In these cases, a detailed specification exists, and the vendor is willing to provide the deliverables and meet a deadline date for a specified figure. Obviously, the vendor assumes most of the risk here. Fixed-bid contracts usually include a payment schedule, too. In my consulting practice, I use the 40-40-20 rule: 40 percent is due on contract signing, 40 percent is due at an agreed-on midpoint in the project, and the remaining 20 percent is due once the final deliverables have been accepted and the company signs off that the contract is complete.

Contract Administration

Once the contract is signed and the vendor begins to deliver the contracted work, contract administration for that vendor has begun. Contract administration is the responsibility of the project manager. My general advice is to have the contract spell out in detail exactly how business will be done — not a detailed list of what will be done for every possible occurrence during the contract period, but rather clear guidelines that everyone understands. The guidelines might include obligations, responsibilities, performance goals and deadline dates, penalties for missed dates, rewards for early delivery, status reporting dates, problem discovery, escalation and resolution, change management procedures, milestone dates, project status meeting dates, acceptance test criteria, cancellation conditions, cancellation policies, and closing criteria.

Contract Cancellation

The contract should clearly spell out the conditions under which the contract may be cancelled. For example, can either party cancel for any reason by simply notifying the other according to a defined procedure? Or does cancellation require both parties' mutual agreement? Cancellation will often be the result of performance not meeting expectations.

Contract Closing

Once the acceptance criteria have been met, a series of events occurs. These are generally debriefing sessions and handoffs of deliverables and documentation. A final payment to the vendor is commonly withheld pending receipt of these items.

CASE STUDY – PIZZA DELIVERED QUICKLY (PDQ)

PDQ is not staffed to provide the skills and experiences needed for this project. Several outside contractors will be needed. That means the project team will comprise technically challenged PDQ personnel and technically experienced outside professionals. That is a challenging mix for the project manager to deal with effectively.

Authority

Authority and responsibility go hand in hand. To have one and not the other makes no sense. How often have you been in situations where you were responsible for making a certain thing happen but had no authority over the resources needed to make it happen or no authority to make and carry out a decision? To be effective, the project manager must have authority over the project. It is his or her job to get the project done on time, within budget, and according to specification. That authority is often delegated, but the project manager is ultimately responsible.

The major difficulty that project managers have is that the project team is not their line responsibility. Team members are assigned based on their expertise but report to other managers, which means that the project manager will have to exercise the best leadership skills and diplomacy to get the job done. The key is in the project planning tasks that schedule resources to windows of time. It is here that the resource manager makes the commitment of people resources. Honoring that commitment within the time allotted reduces the incidence of problems. If the project manager remembers to keep the resource managers involved and aware of all project changes, negotiations will proceed better when circumstances warrant.

Responsibility

There is no question where the responsibility lies. This responsibility cannot be delegated. The project manager assigns task management responsibility to team members. They are then responsible for completing their assigned task within its scheduled window of time and for producing the task deliverables on time according to specification. It is the project manager, though, who is ultimately responsible for completing the project as expected. In conveying this sense of responsibility to each team member, the project manager must exercise sound leadership and management skills. He or she does this by maintaining a consistent level of interest in and communication with each task manager, by involving them and engaging them in planning, change management deliberations, and problem resolution. The project manager will keep everybody on the team informed of project status.

Balancing a Team

Balance is a critical success factor for any team that hopes to successfully complete its project. There are several ways to measure balance and several characteristics of the team that have been used to define balance. Take a simple example — learning styles. Learning styles are measured using an instrument, the Learning Styles Inventory (LSI), which was developed by David Kolb in 1981. Kolb identifies four learning styles:

Assimilating. Assimilators are people who excel at collecting and representing data in crisp logical form. They are focused on ideas and concepts, rather than people. These individuals like to put data and information together into models that explain the situation from a larger perspective. As a result, they are more interested in something making sense logically than they are in any practical value. They are not results-oriented people. These types of individuals are generally found in the more technical or specialist careers, such as developers.

Diverging. These individuals like to look at alternatives and view the situation from a variety of perspectives. They would rather observe than take action. Divergers like brainstorming, and they generally have a broad range of interests and like information to gather. On a project team these people will often display outside-of-the-box thinking and offer suggestions for approaches other than those that have already been identified.

Accommodating. These individuals are results-oriented and want to put things into practice. They are adaptive and can easily change with the circumstances. Accommodators are people persons. They are strong at implementation and hands-on tasks and are good team players. They tend to be action-oriented and more spontaneous than logical. As problem solvers they rely on people for input, rather than on any technical analysis. On the project team you can count on these people to help foster a strong sense of teamwork, and they are often found facilitating the coordination of team members. They are often the peacekeepers as well.

Converging. These individuals like to assemble information in order to solve problems. They like to converge to the correct solution. Convergers are the solution finders but not the solution implementers. Their strength lies in their ability to take concepts, models, and ideas and turn them into practical use. They are not particularly people-oriented and would rather work with technical tasks and problems. They are good at picking the best option among a number of alternatives. On the project team these will be the results-oriented members. They will drive the team into action by helping it focus on which approach to a situation is best and then mobilizing the team into action.

Now suppose you have a team that is loaded with convergers and does not have a single diverger among its members. What do you think might happen? With no one on the team to encourage looking for alternatives (the role of the diverger), you would very likely have a rush to judgment, or "group think," as the convergers press the team into action. I have personally witnessed many situations where a single approach to a problem is presented, and the convergers on the team aggressively suggest that the team go forward with the single proposed solution without even considering whether there is an alternative. Teams involved in high-technology projects are likely to display this behavior.

A team that has balanced learning styles among its members is a team that is prepared to do a very good job at solving problems and making decisions.

CROSS-REF Learning styles are not the only point of balance. Thinking styles, conflict resolution styles, and skills and competencies are also important, but an in-depth discussion of such matters is beyond the scope of this book. For more information about balancing your project team in this manner you can consult Robert K. Wysocki's *Building Effective Project Teams* (New York: John Wiley & Sons, 2002).

Developing a Team Deployment Strategy

Having balance on the team in all of the characteristics discussed in the previous section is certainly a worthy goal, but it is a goal not likely to be reached. In reality, the team is formed more according to availability than to any need to balance its membership. As a result, teams are not balanced but they are the team nevertheless. What's a project manager to do?

First of all, the project manager had better know where the imbalance exists. What characteristics does the team have? Where are its strengths and where are its weaknesses? For example, suppose a confrontation has arisen with the client. I would much rather send an accommodator than a converger to resolve the confrontation. However, there might not be an accommodator on the team. Teams are most likely to be formed without knowledge of this kind of information. It is only after the fact that these imbalances are discovered. On a larger scale, the project manager needs to determine which team members have a greater likelihood of success on which types of work assignments. Build the strategy. If you still have gaping holes, you need a team development plan. That is the topic of the next section.

Developing a Team Development Plan

Your team has been assembled, and you have assessed each member on all of the characteristics important to achieving balance. The picture is not very pretty. There are several areas in which the team is noticeably weak. While your job as project manager is not to be a career or professional development manager of the team members, you still have to get the project done, and the imbalance on the team is a barrier to your success. As project manager, identify the high-risk areas that are not covered by at least one team member who can deal with those types of risks. As part of your risk management plan, put a development plan in place for selected members of the team.

What form might that development plan take? Here are two possibilities:

- You might want to use a conflict resolution management called *masked behavior*. Briefly, it means that you find the person on your team whose normal behavior is as close as possible to the missing behavior. That person then role-plays as though his or her normal behavior were the missing behavior.

- You might consider sensitivity training for all or some of the team. That training involves creating an awareness of the behavior that is lacking and practicing it under supervision. For example, technology professionals are generally not very good people persons. They often lack the traits of an accommodator. Their training might include listening skills, learning how to be a team player, acceptance of change, diversity training, and other related interpersonal skills training.

Establishing Team Operating Rules

Project teams all too often fail to define and agree on the team operating rules. These operating rules define how the team works together, makes decisions, resolves conflicts, reports progress, and deals with a host of other administrative chores. Even before the work of the project begins, the team should agree on how it will work together. When the team is deep into the work of the project is no time to be deciding how they will work together. This section looks at the areas where operating rules are needed, and then covers the specifics of those operating rules.

Situations Requiring Team Operating Rules

The following is a fairly complete list of general situations that may arise during the course of a project and that will require some action on the part of the team. I have grouped them into six general areas:

- Problem solving
- Decision making
- Conflict resolution

- Consensus building
- Brainstorming
- Team meetings

Consider the following questions from *Managing the Project Team: The Human Aspects of Project Management, Volume 3,* by Vijay K. Verma (Project Management Institute, 1997) that must be answered at some point in the project life cycle:

- What has to be done and where? (Scope)
- Why should it be done? (Justification)
- How well must it be done? (Quality)
- When is it required and in what sequence? (Schedule)
- How much will it cost? (Budget/Cost)
- What are the uncertainties? (Risk)
- Who would do the job? (Human resources)
- How should people be organized into teams? (Communication/ Interpersonal skills)
- How will you know if you have done the job? (Information dissemination/Communication)

Each one of these questions will engage one or more of the six action areas listed previously. The team needs to decide ahead of time how it will carry out each of the action areas — that is, what are the rules of engagement. Now take a look at those action areas in more detail and see what is involved on the part of the team.

Problem Solving

There will be many situations during the course of the project work in which the team will be challenged to figure out how to satisfactorily meet the client's needs while maintaining the schedule and the budget within the assigned resources. Some situations will be easily resolved, while others will challenge even the most creative of minds. The problem-solving process is well known, and many variations are in print. Creativity and problem solving go hand in hand. A good problem solver will think outside the box. He or she will conceive of approaches that may have been overlooked. As you will see next, each of the learning styles mentioned earlier in the chapter relates to a different part of the problem-solving model. That means the team must have all learning styles represented in order to solve problems effectively. In this section you will see how those learning styles relate to the problem-solving process.

The model that seems most appropriate for project problem solving is one put forward by J. Daniel Couger in his work *Creative Problem Solving and Opportunity Finding* (Boyd and Fraser Publishing, 1995). The model is shown in Figure 9-1.

Couger's process begins with an outside stimulus: Something has arisen that creates an out-of-control situation in the project and must be rectified. That launches a series of actions that clarifies the situation, identifies and assembles relevant data, gets a number of ideas and approaches on the table, and analyzes the ideas. It then selects the idea that would appear most promising as the way to rectify the situation and return it to normal. Finally, an action plan is put in place and executed (the exit point of the model is the action itself). You will see how all of the learning styles are needed to complete each step in the model. Couger identifies the five steps that make up this problem-solving process:

Step 1: Delineate the opportunity and define the problem. This is a scoping step in which the team members attempt to establish a formulation and definition of the problem and the desired results that a solution to the problem will provide. It helps the team develop the boundaries of the problem — that is, what is in scope and what is out of scope. This step is best performed by team members who have a preference for the assimilator style. These individuals look at the problem independently of any focus on people and try to present the problem at the conceptual level and put it into a logical framework. Their penchant for collecting and concisely reporting data is an early task in this model.

Step 2: Compile the relevant data. With a definition of the problem in hand, the team can now identify and specify the data elements that are needed to further understand the problem and provide a foundation on which possible solutions can be formulated. Again, the assimilator is well suited to this task.

Step 3: Generate ideas. This step typically begins with a brainstorming session. The team should identify as many solutions as possible. This step is the time to think outside the box and look for creative and innovative ways to approach a solution. Ideas will spawn new ideas until the team has exhausted its creative energies. The diverger is well suited to the tasks that take place in this step. The job of this individual is to look at the problem from a number of perspectives. Like the assimilator, the diverger also has an interest in data and information with the purpose of generating ideas, but he or she is not interested in generating solutions.

Stimulus ⟹		Required Learning Styles
Step One	Delineate opportunity and define problem.	Assimilator
Step Two	Compile relevant information.	Assimilator
Step Three	Generate ideas.	Diverger
Step Four	Evaluate and prioritize ideas.	Converger
Step Five	Develop implementation plan.	Accommodator
		⟹ Action

Figure 9-1 Couger's Creative Problem Solving (CPS) model

Step 4: Evaluate and prioritize ideas. In this step the list of possible solutions needs to be winnowed down to the one or two solutions that will actually be planned. Criteria for selecting the best solution ideas need to be developed (that's a job for the converger), metrics for assessing advantages and disadvantages need to be developed (again, a job for the converger), and then the metrics are used to prioritize the solutions. The calculation of the metric value for each alternative and the ranking of the alternatives based on those metric values is a straightforward exercise that anyone on the team can perform. This individual has the ability to take a variety of ideas and turn them into solutions. This person's work is not finished, however, until he or she has established criteria for evaluating those solutions and made recommendations for action.

Step 5: Develop the implementation plan. The solution has been identified, and it's now time to build a plan to implement the solution. This step is a whole-team exercise that draws on the team's collective wisdom for planning and implementation. When it is results that you want, call on the accommodator. His or her contribution will be to put a plan in place for delivering the recommended solution and making it happen. The accommodator is a good person to lead this planning and implementation exercise.

While this five-step process may seem cumbersome and involved, many of the steps can often be executed in a simple and straightforward manner.

Situations requiring a problem-solving effort occur frequently and are often done from start to finish by one team member. Of course, more complex situations will require several team members and the collective creativity of the whole team. The five steps should become second nature to each team member. As team members become familiar with the five steps, the steps will begin to form a commonsense sequence, and they should not be overly burdensome to anyone on the team.

Decision Making

Team members make decisions continuously as they engage in the work of the project. Some of those decisions are obvious and straightforward and may not require the involvement of others; other decisions are more complex and may require the involvement and active participation of the team, the client, and even people outside of the project. There are three major types of decision-making models:

Directive. In this model, the person with the authority — the project manager for the project and the task manager for the task — makes the decision for all team members. While this approach is certainly expedient, it has obvious drawbacks. The only information available is the information that the decision maker possesses, which may or may not be correct or complete. An added danger is that those who disagree or were left out of the decision may not be willing to carry it out or may be resistant to carrying it out. A directive approach is often used when time is of the essence and a decision is needed immediately. It makes no sense to hold a committee meeting to get everyone's input before proceeding.

Participative. In this model, everyone on the team contributes to the decision-making process. A synergy is created as the best decision is sought. Because everyone has an opportunity to participate, commitment will be much stronger than in the directive approach. Obviously, there is an additional benefit to team building — empowerment of the team. Whenever possible, I recommend this participative approach. Because the team members have a chance to participate in the decision-making process, they will be much more committed to the decision that is made and more likely to support it during implementation. From a political perspective, the project manager is much better off using this approach than a directive approach.

Consultative. This middle-ground approach combines the best of the other two approaches. While the person in authority makes the decision, the decision is made only after consulting with all members to get their input and ideas. This approach is participative at the input stage but directive at the point of decision-making. In some cases, when expediency is required, this approach is a good one to take. Rather than having to involve the entire team, the project manager can decide whose input should be sought and then make the decision based on that input. Politically this is a very good strategy, and it can have positive effects on those whose input was sought.

Deciding Which Decision-Making Model to Use

Which model to use in a specific situation is generally a function of the gravity and time sensitivity of the pending decision. Some organizations have constructed categories of decisions, with each category defined by some financial parameters, such as the value of the decision, or by some scope parameters, such as the number of business units or customers affected by the decision. The person responsible for making the decision is defined for each decision category. The more serious the category, the higher the organizational level of the decision maker. Some decisions might be made by an individual team member, some by a task manager, some by the project manager, some by the customer, and some by senior management. Yet others might require a group decision, using either a participative or a consultative approach.

Decision Making and the Learning Styles Inventory

Just as the LSI, discussed earlier in the chapter, relates to the problem-solving process, it also relates to the decision-making process. While it is true that decision making and problem solving are closely related, it is instructive for you to see just how the LSI relates to decision making as well. Problem solving cannot happen without some decisions having been made. In that sense, decision making can be thought of as a subset of problem solving.

NOTE Decision making can also occur outside of the problem-solving context. For example, suppose a project is behind schedule and the design phase is not yet complete. You could start some preliminary programming, but at the risk that when the design is complete, you may have to rework some of the earlier programming. Do you begin programming to make up lost time and take the risk, or do you wait for the design to be finished before you begin programming? This is clearly a decision-making situation and not a problem-solving one.

Decision making is pervasive throughout the life of the project. How will the project team make decisions? Will they be based on a vote? Will they be a result of team consensus? Will they be left up to the project manager? Just how will the team operate?

Determining how decisions are made is only one piece of the puzzle. Another piece is whether the team can make a decision, and if not, what they do about it. Therefore, I want to take a closer look at the decision-making environment that the project team faces.

In their book *Organizational Behavior in Action: Skill Building Experiences* (St. Paul: West Publishing, 1976), William C. Morris and M. Sashkin propose a six-phase model for rational decision making. The six phases in their approach are outlined in the bulleted list that follows. However, as I have indicated, there is a lot of similarity between using the LSI in problem solving and in decision making, and the following list also reflects how the LSI applies to Morris and Sashkin's rational decision making in a way similar to how it applied to Couger's problem-solving process:

Phase I: Situation definition. This phase is one of discovery for the team, clarifying the situation to ensure a shared understanding of the decision the team faces. Phase I requires the services of an assimilator. As part of the process of discovery, the assimilator will collect data and information and formulate the situation and the required decision.

Phase II: Situation decision generation. Through brainstorming, the team tries to expand the decision space. Phase II, the search for alternative decisions, is the province of the diverger. This is a collaborative effort because it continues to involve the assimilator in a definition type of task.

Phase III: Ideas to action. Metrics are devised to attach reward and penalty to each possible decision that might be made. With the alternatives identified, the work can be turned over to the converger in Phase III. His or her job is to establish criteria. This person's work is complete when a plan for implementing the decision is in place in Phase IV.

Phase IV: Decision action plan. The decision has been made, and the development of a plan to implement it is now needed. In Phase IV the accommodator takes over and implements the decision.

Phase V: Decision evaluation planning. This phase is kind of a post-decision audit of what worked and what didn't work. Some lessons learned will be the likely deliverable as well. The team, under the direction of an accommodator, will take an honest look at how effective the decision was.

Phase VI: Evaluation of outcome and process. The team needs to determine whether the decision got the job done and whether another attempt at the situation is needed. Finally, an evaluation of the results in Phase IV puts the work back into the hands of the assimilator. If the expected results were not attained, another round may be required.

Table 9-1 provides a summary of the six decision-making phases and the required learning styles.

CROSS-REF Our discussion has been brief and only a summary of a complex and interesting topic. The decision-making model discussed here is described in more detail in the book *Building Effective Project Teams* by Robert K. Wysocki (New York: John Wiley & Sons, 2002).

Table 9-1 The Six Phases of the Decision-Making Process

PHASE	DESCRIPTION	LEARNING STYLE
Phase I: Situation definition	Discovery phase. The team investigates, discusses, clarifies, and defines the situation. It is important for the team to understand the root causes and evidence that led to the need for a decision.	Assimilator
Phase II: Situation decision generation	Continuation of Phase I. Characterized by brainstorming and searching for new ideas and alternatives for resolving the situation, which should lead to better options for the decision. Above all, the team needs to avoid a rush to judgment.	Diverger
Phase III: Ideas to action	Define the criteria for evaluating the alternative decisions. This involves identifying the advantages and disadvantages of each alternative. Whatever approach is used, the result should be a ranking of alternatives from most desirable to least desirable.	Converger
Phase IV: Decision action plan	Begins once the alternative is chosen. This is the planning phase for the project team. The team determines tasks, resources, and timelines that are required to implement the decision. This phase requires a concerted effort to obtain buy-in from all affected parties.	Converger
Phase V: Decision evaluation planning	Learning opportunity for the project team. The team identifies what did and did not work, as well as areas in which it can improve and how to do so. The value of this discussion lies in the team's willingness to be honest and straightforward with one another.	Accommodator
Phase VI: Evaluation of outcome and process	Focuses on the quality of results. The team evaluates the situation: Was the situation improved satisfactorily, or will another round be required? Was the situation defined correctly, or is revision required? Did the process work as expected, or will it need adjustment for the next attempt?	Assimilator

Conflict Resolution

The next area for which operating rules are needed deals with how the team resolves conflicts. Conflicts arise when two or more team members have a difference of opinion, when the customer takes issue with an action to be taken by the project team, or in a variety of other situations involving two parties with different points of view. In all of these examples, the difference must be resolved. Clearly, conflict resolution is a much more sensitive situation than the decision-making rule because it is confrontational and situational, whereas the decision-making rule is procedural and structured. Depending on the particular conflict situation, the team might adopt one of three conflict resolution styles:

Avoidant. Some people will do anything to avoid a direct confrontation. They agree even though they are opposed to the outcome. This style cannot be tolerated on the project team. Each person's input and opinion must be sought. It is the responsibility of the project manager to ensure that this happens. A simple device is to ask all of the team members in turn what they think about the situation and what they suggest should be done about it. Often this approach will diffuse any direct confrontation between two individuals on the team.

Combative. Some avoid confrontation at all costs; others seem to seek it out. Some team members play devil's advocate at the least provocation. At times this is advantageous — testing the team's thinking before making the decision. At other times it tends to raise the level of stress and tension, when many view it as a waste of time and not productive. The project manager must be able to identify these team members and act to mitigate the chances of these situations arising.

TIP One technique I have used with success is to put such individuals in charge of forming a recommendation for the team to consider. Such an approach offers less opportunity for combative discussion because the combative team member is sharing recommendations before others give reasons for disagreement.

Collaborative. In this approach, the team looks for win-win opportunities. The approach seeks a common ground as the basis for moving ahead to a solution. This approach encourages each team member to put his or her opinions on the table and not avoid any conflict that may result. At the same time, team members do not seek to create conflict unnecessarily. The approach is constructive, not destructive.

A discussion of conflict resolution styles is beyond the scope of this book. You can consult several resources on the topic. Two that I have found particularly helpful are "Conflict and Conflict Management" by Kenneth Thomas in *The Handbook of Industrial and Organizational Psychology* (Hoboken, New Jersey: John Wiley & Sons, Inc., 1983) and *The Dynamics of Conflict Resolution: A Practitioner's Guide* by Bernard S. Mayer (Hoboken, New Jersey: Jossey-Bass, 2000). Of particular importance are the variety of collaborative models that might be adopted.

Consensus Building

Consensus building is a process that a team can follow to reach agreement on which alternative to proceed with for the item (action, decision, and so forth) under consideration. The agreement is not reached by a majority vote, or any vote for that matter. Rather, the agreement is reached through discussion, whereby each participant reaches a point when he or she has no serious disagreement with the decision that is about to be made. The decision will have been revised several times for the participants to reach that point.

Consensus building is an excellent tool to have in the project team tool kit. In all but a few cases, there will be a legitimate difference of opinion as to how a problem or issue should be addressed. There are no clear-cut actions on which all can agree. In such situations the team must fashion an action or decision with which no team members have serious disagreement even though they may not agree in total with the chosen action. To use the method successfully, make sure that everyone on the team has a chance to speak. Talk through the issue until an acceptable action is identified. Conflict is fine, but try to be creative as you search for a compromise action. As soon as no one has serious objections to the defined action, you have reached a consensus. Once a decision is reached, all team members must support it.

If the project manager chooses to operate on a consensus basis, he or she must clearly define the situations in which consensus will be acceptable. The team needs to know these situations.

Brainstorming

Brainstorming is an essential part of the team operating rules because, at several points in the life of the project, the creativity of the team will be tested. Brainstorming is a technique that can focus that creativity and help the team discover solutions. In some situations acceptable ideas and alternatives do not result from the normal team deliberations. In such cases the project manager might suggest a brainstorming session. A brainstorming session is one in which the team contributes ideas in a stream-of-consciousness mode, as described in the next paragraph. Brainstorming sessions have been quite successful in uncovering solutions where none seemed present. The team needs to know how the project manager will conduct such sessions and what will be done with the output.

The method for brainstorming is simple and quick:

1. Assemble those individuals who may have some knowledge of the problem area. They don't need to be experts. In fact, it may be better if they are not. You need people to think creatively and outside the box. Experts tend to think inside the box.

2. The session begins with everyone throwing any idea out on the table. No discussion (except clarification) is permitted. This continues until no new ideas are forthcoming. Silence and pauses are fine.

3. Once all the ideas are on the table, discuss the items on the list. Try to combine ideas or revise ideas based on each member's perspective.

4. In time, some solutions will begin to emerge. Don't rush the process, and by all means test each idea with an open mind. Remember that you are looking for a solution that no individual could identify but that you hope the group is able to identify.

NOTE This is a creative process, one that must be approached with an open mind. Convention and "we've always done it that way" have no place in a true brainstorming session.

Team Meetings

The project manager needs to define team meetings in terms of frequency, length, meeting dates, submission/preparation/distribution of the agenda, who calls the meeting, and who is responsible for recording and distributing the minutes. The entire team needs to participate in and understand the rules and structure of the meetings that will take place over the life of the project. Different types of team meetings, perhaps with different rules governing their conduct and format, may occur.

Team meetings are held for a variety of reasons, including problem definition and resolution, scheduling work, planning, discussing situations that affect team performance, and decision making. The team needs to decide on several procedural matters, including the following:

Meeting frequency. How often should the team meet? If it meets too frequently, precious work time will be lost. If it meets too infrequently, problems may arise and the window of opportunity may close before a meeting to discuss and solve the problem takes place. If meetings happen too infrequently, the project manager risks losing management control over the project. Meeting frequency will vary according to the length and size of the project. There is no formula for frequency. The project manager must simply make a judgment call.

Agenda preparation. When the project team is fortunate enough to have a project administrative assistant, that person can receive agenda items and prepare and distribute the agenda. In the absence of an administrative assistant, the assignment should be rotated to each team member. The project manager may set up a template agenda so that each team meeting covers essentially the same general topics.

Meeting coordinator. Just as agenda preparation can be circulated around to each team member, so can the coordination responsibility. Coordination involves reserving a time, a place, and equipment.

Recording and distributing meeting minutes. Meeting minutes are an important part of project documentation. In the short term, they are the evidence of discussions of problem situations and change requests, the actions taken, and the rationale for those actions. When confusion arises and clarifications are needed, the meeting minutes can settle the issue. Recording and distributing the minutes are important responsibilities and should not be treated lightly. The project manager should establish a rotation among the team members for recording and distributing the meeting minutes.

Daily Status Meetings

For some of you this will seem like overkill and not something you want to engage in. You can already see the expressions on your team members' faces when you announce that there will be daily team meetings. I remember the first time I encountered the daily team meeting. I reacted the same way, but I quickly changed my mind, as I hope you will change yours. This is one of those "try it, you'll like it" cases.

For one thing, the meeting only lasts 15 minutes and everybody stands. The only valid reports are as follows:

- I'm on plan.
- I am x hours behind schedule but have a plan to be caught up by this time tomorrow.
- I am x hours behind plan and need help.
- I am x hours ahead of plan and available to help.

There is no discussion of solutions to schedule slippages. There is no taking of pizza orders for lunch. All of those are taken offline and involve only those who are affected by the topic. The attendees are those team members who have tasks open for work that day.

You'll probably experience a learning curve for this process. My first 15-minute team meeting took 45 minutes, but the team quickly learned to bring the meeting time within the 15-minute limit.

Problem Resolution Meetings

Problem resolution should never be handled in the team status meeting. Rather, a special meeting, attended by those directly involved in the problem or its solution, should be called. The reason you don't deal with problems in the team status meeting is that not everyone in attendance will have an interest in or connection to the problem. You don't want to waste team members' time by having them sit through a discussion of something that does not involve them or interest them. That would be a waste of their time.

The problem resolution meeting should be planned around the problem-solving methodology discussed previously.

Project Review Meetings

These are formal meetings held at milestone events or other defined points in the life of the project. Oftentimes the stage gate that passes a project from one phase to another is used as the time for a project review meeting. These meetings are attended by the project manager, the client, the sponsor, stakeholders, a senior manager who officiates, and two or three other project managers who provide the technical subject matter expertise of the review. The project manager may invite others whose input will be valuable to the review. The meeting focuses on any variances from the plan, and identifying corrective action steps as suggested by the subject matter experts present. If this is not the first project review meeting for the project, there might also be a review of previous corrective action steps.

Team War Room

In the ideal setting the team war room is the physical facility that the team owns during the lifetime of the project. All of the team members are co-located there, and all team meetings take place there. I recognize that this is not possible in many projects, however, so some variations are discussed in the sections that follow.

Physical Layout

Ideally, all of the walls are covered with whiteboards. Depending on the size of the team, the team war room may be one large room that accommodates everyone or several smaller rooms that are adjacent to a larger community-type room for group meetings and presentations. Each team member has his or her own private workspace, but there is a minimum number of partitions. A line of sight between each team member is ideal. The project artifacts are displayed so everyone has immediate access.

Variations

I realize that the preceding physical layout is ideal, but several vendors and consulting companies that I have worked with make it a point to provide such facilities for their teams. I am even aware of clients providing such space when the vendor cannot.

The first ideal to be sacrificed is co-location. In the global marketplace, project teams and the client are often spread over the globe. The cost of face-to-face meetings is prohibitive (travel expenses) and a great waste of time (unproductive time while en route). While this has a few advantages (a 24-hour work day for example), it does create a logistics nightmare for the project manger and team members. Meetings are difficult to schedule and conduct, whereas teleconferences and even video conferences have become affordable and commonplace.

The second ideal to be sacrificed is the co-located team room. Many organizations simply do not have contiguous spaces they can release to a team for the duration of their project. Space is at a premium and has to be shared. In these situations the project artifacts must be mobile rather than fixed. While an inconvenience, this is not a show stopper.

The third ideal to be sacrificed is 100 percent assignment to a project. Commitments, loyalties, and priorities are spread over two or more projects and the home assignment as well.

Operational Uses

A well-planned team war room is not only for the use of the team as it conducts the work of the project, but it also serves other needs of the project. All scoping, planning, kick-off, status, and review meetings will take place there. Depending on the layout, parts of the space may be reserved for use by others outside the project on an as-needed and as-available basis. This will partially alleviate a space shortage problem for some organizations.

Managing Team Communications

Communicating among and between technical team members does not come naturally. Technical people often simply aren't good communicators. In most cases, they would rather spend their time immersed in the technical details of what they are working on. However, for team members to be truly effective, they have to openly communicate with one another. For some, that will be difficult; for others, it simply is a matter of practice. In this section, I examine the importance and role of communications in the effective team.

Managing Communications Timing, Content, and Channels

Getting information to the correct team members at the right time in the project usually determines the success or failure of the project. The project manager must manage the communication process as much as the technical process or risk failure. It isn't possible to manage all the communication in a project; that in itself is more than a full-time job. What the project manager has to do is examine the needs of the project team and make sure that communication occurs at the correct time and with the correct information. The following sections look at those ideas.

Timing

The timing of information can be critical. Problems can arise if the information comes too soon or too late:

■ If the information comes too far in advance of the action needed, it will be forgotten. It's almost impossible to remember information given one year in advance of its use. The project manager has to understand what the various team members need to know and when they need to know it in order to carry out their assignments. Where does this information come from? Like many other things in a project, you can find communication needs in the WBS. As you look through the tasks in the WBS, you will see that team members have to be alerted to upcoming tasks and need to be in communication with the team members whose tasks have precedence to their own. The project manager can make this happen.

■ A second problem in timing is getting the information needed to the project team member after they need it. Remember that project team members may need a few days to assimilate the information you're passing, particularly if you're speaking about a new technology. This requires that you, as project manager, manage the timing carefully so that everyone has as much information as possible and that you give them sufficient time to absorb it and process it so as to get the job done.

Content

The next communications management issue you need to be concerned about is communicating the correct information. This means you must understand what the project team members need to know to be successful. If you don't know what information the team members need, ask them. If the team members don't know, sit down with other of their colleagues and find out what sort of information needs to be passed in order to make the project run smoothly. Sometimes you will know what information is needed intuitively; other times you need to meet with the project team to consider critical information needs. Whichever the case, you need to be in charge of getting the information to your team members at the right time and with the right content.

Choosing Effective Channels

Once you know when the communication needs to occur for the project team to be successful and you have identified the basic communication content, the choice of how to get the information to the team members becomes important. As the project manager, you should stipulate how the team will communicate the information that others on the team need. You have a choice among various channels through which communication can flow. The following list takes a look at each of these channels:

Face-to-face, in-person meeting. A verbal, face-to-face, in-person meeting is usually the absolute best way to communicate. Not only can you get immediate feedback, you can see the person's reaction to information in their nonverbal cues. However, while it is often the best way to communicate, it's not always possible.

Videoconferencing. The cost of teleconferencing has dropped dramatically, and it is now much less expensive to send yourself electronically rather than physically across the country. And don't forget the time savings either. The software available to support these types of meetings has become far more accessible as well. Products such as NetMeeting and WebCast can be very helpful in supporting not only the face-to-face video portion, but also the presentation of slides across the Internet. However, while videoconferencing gives you a chance to see the other people, some people are "telenerds" and don't come off very well on TV. Just be aware that videoconferencing is not the same as in-person, face-to-face communication.

E-mail. E-mail is not, I repeat not, the communication blessing that everyone thinks it is. It does have certain advantages: It is fast, you can read e-mail at your own speed, and I'm sure you all know people who won't respond to voice mail but will respond immediately to e-mail. However, e-mail does have its drawbacks:

Volume. Many people get hundreds of e-mails per day. There's a pretty good chance that the e-mail you sent isn't the single most visible e-mail on the recipient's list, even if you put an exclamation point in front of it. Be aware that e-mail is so ubiquitous that it loses the visibility needed to get important information to other people simply because there is so much other e-mail "noise" out there.

Tone. E-mail tends to be short, much shorter that voice mail, and often people misinterpret the intended tone of the message. It happens. Be aware that the tone conveyed in your e-mail message may not be the one that you would use if you had voice communication.

Quality. Sending an e-mail message doesn't automatically make you a good writer. It's still difficult to send clear information to others in written form.

E-mail is very valuable, but you need to remember the caveats I just listed. While e-mail is a nice invention, it still requires as much management by the project manager as any of the other channels of communication.

TIP Manage the frequency of your e-mail use; don't overuse it. Your messages will end up being dismissed as so much spam, which will defeat your purpose. In addition, manage the distribution list for your e-mails. Because it is so easy just to add another name to the distribution list, resist it. Pretend that you only have so many e-mail coins to spend, and spend them wisely and frugally.

Written materials. Written materials are permanent. That's the good news. If you want to keep it, write it down. However, as with all of these channels, it requires effort to write things down well. It is also difficult for many people to write succinctly. Some use length to make up for good communication. Keep your writing short and clear, which will benefit the project team.

Phone. The phone is great if you actually get someone on it, but a lot of people let the phone ring and dump you into voice mail. (We are conditioned to leave a message and find ourselves surprised when a human actually answers.) The phone has the same good points and pitfalls of all the other channels. Its strength, as with verbal, face-to-face communication, lies in the fact that you can get immediate feedback and exchange ideas quickly. As the project manager, you will be in phone meetings often, either on a one-to-one basis or in a conference call. It's important to manage these calls as you would any of the other channels.

The effective management of communications is a critical factor for successful project management. A complete treatment of this topic is beyond the scope of this book, but an example of this effective management is certainly in order.

Suppose part of your project involves soliciting review comments from a number of people who will be using the process being designed and implemented. You are going to distribute a document that describes the process, and you want them to return their comments and critique what you are proposing. What is the most effective way to distribute the document and get meaningful feedback from the recipients? For the sake of the example, assume that the document is 50 pages long. Your first impulse might be to send it electronically and ask recipients to respond by making their comments directly on the electronic version. If you are using MS Word, you would request that they use the Track Changes feature. Is this the most effective way? It keeps everything in an electronic format and makes it reasonably straightforward to incorporate the changes into the final document, but look at this request from the recipient's point of view. I know from experience that many people do not like to make edits to an electronic document. They prefer marking up a hard-copy version. Your process does not give them that option, which it probably should. The task of incorporating their handwritten feedback is a little more involved than it would be with the electronic markup, but you will likely gain more and better feedback. Getting meaningful feedback is the goal, and you should use whatever means are at your disposal to ensure that happens.

What about the fact that the document is 50 pages long? Is that a barrier to meaningful feedback? I think so. If you agree, then what is the fix? My suggestion is that you dole out the document in bite-size pieces. Does everyone on the distribution list need to see all 50 pages? Maybe not. Maybe you would get more meaningful feedback by parceling out the document based on level of interest and involvement in the process, rather than asking everyone to read and comment on all 50 pages.

The professional project manager is aware of the communication patterns he or she needs to manage to make it possible for the project team to be successful as a unit. The areas to manage include timing, content, and channel. While it's probable that most project managers do a lot of the communication management on an ad hoc basis, it's important to be aware of the different areas of communication that you can manage. The skill of managing communication is just as important as any of the technical skills in project management. As a matter of fact, most surveys I've seen list project communication as the most important of all the areas to manage. By being aware of some of the components of project communication, you can be more effective as a project manager.

Managing Communication Beyond the Team

To be successful as a project manager, you need to communicate not only within the team but also to various stakeholders outside of the team. Your project may seem a success to you, but unless that is conveyed to the right people outside of the team, it won't matter. The question is then "Who are those right people?"

Managing Communications with the Sponsor

The single most important communication for the whole project is the communication you have with the project sponsor. The sponsor is the person who has agreed to give you the necessary resources to complete the project, which makes the sponsor your new best friend for this project. Without sponsor involvement in all phases of the project, you will be in dire trouble. There are a couple of good strategies for managing communications with your project sponsor, which I discuss here.

The first action to take when you are about to start a project is to go to the sponsor and ask what they want to know and when they want to know it. The sponsor is the one who gets to use the information you pass on and is ultimately the person who has to justify the expenditure on your project. The sponsor may want a different type of information than you are used to giving. It doesn't matter. Sponsors pay the bills; they should get what they want in the way of communication.

WARNING Don't tell the sponsor what he or she is going to get. For example, don't start talking about earned value and watch the sponsor's eyes glaze over before they can tell you what they want.

A second consideration is to ensure that the sponsor gets information regularly. Status reports should be sent to the sponsor at least once a week. It's not a good idea to hold on to information concerning the project if it is important to the sponsor. Get the information to the sponsor as fast as possible if it will affect the project.

Now it's time to turn to another topic to consider as a project manager managing communication: upward communication filtering.

Upward Communication Filtering and "Good News"

Upward communication filtering is a strange form of distorting information that is found in almost any type of organizational life. It can also be called the *good news syndrome*. Unfortunately, it can kill a project as fast as any facet of bad communication management. There are two types of upward communication filtering. The first type occurs when the person who is reporting upward — for example, to a sponsor — spins the information or leaves out information so that the communication looks like nothing but good news. For example, instead of saying that a company building has burned down, the person says that everything is under control, that the fire department and insurance company have been called, and that all the people are safe. Sure, some of this information the sponsor needs to know, but a good-news filter is something that puts a positive spin on everything, often at the expense of accuracy.

If something is going badly on a project, let the sponsor know what's going on as soon as possible. It is a good idea to talk about what you plan to do about the problem, but it never pays to filter problems from upward communication.

The second type of upward communication filtering involves withholding information. Perhaps there is a problem that you think can be resolved sometime in the future, so you withhold the current information from the sponsor, thinking that you can fix the problem. Such actions will almost always come back to bite you. Don't withhold information just because you're worried about a reaction. It's better to give all the news to the sponsor than it is to hope you can fix something that is broken, because if you can't fix the problem, it will just get worse and worse. Go ahead; tell the sponsor the truth.

Communicating with Other Stakeholders

A sponsor isn't the only stakeholder outside of the operating project team. A *stakeholder* is anyone who has an interest in the outcome of the project. The other stakeholders may be line managers of people on the team or consumers who are going to be involved in user acceptance tests. The best way to keep them informed is to copy them with the meeting notes from the status meeting.

CASE STUDY – PLEASANTOWN PLAYGROUND PROJECT

Meeting with volunteers is not at all like meeting with paid staff. Volunteers will agree to meet in the evenings or weekends not more than once a week. Meeting attendance may be spotty for some team members. Tasks will not have been completed as planned, with no mention of the slippage until the meeting. That argues in support of overstaffing every critical task until otherwise suggested.

CASE STUDY – PIZZA DELIVERED QUICKLY (PDQ)

Due to the complexity and lack of clarity, daily meetings are essential. For outside contractors this may not be their cup of tea. The challenge to the project manager is to get the firm commitment of the contractors. They must feel like part of the team for this to happen.

That way, all stakeholders will be informed and aware of the project's progress. It's simple enough to do but is often overlooked. The effective project manager makes sure all people who have an interest in the project are informed. If there is a special piece of information that will affect only one stakeholder, then get the information to them immediately. Once again, you start this whole process by asking what the stakeholders want to know and when. Then you find out and provide it.

Ultimately, communication occurs on a project all the time. A professor once said, "You can't *not* communicate." While you can't spend all your time managing it, be aware of the communication needs of your team and stakeholders at all times. The better you are at filling the communication needs of your team members and stakeholders, the better the chance that you will manage a successful project.

Managing Multiple Team Projects

As the applications development business grows, the frequency of projects requiring multiple teams for their execution will also grow. In fact, with the added need for globalization affecting nearly every application, most, if not all, development projects will involve more than one team. This section examines this unique situation and explores several ways to organize, scope, plan, and manage such projects while maintaining the organizational culture throughout.

Most companies present a unique challenge for you to provide exemplary project management tools, processes, and templates without imposing a standard methodology, while at the same time offering suggestions for improving existing practices.

Multiple-Team Projects

The multiple-team projects that populate the organization's portfolio are unlike any other development projects found today. Because of the unique team-centric organizational structure, any project that crosses customer lines results in a multiple-team project. The temptation is to let each team act on its own with some integrating task at the end to "glue" everything together and hope that it works. That is not the approach I take in this book. My approach is more deliberate and planned, as you will see.

A more formal definition is given as follows.

DEFINITION Multiple-Team project

A multiple-team project is any project that requires the involvement of two or more independent teams, who may have their own tools, templates, and processes.

This is a simple definition but it will serve the purposes of this book quite well. The operative word is *independent*. This implies that each team may have its own tools, templates, and processes that it uses for managing projects. The disparity that exists between the teams is what produces the management challenges. Much of the following discussion centers around these disparities and what you can do organizationally to minimize their impact on the project.

How Is a Multiple-Team Project Team Structured?

The multiple-team structure can be represented graphically as shown in Figure 9-2.

Much as in a matrix organization, the team is comprised of members who come from two or more business units (vertical dark bars). Infrastructure team members may join the team as real members (vertical light bars) or as virtual members (horizontal light bars). The size and complexity of the project dictates whether the infrastructure members will be real or virtual. One variation is to have team members from the business units act as liaison to the infrastructure teams (horizontal light bars).

Figure 9-2 The generic multiple-team structure

The Challenges of Multiple Team Projects

For many years the focus in project management has been on the effective management of the project team. Its members were selected based on their expertise relative to the requirements of the project; requirements were gathered and documented; a project plan was built and executed; and customer change requests were proposed and acted upon in the best interest of the customer and the enterprise.

Then along came siloed structures with their unique team-centric orientation. In these organizations, which are typically large organizations, each team focused exclusively on a specific customer group and was able to satisfy their requirements for new and enhanced applications systems. Other teams were infrastructure oriented — for example, database design, enterprise architecture, security, quality assurance, and so on. The teams were usually independent of one another and even developed their own approaches to project management in order to meet what they thought were the unique needs of their customer group. All of that has changed. With companies growing into international markets as well as the added complexities of gaining and sustaining themselves as major competitors in the world marketplace, projects are taking on a different character. Most projects now involve two or more teams for their effective execution. In mission-critical, enterprisewide, and other complex cases, several teams must be brought together in order to successfully deliver the expected results. How to do this effectively without sacrificing the culture that has made organizations great are the topics of this section.

These same challenges extend outside a single department to the entire enterprise. Any organizationally independent business units that practice their own flavor of project management will present the same challenges when they are brought together to work with other business units on the same project.

While you are only concerned about a single project, the fact that you have multiple independent teams working on it makes it appear as though there are really multiple projects. This is a perception that will have to be dispelled if you are to be successful on these very complex endeavors. In all such projects there will be several project leads (one from each team and perhaps one who has overall responsibility for the project). It will be the job of these project leads to build the management infrastructure that is responsible for the overall project.

In today's project management environment, the pace of business initiatives and the lack of resources require many project leads to manage concurrent, multiple, and dependent projects. Years ago this scenario was reserved for the more senior of project leads. Yet today, project leads of all experience and competency levels are called on to manage multiple efforts simultaneously. The following suggestions can help the multiple project leads keep their head "in the midst of the storm" and establish a consistent methodical approach among the inherent chaos of multiple-project team management.

Here are a few thoughts just to get your creative juices flowing.

Working with Fiercely Independent Team Cultures

The teams that define a specific function have each built their own approaches to meeting customer expectations. They have resisted exchanging best practices between teams. In only a few instances have project teams reporting to the same team manager exchanged processes, templates, and tools. I use the term "fiercely independent" to characterize this cultural phenomenon. While that independence may have served customers well, it doesn't scale to projects that involve multiple teams. When such is the case, you have a problem to be reckoned with.

Establishing a Project Management Structure

The team independence has spawned a number of project management approaches and structures. The multiple-team projects are complex and therefore a challenge to manage effectively. The team structure must be chosen to best meet the needs of the project. That structure can be relatively loose or very tight. The nature of the project will influence the choice.

Establishing One Project Management Life Cycle

The first step in establishing consistency and order in a multiple-team project environment is to establish a definitive life cycle for the project. Life cycles (phases) generate certain patterns of thinking with the project team participants. You could call this *contouring behavior*. This becomes very important when your time will be monopolized by multiple team demands. Not having the time to micro-manage project personal behaviors, you need to establish a useful mindset in the project team. Definitive life cycles/phases is a safe and "low-energy level" way of instilling these behaviors and outlook.

The project life cycle, including stage gate approval milestones, should be established at the inception of the project, documented, and become part of the working project schedules. The phases should be used as high-level summary tasks in the actual project plan. It is also a good idea to distribute a definition of the individual phases, their significance, the roles and responsibilities required for each phase, and the clear intent of each phase prior to project kick-off or planning.

If multiple projects are serving the same end, or result, it may be in the project lead's best interest to "sell" them to senior management as a strategy rather than individually disconnected projects. Other contributing projects, not under your auspices, may also be included under the strategy. When classifying a group of projects as a strategy, the following scenarios are far more possible:

- The appointment of a single project manager. This person, by title, would then be responsible for coordinating and securing cross-functional resources, strategic decisions, and general project leadership.

- The establishment of a consistent life cycle/methodology across multiple teams under the strategy

- The appointment of a shared administrative staff for projects under the strategy

- Joint risk analysis and joint resolution strategies

> **CASE STUDY – PIZZA DELIVERED QUICKLY (PDQ)**
>
> Each subsystem could be worked on by a separate team. They cannot operate independently because they are building a single integrated system. A Core Team Structure would seem to be the best fit. The Core Team Members would be both PDQ professionals and outside contractors.

- Proper project scoping (i.e., work is apportioned properly to the team it belongs with; therefore, a more efficient use of resources is achieved)

- Strength in numbers: The project manager under the strategy will benefit from the collective experience and intuition of the group of project team managers. Information sharing is more easily implemented due to the strategic nature of the work.

Defining a Requirements Gathering Approach

Several variables have to be coordinated in order to effectively identify, document, and validate customer requirements. The first variable is the customer. Several customer groups are involved, so their requirements have to be gathered and consolidated with those of the other customer groups. The second variable is the approach to gathering requirements. I can recommend at least six approaches, which are summarized in Table 9-2. Which one or ones are to be used and how the results are to be consolidated are major questions that must be answered.

CROSS-REF Further discussion of requirements gathering can be found in Chapter 3.

Establishing a Scope Change Management Process

Any request for a scope change can, and probably will, affect several other customer groups. Project Impact Statements and the approval process are considerably more complex than they are in single-team projects. At least two levels of approval are needed. One level is at the team level, where not all decisions will be the same across teams. Some will accept the change, others will accept it with compromise, and others will reject it. The other approval is at the project level, where any conflicting decisions from the teams must be reconciled.

Table 9-2 Requirements Gathering Processes

METHOD	STRENGTHS	RISKS
Facilitated Group Sessions	Excellent for cross-functional processes	Use of untrained facilitators can lead to a negative response from users
	Detailed requirements can be documented and verified immediately	Time and cost of planning/executing session can be high
	Resolves issues with an impartial facilitator	
Prototypes	Innovative ideas can be generated	Customer may want to implement a prototype
	Users clarify what they want	Difficult to know when to stop
	Users identify requirements that may be missed	Specialized skills are required
	Customer focused	Absence of documentation
	Early proof of concept	
	Stimulates thought process	
Interviews	End user participation	Descriptions may differ from actual detailed activities
	High-level description of functions and processes provided	Without structure, stakeholders may not know what information to provide
		Real needs are ignored if the analyst is prejudiced

(continued)

Table 9-2 (continued)

METHOD	STRENGTHS	RISKS
Observation	Specific/complete descriptions of actions are provided	Documenting and videotaping may be time-consuming, expensive, and have legal overtones
	Effective when routine activities are difficult to describe	Confusing/conflicting information must be clarified
		Misinterpretation of what is observed
Requirements Reuse	Requirements quickly generated/refined	Significant investment required for developing archives, maintenance, and library functions
	Redundant efforts reduced	May violate intellectual rights of previous owner
	Customer satisfaction enhanced by previous proof	Similarity may be misunderstood
	Quality increase	
	Reinventing the wheel minimized	
Business Process Analysis	Excellent for cross-functional processes	Implementation of improvement is dependent on an organization open to changes
	Visual communication	Good facilitation, data gathering, and interpretation required
	Verification of "what is/what is not"	Time-consuming

Defining the Team Meeting Structure

Multiple-team project structures usually result in additional layers of project management, hence the need for additional team meetings. This structure should be carefully worked out and agreed to by all parties. The danger is meeting overload, which detracts from the real work of the project.

Establishing Manageable Reporting Levels

Multiple-team project management requires high levels of energy and focus over extended periods of time. In order to achieve this, you must consider what reporting levels are required on your projects in order for you to do the following:

- Maintain control over the scope and progress of the project
- Maintain control in the time available, i.e., realistic reporting requirements

Milestone reporting is a way to maintain control over the project yet minimize the amount of time spent in gathering and analyzing the data. Consider the following issues when establishing the project reporting requirements:

- What are the levels of project complexity and urgency?
- What are the levels of project risk, both overall and within each phase?
- What are the skills of the person who will be gathering and reporting data?
- How much time is needed to analyze data after it is reported?
- Is there a clear change management policy in place?
- Is there a clear communication protocol set for the project team?

After answering these questions, determine the reporting levels that will yield results and the detailed information required for management decisions. This must be done in a balanced approach considering the amount of time required from the project team to gather the information and the amount of time required from the project lead to analyze the reporting data.

Searching Out Your Seconds

In this context, second has nothing to do with time. For the purposes here, *Webster's* defines second as "the official attendant of a contest in a duel or boxing match." Although you are not engaged in a duel or boxing match, some projects are not far from either of these. During multiple-team project management, it will be virtually impossible for you to cover all the issues, meetings, and so on that the role requires; therefore, you need to call on the help of those whom you can trust (a second) in keeping your "arms around" the project efforts. Keep in mind the following when considering seconds:

- You may need multiple seconds for the project, such as technical or business-minded seconds.
- Seconds should also be considered confidants.
- Seconds should be well versed in the goals and requirements of the project.
- The role of a second is one of a negotiated relationship.
- Your second will be someone already connected with the project.
- Use the second sparingly and do not use them as a project spy.
- Do not make a regular habit of off-loading work and responsibility on the second.

Building an Integrated Project Plan/Schedule

Because the teams are independent of one another they will come to this project with their own ideas of what constitutes a project plan and schedule. One team's approach may be compatible with other teams but that would be coincidental and not to be counted on. Expect problems regardless of the project organizational structure you adopt. If a standard is to be developed and agreed to by all participating teams, expect an integration problem as teams adjust to the new ways. Plan some time for that adjustment and plan some time to adjust the new standardized process itself.

Sharing Scarce Resources Across Teams

Problems will arise. Schedules will slip. To keep the project moving forward often requires that resources be assigned across team boundaries. If the project organizational structure you have chosen maintains the independent team structure, the project manager will have to negotiate across those team boundaries. The project organizational structure you are using will make those negotiations easy or difficult. Keep this in mind as you choose the organizational structure for the project. Make sure the project team managers are aware of the likelihood of having to assign their members to other teams on a temporary basis as a fix for the scheduling problems that arise.

Managing Team Member Commitment to Their Home Business Unit

Whether or not it is visible to the project manager, team members will maintain a loyalty and attachment to their home team business unit. After all, that is where they get their performance reviews, merit increases, assignments, professional development, and so on. Don't expect that you can do anything to change that attachment. Just be aware of it and keep it in mind as you interact with team members.

Managing Lack of Ownership

One of the most critical success factors for the multiple-team project is the creation of ownership on the part of the customer and the project team members. Get them to participate in as many project functions as possible. That begins with requirements gathering and continues to planning, establishing team operating rules, status meetings, performance reporting, problem-solving meetings, scope change processing, implementation, the post-implementation audit, lessons learned, and other project tasks. The type of project organizational structure you choose will either facilitate this or establish roadblocks. Think through your decision to adopt a given structure and reflect on these ownership areas. How will you establish that ownership in the face of the structure you have decided to use?

Table 9-3 summarizes the preceding discussion, indicating the level of difficulty (L = low, M = medium, H = high) in dealing with each of these challenges for the three project organizational structures discussed in the remainder of this chapter.

Table 9-3 Challenges for Project Organizational Structures

	PROJECT OFFICE	CORE TEAM	SUPER TEAM
Fiercely independent teams	L	M	H
Establishing a project management structure	M	L	H
Establishing one project management life cycle	M	L	H
Defining a requirements gathering approach	H	M	L
Establishing a scope change management process	M	M	L
Defining a team meeting structure	L	L	L
Establishing manageable reporting levels	L	L	M
Searching out your seconds	H	M	H
Building an integrated project plan/schedule	H	M	L
Sharing scarce resources across teams	H	L	L
Managing team member commitment to their home team	H	H	M
Managing lack of ownership	H	L	L

Executing a Multiple-Team Project

You have probably learned from experience that meaningful customer involvement is absolutely necessary for project success. If absolutely necessary for single projects, what level of importance would you place on it for multiple-team projects or multiple-team projects that include globalization? The English language fails here.

The level of complexity is considerably higher than that of the single-team project. In the multiple-team project you probably have multiple stakeholders — several from each team involved in the project. These stakeholder groups will all have their own requirements. Furthermore, each team has their own way of doing things. Is it beginning to sound like a chaotic situation?

You have to approach the situation one step at a time. First, you have to agree on a project team structure. There are three from which to choose: Project Office, Core Team, and Super Team. Once you have agreed to the structure, you can talk about the project management approach to be taken.

Project Office

It is a common practice in organizations to establish a temporary Project Office to manage large or mission-critical projects. Some organizations will even establish a Project Office whenever the team size reaches a certain number (30, for example). The Project Office is just another layer of management to whom the individual project leads report. The Project Office provides general management support and coordination as well as basic administrative services to each of the project leads. You will learn how to adapt the traditional Project Office to accommodate multiple-team projects.

DEFINITION Project Office

A Project Office is a temporary management structure established to coordinate and support the work of two or more independent teams who are concurrently working on a single project that has dependencies across the team task assignments.

NOTE Do not confuse this with a Project Management Office (PMO). A PMO is a permanent structure that supports the work of all projects of a particular type or from a defined part of the organization.

Remember that the Project Office is a temporary structure. It is managed by a Project Office Manager and exists only to serve the needs of a single project.

Once the project is complete the Project Office is disbanded. The Project Office is the top layer of management in a multiple-team project. Its purpose is to coordinate and support the several project teams working on the project and to interact directly with the stakeholder groups and the customers. The Project Office is minimally invasive of the tools, templates, and processes used by the teams assigned to the project. They basically conduct their work using their established artifacts. The role of the Project Office Manager, with the support of a Project Office Administrator, is a coordinating role. In some cases it will be necessary to establish new processes to be superimposed upon existing team processes to handle routine project-level reporting and analysis tasks. A scope change management process would be one example.

Project Office Structure

This structure includes a great deal of administrative and coordinating work, and an administrator position is added to support the Program Office Manager and interact with Project Team Managers for the gathering and dissemination of project information. Data gathering, report preparation, and report dissemination are the primary responsibilities of the Project Office Administrator.

Figure 9-3 shows the basic Project Office structure.

Each project team operates independently with the Project Team Manager responsible for representing the team to the Project Office and for moving information up to that office. The Project Office Manager then consolidates that information and reports back to the project teams and up to the senior management level. Issues, risks, and problems are resolved by the Project Office Manager and the Project Team Managers acting as a committee of the whole. A Project Office Administrator helps the Project Officer Manager collect, summarize, and report information from each team.

Figure 9-3 Project Office structure

Roles and Responsibilities

The roles and responsibilities of the Project Office Manager are listed and briefly discussed in the sections that follow.

Organizing and Managing the Entire Project

The Project Office Manager must bring together under one management structure teams that are accustomed to operating independently but must now operate under a common set of procedures and processes. This is best accomplished through an organizational meeting attended by the managers from each team. A new set of team operating rules will result from this meeting, a set of operating rules that all team leads have agreed to support and follow.

WARNING The Project Office Manager doesn't have any real authority over the teams except as vested in him by the Project Team Managers.

Developing the High-Level Project Plan with the Project Team Managers

The Project Office Manager should collaborate with the Project Team Managers to draft the high-level project plan. Each Project Team Manager can then take that high-level plan as input and work with their team to complete their part of the project plan.

Integrating and Coordinating the Project Plans of Each Team

Several inter-plan dependencies will have to be accounted for and built into a master project schedule. That work will be led by the Project Office Manager in collaboration with all of the Project Team Managers.

Maintaining the Overall Project Schedule

Once the project has been launched, the Project Office Manager will be responsible for monitoring project performance and progress. Adjustments to the project master schedule will have to be made as tasks are completed (ahead of or behind schedule).

The Project Office Administrator is responsible for gathering periodic status updates from each team member and reporting them to the Project Office Manager and the Project Team Managers.

Monitoring and Managing Resource Use

Resource management is a critical responsibility of the Project Office Manager. Adjustments will have to be made to accommodate approved scope change requests and solve other schedule-related problems. This is a most sensitive area and requires the greatest diplomacy and negotiating skills on the part of the Project Office Manager.

WARNING The resolution of project problems and issues may require the reassignment of team members from one team to another for the sake of preserving the project schedule.

Preparing and Distributing Project Status Reports

Project status reports should be submitted by the Project Team Managers and consolidated by the Project Office Manager for submission to the Project Team Managers, various stakeholder groups, customers, and senior IT management. If the Project Office Manager can get the individual teams to submit their updates in a standardized format, that will reduce the labor intensity of their reporting responsibilities.

Planning and Conducting Team Meetings

At the highest level, there will be frequent (perhaps weekly) status meetings, chaired by the Project Office Manager and attended by the Project Team Managers. The Project Team Managers, at their own discretion, will hold meetings with their team members (for some projects that may be daily).

Processing Scope Change Requests

This is a complex task that must be managed by the Project Office Manager or a designated associate. The complexity arises at two levels, as described earlier. Recall that the complexity is at the team level, where differing decisions arise from each team regarding the accommodation of a request, and at the project level, where some resolution and consolidation of the differing opinions will be needed.

WARNING Every change request must be treated as significant until proven otherwise.

You should anticipate that every change request will impact the schedule and resources of every team. The Project Office Manager is responsible for receiving, processing, and closing all scope change requests. This is no small task, as the master schedule and resource allocation must be considered. Given that there are cross-team dependencies, this task must be dealt with using the most intense due diligence.

Solving Project Problems Escalated from the Individual Project Teams

There will be many situations in which a project lead is unable to resolve a problem. Cross-team dependencies will lie at the root of many of the problems. These are beyond the authority of the project lead and must be escalated to the Project Office Manager for resolution.

Negotiating and Resolving Problems Between Teams

Some problems will involve two or more teams. In the event that they are not able to resolve the problem among themselves, it will have to be escalated to the Project Office Manager.

Strengths

The Project Office is a well-established organizational structure. It is used across a number of business situations because it preserves the integrity and processes of the members.

Scales to Very Large Projects

This is a known advantage of the Project Office structure: Intermediate levels of management can be added as size increases. There will be an added reporting load as well, but that contributes to full disclosure across all of the teams and intermediate management layers. Of the three models I discuss here, the Project Office scales to the very largest of projects.

Allows Teams to Maintain Their Practices

Teams are comfortable and most effective when they can use their own processes. Taking them out of that environment will only increase the risk of project failure. At the same time, leaving them to do it their way can also add to the risk of project failure. You can't have it both ways. In any case, using the Project Office structure, they can continue to use their own processes and procedures for the work specific to their team. The Project Office will provide whatever consolidation is needed. For some situations, such as scope change control, another process may need to be superimposed on the existing team scope change management processes. This will provide a cross-team tool for weaving approved scope change requests into the integrated plan.

Weaknesses

Despite its strengths, the Project Office has a number of weaknesses. Those weaknesses center around the integration of independent unit processes. Much of this is absorbed in the Project Office Administrator position.

Managing Across Disparate Practices

The Project Office Manager may have a large management burden in consolidating the input from each of the independent teams. While some standardization may be agreed to by the teams, the Project Office Manager will have to absorb an added management load.

Team Members Will Have to Manage Competing Priorities

This is a potential problem area. Team members will generally defer to their home department when a decision regarding priorities between competing tasks is needed. The Project Team Managers will have to intercede and take a leadership role to keep priorities in line. This will be an uncomfortable position for them to be in because they are often biased toward their home business unit when priority decisions are called for.

May Have to Use a Cumbersome Scope Change Management Process

Scope change requests will have to be processed through each team. Each team must provide some type of impact statement along with alternative ways of accommodating the scope change request. These will have to be reconciled before an overall approval can be granted. An added layer of approvals and project impact will be needed to accommodate this final approval.

Impact on the Project Life Cycle

Table 9-4 summarizes the preceding discussion and provides a bit more detail on how the Project Office structure impacts the project life cycle. Note again that the need to integrate functions dominates the impact.

Table 9-4 Project Office Impact on Project Life Cycle

PHASE	ARTIFACT	SUMMARY COMMENTS
Scoping	(1) Requirements Gathering	(1) Build integrated plan for conducting process. This might be a completely integrated process or one that integrates the results from each team.
Planning	(1) WBS	(1) Integrated plan to develop complete WBS is needed
	(2) Estimation	(2) Needs systems integration estimates
	(3) Dependency Diagrams	(3) To document interproject team dependencies
	(4) Project Schedule	(4) Minor except for resource scheduling
	(5) Risk Management	(5) Straightforward
	(6) Communications	(6) Complex but can be managed
Launching	(1) Team operating rules	(1) Straightforward
	(2) Work packages	(2) Maintain out of Project Office

(continued)

Table 9-4 *(continued)*

PHASE	ARTIFACT	SUMMARY COMMENTS
Monitoring and Controlling	(1) Project performance reports	(1) Coordinate from Project Office
	(2) Scope change management	(2) Must establish a single process
	(3) Problem resolution/escalation	(3) Complex but can be managed
Closing	(1) Requirements validation	(1) Must have an integrated process

Core Team

The second management structure is called the Core Team. It is new and different from the other two management structures I present. Its difference lies in the definition of an intermediate management advisory structure. On the surface it appears to be management by committee, but, in fact, it is not. The intermediate layer of management is responsible for working with all teams that are involved with the project but its main focus is advisory and supportive.

This structure is used by one of my clients. They are a very large international retailer with their IT department highly decentralized around customer groups and infrastructure groups. In other words, they have a very siloed IT organization. Only the most critical of projects are done using the Core Team approach.

DEFINITION Core Team

A Core Team is a temporary structure comprised of a small number of subject matter experts (SMEs) chosen and managed by the Core Team Manager. The SMEs of the Core Team consult, advise, and support the work of all the teams working on the project.

This approach is quite similar to the Project Office, except that there is one additional layer of management above the project managers. The additional layer of management is comprised of the most senior experts in each line of business and technology involved in the project. They report to the Core Team Manager, who has overall responsibility for the project. The Core Team does not do the work of the project but interacts with the Project Team Managers and their teams as advisors. Whereas the Project Office plan was put together in a top down fashion, the Core Team approach is bottom up. Each team builds and documents its project plan. Armed with their plans, the Core Team works with the Core Team Manager to conduct a planning integration session. This session produces an overall project plan with project dependencies identified and date conflicts resolved. Schedule compression is done at these sessions as well.

The structure is also temporary. When the work of the project is done, the structure disbands. The significant feature of this structure is that all the Core Team members are responsible for all of the work of the project. That includes their own team's work and that of all the other teams. That has to be clearly understood and practiced by the Project Team Managers. This is not the time to protect your silo.

Core Team Structure

This structure is not as common as the Project Office structure. It is generally reserved for mission-critical projects and should therefore be used sparingly. It takes the most senior and experienced professionals away from their primary responsibilities and assigns them 100 percent to a single project.

Figure 9-4 shows the basic Core Team structure.

The Core Team is advisory to the Core Team Manager and together with the Project Team Managers manages the work of the individual project teams. This extends the management authority of the Core Team members outside of their normal organizational boundaries. In carrying out this management function they work directly with the Core Team Manager.

NOTE They also act in an advisory, coaching, or mentoring capacity on technical and business matters at the invitation of the individual team members, regardless of the business unit to which they are aligned.

Figure 9-4 Core Team structure

Roles and Responsibilities

The roles and responsibilities of the Core Team are listed and briefly discussed in the sections that follow. Several of the roles and responsibilities are the same as the Project Office structure but adapted to the Core Team structure.

Advising Each Project Team on Technical and Business Matters

At least one of the Core Team members will have detailed knowledge about any business area or technical topic as may be required by the project team members. Having that information come from a closed team — like the Core Team — will ensure a consistency of information and a repeatability that will go a long way to ensuring project success. The Core Team will come to understand the project and be the best source of help in the enterprise to any team member.

Supporting Each Project Team as Needed

The Core Team members by their very nature will be experienced consultants and developers. They will be excellent choices for mentors and coaches to any team member requesting such help. There should not be any boundaries defined by business unit of origin for any team member or Core Team member. This will help spread best practices across organizational boundaries. In the case of a client who is using this model, that has certainly been their experience.

Collaborating with the Core Team Manager as Needed

Besides helping individual team members and Project Team Managers, the Core Team members will be a big asset to the Core Team Manager. Not only will this help extend to business and technical questions but also to more general management situations. The vast experience imbedded in the Core Team gives the Core Team Manager the very best advisory group that could be assembled. They have also worked together before and so are familiar with each other's management styles.

Negotiating and Helping Resolve Problems and Cross-Team Conflicts

The Core Team members will come from the business and technical units represented on the project team and because of that relationship should be in a position to intercede when needed and help resolve problems and conflicts. The Core Team should use this fact as a last resort. They need to establish themselves as leaders and gain the respect of their team members. They won't do that by constantly deferring to the Core Team members to bail them out.

The roles and responsibilities of the Core Team Manager are listed and briefly discussed in the following sections. In all cases these responsibilities are carried out with the support and collaboration of the Core Team Members.

Organizing and Managing the Entire Project

The Core Team must bring together, under one management structure, teams that are used to operating independently. The project managers must agree on the operating rules that bind the teams into a working unit. The teams will be able to maintain much of their independence. Their project managers will decide what processes, tools, and templates must be consistent across all teams. Otherwise, the teams are free to follow their own usual practices.

Developing the High-Level Project Plan with the Project Managers

Each team then completes the plan for its part of the project. Then the Core Team should work as a single team to draft the high-level project plan. There will be dependencies across the teams and these will have to be further planned by the project managers to ensure an orderly completion of the project.

Integrating and Coordinating the Project Plans of Each Team

Several inter-plan dependencies will have to be accounted for and built into a master project schedule. That work will be led by the Core Team Manager and Core Team acting as a committee of the whole.

Maintaining the Overall Project Schedule

Once the project has been launched, the Core Team is responsible for monitoring project performance and progress. The Core Team is mutually accountable for the entire project. For them to focus on their part alone would court disaster for the project; they must work together as a team.

Monitoring and Managing Resource Use

Resource management is a critical component of the project. As required, resources will have to be shared across the teams. Adjustments must be made to accommodate approved scope change requests and solve other schedule-related problems. The Core Team can be very instrumental in helping the Core Team Manager make this happen.

Preparing and Distributing Project Status Reports

Project status reports will be submitted by the Project Team Managers to each other. On a revolving basis, these reports will have to be consolidated by one of their members for submission to the various stakeholder groups, customers, and senior management.

Planning and Conducting Team Meetings

At the highest level, there will be frequent (perhaps daily) meetings of the Core Team chaired by one of their members. At the discretion of the project managers, they will hold meetings (probably daily) of their team members.

Processing Scope Change Requests

This is a complex task that must be managed by all of the Core Team. You should expect that every change request will impact the schedule and resources of every team. The Core Team is responsible for receiving, processing, and closing all scope change requests. This is no small task, as the master schedule and resource allocation must be considered. Given that there are cross-team dependencies, this task must be dealt with using the most intense due diligence.

Solving Problems Escalated from the Individual Project Teams

There will be many situations in which a project manager is unable to resolve a problem. Cross-team dependencies lie at the root of many of the problems. These are beyond the authority of the individual project managers, and must be escalated to the Core Team acting as a committee of the whole for resolution.

Strengths

The Core Team Members are hand-picked and assigned 100 percent to the project. This offers a number of advantages, as described in the following sections.

Hand-Picked by the Core Team Manager

The Core Team Manager is chosen by the CIO or an equivalent senior manager. Obviously, the project will be a mission-critical project. In turn, the Core Team Manager will hand-pick the Core Team. This is very unusual. To give the Core Team Manager the authorization to hand-pick the Core Team speaks to the criticality of the project. Only the most business-critical projects would warrant this approach. Not only that, but the person chosen to lead this project must have an established record of success in the eyes of the senior management team. Not anyone would have achieved this level of credibility. This is a *carte blanche* authority and is not based on availability.

Provides the Best Available Advice to the Core Team Manager

The Core Team will consist of subject matter experts (SMEs) that the Core Team Manager has worked with in the past. They would have established a reputation for credibility and solid delivery skills. Their advice will be respected and listened to by the Core Team Manager. Because they have past experience with the Core Team Manager, their style is known to be compatible and will serve the project well.

Coordinates the Work of Several Project Teams

The Core Team will be the respected experts and will have credibility and great influence over the project team. The Core Team Manager knows this and takes advantage of it as appropriate. This is a distinct advantage over the Project Office structure whereby no such coordinating opportunity is present.

Allows Teams to Maintain Their Practices

This is the same as in the Project Office structure but here it will be impacted by the involvement of the Core Team. The Core Team should act as a buffer between the Core Team Manager and the individual teams. The Core Team will have some influence over the teams from their business unit as well as other business units. They may convince the project teams to change or at least modify the way they conduct their project management affairs. The Core Team Manager can expect some degree of standardization from the efforts of the core team. They will understand that such standardization is a plus for the project and support that position with each of the project teams.

Weaknesses

Even though the strengths significantly reduce the risk of project failure, there are a few weaknesses that have to be dealt with.

May Not Scale to the Largest Projects

At some point the size of the project team gets so large that in order to be representative of the technology and business units involved in the project, the Core Team becomes unwieldy in size. There is evidence that this begins when the size of the Core Team grows beyond 10 persons.

Must Manage Across Disparate Practices

Except for the influence of the Core Team, this is the same as in the case of the Project Office.

Team Members Will Have to Manage Competing Priorities

This is almost the same situation as with the Project Office. The difference is the presence and influence of the Core Team. Its members can play a very important role acting as the glue that keeps the project team members focused on the needs of the project. Continuing to stress the criticality of the project will help the team members keep the project in proper perspective.

Repeatedly Chosen SMEs Does Not Enable Development of New Core Team Members

The cream always rises to the top. The very best SMEs will repeatedly be chosen, so those who aspire to the role of Core Team member will not have many opportunities. Perhaps a position classification can be created that qualifies a person for Core Team membership, perhaps Candidate Core Team member. With that in place, a certain percentage of every Core Team would have to be filled with candidates. That would give at least a few people the opportunity to rise to the top.

Impact on the Project Life Cycle

Table 9-5 summarizes the aspects of the Core Team across the project phases.

Table 9-5 Impact of the Core Team on the Project Life Cycle

PHASE	ARTIFACT	SUMMARY COMMENT
Scoping	(1) Requirements Gathering	(1) Build integrated plan for conducting process
Planning	(1) WBS (2) Estimation (3) Dependency Diagrams (4) Project Schedule (5) Risk Management (6) Communications	(1) Leave each WBS independent (2) Estimate each plan independently (3) Determine project dependencies (4) Integrate project schedules (5) Add integration risks (6) Complex but can be managed
Launching	(1) Team operating rules (2) Work packages	(1) Straightforward (2) Maintain out of Core Team Manager's Office
Monitoring and Controlling	(1) Project performance reports (2) Scope change management (3) Problem resolution/escalation	(1) Coordinate from Core Team Manager's Office (2) Must establish a single process (3) Complex but can be managed
Closing	(1) Requirements validation	(1) Must have an integrated process

CASE STUDY – PIZZA DELIVERED QUICKLY (PDQ)

If the outside contractors are from more than one company, the challenge will be to integrate their processes into one single approach. If I had my choice, I would choose a single vendor for the entire system. Because of the nature of the problem, that may mean choosing a large consulting practice.

Super Teams

The third management structure is called the Super Team. This structure works quite well but requires an experienced project manager.

The Super Team closely resembles teams you have worked on before. Its members are chosen from the enterprise based on skills, competencies, and business or technical orientation. It is driven by the needs of the project. All of this is quite common and well understood by the enterprise, but what if those individual were chosen from independent business units and all came with their own baggage as to how a project should be organized and run? That adds a challenging complexity to what otherwise would have been a relatively simple situation. Such is the case with the Super Team.

DEFINITION Super Team

A Super Team is a temporary management structure that integrates several dependent teams into a single project team managed by a senior-level project manager.

For those cases where team size is not a deterrent to successful project performance, this structure can work quite well. It does require that the project lead be experienced in managing large (even very large) projects. This is not a job for the faint of heart. The team will have one person leading it (a senior member of one of the teams). In most cases, there will be at least one other management layer within the team. These subproject leads are responsible for some of the deliverables. It would be a mistake to organize the subprojects along strict team division lines. The structure of the project should suggest how those subprojects might best be defined. Using the concept of cohesion and coupling would be a best practice that has good application here.

The planning processes that you are already familiar with apply here without revision. It would be my choice to have an experienced planning session facilitator prepare and conduct the Super Team planning session. Expect to spend two or three consecutive days planning the project. The project lead of this superproject should focus on the plan and not on facilitating the planning session. A technographer, who would record all of the deliberations from the planning session, will be indispensable.

The team from which each team member originated is of no consequence in forming a Super Team. While they come from teams that are needed to deliver the project, their association with their home team loses its identity in the Super Team. The final structure that the Super Team takes follows from the functions that the team will have to perform, the size of the team, and the characteristics of the project itself. Often the Work Breakdown Structure (WBS) will be the foundation on which the Super Team organizational structure is fashioned.

Super Team Structure

This structure is nothing more than you would expect for a large project team. The larger the project, the greater the depth of the management structure.

Figure 9-5 shows the Super Team structure.

This is a radical departure from the Project Office and Core Team structures. In the Super Team structure, the team of origin of each project team member is ignored. In its place is a structure that assigns team members to project tasks based on their skill/competency profile. The WBS becomes a tool to determine many of these assignments. As project size grows, intermediate levels of management are created, but they are all functionally oriented, so the Subproject Lead box can actually expand to a hierarchy of boxes, each with a person responsible for a major part of the project deliverables.

Roles and Responsibilities

The roles and responsibilities of the Super Team Manager are pretty much what you would expect of any project manager. They are listed in the sections that follow and briefly described.

Organizing and Managing the Project

There will be one project lead, the Super Team Manager, for the Super Team structure. The Super Team Manager must have solid experience managing large and complex projects. They must negotiate and gain each team's approval of the operating rules that bind the teams into a single working unit. In the Super Team structure, individual teams lose their identity. They are fully integrated into a single project team.

Figure 9-5 Super Team structure

Developing the Project Plan

The senior members from each team should work in collaboration with the Super Team Manager as a single team to draft the high-level project plan. Working with a smaller number of associates for this initial step is sufficient. Once the infrastructure has been established, the full planning team can be assembled to work out the remaining details. The planning task can easily get out of hand, so careful planning is required to ensure that the plan is kept on track and doesn't waste the planning team's time.

Maintaining the Overall Project Schedule

Once the project has been launched, the Subproject Leads are responsible for monitoring project performance and progress. The Super Team Manager is accountable for the entire project and will receive periodic status reports from the Subproject Leads.

Monitoring and Managing Resource Use

Resource management is a critical component of the project. As required, resources will have to be shared across the Subproject Teams. Adjustments must be made to accommodate approved scope change requests and solve other schedule-related problems.

Preparing and Distributing Project Status Reports

Standardized project status reports will be submitted by the Subproject Leads to each other and to the Super Team Manager. These reports will have to be consolidated by the Super Team Manager or a designated project administrator for submission to the various stakeholder groups, customers, and senior IT management.

Planning and Conducting Team Meetings

At the highest level there will be frequent (perhaps daily) meetings of the Subproject Leads chaired by the Super Team Manager. At the discretion of the Subproject Leads, they will hold meetings (probably daily) of their team members.

Processing Scope Change Requests

This is a complex task that must be managed by all of the Subproject Leads. You should expect that every change request will impact the schedule and resources of every team. The Super Team Manager is responsible for receiving, processing, and closing all scope change requests. As appropriate, members of the project team may be pressed into service by the Super Team Manager to analyze the request and report on the impact and alternative actions. This is no small task, as the master schedule and resource allocation must be considered. Given that there are cross-team dependencies, this task must be dealt with using the most intense due diligence.

Strengths

The direct and overall management authority of the Super Team Manager drives the many strengths of this organization.

Managed from a Single Integrated Plan

All parties to the project have participated in building and accepting the project plan and have some ownership of it. As a result, they have a vested interest in the project's success.

Integrated Resource Management Control

Resources are managed from a single pool, as team origin is not considered.

Standardizes on a Set of Tools, Templates, and Processes

The launch phase will include time for the team to decide on its operating rules as well as the set of tools, templates, and processes it will use. This is a great opportunity to press into service the best practices of a number of teams. Based on the nature of the project, some teams may have just the thing to be used.

Weaknesses

Eventually size becomes the enemy and the structure collapses upon itself. A good rule of thumb is to use a project team size of 30 as the trigger to move to the Project Office structure.

Establishing Standardization

From among all of the tools, templates, and processes used by any of the team members, a set of best practices should be chosen. While the variety of options is a strength initially, top closure on the set will require that the team members objectively assess the value and fit to the project, rather than push their own agendas.

Does Not Scale to Very Large Projects

At some point the structure becomes unwieldy and some type of Project Office structure should be used.

Team Members Must Manage Competing Priorities

In order to minimize the risk associated with competing priorities, team members should be assigned 100 percent to Super Team projects. This may not be possible for every team member, especially those with scarce skills.

Impact on the Project Life Cycle

Table 9-6 summarizes the preceding points by project phase.

Selecting Your Project Management Structure

Once the Project Overview Statement, or Project Charter, is in place and has been approved, it is time to start the planning process. At this point it is time to think about selecting the appropriate management structure for your newly assigned project. This is a critical decision and shouldn't be taken lightly. Above all, do not default to the pressure that will come from each team as it pushes to remain independent. As described in the following sections, several variables might impact your decision regarding the best management structure to establish.

Table 9-6 Impact of the Super Team on the Project Life Cycle

PHASE	ARTIFACT	SUMMARY COMMENT
Scoping	(1) Requirements Gathering	(1) Build integrated plan for conducting process
Planning	(1) WBS (2) Estimation (3) Dependency Diagrams (4) Project Schedule (5) Risk Management (6) Communications	(1) Straightforward (2) Straightforward (3) Straightforward (4) Straightforward (5) Straightforward (6) Straightforward
Launching	(1) Team operating rules (2) Work packages	(1) Straightforward (2) Maintain out of Super Team Manager's Office
Monitoring and Controlling	(1) Project performance reports (2) Scope change management (3) Problem resolution/escalation	(1) Coordinate from Super Team Manager's Office (2) Straightforward (3) Straightforward
Closing	(1) Requirements validation	(1) Straightforward

Complexity/Risk

Complexity and risk tend to be positively correlated. That is, usually they both increase or decrease in parallel with one another. The three project structures support increasing complexity and risk in the order Project Office, Core Team, and finally Super Team.

Number of Impacted/Involved Customer Areas

As the number of customer areas increases, the need for coordinating and consolidating disparate points of view also increases. Project size increases the complexity of the task. As the number of impacted/involved areas increases, the three structures should be employed in the order Core Team, Super Team, and finally Project Office. In other words, Core Team works best with smaller projects and Project Office works best with larger projects.

Number of Teams Involved

This is a more serious challenge than increasing numbers of impacted/involved customer areas. Each team brings with it its own tools, templates, and processes, which can present different and often conflicting approaches. The three structures accommodate a growing number of teams in the following order: Core Team, Super Team, and Project Office. This is the same order that applies for an increasing number of impacted/involved customer areas.

Total Project Team Size

This reduces to the number of management layers accommodated by the project team structure. The Core Team works best with smaller team sizes, followed by the Super Team, and finally the Project Office, which supports the largest team sizes. The Project Office accommodates additional layers of management far better than either of the other two structures. Even for the largest of projects there could be Project Offices within the overall Project Office structure.

Type of Systems Project (New, Enhanced)

The best structure for supporting a systems project is a function of the type of systems project. For new systems, my preferred ordering would be Core Team, Super Team, and finally Project Office. Because the system is new, requirements definition and development problems will arise along the way. The Core Team will be the best source of resolution, and their familiarity with the project makes that resolution more efficient and effective. The Super Team should have within its structure technically skilled members as well as business-savvy members. Because resource management is a trait of the Super Team, those resources can be allocated for maximum advantage. Finally, with the Project Office, because of the segregation of its team into independent sub-teams, there is little opportunity to respond organizationally to the issues that arise. Those issues will be handled but not in the most effective manner.

The enhancement projects are a different matter. Here the preferred ordering would be Super Team, Project Office, and finally Core Team. Super Team and Project Office could be interchanged for more comprehensive enhancement projects. The Super Team can be very focused on the exact parts of the system affected by the enhancements. Smaller teams would be the common practice. The Project Office would work well for larger enhancement projects, as more and varied expertise is required. It would be expected to have a wider impact across enterprise systems and hence the broader expertise needed on the team. Finally, in all cases that I can think of, using a Core Team for enhancement projects would be like killing mosquitoes with a sledgehammer — total overkill. There is no need to occupy the best for enhancement projects.

Resource Scarcity/Contention

For this variable you would order the choices from the one that is most accommodating of resource management to the one that is least accommodating. That means the preferred order would be Super Team, Core Team, Project Office. The Super Team ignores the point of origin of its team members. That gives the Super Team Manager the most latitude and flexibility to use the team members in the most effective manner without regard for the home organizational unit of a team member. Next in the order of decreasing flexibility would be the Core Team. Here the Core Team members themselves would be pressed into action to assist the Core Team Manager with resource assignments. Ordered last would be the Project Office, where the silo characteristics would burden the Project Office Manager with negotiations to get approval to move a resource across sub-project boundaries.

Criticality of the Deliverables

As criticality increases risk, containment becomes increasingly important to the Project Office Manager. You want to choose a project management structure that reduces and contains risk as much as possible. The recommended ordering would be Project Office, Core Team, and finally Super Team. In other words, as criticality increases, the tendency would be to move further down the list. The organizational boundaries created by the Project Office will compromise its ability to deal most effectively with critical projects; therefore, it is the choice when criticality is not a variable. The Core Team has the benefit of having subject matter experts on the team. They will be a good source for building the risk management plan. Because the Super Team is really one large team structured around the functionality of the solution, it would seem to provide the most concentrated focus on risk management. The added flexibility of being able to move resources across independent teams increases the viability of the risk management plan. Team members, as needed, add to the effectiveness of the risk mitigation strategies.

Need for an Integrated Project Plan

The ordering here is the same as for the criticality scenario. Ordering from least need for an integrated plan to the most need, the structures would be Project Office, Core Team, and finally Super Team. There is little difference between the Project Office and Core Team with respect to the need for an integrated project plan. Neither structure has one. The presence of the Core Team and the influence it will have over the team members distinguishes it from the Project Office structure; therefore, it might be able to better deal with a given need for the integrated plan. The Super Team is different. Because it is a cohesive single-team structure, it lends itself to the common practices of building a project plan and will therefore best handle the greater needs for an integrated plan.

Need for an Integrated Project Schedule

The ordering here will follow that of the need for an integrated project plan — Project Office, Core Team, and Super Team. The reason is quite obvious. Having an integrated plan means you have an integrated schedule.

Choosing a Management Structure

Table 9-7 summarizes the preceding discussion and can be used to choose the best-fit management structure for your project. In the table, L = Low, M = Medium, and H = High.

The table can be used as follows. Assess the project on each of the variables in terms of Low, Medium, and High. Table 9-8 shows a sample assessment. For the particular project being assessed, its complexity/risk is medium. That favors choosing a Core Team structure. The number of customer areas affected is low, which also favors choosing the Core Team structure. Once the table is complete, a decision must be made as to which team structure is a best fit.

Table 9-7 Project Characteristics Versus Risk for Each Project Organizational Structure

VARIABLES	PROJECT OFFICE	CORE TEAM	SUPER TEAM
Complexity/Risk	L	M	H
Number of customer areas	H	L	M
Number of teams involved	H	L	M
Total project team size	H	L	M
Type of project (new/enhanced)	M/M	L/L	H/H
Resource contention	L	M	H
Criticality of deliverables	L	H	M
Need for integrated plan	L	M	H
Need for integrated schedule	L	M	H

Table 9-8 Example Use of Table 9-7

VARIABLES	PROJECT OFFICE	CORE TEAM	SUPER TEAM
Complexity/Risk	L	**M**	H
Number of customer areas	H	**L**	M
Number of teams involved	H	**L**	M
Total project team size	H	L	**M**
Type of project (new/enhanced)	**M**/M	L/L	H/H
Resource contention	**L**	M	H
Criticality of deliverables	L	**H**	M
Need for integrated plan	L	M	**H**
Need for integrated schedule	L	M	**H**

Seldom will the results of the assessment point to a clear choice. What the assessment does do is indicate areas to which you should pay attention after having made a particular choice. In this example, the choice lies between Core Team and Super Team.

If you choose Core Team, you should be concerned about the following: Size may be a problem in that it might require a Core Team that is too large. If there is a workaround, then that variable can be ignored. The other area of concern will be the need for an integrated plan/schedule. Here the Core Team will have to be called into service during project planning. Their influence over the project teams will be important. They will have to sell the idea of an integrated plan and schedule and then help facilitate the planning session.

If your choice is Super Team, you should be concerned about the following: First of all, none of the variables will adversely affect project success. The downside of this choice is that you will often have difficulty bringing the independent teams into a cohesive unit. Does that outweigh the concerns if you had chosen the Core Team? You should be able to answer that question and hence make the best-fit decision.

Multiple-Team Projects in Summary

The multiple-team project scenario has become more prevalent in the past few years. Despite this prevalence, there are few resources to consult regarding how to handle such projects from a management perspective. It is hoped that this added section of *Effective Project Management* has filled some of that void. Don't assume that multiple-team projects are easy to handle. They aren't. It will take all of your energies as a leader and manager to bring a multiple-team project to successful conclusion.

I have introduced three management structures used by my clients. They have had mixed success. Several variables contributed to success or to failure. I have tried to identify those for you in this chapter. Although you should pay attention to the information provided here, don't look upon my suggestions as the silver-bullet solution. There is no silver bullet, just as there is no substitute for your creative leadership!

Putting It All Together

In this chapter I discussed the team, its membership, the skills needed of the members, and the rules that the team must follow as it goes about the work of the project. Even though you have done your best to put the team together and have set and agreed on the operating rules, much is yet to be done. The team needs to learn how to work together by actually working together. Mistakes will be made, procedures will not always be followed as intended, and the first few team meetings will be clumsy. Learning is taking place, and it must be allowed to do so. The team is passing through a stage called *norming*, where it is learning to work together as teams should. It is a natural phase of development. Unfortunately, you can't wait for the team to become a lean, mean machine. The work of the project must begin.

The next chapter describes how to monitor and report project progress against the plan, and the changes that you can expect as the project work is done.

Discussion Questions

1. You are the project manager. How would you balance your efforts to get the project done with your efforts to help team members use their work on the project to develop themselves professionally?

2. Your project managers have been able to communicate very effectively with all of your clients except one. Getting feedback from this client has always been a nagging problem. What should you do?

3. Identify projects from your past experience that would have benefited from each of the three multiple-team team structures. State your reasons why and describe any concerns that you would have had to face and what you would have done about them.

CASE STUDY – PLEASANTOWN PLAYGROUND PROJECT

4. For the Pleasantown Playground Project, what team structures would you choose and why?

CHAPTER 10

Monitoring and Reporting Project Progress

When you are drowning in numbers you need a system to separate the wheat from the chaff.
— Anthony Adams, Vice President, Campbell Soup Co.

If two lines on a graph cross, it must be important.
— Ernest F. Cooke, University of Baltimore

CHAPTER LEARNING OBJECTIVES

After reading this chapter, you will be able to:

◆ Understand the reasons for implementing controls on the project

◆ Track the progress of a project

◆ Determine an appropriate reporting plan

◆ Measure and analyze variances from the project plan

◆ Use Gantt charts to track progress and identify warning signs of schedule problems

◆ Construct and interpret milestone trend charts to detect trends in progress

◆ Use earned value analysis to detect trends in schedule and budget progress

◆ Integrate milestone trend charts and earned value analysis for further trend analysis

◆ Manage project status meetings

◆ Determine the appropriate corrective actions to restore a project to its planned schedule

(continued)

> **CHAPTER LEARNING OBJECTIVES** *(continued)*
>
> ◆ **Understand the change control process**
>
> ◆ **Manage problem escalation**
>
> ◆ **Reallocate resources to maintain the project schedule**
>
> ◆ **Explain change control across the project landscape**
>
> ◆ **Properly identify corrective measures and problem escalation strategies**

The project plan is a system. As such, it can get out of balance, and a get-well plan must be put in place to restore the system to equilibrium. The longer the project manager waits to put the fix in place, the longer it will take for the system to return to equilibrium. The controls are designed to discover out-of-balance situations early and put get-well plans in place quickly.

You can use a variety of reports as control tools. Most can be used in numeric and tabular form, but I suggest using graphics wherever possible. A well-done graphic is intuitive. It does not require a lengthy explanation and certainly doesn't require a lot of reading. Be cognizant of the fact that senior managers just don't have a lot of time to dwell on your report. Give them what they need as succinctly as possible. Graphics are particularly effective as part of your status report to management. Senior managers generally aren't interested in reading long reports only to find out that everything is on schedule. While they will be pleased that your project is on track, their time could have been spent on other pursuits that require their attention. When projects are not on schedule, they want to know so immediately and see what corrective action you plan to take.

Control versus Risk

At this point, you have put considerable effort into building and getting approval for a project plan that describes in great detail how you will accomplish the goal of the project. The project work has begun, and you want to make sure that it is progressing as planned. To do this, you will institute a number of reports that are designed to indicate exactly how well the project is doing with respect to the plan and how to correct variances from this plan. The first question to consider is the extent to which you want to maintain control through the reports you require.

Purpose of Controls

Controls are actions taken as a result of reports. When implemented, controls are designed to bring actual project status back into conformance with the project plan. These reports are designed to support control activities by drawing attention to certain aspects or characteristics of the project, such as planned versus actual schedule, trends in the schedule, and actual versus planned resource use.

I typically track performance levels, costs, and time schedules. There are three reasons to use reports in your project (Weiss and Wysocki, 1991):[1]

To track progress.   The project manager will want to use a periodic reporting system (at least biweekly, but weekly is best) that identifies the status of every activity scheduled for work since the last progress report. These reports summarize progress for the current period as well as cumulative progress for the entire project.

To detect variance from plan.   Variance reports are of particular importance to management. They are simple and intuitive, and they give managers an excellent tool by which to quickly assess the health of a project. To detect variance, the project manager needs to compare planned performance to actual performance. In larger projects (those with 50 or more activities), reports that indicate everything is on schedule and within the budget are music to the ears of the project manager, but these reports can be too long and boring. Exception reports, variance reports, and graphical reports give management the information necessary for decision making in a concise format.

To take corrective action.   To take corrective action, it is necessary to know where the problem is and to have that information in time to do something about it. Once significant variance from the plan is detected, the next step is to determine whether corrective action is needed and then act appropriately. In complex projects, this requires examining a number of what-ifs. When problems occur in the project, delays result and the project falls behind schedule. For the project to get back on schedule, resources might have to be reallocated. In larger projects, the computer can assist in examining a number of resource reallocation alternatives and help to pick the best solution.

High Control – Low Risk

There is a trade-off between the amount of control (through reports and their frequency) that you can achieve and the protection you buy against out-of-control situations that may arise undetected and, hence, unfavorably affect risk. Simply exerting more controls can reduce project risk.

Low Control – High Risk

At the other extreme, having no controls in place and just assuming that the project work will get done according to the plan is foolish. Critical to project

---

[1]Joseph W. Weiss and Robert K. Wysocki, *5-Phase Project Management: A Practical Planning and Implementation Guide* (Reading, Mass.: Addison Wesley, 1991).

success is knowing that the project is in trouble in time to formulate and implement a get-well plan. Answering the question "How long am I willing to wait before I find out that there is a problem?" may provide the clue about how much control to put in place. I analyze these situations with the milestone trend charts presented later in this chapter.

Balancing the Control System

It is very easy to get carried away with controls and reports. The more controls that are put in place, the lower the project risk, and the less likely it will be for the project to get in trouble. As Figure 10-1 shows, however, there is a point of diminishing returns. Cost aside, there is another impact to consider. To comply with the project controls, project team members will have to spend time preparing and defending progress reports. This subtracts from the time spent doing project work.

The project manager needs to strike a balance between the extent of the control system and the risk of unfavorable outcomes. Just as in the insurance industry, compare the cost of the policy against the dollar value of the loss that would result from the consequences. Figure 10-1 demonstrates the relationship between risk and control. Conceptually, there is a balance point that minimizes the total cost exposure for having chosen a particular level of control.

NOTE Control also implies rigidity and structure, both of which tend to stifle creativity. The project manager should allow the team members some latitude to exercise their individuality. The cost of the control must be weighed against the value of empowering team members to be proactive (hence risk takers).

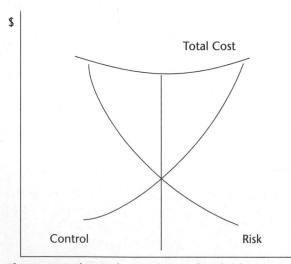

Figure 10-1 The total cost of control and risk

Control versus Quality

Quality does not happen by accident. It must be designed into the project management process. Chapter 2 discusses the Continuous Quality Management and Process Quality Management models. You might want to refer to Chapter 2 to review what those management models are and how they affect quality.

Fortunately, control and quality are positively correlated with each other. If you do not take steps to control the product and the process, you will not enjoy the benefits that quality brings to the equation.

Progress Reporting System

After project work is under way, you want to make sure that it proceeds according to plan. To do this, you need to establish a reporting system that keeps you informed of the many variables that describe how the project is proceeding as compared to the plan.

A reporting system has the following characteristics:

- Provides timely, complete, and accurate status information
- Doesn't add so much overhead time as to be counterproductive
- Is readily acceptable to the project team and senior management
- Warns of pending problems in time to take action
- Is easily understood by those who have a need to know

To establish this reporting system, you will want to look into the hundreds of reports that are standard fare in project management software packages. Once you decide what you want to track, these software tools offer several suggestions and standard reports to meet your needs. Most project management software tools enable you to customize their standard reports to meet even the most specific needs.

Types of Project Status Reports

There are five types of project status reports:

Current period reports.   These reports cover only the most recently completed period. They report progress on those activities that were open or scheduled for work during the period. Reports might highlight activities completed, and variance between scheduled and actual completion dates. If any activities did not progress according to plan, the report should include the reasons for the variance and the appropriate corrective measures that will be implemented to fix the schedule slippage.

Cumulative reports.   These reports contain the history of the project from the beginning to the end of the current report period. They are more informative than the current period reports because they show trends in project progress. For example, a schedule variance might be tracked over several successive periods to show improvement. Reports can be at the activity or project level.

Exception reports.   Exception reports indicate variances from plan. These reports are typically designed for senior management to read and interpret quickly. Reports that are produced for senior management merit special consideration. Senior managers do not have a lot of time to read reports that tell them that everything is on schedule and there are no problems serious enough to warrant their attention. In such cases, a one-page, high-level summary report that says everything is okay is usually sufficient. It might also be appropriate to include a more detailed report as an attachment for those who might want more information. The same might be true of exception reports. That is, the one-page exception report tells senior managers about variances from plan that will be of interest to them, while an attached report provides more details for the interested reader.

Stoplight reports.   Stoplight reports are a variation that can be used on any of the previous report types. I believe in parsimony in all reporting. Here is a technique you might want to try: When the project is on schedule and everything seems to be proceeding as planned, put a green sticker on the top right corner of the first page of the project status report. This sticker will signal to senior managers that everything is progressing according to plan, and they need not even read the attached report.

When the project has encountered a problem — schedule slippage, for example — you might put a yellow sticker on the top-right corner of the first page of the project status report. That is a signal to upper management that the project is not moving along as scheduled but that you have a get-well plan in place. A summary of the problem and the get-well plan may appear on the first page, but they can also refer to the details in the attached report. Those details describe the problem, the corrective steps that have been put in place, and some estimate of when the situation will be rectified.

Red stickers placed on the top-right corner of the first page signal that a project is out of control. Red reports should be avoided at all costs because they indicate that the project has encountered a problem for which you don't have a get-well plan or even a recommendation for upper management. Senior managers will obviously read these reports because they signal a major problem with the project. On a more positive note, the red condition may be beyond your control. For example, there is a major power grid failure on the East Coast and a number of companies have lost their computing systems. Your hot site is overburdened with companies looking for computing power. Your company is one of them, and the loss of computing power has put your project seriously behind in final system testing. There is little you can do to avoid such acts of nature.

Variance reports.   Variance reports do exactly what their name suggests — they report differences between what was planned and what actually happened. The report has three columns:

- The planned number
- The actual number
- The difference, or variance, between the two

A variance report can be in one of two formats:

- The first is numeric and displays a number of rows with each row giving the actual, planned, and variance variables for those variables requiring such calculations. Typical variables that are tracked in a variance report are schedule and cost. For example, the rows might correspond to the activities open for work during the report period, and the columns might be the planned cost to date, the actual cost to date, and the difference between the two. The impact of departures from plan is signified by larger values of this difference (the variance).

- The second format is a graphical representation of the numeric data. It might be formatted so that plan data is shown for each report period of the project, denoted with a curve of one color; the actual data is shown for each report period of the project and is denoted by a curve of a different color. The variance need not be graphed at all because it is merely the difference between the two curves at some point in time. One advantage of the graphic version of the variance report is that it shows any variance trend over the report periods of the project, whereas the numeric report generally shows data only for the current report period.

Typical variance reports are snapshots in time (the current period) of the status of an entity being tracked. Most variance reports do not include data points that report how the project reached that status. Project variance reports can be used to report project as well as activity variances. For the sake of the managers who will have to read these reports, I recommend that one report format be used regardless of the variable being tracked. Top management will quickly become comfortable with a reporting format that is consistent across all projects or activities within a project. It will make life a bit easier for the project manager, too.

There are five reasons why you should measure duration and cost variances:

- **Catch deviations from the curve early.** The cumulative actual cost or actual duration can be plotted against the planned cumulative cost or cumulative duration. As these two curves begin to display a variance from one another, the project manager should put corrective measures in place to bring the two curves together. This reestablishes the agreement between planned and actual performance. This topic is treated in detail later in the chapter in the section "Earned Value Analysis."

- **Dampen oscillation.** Planned versus actual performance should display a similar pattern over time. Wild fluctuations between the two are symptomatic of a project that is not under control. Such a project will get behind schedule or overspend in one period, be corrected in the next, and go out of control in the next report period. Variance reports can provide an early warning that such conditions are likely, giving the project manager an opportunity to correct the anomaly before it gets serious. Smaller oscillations are easier to correct than larger oscillations.

- **Allow early corrective action.** As just suggested, the project manager would prefer to be alerted to a schedule or cost problem early in the development of the problem, rather than later. Early problem detection may offer more opportunities for corrective action than later detection.

- **Determine weekly schedule variance.** In my experience, I have found that progress on activities open for work should be reported on a weekly basis. This is a good compromise on report frequency and gives the project manager the best opportunity for corrective action plans before a situation escalates to a point where it will be difficult to recover any schedule slippages.

- **Determine weekly effort (person hours/day) variance.** The difference between the planned effort and actual effort has a direct impact on both planned cumulative cost and the schedule. If the effort is less than planned, it may suggest potential schedule slippage if the person is not able to increase his or her effort on the activity in the following week. Alternatively, if the weekly effort exceeded the plan and the progress was not proportionately the same, a cost overrun situation may be developing.

Early detection of out-of-control situations is important. The longer you wait to discover a problem, the longer it will take for your solution to bring the project back to a stable condition.

How and What Information to Update

As input to each of these report types, activity managers and the project manager must report the progress made on all of those activities that were open for work (in other words, those that were to have work completed on them during the report period) during the period of time covered by the status report. Recall that your planning estimates of activity duration and cost were based on little or no information. Now that you have completed some work on the activity, you should be able to provide a better estimate of duration and cost. This is reflected in a reestimate of the work remaining to complete the activity. That update information should also be provided.

The following list describes what should actually be reported:

Determine a set period of time and day of week. The project team will have agreed on the day of the week and time of day by which all updated information is to be submitted. A project administrator or another team member is responsible for ensuring that all update information is on file by the report deadline.

Report actual work accomplished during this period. What was planned to be accomplished and what was actually accomplished are often two different things. Rather than disappoint the project manager, activity managers are likely to report that the planned work was actually accomplished. Their hope is to catch up by the next report period. Project managers need to verify the accuracy of the reported data, rather than simply accept it as accurate. Spot-checking on a random basis should be sufficient. If the activity was defined according to the completion criteria, as described in Chapter 2, verification should not be a problem.

Record historical data and reestimate remaining (in-progress work only). Two kinds of information are reported:

- All work completed prior to the report deadline is historical information. It enables variance reports and other tracking data to be presented and analyzed.

- The other kind of information is future-oriented. For the most part, this information consists of reestimates of duration and cost and estimates to completion (both cost and duration) of the activities still open for work.

Report start and finish dates. These are the actual start and end dates of activities started or completed during the report period.

Record days of duration accomplished and remaining. First reported is how many days have been spent so far working on this activity. The second number is based on the reestimated duration as reflected in the time-to-completion number.

Report resource effort (hours/day) spent and remaining (in-progress work only). Whereas the preceding numbers report calendar time, these two numbers report labor time over the duration of the activity. One reports labor completed over the duration accomplished. The other reports labor to be spent over the remaining duration.

Report percent complete. Percent complete is the most common method used to record progress because it is the way we tend to think about what has been done in reference to the total job to be completed. Percent complete isn't the best method to report progress, however, because it is a subjective evaluation. When you ask someone "What percent complete are you on this activity?" what goes through his or her mind? The first thing is most likely "What percent should I be?" followed closely by "What's a number that we can all be happy with?"

To calculate the percent complete for an activity, you need something quantifiable. At least three different approaches have been used to calculate the percent complete of an activity:

- Duration
- Resource work
- Cost

Each of these approaches would result in a different percent complete, so when we say percent complete, what measure are we referring to? If you focus on duration as the measure of percent complete, where did the duration value come from? The only value you have is the original estimate. You know that original estimates often differ from actual performance. If you were to apply a percent complete to duration, however, the only one you have to work with is the original estimated one. Therefore, percent complete is not a good metric.

My advice is to never ask for and never accept percent complete as input to project progress. Always use a calculation. Many software products will let you determine it as either an inputted value or a calculated value. The calculated value that I recommend is based on the number of tasks actually completed in the activity as a proportion of the number of tasks that currently define the activity. Recall that the task list for an activity is part of the work package description. Here you count only completed tasks. Tasks that are under way but not reported as complete may not be used in this calculation.

Frequency of Gathering and Reporting Project Progress

A logical frequency for reporting project progress is once a week, usually on Friday afternoon. For some projects, such as refurbishing a large jet airliner, progress is recorded after each shift, three times a day. I've seen others that were of such a low priority or long duration that they were updated once a month. For most projects, start gathering the information around noon on Friday. Let people extrapolate to the end of the workday.

Variances

Variances are deviations from plan. Think of a variance as the difference between what was planned and what actually occurred. There are two types of variances: positive variances and negative variances.

Positive Variances

Positive variances are deviations from plan indicating that an ahead-of-schedule situation has occurred or that an actual cost was less than a planned cost. This type of variance is good news to the project manager, who would rather hear that the project is ahead of schedule or under budget. Positive variances bring their own set of problems, however, which can be as serious as negative variances. Positive variances can result in rescheduling to bring the project to completion early, under budget, or both. Resources can be reallocated from ahead-of-schedule projects to behind-schedule projects.

Not all the news is good news, though. Positive variances also can result from schedule slippage! Consider budget. Being under budget means that not all dollars were expended, which may be the direct result of not having completed work that was scheduled for completion during the report period.

CROSS-REF I return to this situation later in the "Earned Value Analysis" section of this chapter.

Conversely, if the ahead-of-schedule situation is the result of the project team finding a better way or a shortcut to complete the work, the project manager will be pleased. This situation may result in a short-lived benefit, however. Getting ahead of schedule is great, but staying ahead of schedule presents another kind of problem. To stay ahead of schedule, the project manager must negotiate changes to the resource schedule. Given the aggressive project portfolios in place in most companies, it is unlikely that resource schedule changes can be made. In the final analysis, being ahead of schedule may be a myth.

Negative Variances

Negative variances are deviations from plan that indicate that a behind-schedule situation has occurred or that an actual cost was greater than a planned cost. Being behind schedule or over budget is not what the project manager or reporting manager wants to hear. Negative variances, like positive variances, are not necessarily bad news. For example, you might have overspent because you accomplished more work during the report period than was planned. In overspending during this period, however, you could have accomplished the work at less cost than was originally planned. You can't tell by looking at the variance report.

CROSS-REF More details are forthcoming on this topic in the "Earned Value Analysis" section later in this chapter.

In most cases, negative time variances affect project completion only when they are associated with critical-path activities or when the schedule slippage on noncritical-path activities exceeds the activity's total float. Minor variances use up the float time for that activity; more serious ones will cause a change in the critical path.

Negative cost variances can result from uncontrollable factors such as cost increases from suppliers or unexpected equipment malfunctions. Some negative variances can result from inefficiencies or error. I discuss a problem escalation strategy to resolve such situations later in this chapter.

Applying Graphical Reporting Tools

As mentioned earlier in the chapter, senior managers may have only a few minutes of uninterrupted time to digest your report. Respect that time. They won't be able to fully read and understand your report if they have to read 15 pages before they get any useful information. Having to read several pages only to find out that the project is on schedule is frustrating and a waste of valuable time.

Gantt Charts

As discussed in Chapters 4 and 6, a *Gantt chart* is one of the most convenient, most frequently used, and easy-to-grasp depictions of project activities that I have encountered. The chart is formatted as a two-dimensional representation of the project schedule, with activities shown in the rows and time shown across the horizontal axis. It can be used during planning, for resource scheduling, and for status reporting. The only downside to using Gantt charts is that they do not contain dependency relationships. Some project management software tools provide an option to display these dependencies, but the result is a graphical report that is so cluttered with lines representing the dependencies that the report is next to useless. In some cases, dependencies can be guessed at from the Gantt chart, but in most cases, they are lost.

Figure 10-2 shows a representation of the Cost Containment Project as a Gantt chart, using the format that I prefer. The format shown is from Microsoft Project, but it is typical of the format used in most project management software packages.

Milestone Trend Charts

Milestones are significant events that you wish to track in the life of the project. These significant events are zero-duration activities and merely indicate that a certain condition exists in the project. For example, a milestone event might be the approval of several different component designs. This event consumes no time in the project schedule. It simply reflects the fact that those approvals have all been granted. The completion of this milestone event may be the predecessor of several build-type activities in the project plan. Milestone events are planned into the project in the same way that activities are planned into the project. They typically have FS relationships with the activities that are their predecessors and their successors.

Figure 10-3 shows a milestone trend chart for a hypothetical project. The trend chart plots the difference between the planned and estimated date of a project milestone at each project report period. In the original project plan, the milestone is planned to occur at the ninth month of the project. That is the last project month on this milestone chart. The horizontal lines represent one, two, and three standard deviations above or below the forecasted milestone date. Any activity in the project has an expected completion date that is approximately normally distributed. The mean and variance of its completion date are a function of the longest path to the activity from the report date. In this example, the units of measure are one month. For this project, the first project report (at month 1) shows that the new forecasted milestone date will be one week later than planned. At the second project report date (month 2 of the project), the milestone date is forecasted on target. The next three project reports indicate a slippage to two weeks late, then three weeks late, then four weeks late, and finally six weeks late (at month 6 of the project). In other words, the milestone is forecasted to occur six weeks late, and only three more project months remain in which to recover the slippage. Obviously, the project is in trouble. It appears to be drifting out of control, and in fact it is. Some remedial action is required of the project manager.

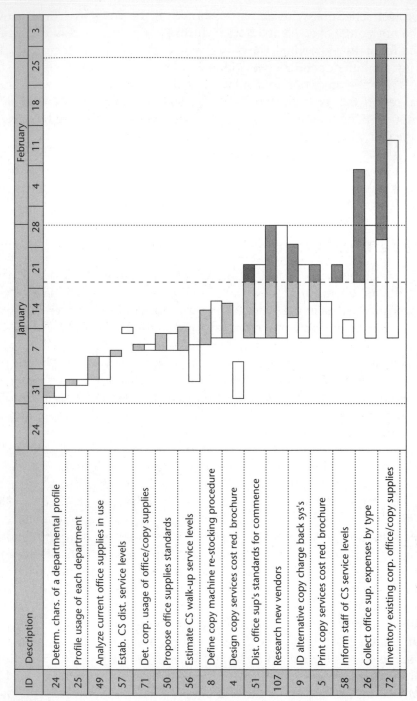

Figure 10-2 Gantt chart project status report

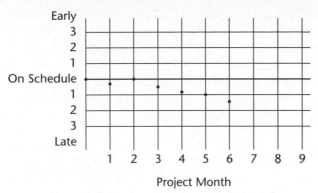

Figure 10-3 A run up or down of four or more successive data points

Certain patterns signal an out-of-control situation. These patterns are shown in Figures 10-3 through 10-6 and are described here:

Successive slippages. Figure 10-3 depicts a project that is drifting out of control. Each report period shows additional slippage since the last report period. Four such successive occurrences, however minor they may seem, require special corrective action on the part of the project manager.

Radical change. Figure 10-4, while it does show the milestone to be ahead of schedule, reports a radical change between report periods. Activity duration may have been grossly overestimated. There may be a data error. In any case, the situation requires further investigation.

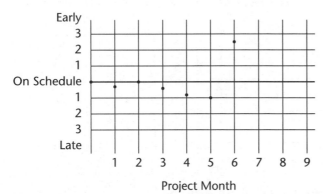

Figure 10-4 A change of more than three standard deviations

Successive runs. Figure 10-5 signals a project that may have encountered a permanent schedule shift. In the example, the milestone date seems to be varying around one month ahead of schedule. Barring any radical shifts and the availability of resources over the next two months, the milestone will probably be reached one month early. Remember that you have negotiated for a resource schedule in these two months, and now you will be trying to renegotiate an accelerated schedule.

Schedule shift. Figure 10-6 depicts a major shift in the milestone schedule. The cause must be isolated and the appropriate corrective measures taken. One possibility is the discovery that a downstream activity will not be required. Perhaps the project manager can buy a deliverable, rather than build it, and remove the associated build activities from the project plan.

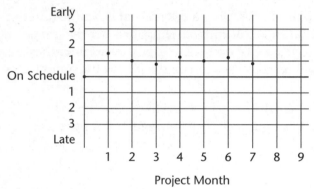

Figure 10-5 Seven or more successive data points above or below the planned milestone date

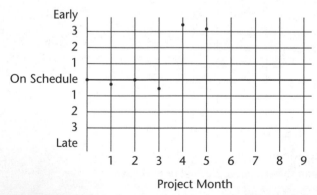

Figure 10-6 Two successive data points outside three standard deviations from the planned milestone date

Earned Value Analysis

Earned Value Analysis (EVA) is used to measure project performance and, by tradition, uses the dollar value of work as the metric. As an alternative, resource person hours/day can be used in cases where the project manager does not directly manage the project budget. Actual work performed is compared against planned and budgeted work expressed in these equivalents. These metrics are used to determine schedule and cost variances for both the current period and the cumulative to date period. Cost and resource person hours/day are not good, objective indicators with which to measure performance or progress. Unfortunately, there is no other good objective indicator. Given this, you are left with dollars or person hours/day, which you are at least familiar working with in other contexts. Either one by itself does not tell the whole story. You need to relate them to each other.

One drawback that these metrics have is that they report history. Although they can be used to make extrapolated predictions for the future, they primarily provide a measure of the general health of the project, which the project manager can correct as needed to restore the project to good health.

Figure 10-7 shows an S curve, which represents the baseline progress curve for the original project plan. It can be used as a reference point. That is, you can compare your actual progress to date against the curve and determine how well the project is doing. Again, progress can be expressed as either dollars or person hours/day.

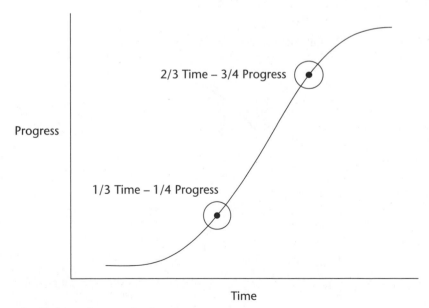

Figure 10-7 The standard S curve

By adding the actual progress curve to the baseline curve, you can now see the current status versus the planned status. Figure 10-8 shows the actual progress curve to be below the planned curve. If this represented dollars, you might be tempted to assume the project is running under budget. Is that really true?

Projects rarely run significantly under budget. A more common reason for the actual curve to be below the baseline is that activities that should have been done have not been, and thus the dollars or person hours/day that were planned to be expended are unused. The possible schedule variance is highlighted in Figure 10-9.

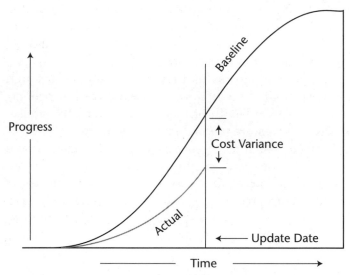

Figure 10-8 Baseline versus actual cost curve illustrating cost variance

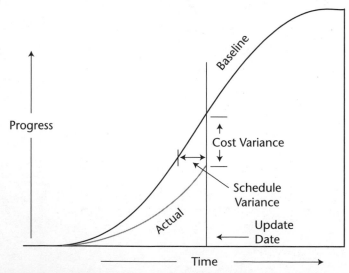

Figure 10-9 Baseline versus actual cost illustrating schedule variance

To determine actual progress schedule variance, you need some additional information. Earned Value Analysis (EVA) comprises three basic measurements: budgeted cost of work scheduled, budgeted cost of work performed, and actual cost of work performed. These measurements result in two variance values: schedule variance and cost variance. Figure 10-10 is a graphical representation of the three measurements.

The figure shows a single activity that has a five-day duration and a budget of $500. The budget is prorated over the five days at an average daily value of $100. The left panel of Figure 10-10 shows an initial (baseline) schedule with the activity starting on the first day of the week (Monday) and finishing at the end of the week (Friday). The budgeted $500 value of the work is planned to be accomplished within that week. This is the planned value (PV). The center panel shows the actual work that was done. Note that the schedule slipped and work did not begin until the third day of the week. Using an average daily budget of $100, you see that you were able to complete only $300 of the scheduled work. This is the earned value (EV). The rightmost panel shows the actual schedule, as in the center panel, but now you see the actual dollars that were spent to accomplish the three days' work. This $400 is the actual cost (AC).

The PV, EV, and AC are used to compute and track two variances. The first is *schedule variance (SV)*. SV is the difference between the EV and the PV, which is –$200 (EV – PV) for this example. That is, the SV is the schedule difference between what was done and what was planned to be done, expressed in dollar or person hours/day equivalents. The second is *cost variance (CV)*. CV is the difference between the EV and the AC, which is $100 in this example. That is, you overspent by $100 (AC – EV) the cost of the work completed.

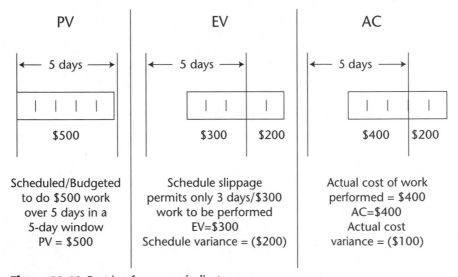

Figure 10-10 Cost/performance indicators

EARNED VALUE ANALYSIS TERMINOLOGY

For those who are familiar with the older cost/schedule control terminology, I have used the new terminology as defined in PMBOK 2000. The old terminology corresponds to the new terminology as follows:

◆ ACWP is the actual cost (AC).

◆ BCWP is the earned value (EV).

◆ BCWS is the planned value (PV).

Management might react positively to the information shown in Figure 10-8, but they might also be misled by such data. The full story is told by comparing both budget variance and schedule variance, shown in Figure 10-11.

To correctly interpret the data shown in Figure 10-9, you need to add the EV data shown in Figure 10-10 to produce Figure 10-11. Comparing the EV curve with the PV curve, you see that you have underspent because all of the work that was scheduled has not been completed. Comparing the EV curve to the AC curve also indicates that you overspent for the work that was done. Clearly, management would have been misled by Figure 10-8 had they ignored the data in Figure 10-10. Either one by itself may be telling a half-truth.

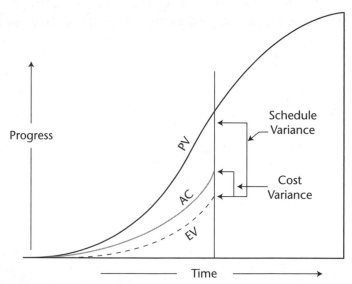

Figure 10-11 The full story

In addition to measuring and reporting history, EVA can be used to predict the future status of a project. Take a look at Figure 10-12. By cutting the PV curve at the height from the horizontal axis, which has been achieved by the EV, and then pasting this curve onto the end of the EV curve, you can extrapolate the completion of the project. Note that this is based on using the original estimates for the remaining work to be completed. If you continue at the rate at which you have been progressing, you will finish beyond the planned completion date. Doing the same thing for the AC shows that you will finish over budget. This is the simplest method of attempting to "estimate to completion," but it clearly illustrates that a significant change needs to occur in the way this project is running.

The three basic indicators yield an additional level of analysis for you. *Schedule performance index (SPI)* and *cost performance index (CPI)* are further refinements computed as follows:

```
SPI = EV/PV
CPI = EV/AC
```

Schedule performance index.   The schedule performance index is a measure of how close the project is to performing work as it was actually scheduled. If you are ahead of schedule, EV will be greater than PV, and therefore the SPI will be greater than 1. Obviously, this is desirable. Conversely, an SPI below 1 indicates that the amount of work performed was less than the work scheduled — not a good thing.

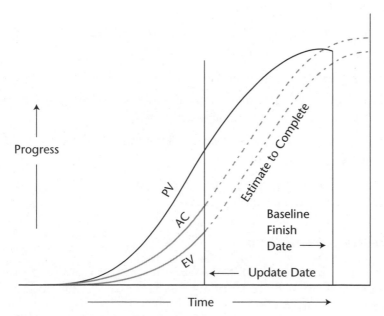

Figure 10-12 PV, EV, and AC curves

Cost performance index. The cost performance index is a measure of how close the project is to spending on the work performed to what was planned to have been spent. If you are spending less on the work performed than was budgeted, the CPI will be greater than 1. If not, and you are spending more than was budgeted for the work performed, then the CPI will be less than 1.

Some managers prefer this type of analysis because it is intuitive and quite simple to equate each index to a baseline of 1. Any value less than 1 is undesirable; any value over 1 is good. These indices are displayed graphically as trends compared against the baseline value of 1.

Integrating Milestone Trend Charts and Earned Value Analysis

Both milestone trend charts and earned value can easily be accommodated within the project life cycle. All of these metrics can be used to track practice-level improvements resulting from a process improvement program. After all, they are where the rubber meets the road.

NOTE This section is adapted from an earlier book of mine, *Effective Software Project Management* (Wiley, 2006).

Integrating Earned Value

At each report date, tasks that are open for work or were scheduled to be open for work can be in one of three situations:

- They are complete and hence have accrued 100 percent value.
- They are still open for work and hence have accrued a percentage of value equal to the proportion of subtasks completed.
- They are still open for work, and no subtasks are completed; hence, they have accrued 0 percent value.

Add all of the accrued value since the last report date to the cumulative project total. Display that data on the baseline S curve.

Integrating Milestone Trend Data

At each report date, the task managers of tasks that are open for work or were scheduled to be open for work should update the project file. The update information will indicate the following:

- The task is reported as complete as of a certain date.

- A certain percentage of the task work is complete (same as earned value report mentioned previously) and an updated estimate to completion is also given.

- No progress is reported.

If project management software is used, the software produces an updated project file with new forecasted dates for the milestones you are tracking. The presentation of the SPI and CPI data over time can be represented using the same format that was used to report milestone trend data. Three examples follow.

Figure 10-13 depicts a common situation. Here the project has gotten behind schedule (denoted by the "S" in the figure) while at the same time being under budget (denoted by the "C" in the figure). That is probably due to the fact that work that was scheduled has not been done and hence the labor costs associated with those tasks have not been incurred.

On rare occasions you might experience the situation shown in Figure 10-14. The project is ahead of schedule and under budget. Less costly ways were found to complete the work, and the work was completed in less time than was planned. If this should ever happen to you, relish the moment. Take whatever kudos your customer or management cares to heap on you. You deserve their accolades. They don't happen often.

Figure 10-15 is the worst of the worst. Nothing more need be said.

Project: ALPHA

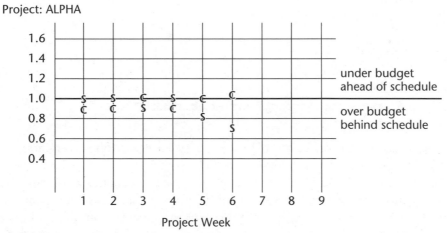

Figure 10-13 A project that is under budget and behind schedule

Project: BETA

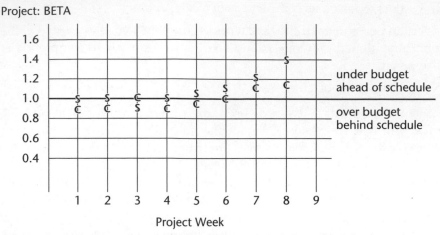

Figure 10-14 A project that is under budget and ahead of schedule

Project: GAMMA

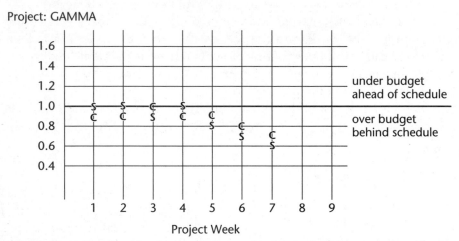

Figure 10-15 A project that is over budget and behind schedule

The same approach can be used to track a project portfolio over time, as shown in Figure 10-16.

The graph shows the SPI values of the individual projects that comprise the portfolio. This will also be a useful graphic for summarizing the practice changes from your process improvement program. If a clear trend is visible at the portfolio level, it is indicative of a successful transition from process to practice.

Portfolio: DELTA Program

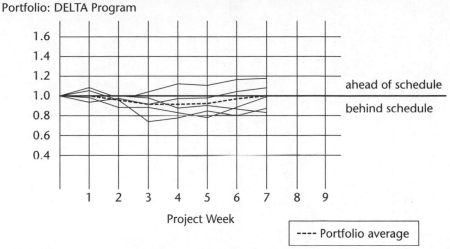

Figure 10-16 Adapting the life cycle for a project portfolio schedule

CROSS-REF Using SPI and CPI values to watch trends in this manner is discussed in more detail in Chapter 20.

Using the WBS to Report Project Status

Because the Work Breakdown Structure (WBS) shows the hierarchical structure of the work to be done, it can be used for status reporting, too. In its simplest form, each activity box can be shaded to reflect completion percentages. As lower-level activities are completed, the summary activities above them can be shaded to represent percent complete data. Senior managers will appreciate knowing that major parts of the project are complete. Unfortunately, the WBS does not contain scheduling or sequencing information. To the extent that this adds to the value of the report, narrative data or brief tabular data can be added to the report. Figure 10-17 shows an example status report using the WBS.

Although this report is rather intuitive, it does not contain much detail. It would have to be accompanied by an explanatory note with schedule and cost detail.

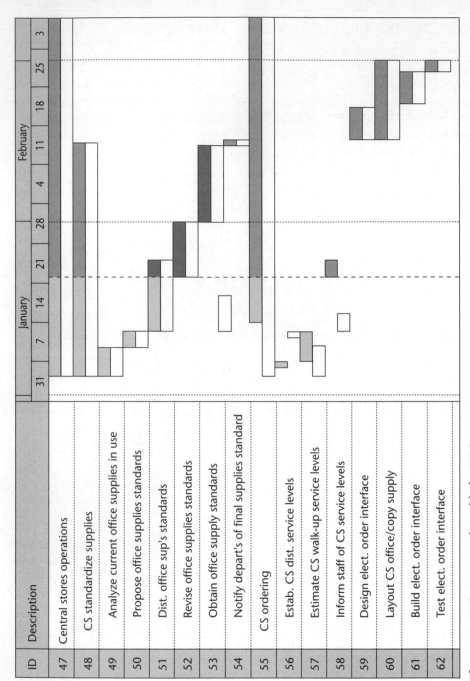

Figure 10-17 Status reporting with the WBS

Deciding on Report Level of Detail

I am often asked questions about the level of detail and the frequency of reporting in regard to project status reports. My feeling is that the more you report, the more likely it is that someone will object or find some reason to micromanage your project. This section examines this issue in more detail by considering the reporting requirements at the activity manager, project manager, and senior manager levels.

Activity Manager

The activity manager will want the most detailed and granular information available. After all, the activity manager is directly responsible for getting the work done. Because he or she manages the resources that are used to complete project work, the activity manager will want to know what happened, what was scheduled to happen, who did what (or didn't do what), why it happened as it did, what problems have arisen, what solutions are within reach, and what changes need to be made. Reports that reflect very detailed information are of use to the activity manager and the project manager but, because of that detail, are of little value to anyone outside of the project team.

Project Manager

The project manager is concerned with the status information for all activities open for work during the report period. Activity reports are for the use of the project manager, who may decide to pass them forward to senior management in his or her report. The activity-level reports can follow a format similar to project-level reports.

Reports for the project manager present data at the activity level and show effects on the project schedule. If project management software is used, the posted data from the activity managers is used to update the project schedule and produce reports on overall project status. Any slippage at the activity level ripples through the successor activities, triggers a new activity schedule, and recomputes project completion dates. These reports display all scheduling information, including float and resource schedule data. In effect, they become working documents for the project manager for schedule adjustments and problem resolution. Because these reports are at a very detailed level, they are not appropriate for distribution beyond the project team. In many cases, they may be for the project manager's eyes only.

Senior Management

I recommend using a graphical exception report structure to report project status to senior management. For many projects, reports at the activity level will be appropriate. For large projects, either milestone-level or summary-task-level reports are more effective. Senior managers have only a few minutes to review any single project report. Keeping a report to a single page is a good strategy. The best report format, in my experience, is the Gantt chart. These charts require little explanation. Activities should be listed in the order of scheduled start date; a line designating the report date should be given; and all percent completed work should be displayed.

TIP If the project is sick, attach a one-page get-well plan to your report. This plan usually is in the form of a narrative discussion of the problem, alternative solutions, recommended action, and any other details relevant to the issue at hand.

Managing Project Status Meetings

To keep close track of progress on the project, the project manager needs information from his or her team on a timely basis. This information will be provided during a project status meeting. At a minimum, you need to have a status meeting at least once a week. On some of the major projects on which I've worked, daily status meetings were the norm for the first few weeks, and then as the need for daily information wasn't as critical, I switched to twice a week and finally to weekly status.

Who Should Attend?

To use the status meetings correctly and efficiently, it's important to figure out who should be in attendance. This information should be a part of your communication plan.

When choosing who should attend, keep a couple of points in mind:

- At first your status team may have a tendency to include people who are needed only in the planning phase. If they don't have a need to know the information, don't make them come to a meeting and sit there without a good reason. You are going to put out meeting minutes anyway, so those people who aren't needed at the actual meeting will get the minutes anyway.

- There will be times in a status meeting when two people get into a discussion and the other people in the meeting aren't needed. If this happens, ask them to conduct a sidebar meeting so that your own status meeting can continue. A *sidebar meeting* is one in which a limited number of people need to participate, and these types of meetings can be done more effectively away from your status meeting. Having everyone in the room listen to these sidebar topics isn't useful.

Ask the people who are going to the sidebar meeting to let you know what happens in the meeting, particularly if what they talk about affects the project. If possible, get a meeting summary from the people, even if it's only a sentence or two long. Circulate this summary to the rest of the team with your minutes so that everyone on the team is kept up-to-date. Typical attendees at sidebar meetings will be the people who must have the problem solved and those who should be able to solve it, or at least those who can escalate it to those who can solve it.

When Are They Held?

Usually, status meetings are held toward the end of the week. Whatever the day, make sure it's the same one each week. People get used to preparing information for a status meeting if they know exactly when the meeting will occur.

What Is Their Purpose?

You hold a status meeting to get information to the whole team. It may be that on large projects the participants in the status meeting are actually representatives of their department. You can't have all the people on a 250-person project team come into a meeting once a week, so make sure that someone is there to represent the rest of the people in their section. The purpose of the meeting is to encourage the free flow of information, and that means ensuring that the people who need to have information to do their jobs get the information at the status meeting. Remember once again that you are going to distribute minutes of the meeting later, so that will take care of the people who aren't in attendance.

TIP Project size may be the determining factor of length, but in general I prefer a one-hour limit. This is the maximum, and an entire hour should not be necessary at every project status meeting. Good judgment is needed here; don't waste people's time.

What Is Their Format?

While the format of the status review meetings should be flexible, as project needs dictate, certain items are part of every status meeting. I recommend that you proceed in a top-down fashion:

1. The project champion reports any changes that may have a bearing on the future of the project.

2. The customer reports any changes that may have a bearing on the future of the project.

3. The project manager reports on the overall health of the project and the impact of earlier problems, changes, and corrective actions as they impact at the project level.

4. Activity managers report on the health of activities open or scheduled open for work since the last status meeting.

5. Activity managers of future activities report on any changes since the last meeting that might impact project status.

6. The project manager reviews the status of open problems from the last status meeting.

7. Attendees identify new problems and assign responsibility for their resolution (the only discussion allowed here is for clarification purposes).

8. The project champion, customer, or project manager, as appropriate, offers closing comments.

9. The project manager announces the time and place of the next meeting and adjourns the meeting.

Minutes are part of the formal project documentation and are taken at each meeting, circulated for comment, revised as appropriate, distributed, and filed in the project notebook (electronic, I hope). Because there is little discussion, the minutes contain any handouts from the meeting and list the items assigned for the next meeting. The minutes should also contain the list of attendees, a summary of comments made, and assigned responsibilities.

A project administrative support person should be present at the project status review meetings to take minutes and monitor handouts. The responsibility might also be passed around to the project team members. In some organizations, the same person is responsible for distributing the meeting agenda and materials ahead of time for review. This advance distribution is especially important if decisions will be made during the meeting. People are very uncomfortable when they are given important information for the first time and are expected to read and understand it, and then make a decision about it, all at the same time.

Managing Change

It is difficult for anyone, regardless of his or her skills at prediction and fore-casting, to completely and accurately define the needs for a product or service that will be implemented 6, 12, or 18 months in the future. Competition, customer reactions, technology changes, a host of supplier-related situations, and many other factors could render a killer application obsolete before it can be implemented. The most frequent situation starts something like this: "Oh, I forgot to tell you that we will also need . . ." or "I just found out that we have to go to market no later than the third quarter instead of the fourth quarter." How often have you heard sentences that start something like those examples? Face it: Change is a way of life in project management. You might as well confront it and be prepared to act accordingly.

Because change is constant, a good project management methodology has a change management process in place. In effect, the change management process has you plan the project again. Think of it as a mini-JPP session.

Two documents are part of every good change management process: the project change request and the project impact statement:

Project change request.   The first principle to learn is that *every change is a significant change*. Adopt that maxim and you will seldom go wrong. What that means is that every change requested by the customer must be documented in a *project change request*. That document might be as simple as a memo but might also follow a format provided by the project team. In any case, it is the start of another round of establishing Conditions of Satisfaction. Only when the request is clearly understood can the project team evaluate the impact of the change and determine whether the change can be accommodated.

Project Impact Statement.   The response to a change request is a document called a *Project Impact Statement*. It is a response that identifies the alternative courses of action that the project manager is willing to consider. The requestor is then charged with choosing the best alternative. The Project Impact Statement describes the feasible alternatives that the project manager was able to identify, the positive and negative aspects of each, and perhaps a recommendation as to which alternative might be best. The final decision rests with the requestor.

Six possible outcomes can result from a change request:

It can be accommodated within the project resources and timelines.
This is the simplest of situations for the project manager to handle. After considering the impact of the change on the project schedule, the project manager decides that the change can be accommodated without any harmful effect on the schedule and resources.

It can be accommodated but will require an extension of the deliverable schedule.   The only impact that the change will have is to lengthen the deliverable schedule. No additional resources will be needed to accommodate the change request.

It can be accommodated within the current deliverable schedule, but additional resources will be needed.   To accommodate this change request, the project manager will need additional resources, but otherwise the current and revised schedule can be met.

It can be accommodated, but additional resources and an extension of the deliverable schedule will be required.   This change request will require additional resources and a lengthened deliverable schedule.

It can be accommodated with a multiple release strategy and prioritizing of the deliverables across the release dates.   This situation comes up more often than you might expect. To accommodate the change request, the project plan will have to be significantly revised, but there is an alternative. For example, suppose that the original request was for a list of 10 features, and they are in the current plan. The change request asks for an additional two features. The project manager asks the customer to prioritize all 12 features. He or she will give the customer eight of them earlier than the delivery date for the original 10 features and will deliver the remaining four features later than the delivery date for the original 10. In other words, the project manager will give the customer some of what is requested earlier than requested and the balance later than requested. I have seen several cases where this compromise has worked quite well.

It cannot be accommodated without a significant change to the project. These change requests are significant. They are so significant, in fact, as to render the current project plan obsolete. There are two alternatives here. The first is to deny the change request, complete the project as planned, and handle the request as another project. The other is to call a stop to the current project, replan the project to accommodate the change, and launch a new project.

An integral part of the change control process is documentation. I strongly suggest that every change be treated as a major change until proven otherwise. To not do so is to court disaster. That means every change request follows the same procedure. Figure 10-18 is an example of the steps in a typical change process. The process is initiated, and the change request is submitted by the customer, who uses a form like the one shown in Figure 10-19. This form is forwarded to the manager or managers charged with reviewing such requests. They may either accept the change as submitted or return it to the customer for rework and resubmission. Once the change request has been accepted, it is forwarded to the project manager, who performs an impact study.

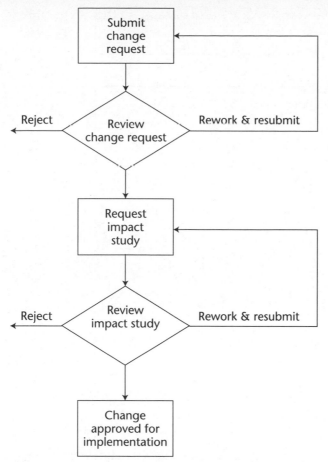

Figure 10-18 A typical change control process

The impact study involves looking at the project plan, assessing how the change request impacts the plan, and issuing the impact study, which is forwarded to the management group for final disposition. They may return it to the project manager for further analysis and recommendations or reject it and notify the customer of their action. The project manager reworks the impact study and returns it to the management group for final disposition. If they approve the change, the project manager will implement it into the project plan.

Project Name
Change Requested By
Date Change Requested
Description of Change
Business Justification
Action
Approved by   Date

Figure 10-19 Change control form

Change Control and the Project Life Cycles

Change has always been viewed with disdain by the traditional project manager and rightly so. Of course, change will not go away just because you don't like it. Change is constant and to think otherwise is foolish. The mark of an effective project manager is learning how to accommodate change within the context of the project management process being used. This section briefly describes each of the five approaches and how change management is handled by each one.

Linear Approaches

This approach is chosen based on the assumption that requirements have been completely and clearly defined and documented. As a result, there should be very little change. If that is not the case and there is a continual stream of change requests from the customer, the project plan and schedule will be severely affected. To minimize the potential impact, a contingency should be put in the schedule, along with a budget to accommodate change should it occur. If there are too many change requests, you might consider changing to an Incremental or Iterative approach. They can accommodate change much better than the Linear approach.

Incremental Approaches

The assumptions here are the same as in the Linear approach. If change requests are forthcoming, they might be handled in the interim between increments, and the plan adjusted going forward. The schedule and budget will still be affected unless there is some prioritization of remaining functions and features that will absorb the change requests.

Iterative Approaches

As you move from certainty toward uncertainty in requirements specification, this is the first approach you encounter that is designed to handle change requests. In fact, they are expected. Most of the change requests arise from the need to clarify functions and features that were not completely or clearly defined during requirements gathering. The schedule and budget should have contingencies to cover such discovery.

Adaptive Approaches

This approach was chosen based on the assumption that some functionality and features have not been identified during requirements gathering and therefore change requests will arise during iteration to complete the requirements. Unlike those that are merely expected, as is the case with the Iterative approach, change requests are required in the Adaptive approach. Change is the only way to get to a complete and acceptable solution. Change requests are discussed during the client checkpoint and prioritized with other features and functions development for later cycles.

Extreme Approaches

In the Extreme approach you are dealing with the most uncertainty, and change to functions and features is also accompanied by changes to scope. Change requests may change the entire direction of the project. The Extreme approach is built on constant change. This is the complete opposite of the Linear approach. While here the focus is on Linear and Incremental change management, there is a counterpart in the Iterative, Adaptive, and Extreme approaches. These are discussed in Chapter 17.

Managing Problem Escalation

Something has happened that put the project plan at risk. Late shipments from suppliers, equipment malfunction, sickness, random acts of nature, resignations, priority changes, errors, and a host of other factors can lead to problems that affect deliverables, deliverable schedules, and resource schedules. The project manager owns the problem and must find a solution.

This situation is very different for the project manager than the case of a change request. When a change request has been made, the project manager has some leverage with the customer. The customer wants something and might be willing to negotiate to an acceptable resolution. That is not the case when a problem arises on the project team. The project manager does not have any leverage and is in a much more difficult position.

When the unplanned happens, the project manager needs to determine the extent of the problem and take the appropriate corrective measures. Minor variations from plan will occur and may not require corrective measures. There are degrees of corrective measures available to the project manager: In trying to resolve a problem, the project manager begins at the top of the following list and works down the list, examining each option until one is found that solves the problem.

There are three levels of escalation strategy: project manager–based, resource manager–based, and customer-based.

Project manager–based strategies.   If the problem occurs within a non-critical-path activity, it can be resolved by using the free float. One example is to reschedule the activity later in its ES to LF window or extend the duration to use some of the free float. Note that this strategy does not affect any other activities in the project. By using total float, you affect the resource schedule for all activities that have this one as a predecessor. Another approach is to continue the schedule compression techniques employed in defining the original project plan. This strategy can affect resource schedules just as in the prior case. The last option open to the project manager is to consider the resource pool under his or her control. Can some resources be reassigned from noncritical-path activities to assist with the problem activity?

Resource manager–based strategies. After the project manager has exhausted all the options under his or her control, it is time to turn to the resource managers for additional help. This help may take the form of additional resources or rescheduling of already committed resources. Expect to make a trade-off here. For example, you might be accommodated now, but at the sacrifice of later activities in the project. At least you have bought some time to resolve the downstream problem that will be created by solving this upstream problem. If the project manager has other projects under way, some trades across projects may solve the problem.

Customer-based strategies. When all else fails, the project manager will have to approach the customer. The first option would be to consider any multiple-release strategies. Delivering some functionality ahead of schedule and the balance later than planned may be a good starting point. The last resort is to ask for an extension of time. This may not be as unpleasant as it seems because the customer's schedule may have also slipped and the customer may be relieved to have a delay in your deliverable schedule, too.

The Escalation Strategy Hierarchy

Our problem escalation strategy is based on the premise that the project manager will try to solve the problem with the resources he or she controls. Failing to do that, the project manager will appeal to resource managers. As a last resort, the project manager will appeal to the customer.

One thing to note here that is very different from the change request situation discussed previously is the leverage to negotiate. As mentioned, the project manager has leverage when the customer has requested a change, but no leverage when he or she has a project problem to solve. The customer has nothing to gain and is therefore less likely to be cooperative. In most cases, the problem can be reduced to how to recover lost time. Six outcomes are possible to this problem situation:

No action required (schedule slack will correct the problem). In this case, the slippage involved a noncritical-path activity and it will self-correct.

Examine FS dependencies for schedule compression opportunities. Recall that you originally compressed the schedule to accommodate the requested project completion date by changing FS dependencies to SS dependencies. The project manager should use that same strategy again. The project schedule will have changed several times since work began, and there may be several new opportunities to accomplish further compression and solve the current problem.

Reassign resources from noncritical-path activities to correct the slippage.   Up to a point, the project manager controls the resources assigned to this project and others that he or she manages. The project manager may be able to reassign resources from noncritical-path activities to the activities that have slipped. These noncritical-path activities may be in the same project in which the slippage occurred or they may be in another project managed by the same project manager.

Negotiate additional resources.   Having exhausted all of the resources he or she controls, the project manager needs to turn to the resource managers as the next strategy. To recoup the lost time, the project manager needs additional resources. They may come in the form of added staff or dollars to acquire contract help.

Negotiate multiple release strategies.   These last two strategies involve the customer. Just as in the case of a change request, the project manager can use multiple-release strategies here to advantage. An example will illustrate the strategy: The project manager shares the problem with the customer and then asks for the customer to prioritize the features requested in the project plan. The project manager then offers to provide the highest-priority features ahead of their scheduled delivery date and the remaining priorities later than the scheduled delivery date. In other words, the project manager gains an extended delivery schedule, but gives the customer something better than the original bargain offered — namely, something ahead of schedule.

Request schedule extension from the customer.   This is the final alternative. Although similar to the multiple-release strategy, it offers the customer nothing in trade. The slippage is such that the only resolution is to ask for a time extension.

The project manager tries to solve the problem by starting at the top of the list and working down until a solution is found. By using this approach, the project manager will first try to solve the problem with resources he or she controls, then with resources the resource managers control, and finally with resources and constraints the customer controls.

Problem Management Meetings

Problem management meetings provide an oversight function to identify, monitor, and resolve problems that arise during the life of a project. Every project has problems. No matter how well planned or managed, there will always be problems. Many problems arise just as an accident of nature. For example, one of your key staff members has resigned just as she was to begin working on a critical-path activity. Her skills are in high demand, and she will be difficult to replace. Each day that her position remains vacant is another day's delay in the project. It seems like an impossible problem. Nevertheless, the project manager must be ready to take action in such cases. The problem management meeting is one vehicle for addressing all problems that need to be escalated above the individual for definition, solution identification, and resolution.

This is an important function in the management of projects, especially large projects. Problems are often identified in the project status meeting and referred to the appropriate persons for resolution. A group is assembled to work on the problem. Progress reports are presented and discussed at a problem management meeting. Problem management meetings usually begin with a review of the status of the activity that resulted in the problem, followed by a statement of the problem and a discussion to ensure that everyone has the same understanding of the problem. At that point the meeting should move into the problem-solving process that was discussed in detail in Chapter 9.

Putting It All Together

Monitoring and controlling the progress of a project won't happen just because the team is committed to the project. There must be an organized oversight process put in place and understood by the client, senior management, the project manager, and all the team members. As you have seen, there are reports for all of these audiences. You have also seen that the extent to which progress reports are necessary and the amount of effort to generate them requires a balance. Requiring too much reporting takes away from the available time to work on the project. Requiring too little reporting puts the project manager at risk of not being able to complete the project within time and cost constraints. You have also seen that there are both numeric and graphic reporting formats. Some managers prefer numeric data, whereas others prefer graphic data. The reporting system you choose must meet the needs of both groups.

Discussion Questions

1. A number of your clients seem to be abusing the change request process. You have seen an increase in the number of frivolous requests.

These, of course, must be researched and resolved, and that takes away from the time that your team members have to do actual project work. From a process point of view, what might you do? Be specific.

2. What are the advantages and disadvantages of confirming the accuracy of status reports filed by your team members?

CASE STUDY – PLEASANTOWN PLAYGROUND PROJECT AND PIZZA DELIVERED QUICKLY (PDQ)

The project work is soon to begin, and you are conferring with your team members to decide on reporting requirements and frequency. Take into account the stakeholders in this project and what their needs might be. Refer back to the two case study background statements in the Introduction for the input you will need to answer the following questions:

3. Who are the people that you need to hear from to determine whether they are satisfied with your progress on this project?

4. How will you get information from your team and distribute it to the other stakeholders for this project?

Closing Out the Project

We judge ourselves by what we feel capable of doing,
while others judge us by what we have already done.
— Henry Wadsworth Longfellow, American poet

We cannot afford to forget any experiences, even the most painful.
— Dag Hammerskjöld, Former Secretary General
of the United Nations

CHAPTER LEARNING OBJECTIVES

After reading this chapter, you will be able to:

◆ **Understand the steps needed to effectively close a project**

◆ **Develop a closing strategy**

◆ **Identify the components of project documentation**

◆ **Conduct a post-implementation audit**

◆ **Explain the significance of each post-implementation audit question**

Steps in Closing a Project

Closing the project is routine once you have the customer's approval of the deliverables. There are six steps to closing the project:

1. Getting client acceptance of deliverables

2. Ensuring that all deliverables are installed

3. Ensuring that the documentation is in place

4. Getting client sign-off on the final report

5. Conducting the post-implementation audit

6. Celebrating the success

This chapter takes a look at each of these steps in more detail.

Getting Client Acceptance

The client decides when the project is done. It is the job of the project manager to demonstrate that the deliverables (whether product or service) meet client specifications. This acceptance can be very informal and ceremonial, or it can be very formal, involving extensive acceptance testing against the client's performance specifications.

Ceremonial Acceptance

Ceremonial acceptance is an informal acceptance by the customer. It does not have an accompanying sign-off of completion or acceptance. It simply happens. Two situations fall under the heading of ceremonial acceptance:

- The first involves deadline dates at which the client must accept the project as complete, whether or not it meets specification. For example, if the project is to plan and conduct a conference, the conference will happen whether or not the project work has been satisfactorily completed.

- The second involves a project deliverable requiring little or no checking to determine whether specifications have been met — for example, planning and taking a vacation.

Formal Acceptance

Formal acceptance occurs in those cases in which the client has written an acceptance procedure. In many cases, especially computer applications development projects, writing an acceptance procedure may be a joint effort by the customer and appropriate members of the project team; it typically is done very early in the life of the project. This acceptance procedure requires that the project team demonstrate compliance with every feature in the client's performance specification. A checklist is used and requires a feature-by-feature sign-off based on performance tests. These tests are conducted jointly and administered by the client and appropriate members of the project team.

NOTE The checklist is written in such a fashion that compliance is either demonstrated by the test or it is not demonstrated by the test. It must not be written in such a way that interpretation is needed to determine whether compliance has been demonstrated.

Installing Project Deliverables

The second step of closing a project is to go live with the deliverables. This commonly occurs in computer systems work. The installation can involve phases, cutovers, or some other rollout strategy. In other cases, it involves nothing more than flipping a switch. Either way, some event or activity turns things over to the customer. This installation triggers the beginning of a number of close-out activities that mostly relate to documentation and report preparation.

Documenting the Project

Documentation always seems to be the most difficult part of the project to complete. There is little glamour and no "way to go!" in doing documentation. That does not diminish its importance, however. There are at least five reasons why you need to do documentation:

   Reference for future changes in deliverables.   Even though the project work is complete, there will be further changes that warrant follow-up projects. By using the deliverables, the customer will identify improvement opportunities, features to be added, and functions to be modified. The documentation of the project just completed is the foundation for the follow-up projects.

   Historical record for estimating duration and cost on future projects, activities, and tasks.   Completed projects are a terrific source of information for future projects, but only if the data and other documentation from them is archived so that it can be retrieved and used. Estimated and actual duration and cost for each activity on completed projects are particularly valuable for estimating these variables on future projects.

   Training resource for new project managers.   History is a great teacher, and nowhere is that more significant than on completed projects. Such items as how the WBS architecture was determined; how change requests were analyzed and decisions reached; problem identification, analysis, and resolution situations; and a variety of other experiences are invaluable lessons for the newly appointed project manager.

Input for further training and development of the project team.   As a reference, project documentation can help the project team deal with situations that arise in the current project. How a similar problem or change request was handled in the past is an excellent example.

Input for performance evaluation by the functional managers of the project team members.   In many organizations, project documentation can be used as input to the performance evaluations of the project manager and team members.

WARNING Care must be exercised in the use of such information, however. In some cases a project was doomed to fail even though the team members' performance may have been exemplary. The reverse is also likely. The project was destined to be a success even though the team members' performance may have been less than expected.

Given all that documentation can do for you, to be most effective and useful, the documentation for a given project should include the following parts:

- Project Overview Statement
- Project proposal and backup data
- Original and revised project schedules
- Minutes of all project team meetings
- Copies of all status reports
- Design documents
- Copies of all change notices
- Copies of all written communications
- Outstanding issues reports
- Final report
- Sample deliverables (if appropriate)
- Client acceptance documents
- Post-implementation audit report

This list is all-encompassing. For a given project, the project manager has to determine what documentation is appropriate. Always refer back to value-added considerations. If the document has value, and many will have good value for future projects, then include it in the documentation. Note also that the list contains very little that does not arise naturally in the execution of the project. All that is added is the appointment of someone to care for and feed the project notebook. This job involves collecting the documents at the time of their creation and ensuring that they are in an easily retrievable form (electronic is a must).

Post-Implementation Audit

The post-implementation audit is an evaluation of the project's goals and activity achievement as measured against the project plan, budget, time deadlines, quality of deliverables, specifications, and client satisfaction. The log of the project activities serves as baseline data for this audit. Six important questions should be answered:

1. Was the project goal achieved?

    a. Does it do what the project team said it would do?

    b. Does it do what the client said it would do?

    The project was justified based on a goal to be achieved. It either was or it wasn't, and an answer to that question must be provided in the audit. The question can be asked and answered from two different perspectives. The provider may have suggested a solution for which certain results were promised. Did that happen? Conversely, the requestor may have promised that if the provider would only provide, say, a new or improved system, then certain results would occur. Did that happen?

2. Was the project work done on time, within budget, and according to specification?

    Recall from the scope triangle discussed in Chapter 1 that the constraints on a project are time, cost, and the customer's specification, as well as resource availability and quality. Here you are concerned with whether the specification was met within the budgeted time and cost constraints.

3. Was the client satisfied with the project results?

    It is possible that the answers to the first two questions are yes, while the answer to this question is no. How can that happen? Simple: the Conditions of Satisfaction changed, but no one was aware that they had. The project manager did not check with the customer to see whether the needs had changed; the customer did not inform the project manager that such changes had occurred.

NOTE I remind you again that it is absolutely essential that the Conditions of Satisfaction be reviewed at every major event in the life of the project, including changes in team membership, especially a new project manager, and changes in the sponsor. Reorganization of the company, acquisitions, and mergers are other reasons to recheck the Conditions of Satisfaction.

4. Was business value realized? (Check success criteria.)

   The success criteria were the basis on which the business case for the project was built and were the primary reason why the project was approved. Did you realize that promised value? When the success criteria measure improvement in profit or market share or other bottom-line parameters, you may not be able to answer this question until some time after the project is closed.

5. What lessons were learned about your project management methodology?

   Companies that have or are developing a project management methodology will want to use completed projects to assess how well the methodology is working. Different parts of the methodology may work well for certain types of projects or in certain situations, and these should be noted in the audit. These lessons will be valuable in tweaking the methodology or simply noting how to apply the methodology when a given situation arises. This part of the audit might also consider how well the team used the methodology, which is related to, yet different from, how well the methodology worked.

6. What worked? What didn't?

   The answers to these questions are helpful hints and suggestions for future project managers and teams. The experiences of past project teams are real "diamonds in the rough"; you will want to pass them on to future teams.

The post-implementation audit is seldom done, which is unfortunate because it does have great value for all stakeholders. Some of the reasons for skipping the audit include the following:

Managers don't want to know.   They reason that the project is done and what difference does it make whether things happened the way you said they would? It is time to move on.

Managers don't want to pay the cost.   The pressures of the budget (both time and money) are such that they would rather spend resources on the next project than on those already completed.

It's not a high priority.   Other projects are waiting to have work done on them, and completed projects don't rate very high on the priority list.

There's too much other billable work to do.   Post-implementation audits are not billable work, and people have billable work on other projects to do.

> **NOTE** I can't stress enough the importance of the post-implementation audit, which contains so much valuable information that can be extracted and used in other projects. Organizations have such a difficult time deploying and improving their project management process and practice that it would be a shame to pass up the greatest source of information to help that effort. I won't mislead you, though — actually doing the post-implementation audit is difficult because of all the other tasks waiting for your attention, not the least of which is probably at least one project that is already behind schedule.

The Final Report

The final project report acts as the memory or history of the project. It is the file that others can check to study the progress and impediments of the project. Many formats can be used for a final report, but the content should include comments relative to the following points:

Overall success of the project.   Taking into account all of the measures of success that you considered, can you consider this project to have been a success?

Organization of the project.   Hindsight is always perfect, but now that you are finished with the project, did you organize it in the best way possible? If not, what might that organization have looked like?

Techniques used to get results.   By way of a summary list, what specific things did you do that helped to get the results?

Project strengths and weaknesses.   Again by way of a summary list, what features, practices, and processes did you use that proved to be strengths or weaknesses? Do you have any advice to pass on to future project teams regarding these strengths/weaknesses?

Project team recommendations.   Throughout the life of the project, there will have been a number of insights and suggestions. This is the place to record them for posterity.

Celebrating Success

There must be some recognition for the project team at the end of the project. This can be as simple as a commemorative mug, a T-shirt, a pizza party, tickets to a ball game, or something more formal, such as bonuses. I recall that when Release 3 of the spreadsheet package Lotus 1-2-3 was delivered, each member of the project team was presented with a videotape showing the team at work during the last week of the project. That was certainly a nice touch and one that will long be remembered by every member of the team.

Even though the team may have started out as a "herd of cats," the project they have just completed has honed them into a real team. Bonding has taken place, new friendships have formed, and mentor relationships have been established. The individual team members have grown professionally through their association with one another, and now it is time to move on to the next project. This can be a very traumatic experience for them, and they deserve closure. That is what celebrating success is all about. My loud and continual message to the senior management team is this: Don't pass up an opportunity to show the team your appreciation. Loyalty, motivation, and commitment by your professional staff are the result of this simple act on your part.

Putting It All Together

You have now completed all five phases of the Traditional Project Management life cycle. I can only hope that the practical tools and techniques I have shared will provide a lasting and valuable store of resources for you to use as you grow in this exciting profession. Whether you are a full-time project manager, an occasional project manager, an experienced project manager, or a wannabe project manager, you should have found value in these pages.

I haven't finished adding to your store of project management tools and processes, however. There is much more to come. For example, in the next chapter, I introduce the topic of critical chain project management as yet another variation on the theme. As you will see, it fills a gap left by TPM that I have ignored so far but cover in the next chapter.

Good luck as you continue on your journey to expand your mind into the many possibilities of effective project management!

Discussion Questions

1. I have advocated the use of a checklist as the acceptance test procedure for establishing that the project is finished. What other type of acceptance test procedure might you suggest? Be specific.

2. Can you suggest a cost/benefit approach to selling management on the value of the post-implementation audit? Be specific.

CASE STUDY – PLEASANTOWN PLAYGROUND PROJECT

3. How will you know when the Pleasantown Playground Project is finished? Did you write some sort of contract with the sponsor at the beginning to ensure that everyone was on the same page as to the exact ending of the project? What are (or could be) the parts of that contract for this project?

CHAPTER 12

Critical Chain Project Management

New ideas are not born in a conforming environment.
— Roger von Oech, President, Creative Thinking

CHAPTER LEARNING OBJECTIVES

After reading this chapter, you will be able to:

- ◆ Explain the difference between the critical path and the critical chain
- ◆ Identify resource constraints and know how to resolve them
- ◆ Use the critical chain approach to project management for single projects

In 1984 Eliyahu M. Goldratt introduced the Theory of Constraints (TOC) in a book entitled *The Goal*. Peter Senge, in his book *The Fifth Discipline* (Currency/Doubleday, 1994), stated that "to change the behavior of a system, you must identify and change the limiting factor," which Lawrence P. Leach, in his book *Critical Chain Project Management, Second Edition* (Artech House, 2005), called the best definition of TOC that he has heard. Still, it was not until the late 1990s that practitioners were able to link TOC to project management. Critical chain project management (CCPM) is the result of the linkage between TOC and project management. CCPM has grown in popularity and is making an impact on project success.

The second edition of this book contained a brief paragraph on CCPM. At the suggestion of several readers, I decided to expand my treatment of CCPM. That is the purpose of this chapter. I am aware that many project management practitioners and writers dismiss CCPM as just another way of managing risk, and suggest that it does not represent any new thinking about project management. It is not my purpose to settle that debate. I merely want to give some space to an idea, an approach, that all project managers will appreciate. The interested reader should consult Leach's *Critical Chain Project Management*.

What Is the Critical Chain?

As mentioned in Chapter 6, the critical path is the longest duration path through the project. It is built by considering only the task dependencies and their individual durations in an additive fashion. CCPM claims that the critical path approach to project management is flawed. Instead, CCPM claims that the focus should not be on the critical path, which is resource-independent, but on the path that is task-dependent and resource-constrained, the so-called *critical chain*. The critical chain is defined as the longest duration path through the project, if you consider both the task dependencies and the resource constraints. *Critical chain project management* is defined as the planning, scheduling, and maintenance of the critical chain throughout the course of the project. Furthermore, by giving priority to the critical chain, the project manager identifies and schedules tasks around the most constrained of the resources, increasing the probability of completing the project in less time than the critical path approach. This chapter includes a simple example to illustrate how that schedule compression happens.

In the critical path approach, resources are allocated first to the critical path, which is known to not be the optimal way to create the shortest schedule. Two concepts form the justification of the CCPM approach, described in the next two sections.

Variation in Duration: Common Cause versus Special Cause

The first concept that justifies the CCPM approach is that there are two basic kinds of variation that you experience in task duration:

Common cause variation.   This is fluctuation in task duration that results from the capacity of the system affecting that task. In other words, this type of variation occurs naturally in nature. For example, if you consider the time it takes an experienced runner to complete a 100-meter race under normal environmental conditions, you might observe times such as 9.85, 9.88, 9.92, and 9.86 seconds. The times are not all the same because the runner (the system) has only a certain capacity for repeatability. There is a natural variation in the actual execution times. Nothing can be done to affect that; it is the nature of the runner. These variations are attributable to common cause variation.

Special cause variation. If we using the same example and the runner is running against a 20-mile-per-hour wind, or at a 5,000-foot elevation, or in 100-degree heat, the recorded times will be even higher and have a greater variation from one another. Those higher recordings are the result of special causes. You can do something to mitigate or avoid special cause variations, but not common cause variations.

What do these mean to the project manager? Common cause variation is accounted for in the contingency attached to each task. Common cause variation occurs naturally and is always present. You live with that and plan accordingly. Special cause variation is dealt with as part of your risk management plan. These are the variations you can manage as project manager.

NOTE Both of these sources of variation have to be accounted for in TPM and in CCPM. However, CCPM takes advantage of common cause variation through the use of the central limit theorem from mathematical statistics, whereas TPM essentially ignores it. It is this use of common cause variation and some statistical properties of variances of additive random variables that enables a CCPM project to actually complete in less time than a TPM approach, even on the same project.

Statistical Validation of the Critical Chain Approach

The second concept that lends credence to the CCPM approach is based in statistical distribution theory. Here you call on a basic concept from statistics that states that the variance of a sum is the square root of the sum of the variances of each of the components in the sum. The square root of the sum of squares is less than the sum itself. That may sound like gibberish to most of you, so let's take a look at how it translates to project duration. Figure 12-1 shows a sequence of four consecutive tasks. Each one has a contingency associated with it (the shaded area after the task). Contingency is defined as the difference in duration between a 50 percent probable estimate and a 90 percent probable estimate. For example, suppose that about half the time a particular activity completes in 10 hours or less. That is the 50 percent probable estimate. In addition, that same activity completes in 15 hours or less approximately 90 percent of the time. That is the 90 percent probable estimate. The difference between the two (15 – 10, or 5 hours) is the contingency.

□ = CONTINGENCY

Figure 12-1 Using contingency can reduce project time.

In the lower part of the figure, I have moved the contingency of each task to the end of the sequence of tasks. Note that the variance of the sum of the contingencies is less than the sum of the variances of the contingencies. Calling on that statistical property has enabled me to shorten the duration of the sequence of tasks. You might say that I haven't really done anything; I've just defined things a little differently. Not quite. I have used the average task duration as the point estimate of task duration. (A point estimate is a single number that represents your best guess as to the real value of the number you are trying to estimate. A range estimate is a low and high number that you believe spans the unknown number you are trying to estimate.) The *average* is that number that the duration will exceed half of the time and be less than half of the time. Because of the variation in duration as a result of common causes, you can expect some of the tasks to take more time than their average duration and some to take less time. That variation is collected into the contingency at the end of the sequence. To bring the sequence in by the shorter time, the project manager has to manage the contingency. So what I have accomplished by collecting the contingencies at the end of the sequence is to change the focus of the project manager to that newly aggregated contingency. The contingency has been made visible, and therefore it is manageable.

A final comparison of the critical path versus the critical chain approaches is valuable. The critical path project manager reacts to a single critical path activity taking longer than it was estimated to take. That excess is immediately translated into a project that will be late by that amount. The critical chain project manager reacts differently. That activity is one of a sequence of activities. Some of them will take longer than their estimated duration, and others will take less time. The project manager reviews the status of the contingency and decides whether to act or to let the statistical variation correct the overage.

I'll have more to say on that later in the chapter by way of the example, but for now it is important to see the distinction and the real strength of CCPM.

The TPM project manager reacts to the performance of a single task in a sequence of dependent tasks and expends management time. The CCPM project manager dismisses that as a waste of time, reasoning that attention should be given to the sequence and not to any single task. CCPM is relying on the statistical properties of a sequence of dependent tasks, whereas TPM is not.

The Critical Chain Project Management Approach

The CCPM approach is identical to the TPM approach up to the point where the project network diagram is defined and the critical path is identified. The traditional project manager would next conduct a resource leveling exercise targeting resource usage on the critical path. At this point, the critical chain project manager develops the critical chain plan. In the discussion that follows, I describe each of the CCPM planning steps for you by way of a simple example, using the sample project shown in Figure 12-2.

Step 1: Creating the Early Schedule Project Network Diagram

Figure 12-2 shows the early schedule for a simple seven-task project. This early schedule is the same one someone using TPM might make. Note that the project duration is estimated at 16 days using the original task duration estimates, which include contingency for each task. Figure 12-2 shows the critical path (C1-C2-C3) for a project manager using TPM, and it is the starting point for resolving any resource contention problems.

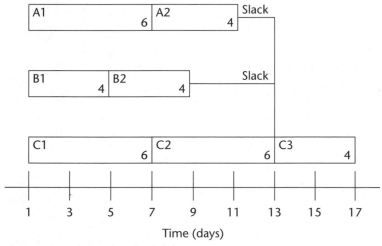

Figure 12-2 The early schedule

Step 2: Converting the Early Schedule to the Late Schedule and Adding Resources

The first thing that a project manager using CCPM does is convert the task schedule to the late schedule, as shown in Figure 12-3. Note that this conversion removes the slack associated with the sequence defined by tasks A1–A2 and B1–B2. In fact, it removes all of the free slack and total slack associated with any task or task sequence in the project. Note also that the 50 percent duration estimates have replaced the original estimates, which included contingency. In doing that, the project duration has been reduced from the original 16 days to 8 days. I have also added the three resources (Duffy, Ernie, and Fran) to the tasks to which they have been assigned. Note that there is a resource conflict with Ernie on tasks A2 and B2. In addition, note that the project duration is reduced to eight days when the contingencies are removed.

Step 3: Resolving Resource Conflicts

In general, resource conflicts are removed by beginning with the task sequence that has the least slack. After resolving that conflict, move to the task path that now has the least slack. Continue in this fashion until all resource conflicts have been resolved. In the example, the critical chain (C1-C2-C3) does not have any resource conflicts. The next task path to consider is A1-A2. In this case, Ernie would be scheduled to work on A2, which means pushing his work on B1 to an earlier date. This resolution is illustrated in Figure 12-4.

The other way to resolve the resource conflict is to have Ernie work on B2; then after Duffy has completed A1, Ernie can work on A2. This resolution is illustrated in Figure 12-5. The second option extends the duration of the project.

Figure 12-3 The late schedule with resource assignments

Figure 12-4 One way to resolve the resource conflict

Figure 12-5 Another way to resolve the resource conflict

This simple example illustrates the major difference between TPM and CCPM. TPM uses the early schedule as the base for all management decisions. CCPM uses the late schedule. TPM focuses only on the critical path and manages in accordance with that. CCPM focuses on the paths with resource constraints and manages in accordance with the best use of the resources. It does so by using the critical path but only to identify the chains with the least slack, and prioritizing resource use based on the minimum slack paths. To protect the scarce resources, CCPM uses the concept of *buffers*, which is the topic of the next section.

Buffers

Now that I have adjusted the late schedule for the resource conflicts, I can add the appropriate buffers to the project schedule. There are many different kinds of buffers and many different purposes for which they are used. I discuss and illustrate three of them with this simple project.

CROSS-REF For a complete discussion of buffers, see Lawrence P. Leach's book *Critical Chain Project Management, Second Edition* (Artech House, 2005).

Defining Buffers

Buffers are segments of time that are placed at the end of a sequence of tasks for the purpose of protecting the schedule of those tasks. Buffers can also be used to protect cost, much like a contingency for unexpected expenses in a budget. The size of time buffers is based on the total duration of the task sequence to which they are attached. Basically, the size of the buffer is determined by calculating the total of the contingencies in the tasks that make up the sequence.

Types of Buffers

Although there are others, in this chapter I focus on the following three types of buffers:

- Project buffers
- Feeding buffers
- Resource buffers

Project Buffers

The project buffer is a time buffer placed at the end of the critical chain to protect the overall project schedule. Its size can be calculated as the square root of the sum of the squared differences between the original task duration estimate and the reduced task duration estimate.

Feeding Buffers

The feeding buffer is a time buffer placed at the end of a sequence of tasks that lead into the critical chain. Its size is calculated the same way as the project buffer size.

Resource Buffers

The resource buffer is different from the previous buffers. It is not a time buffer. It is a flag, usually placed on the critical chain to alert a resource that it is needed. The flag can be placed at intervals such as one week before the resource is needed, three days before the resource is needed, or one day before the resource is needed. Because it does not contain any time interval, it does not affect the project's scheduled completion date. It serves merely to protect the critical chain.

Other Buffers

As indicated earlier, several other buffer types are used, but they relate to a multiproject environment and are beyond the scope of this overview chapter. The interested reader should consult Leach's book *Critical Chain Project Management*. Some of the other pertinent buffers found in Leach's book are as follows:

- **Capacity constrained buffer** — A buffer placed between projects to ensure a specific sequence of projects in a multiproject environment

- **Cost buffer** — A contingency added to a project or sequence of tasks to protect overall cost

- **Drum buffer** — The capacity of a single resource that is scheduled across several projects

Using Buffers

Let's return to the example project shown in Figure 12-4. So far, the project can be completed at the end of the eighth day. Resolving the resource conflict with Ernie did not add any duration to the project. I first put a project buffer after C3, the final task in this project. Its size is the square root of the square of the contingencies in tasks C1, C2, and C3 (or the square root of $9 + 9 + 4$), which is approximately 4.7 days. Next, I add feeding buffers at the end of the sequences A1-A2 and B1-B2. The calculated buffer sizes are 3.6 days for A1-A2 and 2.8 days for B1-B2. Incorporating these buffers into Figure 12-4 results in the schedule shown in Figure 12-6.

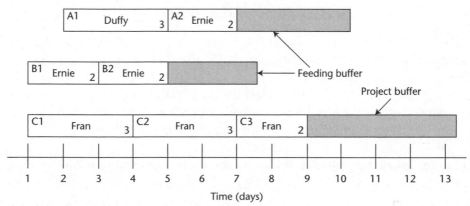

Figure 12-6 Project schedule with buffers added

Note that the CCPM approach gives a project duration (including contingency buffers) of 13.7 days, compared to the TPM approach of 16 days. In other words, extracting the contingency from each task, collecting it at the end of the task sequences, and managing it has saved an average of 2.3 days out of a 16-day schedule. That's about a 14 percent schedule improvement!

Managing Buffers

The CCPM project manager is concerned about the starting time of a sequence of tasks including the critical chain, but isn't concerned about the finish time of the sequences. The finishing times are not even in the CCPM project plan. Instead, the CCPM project manager manages the buffers. In managing the buffers, the CCPM project manager is protecting the actual duration sequence and hence the completion time of the project.

The TPM treats the buffer as nothing more than management reserve, which I discuss in Chapter 6. The only real similarity between a management reserve and a buffer may be in how they are managed. Managing management reserve and managing buffers can follow very similar logic. The three decision trigger levels in buffer management are as follows:

- When the sequence of tasks schedule slips and penetrates into the first third of the buffer

- When the sequence of tasks schedule slips and penetrates into the middle third of the buffer

- When the sequence of tasks schedule slips and penetrates into the final third of the buffer

Let's take a closer look at each of these trigger points and the appropriate action that the CCPM project manager should take.

Penetration into the First Third of the Buffer

Unlike the project manager using TPM who chases every slippage on the critical path or any change in the critical path, the project manager using CCPM is looking at the performance of a sequence and is less likely to act in haste. Penetration into the first third of the buffer means that the cumulative slippage in the sequence is less than one third of the buffer. There is no defensible reason why the CCPM project manager would want to take any action.

TIP The later in the sequence this occurs, the less likely any action will be taken.

Penetration into the Middle Third of the Buffer

Penetration into the middle third of the buffer does call for some action on the part of the CCPM project manager. In this case, the correct action is to investigate the cause of the slippage and put a get-well plan in place. The earlier in the sequence the slippage occurs, the more serious the problem.

Penetration into the Final Third of the Buffer

Penetration into the final third of the buffer is serious regardless of when in the sequence it occurs. Obviously, if it is in the first third of the duration of the sequence, it is very serious. If it occurs late in the final third, there may be little that can be done. In any case, action is called for.

Figure 12-7 illustrates a matrix that can be used to determine schedule slippage severity and the need for action as a function of buffer penetration and distance into the task sequence.

| | | Buffer Penetration | | |
		First Third	Second Third	Final Third
Task Sequence Penetration	**First Third**	NO ACTION	Serious problem; immediate action required	A very serious problem exists; aggressive action is needed
	Second Third	NO ACTION	Define the problem and formulate a solution	Serious problem; implement the solution
	Final Third	Task sequence will be ahead of schedule	NO ACTION	Monitor the situation for any further penetration

Figure 12-7 Buffer penetration and action decisions

To grasp the significance of the penetration matrix, first consider the diagonal from the top-left cell to the bottom-right cell in Figure 12-7. The cells on the diagonal reflect situations where task sequence penetration is about equal to buffer penetration. The statistician would say that is what you should expect on the average. However, the further you move into task sequence penetration (moving down the diagonal), the more you should be paying attention to the team's performance on the work being done on the tasks in the sequence. The nearer you are to the ending tasks in the sequence, the less likely it is that you can formulate and execute a get-well plan should things go poorly. For example, if you are in the second third of the task sequence, it might be a good idea to take a look at the problem situation and formulate an action plan in the event that things deteriorate. The problem is not serious, but it does deserve your attention. In the final third of the task sequence, all you can do is closely monitor things and take action at the slightest aberration in the task sequence schedule.

Below the diagonal I've been discussing is a great place to be. You could even be experiencing a situation where the task sequence will finish ahead of schedule, and the time saved can be passed to the successor task sequence. Above the diagonal are situations you are more used to. If you are in the first third of the task sequence and have penetrated into the second third of the buffer, you have a serious problem that needs immediate investigation and solution implementation. There may be some systemic flaw in the project plan, and early intervention is needed. If the schedule should continue to slip and you find that you have penetrated into the final third of the buffer, you are in real trouble, as the matrix suggests. You could be looking at a significant slippage that may impact the project buffer as well.

Track Record of Critical Chain Project Management

It was not until the 1997 publication of Eliyahu M. Goldratt's book *Critical Chain* (North River Press, 1997) that people began to see the connections between TOC and project management. CCPM has a history of more than 10 years to draw upon for its successes. Leach cites a few of them in his book *Critical Chain Project Management*. They are briefly summarized in the following list:

Honeywell Defense Avionics Systems.   Using critical chain concepts, a team at Honeywell was able to reduce a 13-month project schedule to six months, and they did finish it in six months.

Lucent Technologies.   A project that was scheduled using CCPM was to have taken one year. Many said it couldn't possibly be done in one year. It was, with buffer to spare.

Harris. Harris undertook to build a new manufacturing facility using the CCPM approach. The industry standard for such facilities was 46 months to get the plant up and running to 90 percent capacity. Harris built it and brought it up to 90 percent capacity in 13 months.

Israeli aircraft industry. A particular type of aircraft maintenance requires three months on the average. Using CCPM techniques the maintenance team reduced the average to two weeks.

Better online solutions. A software package was originally planned to be released to the public in August. The TOC schedule cut it down to May 1. The actual delivery date was early April.

These stories do not in any way validate CCPM as better than TPM. It is too early to tell that, but it is a fact that there have been many successes using it. You be the judge. You decide if CCPM wins out over TPM or if it is just another repackaging of PMBOK. I have simply presented another way of managing resources and leave it up to the project team to decide which approach makes more sense, given the situation.

Putting It All Together

This chapter has provided enough of an overview of CCPM to enable you to use it in your projects. Because the overview is brief and applied to a simple project, readers who are more serious about its application will need to dig deeper into it. Again, I heartily endorse Leach's book *Critical Chain Project Management*.

Discussion Questions

1. Assume that your organization is interested in using CCPM along with TPM. What criteria would you use to decide which approach makes more sense for a given project? You might try answering this question by considering some of the characteristics of the project that would lead you to one choice over the other.

2. You are a senior project manager in your company. You have 15 years' experience with them and a solid reputation for delivering successful projects. What might you do, acting on your own, to get your organization to appreciate the value of CCPM? What obstacles might prevent you from going forward with your plan?

PART

II

Adaptive Project Framework

Project management is at a major crossroads. How we choose to go forward will either endear us to our clients or give them more reasons to dismiss project management as irrelevant to their needs. Changes that have taken place in the past few years in the way businesses operate have given us good reason to pause and reflect on whether or not our traditional approach to project management still satisfies the needs of organizations. It is my belief that we are not meeting the needs of contemporary organizations and that we must do something to correct that deficiency. This question has dominated my thinking for several years now. I've had this feeling that the business world is passing us by, and that what we are offering them isn't up to expectations. It's time for some outside-of-the-box thinking.

Part II of this book arose out of that belief and the need to act. I call this new approach the Adaptive Project Framework (APF). It reflects my thinking on an approach to projects that does not fit the traditional project profile. Much of the APF is the direct result of working with project managers who are frustrated with their foiled attempts to adapt TPM to projects for which it was not designed. I warn you now that what you are going to read about in Part II is different. I ask you to be open-minded as you read these chapters. What I have done is take parts from the traditional approach and parts from the extreme approach and integrated them in a way that meets the needs of a type of project that is not served by either the traditional or the extreme approaches. This has resulted in a new taxonomy of projects that ranges from the traditional approach to APF and then to extreme project management. As I discussed in the Introduction, projects also follow a taxonomy that maps directly to these approaches.

If you would like to reduce the cost of projects to your organization, read this part of the book. I believe it is required reading for Project Office directors and managers, program managers, project managers, project leaders, team members, and those who use the services of any of these professionals. Executives will want to read Chapter 13 to learn that something can be done to significantly reduce the high percentage of failed projects without spending any more money. That's right — without spending any more money. The APF does not require any special tools or software or consultant expertise to be implemented. For the traditionalist, the APF should be intuitive. Everything you need is in this book. In fact, I hypothesize that the APF approach introduced here is actually less costly than the traditional processes now in place in every organization.

I first introduce the Adaptive Project Framework at a 60,000-foot level. The first chapter of this part describes the five-phase APF approach and briefly explains each phase. This chapter is an excellent introduction to the APF for senior-level executives, directors, and managers, who will come away with a good grasp and understanding of why the APF is so critically important to our organizations at this time. The following five chapters discuss each of the five phases in detail sufficient for a project team to follow the approach. The final chapter discusses a few variations of the APF and focuses mostly on Extreme Project Management (xPM). xPM is a variation of the APF in that the goal is not clearly specified in xPM, whereas it is in APF. That slight difference leads to a number of variations in the approach. These are discussed in some detail for the practitioner.

In this the fourth edition I introduce a new case study. It is designed to test the very fabric of the APF. I hope you enjoy working with it as much as I enjoyed bringing it to you.

Part II is a work in process. I continue to learn and discover the real power behind the APF as I discuss it with my colleagues and implement it with my clients. How interesting it is to realize that my project to develop a fully functional version of the APF is itself an APF project.

Many strict traditionalist project managers will probably find the APF controversial. I hope to at least get their attention and open their minds to other possibilities. There is an entire class of projects that I believe is not being served by the traditionalist approach. Recent developments in extreme project management address some of those projects. The APF addresses projects that fall in the growing gap between the traditional and agile approaches. In my experience, the majority of projects fall into this middle ground.

I claim full responsibility for the contents and any reactions that follow. If nothing else, I hope to get a number of traditionalists excited enough to take a look at what I am presenting. Perhaps they will help me smooth out any rough edges to the APF and make it a viable tool in their project management arsenal. If you care to comment, contact me at `rkw@eiicorp.com`. I promise you a personal and thoughtful response.

CHAPTER 13

Introduction to the Adaptive Project Framework

It is a mistake to look too far ahead. Only one link of the chain of destiny can be handled at a time.

— Winston Churchill

There is no data on the future.

— Laurel Cutler, Vice Chairman, FCB/Leber Katz Partners

CHAPTER LEARNING OBJECTIVES

After reading this chapter, you will be able to:

◆ Give a general explanation of the APF

◆ Understand the purpose of each of the five APF phases

◆ Apply the APF core values

◆ Describe the types of projects appropriate for the APF

For those businesses that have only recently realized the pain of not having a project management process in place and are struggling to adapt traditional practices to nontraditional projects, I say, "Stop wasting your time!" I'm not advocating the overthrow of the project management world, but rather asking you to stop and consider what has been happening. It's time to pay attention to the signals coming from the changing business environment and discover how to survive the fast-paced, constantly changing, high-quality demands of the new business model.

In the next seven chapters you are going to learn about an approach to project management that dynamically adjusts to the changing characteristics of the project, rather than an approach that follows a static "one-size-fits-all" approach. This adaptive approach will result in far fewer project failures, greater customer satisfaction, and maximum business value for the time and cost invested.

> **NOTE** The Adaptive Project Framework (APF) incorporates selected tools and processes from Traditional Project Management (TPM). Those tools and processes are not repeated here. This part of the book assumes that the reader is familiar with the TPM approach. A quick review of Part I is suggested for those who do not have a working knowledge of TPM.

The project survival strategy that I explore in this groundbreaking part of the book is what I am calling the *Adaptive Project Framework (APF)*. This is definitely not your father's project management. It's new. I don't even use the word management. The APF represents a shift in thinking about projects and how they should be run. For one thing, it eliminates all of the non-value-added work time that is wasted on planning activities that are never performed. Why plan the future when you don't know what it is? In APF, planning is done just-in-time. Sounds like an oxymoron, doesn't it? It is a new mind-set — one that thrives on change, rather than one that avoids it.

The APF is not a one-size-fits-all approach; it continuously adapts to the unique character of the specific business situation as it learns more about that business situation. Based on the principle that form follows function, this strategy adapts some of the tools and processes from TPM (discussed in Part I of this book) and extreme project management (discussed in Chapter 19) to its own special needs. It is a framework based on the principle that you learn by doing, and one that guarantees "If you build it, they will come."

The APF seeks to get it right every time. It is client-focused and client-driven and is grounded in a set of immutable core values. It ensures maximum business value for the time and dollars expended and has squeezed out all of the non-value-added work that it possibly could. As a framework that meaningfully and fully engages the client as the primary decision maker, the APF creates a shared partnership with shared responsibility between requestor and provider. The APF is a framework that works, 100 percent of the time. No exceptions!

Do I have your attention?

Defining the APF

The APF is an iterative and adaptive five-phase approach designed to deliver maximum business value to clients within the limits of their time and cost constraints. The fundamental concept underlying the APF is that scope is variable;

and within specified time and cost constraints, the APF maximizes business value by adjusting scope at each iteration. It does this by making the client the central figure in deciding what constitutes that maximum business value. At the completion of an iteration, the client has an opportunity to change the direction of the project based on what was learned from all previous iterations. This constant adjustment means that an APF project's course is constantly corrected to ensure the delivery of maximum business value. In other words, change is embraced, not avoided.

Planning takes on a whole new meaning in the APF. Initial planning is done at a high level and is component or functionally based. TPM planning is activity- and task-based. In the APF, planning at the micro level is done within each iteration. It begins with a midlevel component or function-based WBS and ends with a micro-level activity and task-based WBS. I like to think of it as just-in-time planning. The underlying strategy to APF planning is not to speculate on the future because such speculation is a waste of time and energy. A key phrase to keep in mind when applying the APF is "when in doubt, leave it out," meaning that you include in your detailed planning only those activities that clearly will be part of the final solution — that is, at each iteration, include in your detailed plan only what you know to be factual. To that end, planning is done in segments whereby each iteration includes work that will require only a few weeks to complete.

The APF had its beginnings in two client engagements that were running concurrently and by coincidence had much in common. The first engagement was with a retailer who wanted to install kiosks in their stores. The kiosks would offer the latest information on product specials, give store location information for their products, and provide other customer services. The second was a software development company that designed and built Internet and intranet applications for their clients.

Even though these two projects were quite different they did have one characteristic in common: Both knew the final goal but neither one knew the solution in detail. The question for both projects was how do you proceed with managing such projects when neither the Requirements Breakdown Structure (RBS) nor the Work Breakdown Structure (WBS) could be established as the basis for the project plan? Both organizations typically followed more or less the traditional linear approach to project management. Both could see that that approach wasn't going to do the job, but what would do the job? Something different was needed. That was the impetus for the development of the APF concurrent with the projects themselves. Both projects completed successfully and APF became a reality.

Since then the APF has been used successfully in a number of different projects. I am aware of its use in developing new financial products for a large insurance company, designing and building computer-based commercials and short subjects, new product R&D for a consumer products company, and others.

I still consider the APF a work in process and will expand and embellish it through my own consulting engagements as well as the experiences shared by others.

The five phases that define the APF are as follows:

- Version Scope
- Cycle Plan
- Cycle Build
- Client Checkpoint
- Post-Version Review

Each of these phases is briefly described in the next section.

An Overview of the APF

The stage is now set to take your first look at the APF. Figure 13-1 is a graphic portrayal of how the APF is structured. Note first that the APF is an iterative process. You iterate within a cycle and between cycles. Every iteration presents the team and the client with a learning and discovery opportunity. The APF is crafted to take advantage of these opportunities. As you continue to study each phase, you will come to realize that is its real strength.

Version Scope

The APF begins with a stated business problem or opportunity. This beginning is the same as TPM. A request has been made to develop a solution to the stated problem or opportunity, and that request has all the earmarks of a project. At this point, you are not at all sure what kind of project this might be or how you might approach it from a methodology perspective. A Conditions of Satisfaction (COS) conversation takes place between the requestor and the provider to define more clearly exactly what is needed and what will be done to meet that need. The result of that conversation is a decision as to which project management approach will be followed: Traditional (covered in Part I), Extreme (covered in Chapter 19), or APF. You have decided that the APF is the approach to be taken, so a project scoping document, specifically, a Project Overview Statement (POS), is written.

A more defined version scope will include a requirements gathering exercise. The result will be either a complete RBS, in which case a traditional approach to project management will be chosen, or an incomplete RBS, in which case an APF approach will be chosen.

VERSION SCOPE

CYCLE PLAN

CYCLE BUILD

CLIENT CHECKPOINT

POST-VERSION REVIEW

Figure 13-1 The Adaptive Project Framework

CROSS-REF I discuss the POS in great detail in Part I, particularly in Chapter 3. See that discussion for more information.

Recall that a POS basically summarizes the Conditions of Satisfaction. It is a brief document (usually one page, maybe an attachment) that contains the following:

- A statement of the problem or opportunity (reason for doing the project)
- A goal statement (what will generally be done)
- A statement of the objectives (general statements of how it might be done)
- The quantifiable business outcomes (what business value will be obtained)
- General comments on risks, assumptions, and obstacles to success

The second deliverable from this phase is a prioritized list of the functionality that has been requested and agreed to in the COS. Both parties recognize that this list may change, but at this point in the project, the list reflects the best information available.

CROSS-REF There are several ways to establish that priority, and I discuss them in Chapter 14. The COS is fully described in Chapter 3.

The third deliverable from this phase is the midlevel Work Breakdown Structure (WBS). For our purposes here, a midlevel WBS is one that shows the goal at level 0, major functions at level 1, and subfunctions at level 2. Generally, such a WBS would have a two- or three-level decomposition. The number of levels is not important. What is important is to have at least one level of decomposition for each functional requirement. At this point anymore WBS detail is not considered useful because that information becomes clear in the Cycle Plan Phase. The traditionalist would have a problem with this because the entire foundation of traditional project planning and scheduling is based on having a complete WBS. I contend that the effort spent creating a complete WBS at this stage is largely a waste of time. Again, I remind you, why plan for the future when you don't know what it is? In this case, the piece that is missing is that you are not exactly sure how you are going to deliver the functionality. You do know what functionality has to be delivered, and you are using that information to generate the midlevel WBS but not the complete WBS. The complete WBS will eventually be generated when enough is known to generate it. That will happen within repeated iterations of Cycle Plan–Cycle Build–Client Checkpoint phases. You will generate it when you need it and not before; and when you do generate it, you will know that it is correct and not a guess.

The fourth deliverable from this phase is a prioritization of the variables that define the scope triangle (time, cost, resources, scope, and quality). This prioritization will be used later as an aid to decision making and problem solving during the Cycle Build Phase.

Cycle Plan

The Project Overview Statement has been written and is presented along with a prioritized list of functionality that the client and the provider believe are needed to take advantage of the business opportunity or solve the business problem. (Again, for a complete discussion of the POS see Chapter 3.) Some high-level planning is done very quickly to prioritize the functionality into a number of time-boxed cycles for development. Typical cycle length is two to six weeks. This cycle length is documented and agreed to by both parties — along with the expectation that it will change as project work commences.

The Cycle Plan Phase will be repeated a number of times before this project is complete. The first Cycle Plan Phase has as input the POS, the prioritized scope triangle, the functionality that will be built in this cycle, and the midlevel WBS. Subsequent Cycle Plan Phases will also have a Scope Bank as input.

CROSS-REF The Scope Bank is introduced in Chapter 16.

Contrary to what you might think, creating the cycle build plan is a low-tech operation. While you could certainly use project management software tools, I have found that a whiteboard, Post-It notes, and marking pens are just as effective. It reduces maintenance of a project file considerably and enables the team to focus on value-added work. This advice may sound heretical to those of you who are software aficionados, so let me explain. Cycle length generally falls within a two- to six-week time frame. There will likely be several small teams (a typical small team will be one architect and two or three software engineers), each working in parallel but independently on a separate piece of functionality. Each of these small teams will plan the cycle build in this phase and then conduct the cycle build in the next phase. Based on this description, a minimal planning effort is all that makes sense.

The cycle planning effort might go something like this:

1. Extract from the WBS those activities that define the functionality that will be built in this cycle.

2. Decompose the extracted WBS down to the task level.

3. Establish the dependencies among these tasks.

4. Partition the tasks into meaningful groups and assign teams to each group.

5. Each team develops a micro-level schedule with resource allocations for the completion of their tasks within the cycle timebox and budget constraints.

There is no critical path to calculate and manage. Traditionalists would have a problem with this. Their approach is based on managing the critical path. You could certainly calculate one here and maintain it, but I believe that is overkill. The cycle is so short that too much planning and analysis leads to paralysis. You don't need to clutter the cycle with non-value-added work. The entire effort can be whiteboard-, Post-It note–, and marker pen-based. A dedicated war room would be helpful (12' by 12' should work fine). The team can post their plans, work schedules, Scope Bank, Issues Log, and so on, and have their daily 15-minute updates, weekly status meetings with the client, and problem-solving sessions here.

Cycle Build

Detailed planning for producing the functionality assigned to this cycle is conducted. The cycle work begins and is monitored throughout the cycle, and adjustments are made as necessary. The cycle ends when its time has expired. Any functionality not completed during this cycle is reconsidered part of the functionality in the next cycle.

The first activity in the Cycle Build Phase is to finish the cycle build schedule and resource allocation. With everything in place and understood by the team, work begins. Every team member has a daily task list and posts task status at the completion of every day. Any variances are caught early, and corrective action plans put in place. Nothing escapes the attention of the project manager for more than one working day. A Scope Bank is created to record all change requests and ideas for functional improvements. An Issues Log records all problems and tracks the status of their resolution.

CROSS-REF The Issues Log is discussed in detail in Chapter 16.

Client Checkpoint

The client and the project team jointly perform a quality review of the functionality produced in the just competed cycle. It is compared against the overall goal of maximum business value, and adjustments are made to the high-level plan and next cycle work as appropriate. The sequence Cycle Plan–Cycle Build–Client Checkpoint is repeated until the time and cost budgets for this version have been expended.

The Client Checkpoint Phase is a critical review that takes place after every Cycle Build Phase is completed. During the cycle build, both the client and the project team will benefit from several discovery and learning episodes. Variations to the version functionality will surface; alternative approaches to delivering certain functionality will be suggested, and the client will learn through his or her continuous involvement with the team. All of this must be considered along with the functionality that was originally assigned to the next cycle. The result is a revised prioritization of functionality for the next cycle. The most important thing to remember is not to speculate on the future. In the next cycle, prioritize only the functionality that you are certain will be in the final solution.

I don't dismiss this as being an easy exercise. It definitely isn't. Most of the difficulty stems from either the client or the project team not approaching reprioritization with an open mind. People tend to get wedded to their earlier ideas and are hard-pressed to give them up in favor of others. To be successful with the APF, both the team and the client must have open minds and not display pride of authorship on any previous functionality that was discussed.

TIP **Change is a critical success factor in the APF.**

One of the greatest benefits from this approach is the meaningful and continuous involvement of the clients. They are the decision makers in all going-forward activities. They are doing it with full knowledge of what has taken place to date and with the collaborative support of the project team. They understand how business value can be achieved by changes in functionality, and they are in a position to take action. The APF encourages the clients to engage in the project even to the level of operating as a co-manager of the project. Their presence is a constant reminder to the team of the business aspects and value of what they are doing and what changes should be made to protect that business value. This client involvement is a very important point to remember. It ensures that what is eventually built will meet client needs.

Post-Version Review

During the Version Scope Phase, you developed measurable business outcomes in discussions with the client. These became the rationale for why the project was undertaken in the first place. Think of these outcomes as success criteria. That is, the undertaking will have been considered a success if, and only if, these outcomes are achieved. In many cases, these outcomes cannot be measured for some time after the project has been completed. Take the case of the project having an affect on market share. It won't happen next Tuesday. It may happen several quarters later, but the time frame is part of the success criteria statement as well.

The budget and time allotted to this version have been spent, and that marks the end of the project. Some functionality that was planned to be completed may not have been completed. The main focus of the post-version review is to check how you did with respect to the success criteria, to document what you learned that will be useful in the next version, and to begin thinking about the functionality for the next version.

What the client and the project team believe to be the best mix of functionality has been built into the solution. The project is done. The deliverables are installed, and the solution is in production status. At this stage, three questions need to be answered:

1. Was the expected business outcome realized?
2. What was learned that can be used to improve the solution?
3. What was learned that can be used to improve the effectiveness of the APF?

The business outcome was the factor used to validate the reason for undertaking the project in the first place. If it was achieved, chalk that one up on the success side of the ledger. If it wasn't, determine why not. Can something further be done to achieve the outcome? If so, that will be input to the functional specifications for the next version. If not, kill the project right now. No need to throw good money after bad money.

There is also a lesson here for everyone. If projects are limited in scope and they fail and there is no way to rescue them, you have reduced the dollars lost to failed projects. The alternative of undertaking larger projects is that you risk losing more money. If there is a way of finding out early that a project isn't going to deliver as promised, cut your losses. The same logic works from cycle to cycle. If you can learn early that a version will not work, kill the version and save the time and cost of the latter cycles.

NOTE TPM would find out a project wasn't working only after all the money was spent, and then a great deal of trouble might be involved in killing the project. The traditional thinking would be "After all, there is so much money tied up in this project, we can't just kill it. Let's try to save it." How costly and unnecessary.

The APF Core Values

As you can see, the APF is more than just a framework. It represents a way of thinking about clients and how to best serve them. The client is the center of attention in an APF project. It is the client who controls the direction of the project and determines where business value can be created. The APF project continues at their discretion and with their approval. This way of thinking is embodied in the six core values described in the sections that follow. These core values are immutable. They must be practiced in every APF project — no exceptions. In time, the APF teams will be recognized for the visible practice of their core values. I have had occasion to work with teams that periodically reward team members for practicing the APF core values. They are that important.

Client-Focused

While I was looking for the appropriate name for this core value, the phrase "walk in the shoes of the client" was always on my mind. It still is an operative part of truly being client-focused. This value is the most important of the core values. The needs of the client must always come first, as long as they are within the bounds of ethical business practices. This value can never be compromised, and it goes beyond simply keeping it in mind. It must be obvious through your actions with one another and with your clients.

Don't think that I am advocating passive acceptance of whatever the client might request. Client-focused also means that you have their best interests at heart. In a spirit of openness, you are obligated to challenge ideas, wishes, and wants whenever you believe challenge is called for. Your goal is to maximize business value to the client even if you have to push back on their wishes. To do otherwise is not part of being client-focused. You want to do the right things for the right reasons and to always act with integrity.

Client-Driven

One of the guiding principles of my business has always been to engage the client in every way that I can. I want them not only to be meaningfully involved, but also to have the sense that they are determining the direction that the project is taking. At the extreme, this value would mean having the client take on the role and responsibilities of the project manager. Such an extreme will not happen very often, but there are occasions when this may be occur. An effective arrangement is to have co-project managers — one from the client and one from your organization. In this arrangement, both individuals share equally in the success and failure of the project. There is a clear and established co-ownership. My own experiences with my clients has shown me that this is a key to successful implementation, and a key critical success factor for a successful project.

Incremental Results Early and Often

In the spirit of prototyping, you want to deliver a working application to the client as early as possible. This early delivery is especially valuable when there is any question that the real needs of the client have not yet surfaced despite your best efforts. The functionality of the first iteration of the application will be very limited but useful in any case. In some cases, the first iteration might be a proof of concept. (See Chapter 19 for more on this point.) It should deliver business value even though it is of very limited functionality. It gives the client an early feel for the final deliverables. Giving the client an opportunity to work with something concrete is always better than asking them to react to some vague concept or sketch on a notepad.

Early and often helps get the client meaningfully engaged and keeps them engaged throughout the project. Without their meaningful participation, an APF project is doomed to failure. They must understand this. If you can't get that involvement, use some other approach; the APF is not the way to go.

Continuous Questioning and Introspection

This speaks to an openness and honesty that must exist between the client and the project manager. Both parties must be committed to making the best business decisions possible. That can only happen with an honest and open dialogue.

Building a solution iteratively affords the opportunity to be creative. It creates the opportunity to adjust as better and more valuable features or presentations are discovered. As the cycle build proceeds, both the client and the project team should always be looking for improvements in the solution or the functionality offered. Look back at previous cycles, and ask whether what was achieved was the best that could have been done. All of this learning and discovery will be captured in the Scope Bank and come together in the Client Checkpoint Phase. Here is where the client and the project team propose, discuss, and approve changes.

A true spirit of openness must exist. Neither party should be afraid to offer or challenge an idea or the real value of some present or future deliverable. I've frequently told teams that if any one of their members had an idea and didn't share it with the rest of the team, I would consider it dereliction of duty. The same is true for the client. The successful practice of this core value is heavily dependent on the existence of a true team environment. And don't forget that the client is part of that team!

Change Is Progress to a Better Solution

One of my colleagues is often heard saying, "You're always smarter tomorrow than you are today." He is referring to improving estimates over time, but his comment applies to the APF as well. The Version Scope Phase begins with the requestor and provider arriving at a definition of what is needed and what will be delivered through the COS experience. Despite their best efforts, all the two parties have done to this point is make the best guess they can as to what will be done. That guess may turn out to be very good, but that is not important. What is important is that by working with the deliverables from the first cycle, both parties will get a better picture of what should be delivered. They will be smarter as a result of their experiences with the early deliverables. The result is to change the project going forward in the next cycle.

Don't Speculate on the Future

The APF strips out all non-value-added work. Guessing only adds non-value-added work back in. Therefore, when in doubt, leave it out. The APF is designed to spend the client's time and money on business value, not on non-value-added work.

If you find yourself building the RBS or the WBS and are guessing at what should be included, you are probably using the wrong approach. The RBS is your best checkpoint against the choice of approach. If there is any guessing at all, you might want to consider the APF as the best-fit approach.

CASE STUDY – PIZZA DELIVERED QUICKLY (PDQ) BACKGROUND

Pizza Delivered Quickly (PDQ) is a family-owned local chain (four stores) of eat-in and home delivery pizza stores. Recently, PDQ has lost 30 percent of sales revenue, due mostly to a drop in their home delivery business. They attribute this solely to their major competitor who recently promoted a program that guarantees 45-minute delivery service from order entry to home delivery. PDQ advertises one-hour delivery. PDQ currently uses computers for in-store operations and the usual business functions but otherwise is not heavily dependent upon software systems to help them receive, process, and home deliver their customers' orders. Dee Livery, their president, has decided to increase their penetration into the home delivery market by locating what she is calling "pizza factories" throughout their market. A pizza factory is not a retail establishment. It receives orders from a central order-taking facility and prepares the pizzas. A delivery truck picks up the baked pizzas and delivers them. Pepe Ronee, their Manager of Information Systems, has been charged with developing a software application to identify "pizza factory" locations and creating the software system needed to operate them. In commissioning this project, Dee Livery said to pull out all the stops. She further stated that the future of PDQ depends on this project. She wants the team to investigate an option to deliver the pizza unbaked and "ready for the oven" in 30 minutes or less or deliver it pre-baked in 45 minutes or less.

(continued)

CASE STUDY – PIZZA DELIVERED QUICKLY (PDQ) BACKGROUND
(continued)

Two software development projects are identified here:

◆ The first is a software system to find pizza factory locations.

◆ The second is a software system to support factory operations.

Clearly the first is a very complex application. It will require the heavy involvement of a number of PDQ managers. The goal can be clearly defined but even then the solution will not be at all obvious. The second focuses on routine business functions and should be easily defined. Off-the-shelf commercial software may be a big part of the final solution to support factory operations.

These are obviously very different software development projects requiring very different approaches. The pizza factory location system will be a very sophisticated modeling tool. The requirements, functionality, and features are not at all obvious. Some of the solution can probably be envisioned, but clearly the whole solution is elusive at this early stage. Exactly how it will do modeling is not known at the outset. It will have to be discovered as the development project is under way. The operations system can utilize commercial off-the-shelf (COTS) order entry software that will have to be enhanced at the front end to direct the order to the closest factory and provide driving directions for delivery and other fulfillment tasks on the back end. The requirements, functionality, and features of this system may be problematic.

Putting It All Together

In this introductory chapter, I have set the stage for the rest of Part II. The rationale behind the APF has been briefly explored, and I have given you the high-level view of what the APF involves. This introduction could well meet the needs of the senior manager who simply wants to understand the APF at a high level. For those at the program or project manager level, you are off to a good start. With that understanding in place, I can now proceed to peel back the layers of the onion — the APF. In Chapters 14 through 19, you will examine and come to understand the most granular of details for each of the five phases and adaptations of the APF. My intent is that you have a working knowledge of the APF when you are finished.

I am truly thankful to have this opportunity to introduce a new way of thinking about an important class of projects. It is my hope that you find it a valuable addition to your project management arsenal.

Discussion Questions

1. Under your leadership, your organization has spent considerable effort to adopt a traditional approach to project management. It has reached maturity level three — that is, there are fully documented project management processes and templates and everyone is following them. PMBOK is the recognized standard. You have earned a good reputation among your management colleagues. You have noticed a number of projects in which the client has requested and gotten approval for several changes throughout the project. These have cost significant money and time, the loss of e-business market share, and the subsequent loss of revenues. As Director of the Project Support Office, you realize that the APF is the approach that should have been taken on this project. You are convinced that by using the APF, these types of projects could have been completed earlier, at less cost, and with much better results. What strategy would you suggest to introduce and institutionalize the APF in your company? What obstacles do you foresee?

2. You are a senior project manager in your company. You have 15 years of experience with them and a solid reputation for delivering successful projects. What might you, acting on your own, do to get your organization to appreciate the value of the APF? What obstacles might prevent you from going forward with your plan? How do you feel about stepping outside the box?

CASE STUDY – PIZZA DELIVERED QUICKLY (PDQ)

3. Generate the RBS for the PDQ factory location software application. Comment on the missing or partially defined functions and features. In generating the RBS, consider such questions as the number of factory locations, where they should be, what criteria should be used to evaluate a location, and how many more delivery trucks will be needed.

CHAPTER 14

Version Scope

Prediction is very difficult, especially about the future.
— **Niels Bohr**

Define the problem before you pursue a solution.
— **John Williams, CEO, Spence Corp.**

CHAPTER LEARNING OBJECTIVES

After reading this chapter, you will be able to:

◆ **Describe the components of the Version Scope Phase**

◆ **Conduct a Conditions of Satisfaction process**

◆ **Write a Project Overview Statement for an APF project**

◆ **Develop a midlevel WBS**

◆ **Prioritize version functionality using one of three methods**

◆ **Prioritize the scope triangle using success sliders**

◆ **Determine the number of cycles and the cycle timeboxes**

◆ **Assign functionality to cycles**

The Version Scope phase is the beginning of the APF (see Figure 14-1). It is a formal set of activities that takes place very soon after a request has been made. There are two major parts to version scope:

A defining part. The defining part can effectively be completed by two parties: a requestor and a provider. These may each be single individuals or small groups that represent the two parties. In either case, the critical factor is that they not only represent their constituency, they also speak for their constituency and can make decisions for the same.

A planning part. The planning part is not unlike the early stages of the TPM planning session. It should be attended by the stakeholders and core project team. The difference here is that the version plan is not a detailed plan. It does not provide a detailed definition of the work to be done or of a schedule to be followed. Those details are part of the cycle plans.

Figure 14-1 Version Scope phase

Defining the Version Scope

You have probably guessed by now that more than one version of the solution is expected, and you are correct. However, you are concerned only with this version and will not reference any future versions of the solution. Information gathered during this version will inform management about any further enhancements they might want to consider in future versions. These future versions are not unlike the normal releases you see in products, services, and systems.

While there are similarities between the TPM and the APF, one major difference is related to scope. Scope creep is the bane of traditional project managers. They put up with it because they have no choice. They know it will happen, and they just have to make the best of it. In APF there is no such thing as scope creep. What occurs is change brought about by discovery, and learning by the team and by the client. What looks like scope creep is really the incorporation of what was previously missing parts of the solution. This change is expected, and the APF is designed to handle it with ease at each client checkpoint.

At this point I want to get into the details of the defining part of the Version Scope phase.

Developing the Conditions of Satisfaction

The Conditions of Satisfaction (COS) are determined by a one-on-one, real-time, face-to-face dialogue between the requestor and the provider. E-mails will never be a substitute for face-to-face dialogue. The problem with e-mail requests and replies is that you are never really sure what the other individual is saying because you don't have the opportunity for immediate feedback or to see nonverbal reactions to the dialogue. With e-mail messages, you assume you understand but you have no way of verifying that you understand correctly.

To further illustrate the point, here is an example from my early days of training IT professionals in project management. I would ask each student to write down his or her definition of *implementation*. They could do it by making a list of what was in and not in the implementation. Would you be surprised to know that there wasn't much agreement from one list to another? IT professionals can hardly say a sentence without using the word implementation, yet they don't really know what they are talking about. With this simple example, it is clear that the message sent is surely not the message received. How serious a communications problem might there be between a requestor (a businessperson) and the provider (a technical person)? Such communications problems can be pretty serious. They could result in the project team having one idea of what the client needs and the client having yet another understanding of what the team is going to deliver. It is so important that both the client and the team have a common understanding of what is needed and what is being delivered that to bypass the COS exercise could be disastrous. The COS, which was introduced in Chapter 3 and is briefly revisited here, solves the problem once and for all.

> **NOTE** The requestor and provider may be individuals or small groups, but they must be representative of the requestor group and the provider group and be empowered to make commitments and decisions for the groups they represent.

Here's a quick review of how the COS works. The COS consists of two conversations. The first one is driven by the requestor, and the second by the provider. Figure 14-2 is a schematic of the process.

Look at the two types of conversation:

Requestor-driven conversation.   The requestor states and describes the request using their language. The provider makes sure he or she understands the request by using questions and eventually feeding back the request in his or her own language. At some point in this conversation, you want the requestor to be able to say to the provider, "You clearly understand what I am asking you to do." The conversation now shifts to the provider-driven conversation.

Provider-driven conversation.   The provider responds by stating and describing what can be done to meet the requestor's request. The requestor asks questions to frame the answer and eventually describes the response in his or her own language. At some point in this conversation, the provider is able to say to the requestor, "You clearly understand what I can provide."

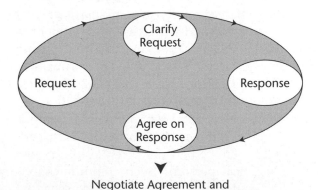

Negotiate Agreement and
Write Project Overview Statement

Figure 14-2 Establishing Conditions of Satisfaction

You should now have agreement and a clear understanding of what is being asked and what can be done. There will be some negotiating to reach agreement, and you shouldn't assume that everything is in sync until finishing the process. Note that the requestor and provider, through their earlier conversations, have established a common language. They each understand the other, which will smooth the negotiating that will take place. This understanding is one of the major benefits of the COS; a clear communication link is now established between the two parties. This communication link is very important now because the project does not have a clear solution. It will take the best efforts of both the project team and the client to fashion a solution that meets the expectations of the client.

The COS process is not a one-time event. It occurs continuously throughout the project. At each client checkpoint, revisit the COS. Because of the learning and discovery that has taken place, something will have surely changed that renders the previous agreement obsolete. This revisiting of the COS is your guarantee of always staying in alignment with what the client needs. It is also the pathway to move the client from what they want to what they need. Remember: The APF embraces change, and here is the place where change enjoys the light of day.

Writing the Project Overview Statement

The output from the COS contains all of the information needed to write the Project Overview Statement.

CROSS-REF The POS is introduced and discussed in detail in Chapter 3.

CASE STUDY – PIZZA DELIVERED QUICKLY (PDQ)

In lengthy discussions with Dee, Pepe Ronee learned that Dee wanted to restore market share by any means possible. She is convinced that will come from the home delivery market. The data supports her conclusion. She challenged Pepe to "pull out all the stops" and do what it takes. From where he stood, Pepe wasn't quite sure how that would be done, but he did have some ideas. Finding additional locations where pizza factories could be established would put PDQ closer to their customer base, which seemed like a good possibility. How those locations would be chosen was not an easily solved problem. Some type of store location model would be needed, but Pepe didn't know whether such systems existed, or if they did, whether they would be a good fit for PDQ. The requirements had not been defined to any level of detail, but Pepe did know that a solution would have to be found through iteration. The APF approach was chosen as the best-fit model.

To quickly review, the POS has five parts:

- Problem/opportunity statement
- Goal statement
- Objectives statement
- Success criteria
- Risks and obstacles

Ideally, the POS is a one-page document. Its primary purpose is to get approval to move forward with the Cycle Plan phase. At this early stage in the project, the last thing you want to do is burden the decision maker with a 70-page tome when all you are asking for is the authority to continue to the next phase.

Some organizations may require a little analysis to validate the business outcome of the proposed project. You have seen a number of attachments included with the POS, such as the following:

- Risk analysis
- Return On Investment (ROI)
- Break-even analysis
- Internal rate of return

These (and any other necessary supporting documents) are all appropriate and should be considered as aids to getting the approval to move forward with midlevel project planning.

Identifying the Business Problem or Opportunity

A well-defined need and a clear solution pathway planned to meet that need define a project that the traditionalist would die for. A rather vague idea of a want coupled with a vague idea of how it will be satisfied define a project that the agilest would die for (an agilest is one who aligns his or her project management approach with Extreme Project Management, or xPM, which is discussed in Chapter 19). Everything in between belongs to the project manager using the APF. The problem or opportunity that your project is going to respond to must already be recognized by the organization as a legitimate problem or opportunity. If anyone in the organization were asked about it, he or she would surely answer, "You bet it is and we need to do something about it." In other words, it is not something that needs a defense. It stands on its own merits.

Defining the Goal of This Version

This goal will be a simple yet definitive statement about what this project intends to do to address the problem or opportunity. It might be a total solution; but to be more realistic, it should be a solution that addresses a major segment of the problem or opportunity. I say this because all too often projects that are far too large in scope are defined. That leaves you vulnerable to scope creep and changes in the environment that render the global solution ineffective or irrelevant. By defining the goal of this version to be a reachable target, rather than a lofty or unattainable ambition, you protect the client and the team from scope creep. I am sure that unrealistic goal defining is directly correlated with the high incidence of project failure. Although it may sound too pedestrian, I believe that you will be far more successful in the long run by biting off less than you think you can chew. Don't ask for heroic efforts, just successful ones.

Writing the Objectives of This Version

By way of analogy, think of the goal statement as a pie, and the objective statements as slices of the pie. All of the slices that make up the pie are the objective statements. If you would rather have a mathematical interpretation, think of the objectives as necessary and sufficient conditions for the attainment of the goal. In either case, the objective statements provide a little more detail about how the goal will be achieved. They are the boundary conditions, if you will. Expect to write six to eight objective statements to clarify your goal statement.

Defining the Success Criteria

The success criteria (or *explicit business outcomes*) are quantitative statements of the results that will be realized from having successfully completed this project. They are formulated in such a way that they either happened or they didn't happen. There will be no debate over attainment of success criteria. Statements like "Gross profit margins will increase from their current average of 11 percent per month to an average of at least 14 percent per month by the end of the second quarter of production using the new system" are acceptable. Statements like "Increase customer satisfaction" are not. Generate two or perhaps three success criteria for your project. Success criteria generally fall into three categories:

- A metric related to an increase in revenues
- A metric related to a reduction or avoidance of cost
- A metric related to an improvement or increase in services

Listing the Major Risks

Put yourself in the shoes of the financial analyst who might ask, "I am being asked to invest $10 million in a new system that is supposed to cut operating expenses by 5 percent per month. What risks are you exposed to that might prevent you from achieving that ROI?" What would you tell the analyst? That is what you list as the major risks. You might also make senior managers aware of the fact that certain staff skill shortages are going to be a problem or that the reorganization of sales and marketing will have to be complete or there will be serious consequences during system implementation.

Holding a Fixed-Version Budget and Timebox

In the APF the budget and timebox are fixed. The *timebox* refers to the window of time within which the project must be completed. This timebox includes all cycles, which have their own timeboxes, too. I suggest trying to keep a version timebox to less than six months. Any longer and you invite many of the problems that plague the traditionalist. There are no rolling schedules. There is no going back to the well for another budget increase. One of the objectives in an APF project is maximizing business value under fixed time and cost constraints. Period. This is a very different approach to the project than the traditionalist would take. As long as the client is satisfied that the maximum business value has been attained for the time and dollars expended, the project was successfully completed. If the client and the project team pay attention, this result can be achieved every time. No exceptions!

Unfortunately, the maximum business value they attain may not meet the success criteria, but that is an issue for the client to deal with and should not determine the success or failure of the APF approach. Whatever didn't get done in this version will have to be left for the next version or not at all. Hence, you have another reason to keep scope to a feasible minimum and the timebox to less than six months. Those restrictions reduce occasions where schedules are extended or more dollars are needed. Those restrictions, therefore, also reduce the financial loss to the organization compared to the traditional approach. With the APF you can kill a bad project much earlier than you can with the traditional approach, and that accounts for the dollar savings.

CASE STUDY – PIZZA DELIVERED QUICKLY (PDQ)

The same template that was used to create the POS for the traditional project is used for the adaptive project. The figure included with this case study sidebar is the POS for PDQ.

PROJECT OVERVIEW STATEMENT	Project Name	Project No.	Project Manager
	Home Delivery System	IT-07-01	Pepe Ronee

Problem/Opportunity

30% of market share in the home delivery business has been lost to a national chain moving into PDQ's market

Goal

Restore market share to its previous high no later than 12 months after implementing the Home Delivery System

Objectives

Fully automate the order entry to order fulfillment process.
Acquire 2 store locations and establish pizza factories at those locations

Success Criteria

1. Reduce order entry to order fulfillment time to 45 minutes maximum for baked pizza and 30 minutes maximum for unbaked pizza.
2. Total development and first 5 year maintenance costs will not exceed $12m.

Assumptions, Risks, Obstacles

Competition has not permanently captured the home delivery market from PDQ.
30 minute delivery time cannot be achieved with present business model.

Prepared By	Date	Approved By		Date
Pepe Ronee	6/03/07	Dee Livery		6/04/07

PDQ POS

(continued)

CASE STUDY – PIZZA DELIVERED QUICKLY (PDQ) *(continued)*

First note that the Problem/Opportunity Statement is a fact. That is an important characteristic of every POS. The Problem/Opportunity Statement must stand on its own. It must not be a debatable statement. Furthermore, the statement can be changed from a problem to an opportunity. Pick the format that makes the most sense. Stated as a problem it is more powerful.

The Goal Statement is straightforward. Note the absence of a specific date. Phrasing it as a duration makes more sense because you do not control the start date. The two Objective Statements are all that is needed because the solution is not very well defined at this early stage. As the project progresses, the Objective Statements might be revised in the light of new knowledge discovered in one of the cycles.

The Success Criteria are quantitative statements of what characterizes a successful outcome.

In the final section of the POS I've provided an assumption and a risk statement. These are usually high-level statements that senior management would take an interest in. They may be able to mitigate the situation somewhat. At least they would be cognizant of your concerns.

CASE STUDY – PIZZA DELIVERED QUICKLY (PDQ)

The budget and time constraints for this project are typical of all APF projects. In this case Pepe knows the full five-year budgeted cost of this project. For any solution that might be proposed, the development and maintenance costs can be calculated. In other words, scope is a variable. In working with Dee, the greatest business value (as she would define it) will be delivered within the time and cost constraints. As the project commences Dee might change her mind about the time and cost constraints but for the time being Pepe must work within those parameters.

Planning the Version Scope

This planning function will look quite similar to what the traditionalist would do. In the APF. however, you stop the process earlier than the traditionalist would. The APF version plan extends only to the mid level, whereas the traditional plan would extend to the low level. In the APF you plan only to the level that you know will happen. Anything below that level is playing with the future, and the project manager using the APF doesn't play with the future.

APF planning is just-in-time planning. The following sections describe the details of the planning part of the Version Scope phase.

Developing the Midlevel WBS

The input to planning this version is the midlevel WBS. The midlevel WBS identifies the functionality that will be built in this version. It is a noun-type decomposition of the goal statement.

CROSS-REF Refer to Chapter 4 for a refresher on the noun-type decompositions.

The midlevel WBS does not show the tasks that have to be done to build that functionality. To complete the WBS down to that level at this point in time would define work that might never be done. In the APF, you don't know enough about the future to spend the time creating the full WBS to that level of detail. Over the course of all of the cycles, you may end up generating the complete WBS, but you don't know that for sure. In the APF, you build the WBS detail when you need it. For the purposes here, you simply decompose the WBS to a level at which you can reasonably estimate the time and resources needed for each piece of functionality. These are neither top-down estimates nor bottom-up estimates. You simply need a reasonable guesstimate.

The techniques described in Chapter 4 can be used here to build the midlevel WBS. Typically, the midlevel WBS is detailed down to level 2, but this is not mandatory. Level 2 would consist of subfunctions, but they are still noun-type statements. If you find yourself decomposing using verb-type statements, you have gone too far. In the APF midlevel WBS, the lowest level of detail is still a definition of what needs to be built (functionality), rather than how it is built. This is an important distinction. To define how to build something that may not even be built is a waste of time. Again, why plan the future when you don't know what it is?

Prioritizing the Version Functionality

Using the midlevel WBS as a starting point, the core team, along with representatives from the requestor organization, must determine the priorities of the subfunctions identified in the midlevel WBS. Before you can determine the priorities of the various functionalities, you need a criterion on which to make those priority decisions. Some possibilities are risk, complexity, duration, business value, or dependencies. The following sections take a look at each of these and discuss some of the reasons why you might want to use it.

CASE STUDY – PIZZA DELIVERED QUICKLY (PDQ)

Pepe Ronee defines the project as having two objectives:

◆ The first is to fully automate the order entry to order fulfillment process. Pepe thought it highly probable that a commercial product might be adaptable to their needs and that an early effort with a Request for Information (RFI) was appropriate. In the spirit of the APF, no further planning for this objective would be done until the results of the RFI had been evaluated and next steps identified. The TPM approach would probably include a requirements gathering exercise followed by a complete Request for Proposal (RFP). To the APFist that would be a waste of time. No speculation is allowed in the APF.

◆ The second objective is to acquire two store locations and establish pizza factories there. This is the real APF part of the project. The first question is, where should these pizza factories be located? The answer to that question requires some form of store location model. Exactly how to do that was not known by Pepe or Dee. Another RFI was called for. The figure that accompanies this case study sidebar is the WBS that reflects this approach.

Midlevel WBS

Risk

This criterion suggests that high-risk functionality has the highest priority and that low-risk functionality has the lowest priority. Why? The reasoning goes something like this: If you get started on the tough stuff early and you have problems, you'll have time to make any midproject corrections. If you leave it until later, you may not have time to solve it before the version timebox expires.

Complexity

This criterion says that highly complex functionality has the highest priority and that low-complexity functionality has the lowest priority. Why? The rationale here is exactly the same as the risk criterion.

Duration

This criterion says that short-duration functionality has the highest priority and long-duration functionality has the lowest priority. Why? If the driving strategy is to get something to the client ASAP, this criterion does the job. It also keeps the client's interest at a high level. You don't want them to wait three months before you produce some working piece of the solution, and this strategy enables you to get back to them quickly. They have something to inspect, and you get some input for the next cycle. As you move further into the cycles, cycle length can increase because by that time you will have the committed interest of the client and longer cycles will not be a problem for them.

Business Value

This criterion states that high business value has the highest priority and low business value has the lowest priority. From a business perspective, this criterion makes perfect sense. Get the most business value into the solution ASAP and start to reap the benefits.

Dependencies

There will be cases where the functions and even subfunctions between two or more functions are dependent upon one another. For example, subfunction A1 in function A must be in place in order for subfunction B2 in function B to work. Dependencies like the example may suggest that subfunctions A1 and B2 be in the same cycle build.

So which criterion do you use? If you guessed that the answer is "it depends," you are partially right. Actually, the best strategy is to defer to the client for the answer. Of course, you as project manager had better provide a detailed analysis of the pluses and minuses of each option. Still, this decision is really a business decision, and the client is in the best position to give the answer. In any case, the functionality is prioritized.

CASE STUDY – PIZZA DELIVERED QUICKLY (PDQ)

The midlevel WBS suggests the activities that could be undertaken in the first cycle. There are three: Request for Order Fulfillment Process, Requirements Gathering for the Order Fulfillment Process, and Request for Store Location System. Anything else would be speculative and not in keeping with the spirit of the APF. The two RFIs are done in order to determine what is out there that might be useful and to get ideas for RFP development as appropriate. The Gather Requirements activity is needed in any case because it will define the solution as best it can be defined at this early stage. It will also provide information for an eventual RFP, if that is the direction chosen. None of these three activities waste time or resources. The APF has a fixation about wasting time.

Prioritization Approaches

Before leaving this topic, I need to spend a few lines on what that prioritization looks like. The choice of how you establish the priority order of the subfunctions is entirely up to the client and the team. If you need some suggestions about the rule to use to prioritize, the following sections offer three suggestions by way of examples.

Forced Ranking

The first approach to prioritizing is called *forced ranking*. Suppose 10 pieces of functionality have been requested. Number them 1 through 10 so that you can refer to them later. In addition, suppose that the client has a panel of six managers (A through F), and each is asked to rank the functionality from most important (1) to least important (10). They can use any criteria they wish, and they do not have to describe the criteria they used. The results of their rankings are shown in Table 14-1.

The individual rankings from each of the six members for specific functions (or subfunctions) are added to produce the rank sum for each function (or subfunction). Low values for the rank sum are indicative of functions (or subfunctions) that have been given high priority by the members. For example, Function 7 has the lowest rank sum and is therefore the highest-priority function. Ties are possible. In fact, the preceding example has two ties (1 and 4, 6 and 9). Ties can be broken in a number of ways. I prefer to use the existing rankings to break ties. In this example, taking the tied function with the lowest rank score and moving it to the next lowest forced rank breaks a tie. For example, the lowest rank for Function 1 is 6, and the lowest rank for Function 4 is 8. Therefore, the tie is broken by giving Function 1 a rank of 2 and Function 4 a rank of 3.

Table 14-1 Forced Ranking of 10 Pieces of Functionality

FUNCTIONALITY #	A	B	C	D	E	F	RANK SUM	FORCED RANK
1	2	5	3	2	1	6	19	2
2	4	3	2	7	9	10	35	6
3	7	4	9	8	6	3	37	7
4	1	8	5	1	2	2	19	3
5	3	6	8	4	7	5	33	5
6	8	9	10	9	10	8	54	9
7	5	1	1	3	3	4	17	1
8	6	2	4	5	4	1	22	4
9	10	10	7	10	8	9	54	10
10	9	7	6	6	5	7	40	8

Must-Haves, Should-Haves, Nice-to-Haves

The second prioritization approach is a bit less demanding. Here you simply create three buckets: the must-haves, the should-haves, and the nice-to-haves. Every piece of functionality is assigned to one and only one bucket. Be careful with this exercise because there is a temptation to make everything a must-have. To prevent that from happening, you might put a rule in place that every bucket must have at least 20 percent of the functionality in it. Adjust the percentage to suit your taste.

Q-Sort

The third approach to prioritizing is called the *Q-Sort*. This approach discussed by William E. Souder in *Project Selection and Economic Appraisal* (New York: Van Nostrand Reinhold, 1984) starts out much like the previous one. Functions (or subfunctions) are divided into two groups: high priority and low priority. The high-priority group is then divided into two groups: high priority and medium priority. The low-priority group is also divided into two groups: low priority and medium priority. The next step is to divide the high-priority group into two groups: very high priority and high priority. The same is done for the low-priority group. The decomposition continues until all groups have eight or fewer members (see Figure 14-3). As a last step, you could distribute the medium priority projects to the other final groups.

Figure 14-3 An example of the Q-Sort

Prioritizing the Scope Triangle

You are probably wondering why you would want to do this or even what it means to prioritize the scope triangle. First, I want to define the scope triangle, and then you can begin to explore what it means to prioritize it and why we want to do that. Figure 14-4 is the scope triangle used in the APF. It's the same one that was introduced in Chapter 1 and is reproduced here for your convenience.

Figure 14-4 The scope triangle

Recall that the scope triangle consists of five variables: time, cost, resource availability, scope, and quality. To understand the triangle, think in terms of geometry. There is a triangle whose area is defined by scope and quality. The triangle is bounded by the three sides defined by time, cost, and resource availability. The sides are exactly long enough to bound the area defined by scope and quality. This triangle also represents a system in balance because of its geometric properties. If any one of these variables should change (e.g., the client wants the deliverables earlier than originally planned or a scarce resource leaves the company and will be very difficult to replace), the length of its line will decrease, and the three sides of the triangle could no longer encompass the area represented by scope and quality. In that case, one or more of the other variables must also change in order to bring this system back into balance.

In the APF, this scope triangle is used as your model for decision making. You first have to prioritize the five variables that define the triangle. The highest-priority variable will be the one that you change only as a last resort. For example, suppose you are developing a new release of a commercial software package, and getting to market first is very important to your business strategy. Time will be your highest-priority variable. Cost might be your second priority because the price points for this type of product are well established by the competition.

A useful tool for establishing the scope triangle priorities was developed by Rob Thomsett in his book *Radical Project Management* (Prentice Hall, 2002). Called *success sliders*, I have adapted it to the scope triangle, as shown in Figure 14-5.

OFF ←———|——◢▲◣|———→ ON   SCOPE: Stakeholder satisfaction

OFF ←———|———|◢▲◣——→ ON   SCOPE: Met project objectives

OFF ←———|———◢▲◣——→ ON   SCOPE: Delivered expected business value

OFF ◢▲◣———|———|———→ ON   SCOPE: Did not exceed agreed budget

OFF ←———|———|———◢▲◣ ON   SCOPE: Delivered the product on time

OFF ←———◢▲◣———|———→ ON   SCOPE: Met all quality requirements

OFF ←———|———|◢▲◣——→ ON   SCOPE: Met resource availability

Figure 14-5 Success sliders for the scope triangle

Think of each of these sliders as a dimmer switch. Accompanying each criterion is a dimmer switch that is set to ON or OFF, or any spot in between. If the dimmer switch is set to ON, then the constraint is binding. In other words, there is no room for compromise. That constraint must be met. For example, if the dimmer switch for the delivery date of the product were set to ON, that date is firm and may not be compromised. If the dimmer switch is set to OFF, the constraint is not binding. For example, if the dimmer switch for budget were set to OFF, that means the budget constraint is not binding and more dollars can be made available for good business reasons. If the dimmer switch is set somewhere between ON and OFF, the sponsor is willing to negotiate that constraint. The closer the setting is to either endpoint, the more or less flexible the sponsor is willing to be. To determine the settings, the stakeholder(s) should be asked for their individual opinions. The sponsor will use that data to make the final determination as to the settings.

Determining the Number of Cycles and Cycle Timeboxes

This task can be as simple or as complex as you care to make it. You don't need to make a lifetime project out of this step, so for a first pass, I suggest that you think in terms of four-week cycles and simply compute how many of them you can fit into the version timebox. Later, when you assign functionality to each cycle, you may want to adjust cycle length to accommodate the subfunctions that will be built in a particular cycle. If you want to be a little more sophisticated, take a look at the durations of the prioritized functionality and determine cycle length from that data. In this approach, you may vary cycle length so as to accommodate functionality durations of varying lengths. If you want to get even more sophisticated, take a look at dependencies between pieces of functionality, and sequence the development effort across cycles with those dependencies in mind.

There are a number of ways to proceed here. Choose the one that is the best for your needs. The most important consideration is the core value, which says to deliver incremental results early and often. Once you complete the Version Scope phase with your clients, they are excited about the project. They want to see results, and to have them wait for even eight weeks may dampen their enthusiasm. For that reason, you should think in terms of quick deliverables early in the cycles and leave more extensive build activities for later cycles. The early part of the project is the best time to capture the involvement of the client. Don't miss that opportunity.

Assigning Functionality to Cycles

Using the established priorities, simply map the functionality into the cycles, and then step back and ask the following questions about what you have just done:

- Based on the dependencies between functionality and the resources available, does this assignment make sense?
- When you finish the first few cycles, will you have a working version of part of the final solution?
- Can you improve on this assignment if you vary cycle length for the early cycles?
- Does this assignment fully utilize your resources in the early cycles?
- Are you practicing the core value to "deliver incremental results early and often"?

There is no substitute for common sense, and you always want to do what is right. Don't make the mistake that a traditionalist might make if they were making the assignments. Don't plan the details down to the last cycle. You really have no idea what will take place in the late cycles. Focus on the first few cycles and do what makes sense for them. You'll worry about the later cycles in due time.

CASE STUDY – PIZZA DELIVERED QUICKLY (PDQ)

For this project the total cycle length is 12 months from the start. In the absence of any other information, Pepe sets the number of cycles at 15 and the cycle length at four weeks, except for the first two cycles. This will change, but spending anymore time on it than they just did is a waste of time. The deliverables from the first cycle will provide further insight into later cycles and their length.

Writing Objective Statements for Each Cycle

These objective statements are primarily for the benefit of the clients and their management. You need to be able to tell them what they can expect at each cycle. The objectives have to make business sense, and that means you may need some further modification of the assignments to each cycle as a result of the client having reviewed and commented on your plan so far. You also want to make sure that the client can do something productive with the deliverables from each cycle. Those deliverables are your key to further modifications of the version scope that will be discussed at the Client Checkpoint phase following the completion of a Cycle Build phase.

Putting It All Together

I hope you are beginning to get a feel for what the APF has to offer and how it differs from the traditionalist approach. So far, you've examined only the first phase of the APF. Some of it is similar to the traditionalist approach, but some of it is quite different. For example, the APF uses the WBS but not to the extent that the traditionalist approach does. Traditionalists develop a complete WBS because they have to show all of the work needed to complete the project. After all, that's what the definition of the WBS says you have to do. The project manager using the APF would say that's great as long as you know all of the work that has to be done. In the APF you don't know all the work that has to be done, so you are taking some liberties with the WBS. You are going to define only the early work that has to be done (the topic of the next chapter). Some of that later work, even though you think you know what it is, may not be done. Why worry about it? You'll take care of that part of your planning when you need to, and right now you don't need to.

At this point you have done all of the planning that you are going to do for the version scope. In the next chapter, you complete the planning for the next cycle.

Discussion Questions

1. From what you know so far about the APF, do you see a conflict between process and people? Explain.

2. Clients are always reluctant to get too involved in planning. What might you do to sell them on the idea that their full involvement in the APF is needed for this effort to succeed?

CASE STUDY – PLEASANTOWN PLAYGROUND PROJECT

3. Referring to the Pleasantown Playground Project case study in the Introduction, how might you define the version scope if you were to use the APF instead of TPM? Be careful to differentiate between functions and features that you know will be in the final solution versus those that would be nice to have.

Cycle Plan

*You've got to think about "big things" while you're doing small
things, so that all the small things go in the right direction.*
— Alvin Toffler

CHAPTER LEARNING OBJECTIVES

After reading this chapter, you will be able to:

◆ **Create a low-level WBS for a cycle**

◆ **Apply the WBS completion criteria to the low-level WBS**

◆ **Understand the problems associated with APF micromanagement**

◆ **Estimate resource requirements**

◆ **Sequence the low-level WBS tasks**

This chapter bears remarkable similarity to the TPM approach. In fact, everything we do in this chapter, the traditionalist will also do (see Figure 15-1). There
are two differences, however: One, the traditionalist will do cycle planning for
the entire project using a complete version of the WBS. As noted in the previous
chapter, the project manager using the APF (APFist) works only on the part of
the WBS that corresponds to the work that will be done in the upcoming cycle.
Anything beyond that would be conjecture on the part of the APFist. Two, the
traditionalist will use project management software, whereas the APFist will use
a whiteboard, Post-It notes, and marking pens. The APFist could use project
management software, but it is not necessary. In fact, using project management
software to do cycle planning is like killing mosquitoes with a sledgehammer.

Remember that cycle length is typically around two to six weeks, and that is the window of time during which the APFist is doing cycle planning. Because TPM and the APF are so similar in this planning stage, there is some repetition of material in the first part of this chapter. This repetition is needed to keep the presentation flowing smoothly, but I will keep it to a minimum.

NOTE If you are an APFist and you still want to use project management software, be my guest. Just remember that you have to feed and care for the monster that you create. Ask yourself whether the time spent doing that is really value-added time. Two years ago I don't think you would have heard me say anything like that. Then I worked with a few major clients and watched and participated with them as they integrated the approach just described. It works and it really does save time.

Figure 15-1 Cycle Plan Phase

Developing a Low-Level WBS for This Cycle's Functionality

Our starting point for the cycle plan is the midlevel WBS we created in Chapter 14. Figure 15-2 shows a generic version of the midlevel WBS. We decomposed the WBS down to the second level, which is still expressing the WBS in terms of deliverables — the functionality that was identified in the Version Scope Phase. In this phase we will extract from the midlevel WBS the functionality that will be worked on during the cycle we are now planning. It is that part of the WBS that becomes the basis of our cycle plan and that we will decompose down to the low level. This level is where we define the WBS down to the task level. This decomposition will be defined in terms of verb-type statements, rather than the noun-type statements that are characteristics of the midlevel WBS, which is repeated here for easier reference.

So far the midlevel WBS is deliverables-oriented (subfunctions). We will create the low-level WBS for each of the subfunctions assigned to this cycle. To do that, we have to decompose deliverables into activities and finally into tasks that must be done to produce the deliverables. The top-down approach is my clear choice for how to do this. Start with any subfunction and ask yourself, "What major activities (segments of work) must be done in order to deliver this subfunction?" Think in the broadest sense, and come up with three to five activities. At this level you are defining work, and that means a verb statement. Make sure these activities are defined at a high enough level so that you can easily tell when they are all completed and when the subfunction is completed. Continue this decomposition of activities until certain completion criteria have been met. Once an activity meets the completion criteria, we call it a task. No other activity will have this property, so the term *task* is a precise term in our project management vocabulary.

Figure 15-2 Midlevel WBS

Because we are dealing with a project whose complete solution is not known, you will encounter activities that cannot be completely defined to the task level. Don't force this decomposition. Simply acknowledge it, mark it as incomplete, and move on. Later cycles will address the missing decomposition. The APFist does not speculate or guess, which leads to wasted time and resources.

CASE STUDY – PIZZA DELIVERED QUICKLY (PDQ)

The first figure included with this case study sidebar is the specific midlevel WBS for the PDQ Home Delivery System Project.

Midlevel WBS for the PDQ Home Delivery Project

The team size is such that the two RFIs and the requirements gathering activity will be undertaken in the first cycle. At the task level both RFIs have the same list:

◆ **Identify potential vendors**

◆ **Develop RFI document**

◆ **Distribute RFI document**

◆ **Analyze RFI responses**

◆ **Develop potential list of vendors**

The requirements gathering activity has a more detailed WBS, as shown in the second figure included with this case study sidebar.

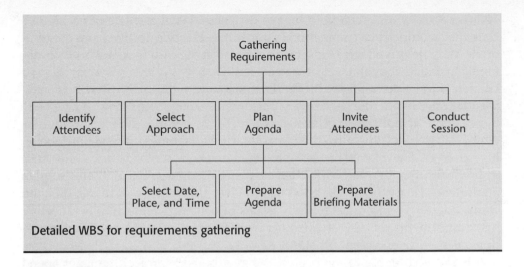

Detailed WBS for requirements gathering

CROSS-REF The completion criteria are fully discussed in Chapter 4.

Micromanaging an APF Project

Remember that every activity you define in the low-level WBS must be managed. That opens up the possibility of micromanagement. You want to make sure that the final decomposition isn't at such a granular level that you are forcing yourself to be a micromanager.

WARNING Understand at the outset that micromanagement is an easy trap to fall into in an APF project. The APF is a creative approach. It seeks to complete a solution to a specific problem. That requires creativity and not tight management controls. Let the team and the client have plenty of room to exercise their creative juices.

Best APF practices suggest that you manage an individual's work down to units of one week. For example, Harry is going to work on an activity that requires 10 hours of effort. The activity is scheduled to begin on Monday morning and to be completed by Friday afternoon. Harry has agreed that he can accommodate the 10 hours within the week given his other commitments during that same week. Harry's manager (or the project manager) could ask Harry to report exactly when during the week he will be working on this

10-hour activity and then hold him to that plan. What a waste of everyone's time that would be, not to mention an insult to Harry's abilities and commitment. Why not give Harry credit for enough intelligence to make his commitments at the one-week level? No need to drill down into the workweek and burden Harry with a microplan, and his manager with the burden of managing that microplan. The net result of this micromanagement may, in fact, be to increase the actual time to complete the activity, because Harry is now burdened with complying with the unnecessary management oversight done by his manager. The exemplary APF project manager will place more confidence in the team member, knowing that the processes are in place to ensure plan attainment. Harry, being the good team player that he is, will report daily on status and let you know about any issues or concerns regarding his meeting his commitments for delivery. In other words, you manage Harry on an exception basis, and you accept his status reports.

It is more valuable to the project to have the APF project manager spend time encouraging that behavior from Harry than it is to waste the time micromanaging Harry. If it should happen that Harry doesn't deliver against the commitment, there will certainly be a conversation between him and the project manager about future assignments and how progress will be managed. As you can see from this example, the APF defines a structured framework; and within that framework, it gives maximum latitude to the team members.

Once the low-level WBS has been deemed complete and all task durations have been estimated, print the unique name of each task and its duration on a separate Post-It note. For added efficiency, you might color-code the Post-It notes, with each function getting a different color. You will see the value of this later in the phase. If you are still using project management software, enter the name of each task and its duration into the package. Print the PERT diagram, which will produce a columnar display of the tasks because no dependencies have been specified. You can then cut out each task node and tape each one to a Post-It note.

By defining project tasks according to the completion criteria, you should have reached a point of granularity with each task so that it is familiar. You may have done the task or something very similar to it in a past project. That recollection, that historical information, gives you the basis for estimating the resources you will need to complete the tasks in the current project. In some cases, it is a straightforward recollection; in others, it is the result of keeping a historical file of similar tasks. It may also be the advice of experts.

Estimating Task Duration

For each task, estimate the clock time (duration) it would take with normal resources to complete it. Don't get heroic here. This estimation is no different from what the traditionalist would do at this point. Just think of the average skilled person working on the task at a normal pace with all of the interruptions and so on that typically get in the way. That is the duration you want to record for this task. Record this duration in the software tool if you are using one.

CROSS-REF   Chapter 5 provides the tools you need to complete this level of estimation.

Estimating Resource Requirements

There are two ways to approach this estimation: by skill or by person. You may not have your team assembled yet and may have to estimate resource requirements by skills needed. If you do have your team together, which you most likely will at this point in the project, they will participate in the cycle plan, and by person is OK. Add their name to the Post-It notes for the tasks they will work on. Alternatively, you might consider color-coding the Post-It notes so that each color represents a different person. Be creative because this visual display will be the foundation of all further planning and plan adjustments for this cycle. These strategies may be low-tech, but believe me, they work! For the high-tech folks, add this information to the software tool and print the PERT diagram. You can then cut out each node, and you will be in the same place as the low-tech folks.

Types of resources include the following:

People.   In most cases, the resources you will have to schedule are human resources. This is also the most difficult type of resource to schedule.

Facilities.   Project work takes place in locations. Planning rooms, conference rooms, presentation rooms, and auditoriums are but a few examples of facilities that projects require. The exact specifications as well as the precise time at which they are needed are some of the variables that must be taken into account. The project plan can provide the detail required. The facility specification also drives the project schedule based on availability.

Equipment.   Equipment is treated exactly the same as facilities. What is needed and when it is needed drive the activity schedule based on availability.

Money.   Accountants would tell you that everything is eventually reduced to dollars, and that is true. Project expenses typically include travel, room and meals, and supplies.

Materials.   Parts to be used in the fabrication of products and other physical deliverables are often part of the project work, too. For example, the materials needed to build a bicycle might include nuts, bolts, washers, and spacers.

Determining Resource Requirements in the WBS

The planning team includes resource managers or their representatives. At the time the planning team is defining the WBS and estimating task duration, they will also estimate resource requirements.

I have found the following practice effective. First, create a list of all the resources required for the cycle. For people resources, list only position title or skill level. Do not name specific people even if there is only one person with the requisite skills. Envision a person with the typical skill set and loading on the project activity. Task duration estimates are based on workers of average skill level, and resource requirements should be also. You will worry about changing this relationship later in the planning session. Second, when the WBS is presented, resource requirements can be reported, too.

Identifying a Specific Resource Needed

The need for a specific resource will occur quite often. When the situation arises, you are faced with the question "Should I put that specific person in the plan?" If you do and if that person is not available when you need him or her, how will that affect your cycle plan? If he or she is very highly skilled and you used that information to estimate the duration of the task for which that person would be responsible, you may have a problem. If you cannot replace him or her with an equally skilled individual, will that create a slippage that dominoes through the cycle schedule? Take your choice. It's often a good idea to have a contingency plan if you can't get a specific resource at exactly the time when you need him or her.

You now have estimated the parameters needed to begin constructing the cycle schedule. The task duration estimates provide input to planning the order and sequence of completing the work defined by the tasks. Once the initial schedule is built, you can use the resource requirements and availability data to further modify the schedule.

Sequencing the Tasks

Now we are going to put all the pieces of the puzzle together for a first look at what we have. Arrange these tasks in the shape of a network diagram from left to right on the whiteboard, showing their dependencies with the marking pens. You can follow the same procedure used in Chapter 6. You want to scale the display on a timeline so that you will know if you are meeting the cycle timebox constraint. The high-tech folks won't be able to resist the temptation and will go ahead and put these dependencies into the software tool. They will let the tool tell them when the critical path ends. That's fine; just remember that the cycle task duration is only two to six weeks, so the task list will be short. Be careful not to create a monster in your software tool, because you will have to feed it throughout the cycle to get any return for your investment of time.

The tasks are few in number, and you know the resources availability of your team members. The APF works best when the resources are assigned 100 percent to the cycle. If that is the case, you should have total control over their schedule. That means you can create the cycle schedule with both dependencies and resource schedules taken into account. The traditionalist seldom has that luxury.

CASE STUDY – PIZZA DELIVERED QUICKLY (PDQ)

The first cycle is rather straightforward. There will be three parallel swim lanes — one for each RFI and one for requirements gathering. The figure accompanying this case study sidebar shows the task sequence for this cycle.

The first cycle length is two weeks, which should be ample time to complete all three swim lanes. There is a dependency across swim lanes but that cannot be avoided. Because of the parallelism of tasks between the two RFI swim lanes, resources can be moved as needed. If the three swim lanes should finish before the two-week timebox, the cycle should be ended and you should move to the Client Checkpoint Phase. Don't waste time! That is not in keeping with APF practices.

(continued)

First cycle task sequence

Putting It All Together

We've come as far as we can with the cycle plan. It is now time to go into execution mode. There are a few more cycle plan details to figure out, but these are better left as the starting activities in the Cycle Build Phase, which is discussed in the next chapter.

Discussion Questions

1. Suppose your team has one person who can't do without the support of a software tool and another who is violently opposed to using them. You are the project manager. How might you resolve this dilemma?

2. Make a list of the advantages and disadvantages of using and not using a project management software tool for this phase of the APF. Discuss your findings. Does either approach win out over the other? In what ways?

CASE STUDY – PLEASANTOWN PLAYGROUND PROJECT

3. Suppose you were to use the Pleasantown Playground Project case study results from Discussion Question 3 in Chapter 14 to build your cycle plan. What risks might result from having isolated these tasks from the rest of the WBS? How would you mitigate these risks? Be specific.

Cycle Build

Try several solutions at once. Maybe none of them, alone, would solve the problem, but in combination they do the job.

— **Ray Josephs, President, Ray Josephs Associates, Inc.**

No matter how complicated a problem is, it usually can be reduced to a simple, comprehensible form, which is often the best solution.

— **Dr. An Wang**

CHAPTER LEARNING OBJECTIVES

After reading this chapter, you will be able to:

◆ **Build a micro-level WBS**

◆ **Create a micro-level network schedule for the cycle build**

◆ **Display and update the micro-level resource schedule**

◆ **Understand the purpose of the Scope Bank**

◆ **Use the Scope Bank to record change requests**

◆ **Use the Issues Log to record and resolve cycle build problems**

The Cycle Plan Phase works best as a team event, but I realize that some project teams might not be fully staffed and able to participate in the Cycle Plan Phase. For that reason, I have left the remaining details of the cycle plan for this phase. The Cycle Build Phase is an event that requires the presence of the entire team from the very start of the phase. You left the Cycle Plan Phase with a first pass at the cycle build schedule. You start this phase by continuing to work with the schedule and complete the last details of scheduling in this phase. Figure 16-1 graphically displays the Cycle Build Phase.

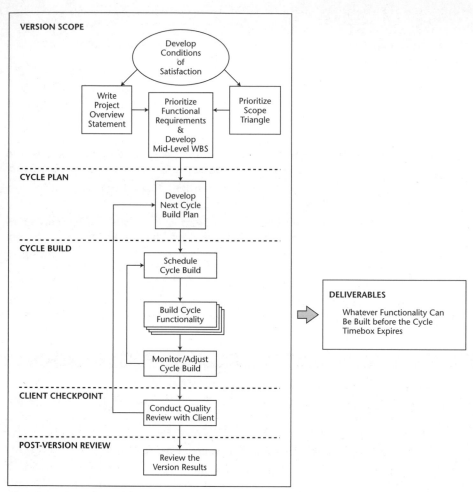

Figure 16-1 Cycle Build Phase

Creating a Micro-Level Schedule and Finalizing Resource Assignments

The team begins the creation of the micro-level schedule by further decomposing the tasks that make up this cycle's functionality to the subtask level. This process is a top-down whole-team exercise, and it follows the same process that is discussed in Chapter 4. Once the micro-level WBS has been created, perform two basic tasks:

■ Make Post-It notes for each of these subtasks and lay them out in a network diagram as shown in the upper portion of Figure 16-2. Note that the network diagram is time-scaled. This time scaling is important because it is going to replace what otherwise would have been a schedule produced by a project management software package.

■ At another spot on the whiteboard (ideally below the network diagram and on the same time scale), lay out a grid that shows the timeline on a daily basis across the columns, and have one row allocated to each resource. The resources for this example are Duffy, Ernie, and Fran. Show all seven days on this grid. For any workday or half workday in this cycle for which a resource will not be available for cycle build work, put an X or some other indicator of unavailability in the corresponding cell or half cell. (I have used shading to indicate unavailability in the figure.) This grid is your resource calendar for this cycle.

> **TIP** Half-day units are the smallest unit of time that I build my plan around. Smaller units just create non-value-added work and begin to border on micromanagement.

The lower part of Figure 16-2 gives an example grid for the network diagram. For this example, the tasks in this cycle build were A, B, and C. The subtasks, which are what you are scheduling, are A1, A2, B1, B2, C1, C2, and C3.

Before you finalize the micro-level schedule, check whether the initial schedule and resource assignments allow the team to complete the cycle within the cycle timebox. You can do this by inspecting the scaled timeline you created in the Cycle Plan Phase. If the current schedule doesn't meet the cycle timebox, look for alternative resource assignments that bring the schedule inside it. Look for resources that are not assigned for periods of time. They can either take over a task or help another resource complete a task earlier than currently scheduled. What you are doing is manual resource leveling in a way that makes more sense than the approach taken by most software tools. Some of the ideas presented in Chapter 12 may be useful for this work.

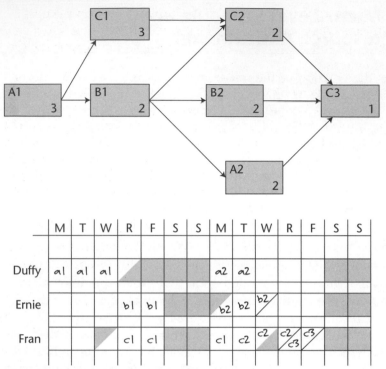

Figure 16-2 An example micro-level schedule

Once you have met the cycle timebox constraint, you are ready to finalize the information on the grid. For each resource, simply transfer to the grid the information that shows what task he or she is working on, what day he or she expects to start it, and what day he or she expects to end it. Every morning you will have a team status meeting during which you compare what was completed the previous day with what the grid had scheduled for that day. Any adjustments to the plan are made on the grid. Resources can be moved to meet schedule delays. Because you still have the Post-It note network diagram on the whiteboard, you will be able to see whether schedule delays will cause any other delays downstream in the plan, and you can adjust accordingly.

Take a look at a few important points with regard to Figure 16-2:

- First, when scheduling resources, try to keep them busy for consecutive days. That makes it easier if you need to replace an individual on the team.

- Second, notice when a resource is not busy (for example, Duffy is available for a half-day on Thursday of the first week). While this is early in the cycle, it may provide a resource that can help either Ernie or Fran, or help the team recover from a slippage or a problem.

- Finally, note that in the second week Duffy and Ernie are available to perhaps help Fran complete C2 when Fran is unavailable on Wednesday afternoon. If that can be scheduled, C3 may be able to be completed early. This means that the cycle would be completed ahead of schedule. Alternatively, that staffing adjustment might provide a way to make up for earlier slippages.

This grid should be permanently displayed in the team war room. It will be the focal point of daily team meetings. As status is being reported, the team can refer to this schedule and make any changes to the latter parts of the schedule. The most important benefit to having it displayed is that it is visible and accessible to the team. The only negative you have to worry about is that there is no backup for this approach. The fact that the team war room is reserved for the exclusive use of the team and is secure will mitigate most of the risk but not all of the risk.

TIP I have made it a practice to have one of the team members, when he or she is not otherwise busy, update an electronic version of the data posted in the team war room. Because this is only for backup, it doesn't need to be saved in a high-powered software application. A word processor or a spreadsheet package will do just fine. I have even used Visio on occasion.

The reason why using Post-It notes and the grid works is that the cycle length is short. The example cycle is only two weeks long, but even if it were three or four weeks long, the same approach would work. Even though I have used project management software packages extensively, I still find this low-tech approach to be far more intuitive than any software display. The entire team can see what's going on and figure out how to resolve scheduling problems in a very intuitive manner. Try it.

This approach would never do well in TPM for the following reasons:

- The network diagram would take up too much real estate and is generally not available from the software package, and not because it can't be generated. We all know that it can, but the labor to create it just doesn't justify it.

- Resource balancing is the other side of the coin. On the whiteboard it is easy. In a software package, who knows what happens when you try to level resources? Most popular project management software packages level resources using an algorithm that starts at the beginning of the project and works on the critical path, moving the task schedule out in time to remove any over-allocations of resources. That sounds all right, but in my experience, it has produced some rather bizarre resource schedules that put the project completion date past the date required by the client. Because you are working with a cycle of only a few weeks, you can easily represent the problem on the grid and create a workable resource schedule that meets client timeline requirements for this cycle. You want to see the problem, and a software package just doesn't measure up.

Writing Work Packages

By inspection you will be able to identify the critical tasks for which work packages will be needed. The aficionados will want to use a software tool to locate the critical path. That's fine, but don't let the tool do the thinking for you. The critical-path tasks are only some of the tasks for which a work package will be written. The actual decision as to which tasks you finally decide to create work packages for is based not just on how those tasks fit into the cycle schedule but who is working on them, what level of risk is associated with the task, whether or not the assigned resources are scarce resources, and a host of other factors. I would rather have you use reasoning to arrive at your decision than default to the software tool. There is no substitute for thinking.

For every critical task in the cycle plan, it is a good insurance policy to have the person responsible for the subtasks develop a brief step-by-step description of what they plan to do to complete the subtask within the allotted time. Remember that these subtasks are of short duration (only a few days) and quite simple to understand. The description should be one or two sentences. Don't add a lot of narrative, which may turn out to be lost effort and time. Don't waste time! If you lose that person or have to reassign the subtask, the person who takes over can continue with minimal loss of time.

You might also want to create work packages for high-risk tasks or tasks for which there is little experience among the team members. I tend to write work packages for tasks that require a scarce resource. If you lose that resource, perhaps you can replace it with less skilled resources and depend on the work package to help them over the tough spots. If formatted correctly, the task manager can use this work package to post progress and record any other information that might be useful in the event that he is not able to continue with the cycle build.

Building Cycle Functionality

Work is now under way to build the functionality prioritized for this cycle. Even though the cycle is short and the build not very complex, things will not go according to plan. About this time, the APFist is thankful that not a lot of time was spent planning, and takes the unexpected in stride. Something unexpected is sure to happen. A person gets sick or leaves the company; a vendor is late in shipping or ships the wrong hardware or goes out of business. These are the same kinds of risks that the traditionalist faces, but for them the results are far more catastrophic than they are for the APFist.

Depending on the severity, the APFist either finishes the current cycle or, for the really major problems, cancels the current cycle and immediately moves into the Cycle Plan Phase for the next cycle. In rare cases, he or she may jointly decide with the client to cancel the version and start all over, if at all.

NOTE Note that by making these decisions at this point in the process, the APF approach wastes the minimum amount of time and money as compared to the traditionalist approach.

Monitoring and Adjusting the Cycle Build Schedule

The team will have morning team status meetings every day — no exceptions. The meeting need not last more than 15 minutes. Everyone is standing and everyone gives his or her status report. If the status is behind, each member should report what he or she plans to do to catch up. Issues that affect only certain members of the team are taken "offline" by the affected persons so as not to waste the time of the entire team. Those who are ahead of plan become a resource for the others. You are talking here about minor adjustments to a few weeks of work. There are no big surprises.

To help monitor and adjust the cycle build schedule, the team will use three tools continually throughout the Cycle Build Phase:

- Scope Bank
- Issues Log
- Prioritized Scope Matrix

Maintaining a Scope Bank

The process of discovery and learning by the team is continuous throughout the cycle. Any new ideas or thoughts on functionality are simply recorded in the Scope Bank and saved for the Client Checkpoint Phase. The Scope Bank can physically be a list posted in the team war room, or some electronic form (spreadsheet or word processing document). Whichever form you decide to use, make sure it is visible to the team. Changes to scope are never made during a cycle. The cycle plan is adhered to religiously. There are no schedule extensions or additions of resources within a cycle. Whatever can be done is done. All of these extraneous items are taken up in the Client Checkpoint Phase.

CASE STUDY – PIZZA DELIVERED QUICKLY (PDQ)

The project has moved along pretty much according to schedule except for the requirements gathering swim lane. The other two swim lanes are on schedule and will finish by the end of the cycle. It is now the second day of the second week. The cycle is scheduled to end on the fifth day of the week. Requirements gathering will not be complete until the second day of the third week. The schedule slippage was the result of Pepe having difficulty scheduling the actual requirements gathering session. Critical people were not available until the third week. What do you do? Thinking about the answer to this is deferred to a Discussion Question at the end of the chapter.

The following fields make up the Scope Bank:

- Date posted
- Posted by
- Brief description of scope item
- Assigned to
- Date scheduled for action
- Recommended action
- Reason for recommendation

The Scope Bank is posted in the team war room. The first three items are completed by the person who initiated the scope item. At the next team meeting, someone is assigned to investigate the scope item further. He or she reports back at the team meeting on or before the date scheduled for action. The report consists of a recommended action and a reason for the recommendation. The date scheduled for action is changed to the date of the next client checkpoint. Until that time, this information remains in the Scope Bank to be acted upon at the client checkpoint.

Maintaining an Issues Log

Despite all of the team's due diligence in putting the micro-level schedule together, there will be problems. You don't need to enumerate what they might be — you know them by now. The bigger issue for the APF is how to handle them within the context of a learning and discovery framework.

CASE STUDY – PIZZA DELIVERED QUICKLY (PDQ)

At one of the team meetings Pepe talked about a street vendor who drove his van around the neighborhood and throughout the business district offering made-to-order hot dogs and hamburgers to people on the street. While the idea is not new, it got Pepe thinking about a van that could prepare and bake pizza for home delivery. That would eliminate some of the order entry to order delivery time by combining the driving to a delivery site with the preparation of the pizza. The pizza could be baked or unbaked. Surely that would save some precious time. The idea was posted in the Scope Bank for consideration at the next client checkpoint.

The fields that make up the Issues Log are as follows:

- Date posted
- Date scheduled for resolution
- Posted by
- Assigned to
- Brief description of issue
- Current status of issue
- Next step

The Issues Log is posted in the team war room and lists the problems and issues that the team has encountered during the cycle. Because the list is continually changing, I recommend that it be handwritten (I use nonpermanent marking pens) in a convenient location on the whiteboard. That facilitates updating and keeps it always visible to the team. It contains the information shown in the preceding bulleted list and is updated daily. The items in the Issues Log need resolution, and there should be a plan to resolve them. The person to whom the issue was assigned is responsible for developing that plan and keeping the team informed through daily team meetings of the status and next steps of the plan.

CASE STUDY – PIZZA DELIVERED QUICKLY (PDQ)

The delay in scheduling the requirements gathering session alerted the team to potential scheduling problems later in the project. The biggest concern was any delays in scheduling client checkpoints. Those would put the team at risk in that they would be held back in getting the next cycle under way. The issue was posted on the Issues Log and assigned to Pepe. The actual Log Entry is shown in Table 16-1.

Table 16-1 Issues Log Entry

DATE POSTED	DATE TO BE RESOLVED	POSTED BY	ASSIGNED TO	DESCRIPTION	STATUS	NEXT STEP
6/15/07	6/22/07	Pepe	Pepe	Key client representatives have very busy schedules and will create problems in the timely scheduling of client checkpoints.	New	Ask Dee for some resolution.

Using a Prioritized Scope Matrix

Any additions to either the Scope Bank or the Issues Log must take into account the prioritization of the project constraints.

CROSS-REF For more information, refer to Chapter 14, which discusses how the prioritization is done. Here I discuss how to apply it.

- For the Scope Bank entry, which was either a change request or an idea, a project impact statement should accompany the entry. At this point the impact statement should include comments relevant to the constraints that will be impacted if the change request or idea is incorporated in the version scope. There may be alternative ways to satisfy the change request or idea, and each of these should also have an impact statement relative to the constraints. Remember that the impact statement is brief. Don't get side-tracked writing the perfect document in the king's best English. Just get the basic information recorded in the Scope Bank. Do it at the time the change request or idea is new, so that a good idea is not lost with the passage of time.

- For the Issues Log entry, which is the statement of a problem or a condition that has arisen, the Prioritized Scope Matrix serves a different purpose. There will typically be a sense of urgency with an Issues Log entry. If it affects the current cycle, something must be done ASAP. Here is where the prioritized constraints help you, in that they help you focus your efforts at finding a solution within the constraints available to you. These constraints will help you avoid wasting time pursuing solutions that are not feasible in the minds of the stakeholders and sponsor.

Holding Team Meetings

The entire project team meets every morning for about 15 minutes. These are stand-up meetings where status is reported. Each task leader should state where he or she is with respect to the timeline (ahead, on target, or behind) and whether his or her team is ahead or behind, by how many hours or days. If the team is behind, they should briefly state their get-well plan. If anyone in the meeting is able to help, that person should say so and take that conversation offline. Problems and issues are not discussed in the team meeting except to add them to the Scope Bank and Issues Log. Their resolution or further clarification should be dealt with by the affected parties offline. Do not use team time to discuss things that are of interest to only a few members.

For larger teams (more than 20 members) there is an exception to what I just outlined in the previous paragraph. Such teams generally have task leaders who have a few team members responsible to them for their work. In such cases the task leaders should meet daily and inform their team of the outcome of those meetings. Once a week the entire team should gather for a team meeting.

TIP While the project manager might be the first choice for leading the team meetings, this is not necessary. Rotating the person who leads the team meeting is a good idea. It gives others a chance to develop that skill.

Status Reports

Project status is always posted in the team war room and is kept up-to-date. Anyone who has an interest or a need to know can always go there for the details. Brief written status reports should be available for the client at the end of each cycle, and more lengthy reports to senior management at the end of the version. While the project is under way, I tend to place responsibility for status reporting outside of the extended project team into the hands of the client. Placing it with the client maintains the core value of a client-focused and client-driven approach. Ownership is in the hands of the client, not in the hands of the project manager or project team. That is as it should be. The reason for this recommendation is that it puts the client in a position of responsibility for reporting the status of their project to senior management. It now becomes a business-type report, not a project-type report.

Putting It All Together

With a few exceptions, the Cycle Build Phase looks just like the traditionalist approach. Note, however, that the cycle plan and functionality are not tampered with. Whatever doesn't get done within the cycle is reconsidered for the next or some future cycle. Change management, which is a big issue for the traditionalist, doesn't even come up in the APF. It is imbedded in the Client Checkpoint Phase as a routine activity. In the next chapter, you'll examine the Client Checkpoint Phase. It is the critical piece that makes or breaks the APF.

Discussion Questions

1. Make a list of the advantages and disadvantages of using a high-tech approach versus a low-tech approach in this phase of the project. Discuss your findings. Does either approach win out over the other? In what ways?

2. Clearly, this phase is very dependent upon the people on your team. The APF gives team members great discretion in completing their work. If you were managing an APF project, how would you balance your need to know against the need to empower team members to do their work? Be specific.

3. Compare what happens with a TPM project and an APF project when a team member is taken off the team and is no longer available. What are the effects on each approach? Which approach is least affected by such a change? To do this comparison, consider a full TPM plan versus an APF cycle plan.

CASE STUDY – PIZZA DELIVERED QUICKLY (PDQ)

4. Through no fault of Pepe or the Home Delivery System team, the requirements gathering session is scheduled to occur on the second day of the third week. Critical people were not available until then. What do you do? If there are alternatives, what are they ? Which one will you choose and why? Be creative!

5. How would you resolve the issue regarding scheduling busy people so as to minimize the impact on the project schedule? Be specific.

Client Checkpoint

Any plan is bad which is not susceptible to change.
— Bartolommeo de San Concordio, Florentine painter and writer

---

CHAPTER LEARNING OBJECTIVES

After reading this chapter, you will be able to:

- ◆ Explain the significance of each input to the client checkpoint
- ◆ Assess the status of the completed cycle relative to its plan
- ◆ Describe the inputs to the next cycle plan
- ◆ Explain the outputs of the client checkpoint

This is the very heart of the APF. Here the client and the project team confer openly about what has been done so far, what still needs to be done, and what new learning and discovery have taken place in the just completed cycle. The next cycle functionality is discussed and the cycle begins again with the Cycle Plan Phase.

One of the real advantages of the APF over other approaches is that the client is involved as a principal and decision maker at all critical junctures in the project. Because cycle length is so short and so controlled, little can go wrong that is not easily corrected. Within the cycle itself, not even a day passes without the team taking stock of where it is compared to where it was planned to be, adjusting accordingly. Such is also the case between cycles. Little can go wrong that cannot be corrected, and few dollars and little time are wasted because of the APF's structure. It is here that the team and the client spend valuable time looking at what was done, reflecting on what was discovered and learned since the last checkpoint, and planning the functionality that will be built in the next cycle.

As you will see, this introspection with client and project team fully engaged is a very thorough process. If properly done, it is unlikely that anything significant will be missed. Figure 17-1 is a graphical display of the Client Checkpoint Phase.

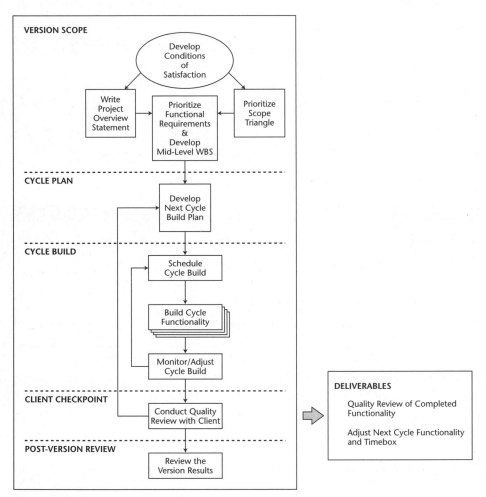

Figure 17-1 Client Checkpoint Phase

Inputs to the Client Checkpoint

The following lists the inputs to the Client Checkpoint Phase:

- Planned versus actual functionality added
- Scope Bank

Planned versus Actual Functionality Added

For the cycle just completed, the cycle plan called for a specific list of functionality to be added to the deliverables. No changes were made during the cycle, so it is possible that not all the planned functionality actually made it into the deliverables. There are several reasons for that, which I will not discuss; they are obvious (schedule slippages that could not be recovered, a discovery that rendered the functionality unnecessary). Any functionality not completed in the just completed cycle will be prioritized along with this cycle's functionality and any adjustments made in the cycle plan going forward.

Scope Bank

First discussed in Chapter 16, the *Scope Bank* is the cumulative depository of all the ideas and proposed changes that were generated during all previous cycles and have not yet been acted upon. Some of them were incorporated in previous cycles and are no longer in the Scope Bank, and some were not incorporated and are still there. In any case, the current contents are all the items not previously acted upon. There may be cases where ideas suggested earlier that were not incorporated may now be viable. That is the reason the Scope Bank is cumulative.

NOTE The only time anything is deleted from the Scope Bank is when it is incorporated into the solution.

Questions to Be Answered During Client Checkpoint

The following is a list of the questions to be answered during the Client Checkpoint Phase:

- What was planned?
- What was done?

- Is the version scope still valid?
- Is the team working as expected?
- What was learned?

What Was Planned?

The answer to this question is nothing more than a list of the objectives and functionality that were planned to be completed during the previous cycle.

What Was Done?

This answer is nothing more than a check-off list of the objectives and functionality completed. Comments often accompany the check-off because some items may not have been completed as planned. Subfunctions may have been left undone, and there may be good reasons for that. In such cases, the Scope Bank should reflect the situation.

Again, the only questions to be answered here are these: Did the cycle meet its objectives? Did the cycle meet its planned functional specifications? If no, where are the variances? The answers will provide input into planning for the objectives of the next cycle and the functionality to be built in the next cycle. Remember that you already specified objectives and functionality for the next cycle in the Version Scope Phase, so you have the original scope and potential revised scope to consider as you decide what the next cycle will contain.

NOTE TPM defines a formal change management process that can be invoked at any time in the project. In the APF, the change process is imbedded in the client checkpoint. The only changes that are accommodated in the APF occur between cycles. No changes to scope are incorporated within an ongoing cycle. Any and all change requests are filed into the Scope Bank for consideration at the next client checkpoint.

Is the Version Scope Still Valid?

Armed with the information discussed in the previous two sections, you now can ask a very basic question: Is the version scope still valid? If yes, you are on the right track. If not, you need to revise accordingly. Revisions to version scope can be significant. In some cases revisions may be so significant that the correct business decision is to kill the current project, go back to the drawing board, and start over again. The cost of killing an APF project will always be less than the cost of killing a TPM project because the TPM spends money and time on functionality that may not remain in the solution. APF, conversely, almost guarantees that all functionality that is built will remain in the application. More to the point, TPM projects are often killed, if at all, very late in the game when all the money is spent. APF projects are killed at a point where it becomes obvious that the solution will not be acceptable. That will generally happen while there is still money and time left in the budget.

Is the Team Working as Expected?

Real teamwork is a critical success factor in the APF. A lot of worker empowerment is threaded throughout it. If you count the frequency of the use of the word *I* compared to the use of the word *we*, you will have a pretty good metric for measuring team strength. The formula would be as follows:

```
Team Strength = number of We's/(number of I's plus number of We's)
```

You would like to see this number hovering around 1. The APF team needs to work in an open and honest environment for this to happen. That means every team member must be forthright in stating the actual status of their project work. To do otherwise would be to violate the trust that must exist among team members. The project manager must ensure that the working environment on the project is such that team members are not afraid to raise their hand, say they are having trouble, and ask for help. To do otherwise would be to let the teammates down.

What Was Learned?

This question is perhaps the most important one of all. Here is where the process will be reviewed to provide more value to the client. The new ideas that are generated here could not have come about through the TPM approach. This point in the process is where the APF, and xPM, in all fairness, really shine. Both the APF and xPM obtain their value from learning by doing.

Adjusting Functionality for the Next Cycle Plan

Once the answers have been given to the preceding questions, it is time for the client and the project team to look forward to the next cycle. The inputs to the next cycle planning activity are as follows:

- Any functionality completed during the previous cycle
- Any functionality planned but not completed in the previous cycle
- The functionality planned for this cycle

- The functionality planned for all the cycles beyond the next one
- All learning and discovery that took place in all previous cycles (Scope Bank)
- Any items still remaining on the Issues Log
- Any changes that took place in the business environment during the previous cycles

From these inputs, you generate the following outputs from the Client Checkpoint Phase:

- Updated functionality list
- Reprioritized functionality list
- Next cycle length

Updated Functionality List

You started this whole process with the Conditions of Satisfaction (COS), and it is to the COS that you now return. The only question to be answered here is this: Are the COS still valid? If yes, continue on. If not, revise accordingly. These revisions are the planned functionality for the next cycle.

The client and the team should spend most of a day in frank and honest conversation, considering all of these factors and then agreeing on the functionality that will be planned for the next cycle. Do not underestimate the value that can come from the sharing of learning and discovery. That will be your most important information because it helps both parties understand what this solution is really all about and what should be offered as a final solution. This part of the process is no trivial task.

Reprioritized Functionality List

The process that was used in the first cycle to prioritize functionality can be repeated here. The criterion that was used to determine the priority may be the same or different. Again, take advantage of all the learning and discovery from the previous cycles.

Next Cycle Length

The initial estimates of functionality duration for those functions planned for the next cycle may require a change in cycle length. Remember to be true to the overall timebox for the version. That cannot be adjusted.

CROSS-REF See Chapter 14 for a more detailed discussion on prioritizing functionality and working with cycle length and timebox constraints in the APF.

CASE STUDY — PIZZA DELIVERED QUICKLY (PDQ)

Recall from Chapter 16 that Pepe added an idea to the Scope Bank. The idea was to have pizza baked on a pizza van that was circulating in the market area. While traveling to the customer site, the pizza could be prepared and baked. The idea was that it would be delivered sooner due to the overlap of preparation time and delivery time. He introduced the idea at the client checkpoint. Dee was thrilled at the idea.

Fortunately, the requirements gathering activity was a few days away from completion and this new idea could be factored into that activity. The second cycle consisted only of the requirements gathering activity, and one week was scheduled for its completion.

Fast forward to the next Client Checkpoint. The requirements gathering activity was completed, but there was a new wrinkle to the project.

MEMORANDUM

DATE:	June 9, 2007
FROM:	Dee Livery
TO:	All PDQ Employees
SUBJECT:	Status Report

I just wanted to update you on the company-wide business improvement project. As you know, we hired Hype, Hype, and Morehype, a local marketing research and planning company, to ascertain our situation in the marketplace and our business processes. I have seen the draft of their report and wanted you to be aware of certain steps I feel are necessary and must be implemented without further delay.

Their final report will be distributed next week but I wanted you to hear from me before copies of that report begin to circulate. First of all, they have done an admirable job of addressing all of our major issues. They were a good choice. Here are the salient points in their report:

From their interviews, competitor surveys, and analyses, they have verified that we do have the best pizza in our market area. We ranked higher than the competition in all categories (taste, variety, appearance, price, and quality of ingredients). The survey also suggested that we add a selection of oven-baked sandwiches to our menus.

From the same market survey we were second only to our major competitor in our home delivery service. The survey pointed out that our time to deliver and pizza temperature at delivery were the only areas needing improvement.

(continued)

CASE STUDY – PIZZA DELIVERED QUICKLY (PDQ) *(continued)*

The market survey also asked about delivery of unbaked pizzas. The results were as follows:

We would definitely use the service	28%
We would probably use the service	31%
Not sure if we would use the service	20%
We would probably not use the service	10%
We definitely would not use the service	11%

The unbaked pizza market is not served by our competitor, and we should move immediately to take advantage of this window of opportunity. From the analysis of our sales data over the past 30 months, we learned that our home delivery sales began to drop a few months after our competitor moved into the market and has continued to drop at a fairly steady pace. Over the past 18 months, we have lost more than 30 percent of our revenues in the home delivery business. That impact has hit all four of our stores about equally. Our eat-in and carry-out sales have remained steady over that same period of time.

The summary-level data is as follows.

STORE #1 (OPENED IN 1999)	2005		2006		2007
	JAN/JUNE	JULY/DEC	JAN/JUNE	JULY/DEC	JAN/JUNE
In	$1.2M	$1.3M	$1.3M	$1.2M	$1.3M
Del	$0.7M	$0.5M	$0.5M	$0.4M	$0.3M

STORE #2 (OPENED IN 1992)					
In	$1.2M	$1.1M	$1.1M	$1.1M	$1.0M
Del	$0.8M	$0.6M	$0.5M	$0.5M	$0.4M

STORE #3 (OPENED IN 1975)					
In	$1.1M	$1.0M	$1.0M	$0.9M	$1.0M
Del	$0.7M	$0.9M	$0.8M	$0.7M	$0.6M

CASE STUDY – PIZZA DELIVERED QUICKLY (PDQ) (continued)

STORE #4 (OPENED IN 1984)	2005		2006		2007
	JAN/JUNE	JULY/DEC	JAN/JUNE	JULY/DEC	JAN/JUNE
In	$0.7M	$0.7M	$0.8M	$0.9M	$0.9M
Del	$0.7M	$0.8M	$0.8M	$0.6M	$0.5M

ALL					
In	$4.2M	$4.1M	$4.2M	$4.1M	$4.2M
Del	$2.9M	$2.8M	$2.6M	$2.2M	$1.8M
TOTAL	$7.1M	$6.9M	$6.8M	$6.3M	$6.0M

Our major competitor began opening stores at the rate of one per month beginning in January 2004. They now have 20 stores. Every PDQ store has lost home delivery sales over that 18-month period and continues to lose sales. In-store sales, which includes take-out, has held fairly steady over the past 18 months.

Our marketing consultants have shown how an advertising campaign would boost sales. They also suggest a discount coupon program to introduce our new home delivery services. I like their ideas and recommend we try them out.

The business process improvement program has identified two problems. First, we need to implement a preparation area where pizza ingredients are sliced, chopped, diced, and otherwise prepared for the production line. Because our kitchens are already cramped for space, I am going to use the four pizza vans for that staging area. They will service all four stores' inventory needs from the two pizza factories. The pizza factories will have the main inventory that supplies the pizza vans, which will carry inventory destined for the stores and their own production needs. This is expected to be a continuous service.

Second, in order to make room for growth, we need to replace the ovens in all four stores. The new ovens will be rotary ovens that occupy the same footprint as our current ovens but can handle 50 percent more volume. I've had several of our regular customers sample the pizzas baked in these new ovens. As long as we baked the pizzas on pizza stones they didn't notice any differences. Customers who order unbaked pizzas will be given a complimentary pizza stone for their future orders of unbaked pizza. The ovens are on order and will be delivered in one month.

(continued)

Our major competitor has just introduced 30-minute order entry to order delivery time. We do not have any details about how they intend to meet that goal, but we must counter their program with one of our own.

Based on all of this information and my 30 years of successful experience in this business, I have made an executive decision as to how we are going to proceed. The details will follow but here is an outline of the actions we are going to take:

We will open two pizza factories to add capacity to our home delivery line of business. The four existing stores will continue to offer home delivery. Two take-out businesses recently closed, and their fully equipped properties were put on the market with five-year renewable leases with an option to buy at any time. One was the German store Schnitzels-R-Us, and the other was the Cambodian store Sprouts-To-Go. Their locations are very strategically located in our growing market areas. I have signed a leasing agreement for both of those properties. They are available immediately.

I have been informed by our longtime supplier that they are outfitting trucks to bake pizzas for a small chain on the West Coast. I talked with the owner of that chain who said that the early sales figures exceeded their forecasts. I have asked our vendor to customize four of these pizza vans for us. They will be delivered in six weeks. Two of them will operate out of our existing four stores and the other two out of our new pizza factories. We'll continue to use the four vans that now service our four stores. At this time they will not be retrofitted to bake pizzas but that option is open to us if it is deemed to be a good business decision. This will be the pilot for further expansion of pizza factories and/or pizza vans.

We have been studying our telephone system. It needs to be replaced with a system that receives all orders from a single number and routes them to the appropriate store, factory, or pizza van for processing.

We need a point-of-sale (POS) system to handle all data collection (in store, pick-up, and home delivery) and analyze the information to help us make further decisions about pizza factory locations and pizza vans. The network that will service our business going forward must link all information and physical systems into a single system. We haven't used information technology to our advantage in the past, but we must do so in the future if we intend to succeed in this highly competitive business. I need your teams to be limited only by their own creativity.

Because all orders are routed to a store, pizza factory, or pizza van, we will need a hardware/software/communications/data system to handle all scheduling and routing in real time.

Inventory replenishment will require an order to be routed from the store to the appropriate pizza van for fulfillment. This order should be initiated by the POS system because it will be constantly monitoring store inventories as a result of orders.

CASE STUDY – PIZZA DELIVERED QUICKLY (PDQ) *(continued)*

We will also announce a 30-minute order entry to order delivery service as soon as we get our pizza factories and pizza vans in operation. This will be announced through a major advertising blitz in our markets.

I recognize that this action preempts the work you are now doing. Please be assured that your work to date with the marketing consultants has been exemplary and has solidified my thinking and made these decisions possible. Your work is far from done, and we will need to closely monitor our sales and performance to ensure we can reach our goal of recouping and surpassing the lost revenues from the past 18 months.

As always, my door is open to all of you and I welcome your input. We have a significant challenge ahead of us and the business needs all of us pulling together as a team.

Signed

Dee

The traditionalists would throw up their arms in disbelief. The APFists would shout with joy. First of all, there certainly is no lack of customer involvement. Dee is really excited and fully engaged. A strategy to contain her exuberance may be called for. Fast is good, but too fast can lead to errors of judgment and bad decisions. Nevertheless, a solution is coming together and everyone should be thankful.

Putting It All Together

In this chapter I have tried to give you an understanding of how important the Client Checkpoint Phase is to the success of an APF project. As already discussed, the APF embraces change, and it is through change that you can converge on a solution that delivers maximum business value for the time and money invested. All of the change that occurs in the APF occurs in the Client Checkpoint Phase. There is no separate change management process as there is in the traditional approach. Make the Client Checkpoint Phase the high spot of your APF experience and you won't go wrong. This phase is the last phase in a loop that returns back to the Cycle Plan Phase. The loop cycle plan–cycle build–client checkpoint repeats itself for as many cycles as have been planned within the version timebox.

In the next chapter, you will learn how to close the version project with the Post-Version Review.

Discussion Questions

1. A member of your team is a systems analyst from the old school and just cannot adjust to the APF. Her problem is that the client has decision-making authority over the direction that your software development project is taking and the client is, shall we say, technically challenged. How would you handle this dilemma?

2. You are the project manager for one of your company's first APF projects. You are having trouble getting the client's involvement. What would you do?

CHAPTER 18

Post-Version Review

The only thing we know about the future is that it is going to be different.
— Peter F. Drucker

CHAPTER LEARNING OBJECTIVES

After reading this chapter, you will be able to:

◆ **Explain the significance of the Post-Version Review**

◆ **Describe the deliverables from a Post-Version Review**

◆ **Conduct a Post-Version Review**

◆ **Extract lessons learned from the version project**

Just as the traditionalist conducts a post-implementation audit at the end of the project, so also does the APFist conduct a Post-Version Review at the end of the current version (see Figure 18-1). There are a number of similarities between a post-implementation audit and a Post-Version Review, but there are differences, too. The traditionalist is looking for final closure on the project, whereas the APFist is looking for ways to further increase the business value of the solution. In other words, the APFist is never looking for final closure; instead, he or she is always looking for more business value. The version just completed is just another step toward increasing business value. In that sense, the APF is quite like the production prototype because it consists of a never-ending cycle of repeated solution improvements. The only ending that is ever encountered is to retire the solution altogether.

Figure 18-1 Post-Version Review Phase

This chapter describes the series of actions that take place in the APF Post-Version Review.

Checking Explicit Business Outcomes

The only true measure of success of an APF project is the delivered business value. Meeting a schedule or a cost figure or some specification written at the beginning of the project is only incidental to the delivered business value.

The project was justified on the basis of explicit business value as defined by specific business outcomes. The Post-Version Review Phase is the time to verify whether the project has achieved these outcomes. Oftentimes, however, these outcomes cannot be measured until weeks, months, or even quarters have passed since the version was put into production status and the success criteria can be measured. This part of the review is no different from the traditional approach. The project has finished, and the team will be disbanded for reassignment to other projects. Waiting on the validation of a business outcome is related to the business reason for doing the project and in no way affects the team. Depending on that business outcome, another project focused on the same application may be commissioned and a new team assembled to do that work.

Reviewing Lessons Learned for Next Version Functionality

By now you understand that learning and discovery are very important parts of the Client Checkpoint Phase because that phase leads the client and the team to adjust the cycle plans going forward. Similarly, in the Post-Version Review Phase, the client and the team consider all discovery and learning experiences with a view toward the next version's functionality, on the assumption that there will be a next version. This information is the major input to the Version Scope Phase for the next version. The analysis of this information is a major part of the business validation of that next version.

CASE STUDY – PIZZA DELIVERED QUICKLY (PDQ)

The project ended at the end of the twelfth project month. Notice I did not say the project completed at the end of the twelfth project month. Time and budget are the constraining factors in an APF project. Dee, Pepe, and the team actually were quite successful. At the end of the twelfth project month the following solution was delivered:

◆ Two pizza factories were in full operation.

◆ Four pizza vans were in operation.

◆ A centralized computer-based order entry system was in place.

◆ The first production version of a centralized order routing system was in place.

◆ The first production version of an order delivery system was in place.

◆ An automated inventory control and reordering system was in place.

Much remained to be done, but at least an initial system was in place and was providing valuable operational data for Version 2. Both the order routing system, which sent an order to the location that would prepare the pizza (existing store, pizza factory, or pizza van), and the order delivery system, which sent a completed order to the delivery method (store location or pizza van), were built on heuristic logic. Such solutions are driven by experience and the data that describes that experience. The algorithms would be adjusted based on operational data. Version 2 would use that data to improve the affected systems.

> **CASE STUDY – PIZZA DELIVERED QUICKLY (PDQ)**
>
> **Dee was an ideal client. She stayed involved and actively made suggestions for improving the solution. This project simply reinforced the importance of meaningful customer involvement and the avoidance of speculation. Dee introduced a number of significant changes in direction, and any attempt to forecast the future of the project for the sake of a plan would have been wasted effort.**

Assessing APF for Improvements

So far, the lessons learned have focused on the solution (that is, the product) of the just completed version. The other type of lessons learned focuses on the process that was followed to create the solution and asks such questions as "How well did APF work?" and "How well did the client and the team follow the APF?" In answering these questions, the client and the team offer suggestions for improvement of the process and the practice of the process. As you can see, the APF has a built-in, continuous quality improvement process.

Putting It All Together

Clearly, the Post-Version Review is focused on the business value of what was just completed and on the business value of any future versions that might follow, which is as it should be. A guiding principle of the APF is to deliver maximum business value. I have shown how this applies to a critique of the solution just delivered and to a preparation for any version that might follow.

In the next chapter, the final chapter in Part II, you will look at some variations that might be encountered and how the APF can be adapted to fit.

Discussion Questions

1. You have completed your first APF project. Compare and contrast the traditional and APF approaches when both of them reach this same point.

2. What differences might you see if it were possible to do the same project twice — once using the traditional approach and once using the APF? Be specific. How might project differences affect your comparison? Again, be specific.

CASE STUDY – PIZZA DELIVERED QUICKLY (PDQ)

3. What situations might you envision in which TPM would be a better choice than the APF for PDQ? Be specific.

CHAPTER 19

Extreme Project Management and Other Variations to APF

Clearly no group can as an entity create ideas. Only individuals can do this. A group of individuals may, however, stimulate one another in the creation of ideas.
— **Estill I. Green, former VP, Bell Telephone Laboratories**

An eXtreme project is a complex, self-correcting venture in search of a desired result.
— **Doug DeCarlo**

CHAPTER LEARNING OBJECTIVES

After reading this chapter, you will be able to:

◆ **Embed the APF in other approaches**

◆ **Use the APF for proof of concept**

◆ **Adapt the APF to revise the version plan**

◆ **Identify an extreme project**

◆ **Describe the four phases of the Extreme Project Management approach**

◆ **Understand how Extreme Project Management clarifies the goal and converges to a solution**

As its name implies, the APF is adaptive. You have seen that in several ways:

■ Specifying the number of cycles

■ Determining cycle length

■ Changing functionality priorities at each client checkpoint

- Building in changes in functionality (adding new, modify existing, or deleting) at each client checkpoint

You have also seen how the APF not only anticipates these adaptations but also expects them. However, the APF is far more adaptable than even the situations in the preceding list indicate. There are three other adaptations you should be aware of, and these are the topic of this short chapter. The first two are brief topics and demonstrate how the APF can be used as a proof-of-concept tool and to revise the version plan. These are discussed first. Then I draw a comparison between the APF and Extreme Project Management (xPM). The two are closely related approaches to managing projects when the solution is not known (APF), and when neither the solution nor the goal is known (xPM).

> **NOTE** You will probably find other reasons to adapt the APF. Feel free to do that. The APF is not a rigid structure to be followed without question. The bottom line is to do what is right for the client. If that flies in the face of some established process or procedure, you need to take a serious look at the process or procedure. It may not be serving your needs.

Proof-of-Concept Cycle

There will be situations where the business case has not been sufficiently made to get approval to build the first version. In much the same way you have used prototyping to help with the client definition of functionality, you can use the same concept in the first cycle by making the first cycle of the APF a proof-of-concept cycle. That proof of concept could entail any of the following:

- The creation of a prototype
- A feasibility study
- The writing of use cases
- Storyboarding
- Any other activity to demonstrate business value

Note that it is very important that you not drag this activity out too long. Client interest and the interest of the approving manager will wane. You need to strike quickly while the iron is hot.

Revising the Version Plan

Sometimes the initial version scope misses the mark. You will see evidence of this via a significant number of discoveries and lessons learned in the first few cycles. These discoveries and lessons can create a big disconnect between the original direction of the project and the corrected one that is now indicated. In other words, continuing on the course suggested by the current version scope is a waste of time and money. Remember that you built a midlevel WBS and are making your cycle plans around that WBS. Too many changes brought on by learning and discovery may render much of the WBS out of sync. Revising the version plan is clearly a subjective decision. I would err on the side of revision rather than stick with a plan that may be heading in the wrong direction. The APFist is hard-pressed to do anything that may be a waste of the client's time or money. The APFist would conclude that the plan is off course and should be abandoned immediately. The correct action is to revise (or even replace) the current version plan and basically start over.

NOTE At this early point in the project, do not be afraid to kill the plan. In almost every case I can think of, you will be making the correct decision.

Embedding the APF in Other Approaches

So far I have discussed the APF as a standalone approach. However, its adaptable nature enables it to be embedded in other approaches. Take a simple case — suppose you have gathered and documented your requirements, and everything looks complete except for one piece of functionality. You are not sure how to build it, but it is an essential part of the solution. The TPM approach fails miserably. You could approach the project as a pure APF project, but that wouldn't do it justice either. Here's another way to tackle such projects.

Take the TPM approach and build the Work Breakdown Structure (WBS), but leave the unknown piece of functionality as a high-level activity. For the purpose of TPM planning, it will be treated as a task, although you know that in fact it is not a task. Bear with me, though. Build the network diagram and schedule with that unknown piece of functionality taking the role of a task. When you build the schedule, the task will appear according to its predecessor and successor relationships. It will have an early start and late finish date. You can calculate the part of the budget that can be spent on it as well. Now you have a start date and a completion date and a budget to find this missing piece of the solution. That is an APF project, and it is embedded in a TPM project.

Extreme Project Management

The third variation that I will discuss is Extreme Project Management (xPM). xPM and the APF both originated at about the same time, so it is difficult to say which is a variation of the other from a chronological point of view. In any case, xPM handles situations in which the goal is not clearly defined and therefore the solution cannot be defined either. On the continuum of project management approaches, the traditional approach occupies the structured end, where there is the most clarity with respect to both the goal and the solution. xPM is at the unstructured end, where there is the least clarity with respect to the goal and the solution. The APF occupies the middle position.

This section defines the extreme project and gives a high-level overview of the four phases that constitute the xPM approach. As such, it is a good starting point for the executive or manager who simply needs to become familiar with the xPM approach.

Defining an Extreme Project

The best way to define an extreme project is to consider its characteristics, which are discussed in the following list:

High speed.   The types of projects that are suited to xPM are groundbreaking, innovative, critical to an organization's future, and otherwise very important to their sponsors. That means that the results are wanted ASAP. Fast is good, and you will be around tomorrow to talk about it. Slow is bad, and you will be looking for something else to do with the rest of your life. Time, or faster, to market is a critical success factor in every extreme project business endeavor.

High change.   The uncertainty about the goal or the solution means that as the project is under way, learning and discovery, just as in APF projects, will happen. It happens with more regularity and frequency in xPM than in APF projects. The APF changes can be thought of as minor in comparison. The changes in an extreme project may completely reverse the direction of the project. In some cases, the changes might mean canceling the current project and starting two or more projects based on the learning and discovery to date with the now cancelled project. For example, R&D projects are extreme projects, and a discovery in one cycle may cause the team and the client to move in a totally different direction in the next and later cycles.

High uncertainty.   Because an extreme project is innovative and research-oriented, no one really knows what lies ahead. The direction chosen by the client and the project team might be 180 degrees out of phase with what they should be doing, but no one knows that. Furthermore, the time to complete the extreme project is not known. The cost to complete an extreme project is not known either. In short, there will be a lot of trial and error, and a lot of false starts and killed projects.

These characteristics will strike fear into the hearts of most, if not all, project managers. Make no mistake, extreme projects are extremely challenging. Their failure rate will be high. Many will be canceled before they are completed. For those that are successful, what they deliver may not at all reflect what they thought they would deliver. In other words, the actual goal achieved may be quite different from the goal that was originally envisioned. That is the nature of extreme projects, and that is where we begin our investigation of how xPM applies to them.

Overview of Extreme Project Management

By its very nature, xPM is unstructured (see Figure 19-1). xPM and the APF are both variations of the same theme: learning and discovery move the project forward. The idea is an adaptation of the Flexible Project Model introduced in 2000 by Doug DeCarlo in his eXtreme Project Management Workshop. Recall that the difference between xPM and the APF is that the latter requires a clearly defined goal, whereas xPM does not. As Figure 19-1 illustrates, xPM consists of four phases, which I am calling INitiate, SPeculate, Incubate, and REview (INSPIRE).

xPM is an iterative approach, just as the APF is an iterative approach. xPM iterates in an unspecified number of short cycles (one- to four-week cycle lengths are typical) in search of the solution (in other words, the goal). It may find an acceptable solution, or it may be cancelled before any solution is reached. It is distinguished from the APF in that the goal is unknown, or at best, someone has a vague, but unspecified, notion of what the goal consists. Such a client might say, "I'll know it when I see it." That isn't a new revelation to the experienced project manager; they have heard that many times before. Nevertheless, it is their job to find the solution (with the client's help, of course).

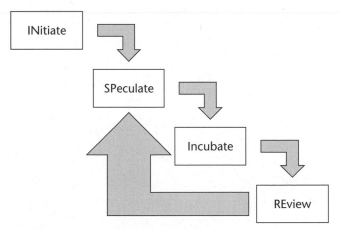

Figure 19-1 Extreme Project Management

The APF is further distinguished from xPM in that xPM requires the client to be more involved within and between cycles, whereas the APF requires client involvement between cycles. Drug research provides a good example of the extreme project. Suppose, for example, that the goal is to find a natural food additive that will eliminate the common cold. This is a wide-open project. Constraining the project to a fixed budget or fixed timeline makes no sense whatsoever. More than likely, the project team will begin by choosing some investigative direction or directions and hope that intermediate findings and results will accomplish two things:

- The just-finished cycle will point to a more informed and productive direction for the next and future cycles. In other words, xPM includes learning and discovery experiences just as the APF does.

- Most important of all, the funding agent will see this learning and discovery as potentially rewarding and decide to continue the funding support.

There is no constrained scope triangle in xPM as there is in TPM and APF projects. Recall that those TPM and APF projects have time and funding constraints that were meaningful. "Put a man on the moon and return him safely by the end of the decade" is pretty specific. It has a built-in stopping rule. When the money or the time runs out, the project is over. xPM does have stopping rules, two of them, but they are very different:

- The first one says that the project is over when the solution is found. Success!

- The second one says the project is over when the sponsor is not willing to continue the funding. The sponsor might withdraw the funding because the project is not making any meaningful progress. It is not converging on an acceptable solution. In other words, the project is killed. Failure!

The next sections take a high-level look at the four phases of xPM.

INitiate

The INitiate phase is a mixture of selling the idea, establishing the business value of the project, brainstorming possible approaches, forming the team, and getting everyone on board and excited about what they are about to undertake. It is definitely a time for team building and creating a strong working relationship with the client.

At this point, someone has an idea for a product or service and is proposing that a project be commissioned to investigate and produce it. Before any project will be launched, management must be convinced that it is an idea worth pursuing. The burden of proof is on the requestor. He or she must document and demonstrate that there is business value in the undertaking. The Project Overview Statement (POS), which you used in both TPM and the APF, is the documentation I recommend to sell the idea. There are some differences in the xPM version of the POS.

Defining the Project Goal

Unlike the goal of an APF project, the goal of an extreme project is not much more than a vision of some future state. "I'll know it when I see it" is about the only statement of the project goal that could be made, given the vague nature of the goal as envisioned at this point in time. It has all the characteristics of an adventure in which the destination is only vaguely defined. You have to understand that the goal of an extreme project unfolds along the journey. It is not something that you can plan to achieve; it is only something that you and the client discover along the way. That process of discovery is exciting. It will call upon all of the creative juices that the team and the client can muster. Contrast this to the project goal in an APF project. In the APF, the goal is known; it's the solution that evolves as the project unfolds. In general, the client is more directive in xPM, whereas the team is more directive in the APF.

At this early stage, any definition of the project goal should be that vision of the future. It would be good at this point to discuss how the user or customer of the deliverables will use the product or service. Don't be too restrictive. Keep your options open — or "keep your powder dry," as one of my colleagues would say. Forming a vision of the end state is as much a brainstorming exercise as it is anything else. Don't close out any ideas that may prove useful later.

xPM Project Overview Statement

An example will help ground some of these new ideas. Suppose the project is to find a cure for the common cold. As discussed in earlier chapters of this book, the Project Overview Statement is a critical document in both the TPM and APF approaches, and so it is again in xPM projects. However, because the goal was known in both TPM and APF projects but is not known in xPM projects, there will be some differences in the POS. These differences are best illustrated by way of example. Figure 19-2 is the POS for the project to find a cure for the common cold.

PROJECT OVERVIEW STATEMENT	Project Name Common Cold Prevention Project	Project No. 02 - 01	Project Manager Carrie deCure

Problem/Opportunity

    There does not exist a preventative for the common cold.

Goal

    Find a way to prevent the occurrence of the common cold.

Objectives

    1. Find a food additive that will prevent the occurrence of the common cold.

    2. Alter the immune system to prevent the occurrence of the common cold.

    3. Define a program of diet and excercise that will prevent the occurrence of the common cold.

Success Criteria

    The solution must be effective for persons of any age.

    The solution must not introduce any harmful side effects.

    The solution must be affordable.

    The solution must be acceptable to the FDA.

    The solution must be easily obtained.

    The solution must create a profitable business oppurtunity.

Assumptions, Risks, Obstacles

    The common cold can be prevented.

    The solution will have harmful side effects.

Prepared By Earnest Effort	Date 2-14-2007	Approved By Hy Podermick	Date 2-16-2007

Figure 19-2 POS for the project to find a cure for the common cold

    The following list looks at each of the elements of this xPM POS to illustrate the differences between this sort of POS and that used in a TPM or APF approach.

    Problem or opportunity statement. Nothing unusual here. This is a very simple statement of a problem that has plagued health care providers and moms since the dawn of civilization.

    Goal statement. This particular project is taking a calculated (or maybe wild a**) guess that they can establish a preventative barrier to the occurrence of the common cold. Unlike the goal statements in TPM and APF projects, no time frame is specified. That would make no sense for such a research project.

Objective statements.   These objective statements identify broad directions that the research effort will take. Notice that the format does not fit the S.M.A.R.T. characteristics defined in Chapter 3. In most cases, these objective statements will provide some early guidance on the directions the team intends to pursue. Unlike TPM and APF projects, these objective statements are not a necessary and sufficient set of objectives. Their successful completion does not assure goal attainment. In fact, some of them may be discarded based on learning and discovery in early cycles. Think of them as guideposts only. They set an initial direction for the project. Because the goal is not clearly defined, you can't expect the objective statements to play the role that they do in TPM and APF projects.

Success criteria.   The goal statement might do just as well as any success criteria, so this part of the POS could be left blank. In this case you have set bounds around the characteristics of an acceptable cure.

Assumptions, risks, and obstacles.   There is no difference between xPM, TPM, and the APF when it comes to this section. The statements given in the example lean heavily toward assumptions. Having to make such assumptions happens to be the nature of this project.

Establishing a Project Timebox and Cost

Contrary to an APF project, an extreme project is not constrained by a fixed time frame or cost limit. It is best to think of the xPM time and cost parameters as something that provides the project team with guidance about the client's expectations. It is much like having the client say, "I would like to see some results within N months, and I am willing to invest as much as $\$X$ to have you deliver." In reality, at each REview phase the decision to continue or abort is made. That decision isn't necessarily tied to the time and cost parameters given earlier by the client. In fact, if exceptional progress toward a solution is made, then the client may relax either or both of the time and cost parameters. Put another way, if the progress to date is promising, more time and/or money may be put at the team's disposal.

Establishing the Number of Cycles and Cycle Length

In the beginning, short cycles are advisable. In the early cycles, new ideas are tested, and many will be rejected; proof of concept may be part of the first few cycles. The team should not be committing to complex activities and tasks early on. As the team gains a better sense of direction, cycle length may be increased. Specifying cycle length and the number of cycles up front merely sets expectations as to when and how frequently the REview phase will take place. At each occurrence of a REview phase, cycle length and perhaps the number of cycles remaining may be changed to suit the situation. In an exploratory project, it would be a mistake to bind the team and the client to cycles that do not relate to the realities of the project. Remember that flexibility is the key to a successful xPM project.

Trade-Offs in the Scope Triangle

Despite the fact that xPM is unstructured, it is important to set the priorities of the variables in the scope triangle. As project work commences and problems arise, which variable or variables are the client and the team willing to compromise? As discussed in Chapter 1, the five variables in a project are as follows:

- Scope
- Quality
- Cost
- Time
- Resource availability

Which of these is least likely to be compromised? Which would you choose to compromise first if the situation warranted it? The answer should depend on the type of project. For example, if the project involves conducting research to find a cure for the common cold, quality is the least likely to be compromised and time might be the first to be compromised. But what if you knew that a competitor was working on the same project? Would time still be the first variable to compromise? Probably not. Cost might take its place because time to market is now a critical success factor.

Scope is an interesting variable in extreme projects. Consider the common cold cure example again. Hypothetically, what if you knew that the competition was also looking for a cure for the common cold and that being first to market would be very important? In an earlier cycle, the team discovered not a cure for the cold but a food additive that arrests the cold at whatever stage of development it happens to be. In other words, the cold will not get worse than it was at the time the additive was taken. The early discovery also holds great promise to morph into the cure that you are looking for, but you need time to explore it. You feel that getting the early result to market now may give you a strategic barrier to entry, give the competition reason to pause, and buy you some time to continue toward the original goal. Therefore, scope is reduced in the current project and it is brought to a successful completion. A new project is commissioned to continue on the path discovered in the earlier project.

SPeculate

This phase defines the beginning of a new cycle and will always start with a brainstorming session. The input will be either a blank slate or output from the previous SPeculate-Incubate-REview cycle. In any case, the project team, client, and final user of the product or service should participate in the brainstorming session. The objective of this session is to explore ideas and identify alternative directions for the next Incubate phase. Because an extreme project has a strong exploratory nature about it, no idea should be neglected. Several directions may eventually be pursued in parallel in the next cycle. Cycle length, deliverables, and other planning artifacts are defined in the SPeculate phase as well.

The word *speculate* conjures up deep thinking, carrying out due diligence on several alternatives, the choosing of one or more of those alternatives, and then simply taking your chances. You should hear yourself saying, "I wonder if this would work?" That is what the SPeculate phase of xPM is all about.

Defining How the Project Will Be Done

The initial sense of direction for the team to take in the first cycle of an extreme project can vary considerably. A good approach is to use the POS objective statements as a guide. The POS can continuously be updated to reflect the current view of the project, and its objective statements can serve as a guide to what will be done. In later cycles, the team and the client will have the benefit of learning and discovery from the prior cycles. For the sake of discussion, I want to treat those two situations separately. In this section of the chapter, assume you are planning the first cycle. In some of the following sections, you will look at the SPeculate phase for the second and subsequent cycles.

Conditions of Satisfaction

The Conditions of Satisfaction are described in detail in Chapter 3 and are not repeated here. While the COS is a tool that produces a required deliverable in TPM and the APF, its use in xPM is optional. The COS lose their value as the goal becomes more and more elusive. If the client has only a vague idea about the goal, no amount of discussion around needs and deliverables will clarify the situation for either party, and the other planning artifacts described in the text that follows may be more useful in the initial SPeculate phase.

If you choose to use the COS in your xPM project, think of it as more of a brainstorming process. The project team and the client can investigate ideas en route to generating a list of what will be done in this cycle.

Scenarios, Stories, and Use Cases

The technical perfectionist would probably define these terms as different from one another, but for my purposes they are synonymous. All three can be defined as descriptions of how a person might use the application. Because the application may be feature-rich, there can be, and usually will be, several such descriptions. If done correctly, these descriptions will be comprehensive regarding how the application can be used. The descriptions can then be prioritized and assigned to the appropriate development cycles. There is no practical limit to the number of such situations that are documented. In the case of technology projects, such as Web site development, the client may be more comfortable telling you how they envision someone using the deliverable and what they can do at the Web site than they would be trying to help you write a functional specification. The advantage in using scenarios, stories, and use cases is that the view you are building is from the user side, not from the technology side.

Prioritizing Requirements

The collection of scenarios, stories, and use cases provides insight into the requirements that the deliverable should meet. For the client, it is far easier to prioritize the collection than it is to prioritize the requirements. Prioritization is the next step in the SPeculate phase. There are several ways to produce a prioritized list of items in the collection. Chapter 14 discusses three such methods: forced ranking; must-haves, should-haves, and nice-to-haves; and the Q-Sort. Refer to Chapter 14 for the details on those methods.

Here are other aspects of the prioritization that need to be considered:

- First, there can be a great number of items in the collection; so many, in fact, that approaches like forced ranking are not practical. Forced ranking doesn't scale very well. A compromise approach might involve grouping the items based on their relationship to specific functions and then prioritizing between and within the functions. The strategy here would be to assign all of the items related to a specific function to a subteam for their consideration and development. Several subteams could be active in any given cycle.

- Second, depending on how well the goal is understood, it might be wise to plan the initial SPeculate phase so that as many options and alternatives as possible can be investigated. The strategy here is to eliminate those alternatives that show little promise earlier rather than later in the project. That enables more resources to be brought to bear on approaches that have a higher probability of success.

- Finally, where appropriate, prototypes might be considered as part or all of the first-cycle deliverables. Here the strategy is to prioritize items in the collection or functions by not spending too much time developing the real deliverable. Familiarizing the client with the prototype may provide sufficient information to enable not only a reduction in the number of items in the collection, but also a prioritization of those items or functions that show promise. A good example is a typical B2C application. The prototype will show the various ways that a customer can interact with the application. Upon examination, the client adds to that list or deletes from that list as they experience what the customer would experience when interacting with the application.

Think of the first cycle or two as exploratory in nature. Their purpose is to discover the directions that show promise and focus later cycles on them.

Identifying the First Cycle Deliverables

Once the prioritization is done, it is time to decide how much of that prioritized list to bite off for the initial cycle. Remembering that you want shorter cycles in the early part of the project suggests that you limit the first-cycle deliverables to what you can reasonably accomplish in a week or two.

> **NOTE** By taking this approach you are keeping the client's interest up, which is important. The APF follows the same strategy. Once the client has been fully engaged in the project, later cycles can be lengthened.

Because your team resources are limited, you have to face the question of depth versus breadth of deliverables. In other words, might it be better to extend the breadth to accommodate more functions by not delving deep into any one function? Produce enough detail in each function in this initial cycle to get a sense of further direction for the function. You may learn from only a shallow look at a function that it isn't going to be part of the final solution. This shallow look enables you to save labor that would have been spent on a function that will be discarded, and to spend it on more important work.

Go/No-Go Decision

Because the initial cycle can be exploratory, the sponsor must have an opportunity to judge the soundness of the initial cycle plan and decide whether it makes sense to proceed. It is entirely possible that the original idea of the client cannot be delivered with the approach taken in the first cycle, and the first cycle leads the client to the decision that the idea doesn't make any sense after all. Some other approach needs to be taken, and that approach is not known at this time. The go/no-go decision points will occur at the end of each cycle. Decisions to stop a project are more likely to occur in the early cycles than in the later cycles. One should expect later cycles to have the benefit of earlier results that suggest that the project direction is feasible and should be continued.

Planning for Later Cycles

Later cycles will have the benefit of output from a REview phase to inform the planning activities that will take place in the SPeculate phase that follows. Each REview phase will produce a clearer vision and definition of the goal.

That clearer vision translates into a redirection of the project, which translates into a new prioritized list of deliverables for the coming Incubate phase. The newly prioritized deliverables list may contain deliverables from previous cycles that were not completed, deliverables that have not yet been part of an Incubate phase, and deliverables that are new to the project as a result of learning and discovery that occurred in the most recently completed Incubate phase. In any case, the revised prioritized deliverables list is taken into consideration as the team plans what it will do in the coming Incubate phase. It is now in the same position as it was in the very first SPeculate phase. What follows then is the assignment of deliverables to subteams, and the scheduling of the work that will be done and who will do it.

Incubate

The Incubate phase is the xPM version of the Cycle Build Phase in APF. There are several similarities between the phases and some differences as well. Consider the following points:

- Even though the Incubate phase has a prioritized list of deliverables that are to be produced in this cycle, xPM still must maintain the spirit of exploration. It is a learning and discovery experience that may result in midcycle corrections that arise from that exploration.

- The APF, conversely, does benefit from learning and discovery as it proceeds with the cycle plan but it does not vary from the plan. The learning and discovery are input to the client checkpoint and that is where plan revisions take place.

These points reflect an important distinction between xPM and the APF.

Subteams, working in parallel, will execute the plan developed in the previous SPeculate phase. The environment has to be very open and collaborative for this phase to be successful. Teams should be sharing ideas and cross-fertilizing discoveries and learning moments with one another. This is not just a time to execute a plan; it is a time for exploration and dynamic interchange. Midphase corrections with the collaboration of the client are likely as the subteams learn and discover together. New ideas and a redirection or clarification of the goal is likely to come from these learning and discovery experiences as well.

Assigning Resources

The Incubate cycle begins with an assignment of team members to each of the deliverables that have been prioritized for this cycle. The assignment should take place as a team exercise. That team involvement is important because of the exploratory nature of xPM cycles. Team members need to express their interest in one or more deliverables and share their ideas with their fellow team members. This assignment time can also be an opportunity for team members to recruit others who share their same interests and would like to develop the deliverable with them. The project manager should not pass up the opportunity to create a synergy among team members with similar interests, as well as between subteams that will be working in parallel on different deliverables. Any opportunity to create a collaborative work environment only increases the team's chances of success.

Establishing Cycle Plan

With the subteams in place and with their assignments made, the subteams can plan how they will produce the deliverables assigned to them. Deciding how a team produces the deliverables is exactly the same as discussed in Chapter 16. In fact, many of the same tools discussed in Chapter 16 can be used to help establish a cycle plan here with equal effectiveness. For example, Chapter 16 presents the cycle plan as a time-sequenced whiteboard diagram showing a day-by-day schedule of what is going to be done and by whom.

NOTE However, never forget the differences of a cycle plan in xPM. In xPM, the team has to be ready for changes at any time. Exploration will often bring the team to a point where a change of direction makes sense. When these situations arise, the team needs to collaborate with the client and decide how to go forward.

Collaboratively Producing Deliverables

Collaboration goes to the very essence of xPM. Collaboration among subteams must occur. The example given earlier is one such instance. I spoke earlier in the chapter about the exploratory nature of an xPM project. Because the project is exploratory, no one has a lock on the solution. Even the goal is somewhat elusive. That means the goal and the solution can be attained only through a solid team effort — a collaborative effort. There is a great deal of similarity between xPM projects and brainstorming. One idea may not be of much value when taken individually. However, combine it with one or more other ideas and suddenly there is value. The quote at the beginning of the chapter from Estill I. Green, former vice president of Bell Telephone Laboratories, is relevant here: "Clearly no group can as an entity create ideas. Only individuals can do this. A group of individuals may, however, stimulate one another in the creation of ideas."

REview

The REview phase is very similar to the Client Checkpoint Phase in the APF. All of the learning and discovery from the just-completed Incubate phase are brought together in another brainstorming session. Shared will be answers to questions such as the following:

- What did you learn?
- What can you do to enhance goal attainment?
- What new ideas arose and should be pursued?
- What should you do in the next cycle?

The most important decision is whether or not the project will continue. This is a client decision. Have the results to date met with their expectations? Is the project moving toward an acceptable solution? These answers will determine whether or not the project continues to the next cycle or is canceled. The APF and xPM share this go/no-go decision point at the completion of each cycle. The APF is less likely to result in a cancellation because so much more is known about the solution. xPM, conversely, is so exploratory and research-based that cancellations are far more likely.

Each cycle of an xPM project ends with a review of the just-completed Incubate phase. It is a meeting attended by the client and the project team. The purpose of the REview phase is to reflect on what has just happened and what learning and discovery have taken place. The output is a definition of the next cycle's activities.

Applying Learning and Discovery from the Previous Cycle

Early in the sequence of cycles, the client and the team should expect significant findings and major redirections of further efforts. As the project moves into later cycles, the changes should diminish in scope because the project team should be converging on a more clearly defined goal and an acceptable solution to reach it.

> **NOTE** This part of the xPM process differs from the APF because in the APF the goal has always been clearly defined; it is the solution that becomes clearer with each passing APF cycle.

Revising the Project Goal

The first order of business is for the client and the project team to revisit the previous goal statement from the prior REview phase. Ask the following questions:

- What has happened in the just-completed Incubate phase?
- What new information do you have?

- What approaches have you eliminated?
- What new discovery suggests a change in goal direction and definition?
- Are you converging on a more clearly defined goal?

This revision of the project goal is an important step and must not be treated lightly. The client and the team need to reach a consensus about that new goal statement. Update the POS with the new goal statement.

Reprioritizing Requirements

The second order of business is for the client and the project team to revisit deliverables and requirements. The following questions should be asked here:

- How does the new goal statement affect the deliverables list?
  - Should some items be removed?
  - Should new items be added?
- How is the functionality embedded in the new goal statement affected?

The answers to these questions enable the client and the project team to reprioritize the new requirements. Update the POS to reflect any changes in the objective statements.

Making the Go/No-Go Decision for the Next Cycle

Will there be a next SPeculate-Incubate-REview cycle? Equivalently, the question could be this: Are you converging at an acceptable rate on a clearly defined goal and acceptable solution? The client will consider this question in the face of the money and time already spent. Does it make business sense to continue this project? The updated POS is the input to this decision.

Comparing Project Approaches

Figure 19-3 summarizes much of what has been discussed in the first two parts of this book. It is interesting to compare and contrast all three approaches. The first thing to note is that these three approaches span the entire project landscape. TPM covers those cases where the goal and how to reach it are clearly known. At the other end of the spectrum is xPM, which covers those projects whose goal is not clearly known and, therefore, whose solution is not known either. All other cases fall in between the two and are covered by the APF. The APF and xPM require multiple cycles in order to bring the solution into focus (APF) or to bring the goal and the solution into focus (xPM).

TPM	APF	xPM
One cycle	Fixed # of cycles	Unknown # of cycles
Fixed budget & time	Fixed budget & time	Variable budget & time
Fixed scope	Variable scope	Unknown scope
Complete WBS	Mid-level & JIT WBS	No WBS
Complete plan	JIT plan	JIT plan
Change intolerant	Change embraced	Change necessary

Figure 19-3 A comparison of the three approaches

The scope triangle applies equally to both TPM and the APF, but not xPM. The xPM budget and time frame are variable, and hence the scope triangle does not apply there. The scope and its accompanying WBS are different for all three. Because scope is known and fixed in TPM, a complete WBS can be built and a complete plan generated from it. In the case of the APF, only a certain level of detail is known, so the midlevel WBS reflects that level of clarity. Within a cycle, however, a lower-level WBS can be built for APF projects and a plan generated to build that cycle's functionality. In the case of xPM, the scope is unknown, and hence no meaningful WBS can be generated. Only within an xPM cycle can a plan be generated for the functionality to be explored in that cycle.

The most important message I can offer you is this: "Do not force your project into an approach. Let the characteristics of the project suggest the approach to be taken."

Putting It All Together

One noticeable difference between the traditional approach and the APF approach is that the APF is a thinking person's approach, whereas the traditionalist approach often tends to be the blind following of a recipe with the expectation that everything will turn out fine. For example, the APF requires continuous and meaningful involvement on the part of the client. A clear joint ownership by the client and the team is built into the APF. That is not the case with the traditionalist approach. The traditionalist approach can be followed with little or no involvement by the client.

This chapter ends my presentation of the APF. It is an exciting and invigorating approach to those projects that don't quite fit the mold of the traditional approach. I hope that this brief introduction to the APF will encourage my colleagues to ponder what I have said here and add their own take on the APF. It is an idea whose time has come, and it should be taken seriously by the project management community.

When it comes to starting an extreme project, you have learned that the good habits formed in TPM and the APF carry over into xPM. There is no need to learn anything new in order to get an extreme project under way. The POS will be used here just as it is used in TPM and the APF. You want to get approval to work on your project, and you have a selling job to do. You are armed with the POS as your best strategy regardless of the type of project to be undertaken.

Finally, the best advice I can give you when you are doing an extreme project is to be open-minded. The habits that you formed in traditional project management may have great application in extreme projects, but they might not. You will be called on to be adaptive. Keep the goal of your extreme project in mind, and use or adapt whatever you can from your earlier experiences with traditional or adaptive projects.

You should now have a better understanding of how this unstructured xPM approach can, in fact, converge on the goal. The learning and discovery that takes place in a cycle gives the client and the project team the information it needs to rethink how it will move forward at the next cycle. The decision to move forward is a collective decision made by the client with the advice of the project team.

The ability of the team and the client to decide how to move forward is heavily dependent upon their ability to reconsider the prioritization of functionality. The learning that has taken place is the major contributor to their ability to reprioritize. That learning brings clarity to the final goal specification, and that clarity helps the client and the team to eliminate functionality that is out of scope with that now clearer goal, as well as to identify functionality that is critical to the more clearly defined goal.

Discussion Questions

1. Suppose a project should have used a traditional approach, but you used the APF. Comment on what might be different. Would the traditional approach have given you a better outcome? Why or why not? Be specific.

CASE STUDY – PIZZA DELIVERED QUICKLY (PDQ)

> 2. What situation would enable you to embed an APF approach in a TPM approach? In other words, what conditions would you expect to see for that approach to be feasible? Give an example and be specific.

3. How does xPM differ from the APF? Discuss the differentiating characteristics of each.

4. Can the APF be used on an extreme project? Why or why not? Be specific.

5. In the formative stages of a project, are there any distinct advantages to using xPM over the APF for an extreme project? If so, identify them.

6. In the formative stages of a project, are there any distinct disadvantages to using the APF over xPM for an extreme project? If so, identify them. In considering your answer, think about what is actually known versus what may be only speculation, and how that might create problems.

7. As a class exercise, identify three xPM projects and write the POS for one of them.

8. Is the APF or xPM more likely to waste less of the client's money and the team's time if the project is killed prior to completion? To answer the question, you have to consider when the decision to kill the project is made in the APF versus xPM projects and what is known at the time the decision is made. Defend your position with specifics.

Organizational Considerations

I have completed my discussion of the three approaches to project management: TPM, APF, and xPM. In the previous two parts, I discussed when to use the traditional, adaptive, or extreme approaches and how to use each one. There are two remaining topics that I believe are critical to your understanding of the place of projects in the organization:

- The first is project portfolio management. Many organizations are changing their focus from the individual project to the collection of projects under way or proposed in the organization.

- The second is the Project Support Office (PSO). If any of the three approaches are to succeed in the organization, it will be because the organization has an effective support function in place.

Part III consists of two chapters. In Chapter 20, I take a look at the project portfolio with specific focus on what it is, how it is formed, and how it is managed. Chapter 21 discusses how organizations can support the project effort. I discuss what the PSO is, what functions it performs, what roles and responsibilities it has, how it is organized, and how to form one.

Part III is intended to give you an awareness of these two contemporary aspects of the enterprise — the project portfolio and the Project Support Office. Both can contribute to the success of TPM, APF, and xPM. It is important that you understand the roles, responsibilities, and functions of each, because they will impact your ability to be successful with project execution.

CHAPTER 20

Project Portfolio Management

He who attempts too much seldom succeeds.
— **Dutch proverb**

A good way to outline a strategy is to ask yourself: "How and where am I going to commit my resources?" Your answer constitutes your strategy.
— **R. Henry Miglione, Oral Roberts University,**
An MBO Approach to Long-Range Planning

CHAPTER LEARNING OBJECTIVES

After reading this chapter, you will be able to:

◆ **Understand current practices in corporate project portfolio management and how they are applied**

◆ **Know how to deliver explicit business value through a strategically aligned project portfolio**

◆ **Adapt the concepts and practices of project portfolio management**

Organizations that invest in information technology projects, whether hardware-focused, software-focused, or both, must have a plan for investing in these projects. The dollars needed to fund these projects almost always exceed the dollars available. How should an organization decide which projects should be funded and which shouldn't be funded? Is this a short-term decision that looks only at the coming budget cycle, or is there some long-term strategy that spans multiple budget cycles? How can the funding agency determine whether an IT investment is a good investment? Can some criteria be applied?

The answers to these questions are simple in some cases and extremely difficult in others. This chapter uses a life-cycle approach that traces the life of a project through the portfolio management process.

Introduction to Project Portfolio Management

In this first section, I set the foundation for our exploration of project portfolio management. While everyone knows what a project is, not everyone may understand that not all projects come under the purview of the portfolio management process. Just what types of projects will be candidates for the project portfolio is a very basic tenet for every portfolio. You need to have a clear understanding of what a portfolio is, and in some situations more than one portfolio is advised. I want to make sure everyone is on the same page before I launch into the depths of a portfolio management discussion. In this section, I present a conceptual overview of the portfolio management process. Subsequent sections describe each part of the process in detail.

Portfolio Management Concepts

I first want to take another look at the idea of a project. The definition of a project comes from earlier discussions in this book, but not all projects belong in the portfolio. The word *portfolio* probably conjures up several different ideas. I have a simple definition that will put everyone on the same page.

What Is a Portfolio Project?

In Chapter 1, I defined a project in the following way:

> *A project is a sequence of unique, complex, and connected activities having one goal or purpose that must be completed by a specific time, within budget, and according to specification.*

This is a technical definition, and it tells you quite a bit about the type of work that can legitimately be called a project, but when you are dealing with a portfolio, it doesn't tell the whole story. Because you are constructing a portfolio of projects, you need to define the types of projects that qualify for inclusion in the portfolio. Not all projects will be managed as part of a portfolio. What about small, routine projects that are done as part of normal business operations? Certainly they will not fall under the portfolio management process. They are already included in the operations budget of their respective business units. Conversely, how big, complex, and expensive does the project have to be before you will consider it for the portfolio? No matter how specific you are in establishing the qualification criteria, a certain amount of subjectivity will be involved. For example, consider complexity in the case of the selection and purchase of a desktop computer. If you are technically savvy, the purchase of the computer is a simple task and would not be considered a project. If you are technically challenged, however, then the purchase of a computer clearly is a project and a complex one at that.

That said, it seems clear that you would want to set a minimum effort, cost, and even value to those projects that will be considered for inclusion in the portfolio. These are certainly subjective calls on your part, but you must be able to make a case for a project that will be proposed for the portfolio and one that won't.

NOTE What about capital budget projects? Regardless of their dollar value, some organizations require that all capital budget projects be approved and constitute a line item in the capital budget. In effect, the capital budget is a portfolio of projects, whereby each project defines a piece of capital equipment that the requestor is asking to purchase.

What Is a Project Portfolio?

The simple definition of a project portfolio is as follows:

A project portfolio is a collection of projects that share some common link to one another.

The operative phrase here is "share some common link to one another." I want to explore that idea in more detail. I already have given one example of projects that share a common link in the Note about capital budgets in the previous section. That link could take many forms. At the enterprise level, the link might be nothing more than the fact that all the projects belong to the same company. While that may be true, it is not too likely the kind of link you are looking for. Some more effective and specific links might be the following:

- The projects may all originate in the same business unit or functional area — for example, information technology.
- The projects may all be new product development projects.
- The projects may all be funded out of the same budget or from the same resource pool.

Whichever way you choose to define the link, one thing is almost certain: Whatever resources you have available for those projects will not be enough to meet all project requests. Some choices have to be made, and that is where project portfolio management takes over.

To further complicate the situation, you might need to establish different types of portfolios. For example, all of the capital projects with a value above $500 could form a portfolio. More specifically, the portfolio could cover only technology capital projects above $500. Systems development projects longer than six months with a total cost above $500,000 might be another type of portfolio. At this point in the discussion you can see that whatever portfolios you choose to establish, they will consist of projects that share similar characteristics.

What Is Project Portfolio Management?

Credit for establishing the field of modern portfolio theory belongs to Henry Markowitz, an economist at the City University of New York. He first presented his theory in the *Harvard Business Review* in 1959. In later years, he was awarded the Nobel Prize in Economics for his discoveries. It wasn't until the 1990s that his theories were extended from the investment portfolio to the project portfolio. Many of the approaches I talk about later in this chapter have their conceptual roots in his earlier works.

Our working definition of project portfolio management is as follows:

Project portfolio management includes establishing the investment strategy of the portfolio, determining what types of projects can be incorporated in the portfolio, evaluating and prioritizing proposed projects, constructing a balanced portfolio that will achieve the investment objectives, monitoring the performance of the portfolio, and adjusting the contents of the portfolio in order to achieve the desired results.

The Major Phases of Project Portfolio Management

No matter how you slice and dice it, project portfolio management consists of five phases, as shown by the shaded boxes in Figure 20-1.

1. Establish
2. Evaluate
3. Prioritize
4. Select
5. Manage

In the diagram, I have embedded a generic project in the phases to illustrate the principles involved and the possible courses of action that a project may take over the course of its life. All of the discussions that follow in the remaining sections of this chapter are based on this diagram.

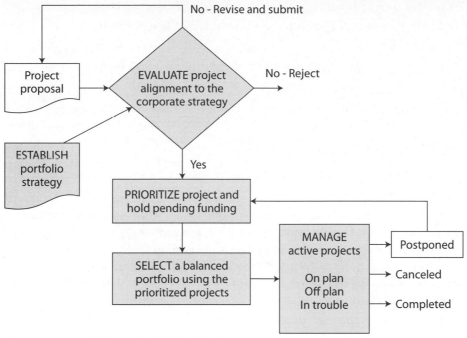

Figure 20-1 Portfolio project life cycle

Also shown in Figure 20-1 is the changing status of a project as it moves through this life cycle. Note that there are eight different stages that a project may be in during this life cycle:

Proposed. A proposed project is one that has been submitted to the portfolio with a request that it be evaluated regarding its alignment to the portfolio strategy. A project that does not meet the alignment criteria may be either rejected out of hand or returned to the proposing party for revision and resubmission. Projects that are returned for revision are generally only in minor noncompliance, and following the suggested revisions should meet the alignment criteria.

Aligned. A proposed project is aligned if it has been evaluated and determined to be in alignment with the portfolio strategy. Once it has been determined to be aligned, it will be placed in one or more funding categories for future consideration. At this stage, the proposing parties should begin preparing a detailed plan. The plan will contain information that helps the portfolio manager make a final determination regarding project funding and, hence, inclusion in the portfolio.

Prioritized. An aligned project is prioritized if it has been ranked along with other projects in its funding category. This is the final stage before the project is selected for the portfolio. If it is high enough in priority in its category, it will be funded and included in the portfolio.

Selected.   A prioritized project has been selected if it is in the queue of other prioritized projects in its funding category and is awaiting funding authorization. This is a temporary stage, and funding is certain at this point.

Active.   A selected project is active if it has received its funding authorization and is open for work. At this stage, the project manager is authorized to proceed with the recruiting and assignment of team members, scheduling of work, and other activities associated with launching the project.

Postponed.   An active project is postponed if its funding authorization has been temporarily removed. Such projects must return to the pool of prioritized projects and be selected once again in order for its funding authorization to be restored. The resources allocated to a postponed project are returned to the funding category from which they originated. The resources may be reassigned to the postponed project later or may be allocated to the next project in the queue of that funding category.

Canceled.   An active project is cancelled if it has failed to demonstrate regular progress toward its successful completion. Depending on the stage in which the project was cancelled, there may be unspent resources. If so, they are returned to the funding category from which they originated. Those funds then become available for the next project in the queue of that funding category.

Completed.   A project is completed if it has met all of its objectives and delivered business value as proposed.

A project may find itself in any one of these eight stages as it proceeds through the five phases of the project portfolio management life cycle. The following sections of this chapter cover each one of the five phases in more detail.

Establishing a Portfolio Strategy

The first step in portfolio management is deciding the strategy for the portfolio. That strategy is an investment strategy. That is, how will the enterprise's funding be spread across the portfolio? Once this investment strategy is in place, the enterprise will have a structure for selecting the investment opportunities that will be presented in the form of project proposals. This is really a type of strategic planning phase in which the portfolio manager or the portfolio management team decides how it will allocate its project budget to various general categories of project investment.

> **NOTE** I use the term *portfolio manager* to represent the decision-making body, whether it is one individual or a team.

Several models are easily adapted to this phase. In this chapter I examine five popular models:

- Strategic Alignment Model
- Boston Consulting Group Products/Services Matrix
- Project Distribution Matrix
- Growth versus Survival Model
- Project Investment Categories

Each model has desirable characteristics that meet the organization's need for good investment strategies. The strategy itself is determined by the dollar or resource investment (people, machines, facilities, and so on) the company is willing to make in each of the funding categories defined by the various models. Once this strategy is in place, a final question must be answered: Which projects will be funded in each of these categories? The answer to that question is found in the next three phases of the model.

Prior to releasing the investment plan, two questions should be answered by the portfolio manager:

- Will projects be partially funded in order to include more projects in the portfolio, or will projects be funded only at the level of their request?
- If an investment category has excess resources after project funding decisions have been made, can those resources be reallocated to other investment categories without compromising the portfolio strategy, and if so, how will they be reallocated?

If possible, it is good to make these decisions before the situations arise. The rules need to be clear so that all parties are informed ahead of time.

Strategic Alignment Model

The first model is the Strategic Alignment Model. This model makes good sense because it attempts to align projects with the direction the enterprise has decided to follow. In other words, it aligns projects with those things that are important to the enterprise. Figure 20-2 graphically depicts this model.

Figure 20-2 Strategic Alignment Model

Value/Mission

The *value/mission* is a very brief statement of why the enterprise exists. It could be stated in terms of an end state that the enterprise hopes to achieve or simply be a statement of who the enterprise is. Whichever form is used, this statement is unlikely to change, at least not in the foreseeable future.

Goals

To achieve its end state or accomplish its mission, the enterprise has to engage in certain major efforts. These are likely to be multiperiod or multiyear efforts designed to accomplish major results. They might never be attainable (eliminating world hunger, for example) or they might be achievable over long periods of time (finding a cure for cancer or a preventative for the common cold, for example). Any of these are good examples of goal statements. The important thing to remember is that they must be stated in a fashion that links them directly to one or more of the corporate objectives.

Objectives

There will be many approaches to the realization of each goal. Each approach is called an *objective*, which might be a one-year effort or could span several years. Again, take the example of the preventative for the common cold. Objectives might include investigating possible food additives or modifying the immune system or finding a drug that establishes immunity to the cold. All three of these objectives can launch a number of tactics.

Tactics

Tactics are the short-term efforts, usually less than one year in duration, designed to meet one or more objectives. These are the projects that will be proposed for the portfolio. A project that relates to only one objective will be less attractive to the portfolio manager than a project that relates to several objectives. Similarly, a project that relates to a lower-priority objective will be less attractive than a project that relates to a higher-priority objective. Later in the chapter, in the section "Selecting a Balanced Portfolio Using the Prioritized Projects," you will see how this works with some examples.

How Are You Going to Allocate Your Resources?

The application of this model is quite straightforward. The enterprise must decide what resources will be allocated to each goal and to the objectives that support that goal. With that decision made, the enterprise accepts project proposals from its various departments regarding what projects they wish to undertake and how those projects relate to the goals and objectives of the enterprise. Obviously, there won't be much interest in supporting projects that do not further the goals of the enterprise.

Boston Consulting Group Products/Services Matrix

The Boston Consulting Group (BCG) Matrix is a well-known model that has been used for several years. It defines four categories of products/services based on their growth rate and competitive position, as shown in Figure 20-3.

Cash Cows

These are well-established products/services that have a strong market share but limited growth potential. They are stable and profitable. Projects that relate to cash cows are important to the organization because the company will want to protect that investment for as long as it maintains that market position.

Dogs

Because these products/services are not competitive and have little or no growth potential, any projects related to them should not be undertaken. The best thing an organization can do with dogs is phase them out as quickly and painlessly as possible. Don't throw good money after bad!

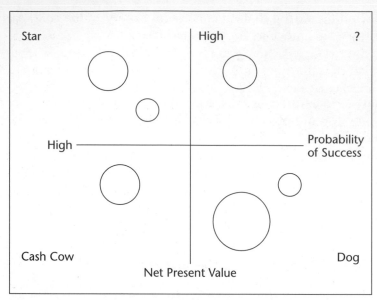

Figure 20-3 BCG Products/Services Matrix

Stars

These are products/services that have strong market positions and clearly strong growth potential. Projects related to stars are good investment opportunities. Stars are the future cash cows.

?

The question mark represents the starting point of the model. Products/services that are untested in the market but appear to have strong growth potential are worthy of spending R&D dollars. Projects linked to those efforts are good investment opportunities. The objective is to turn them into stars and then cash cows.

How Are You Going to Allocate Your Resources?

The answer to this question depends on the current market position of the enterprise, the business outlook, and a variety of other considerations. Except for the dogs, the other three categories will have some level of investment. If the industry is stable, such as cement manufacturing, more resources might be spent on the cash cows to ensure that they maintain their market position, fewer resources on the stars because the enterprise will always want to keep some growth opportunities in the pipeline, and even fewer on the ? because the industry isn't in the research and development mode. In a volatile, high-growth, high-tech industry, the allocations might be very different. More resources will be spent on the stars and ? and fewer on the cash cows. Cash cows have a very short useful life, and any investments in them are risky.

Project Distribution Matrix

Simple, yet elegant in its simplicity, the Project Distribution Matrix, shown in Figure 20-4, says that there must be a mix of projects in the portfolio. This mix will be dictated by the skill inventory of those who work on the projects, as well as the needs of the organization to attain and sustain market share. It can be used in conjunction with the models shown previously to ensure that a healthy mix is present in the project portfolio. The Project Distribution Matrix is similar to the Strategic Alignment Model in that it defines a rule for classifying projects. The rule is a two-way classification, as shown in the figure.

New – Enhancement – Maintenance

The columns of the matrix classify projects according to whether they are New, Enhancement, or Maintenance.

Project Focus	New	Enhancement	Maintenance
Strategic			
Tactical			
Operational			

Figure 20-4 Project Distribution Matrix

New.   A new project is one that proposes to develop a new application, process, or product.

Enhancement.   An enhancement project is one that proposes to improve an existing process or product.

Maintenance.   A maintenance project is one that simply proposes to conduct the normal care and feeding of an existing operation, which could include fixing errors that have been detected or otherwise updating some features that have become obsolete or are part of a process that has been changed.

Strategic – Tactical – Operational

The rows of the matrix classify projects based on their role in the enterprise:

Strategic.   A strategic project is one that focuses on the strategic elements of the enterprise. Applications that extract basic data from businesses, society, and the economy and translate that data into policy formulation are examples of strategic projects.

Tactical.   Tactical projects are projects that look at existing processes and procedures and propose ways to make improvements by changing or replacing the process or procedure.

Operational.   Operational projects are those that focus on existing processes and try to find ways to improve efficiency or reduce costs.

How Are You Going to Allocate Your Resources?

The application of this model is also quite straightforward. The enterprise that has defined a project classification rule must now decide what resources will be allocated to each of the nine categories. With that decision made, the enterprise accepts project proposals from its various departments as to what projects they wish to undertake. A feature of this model is that it can be tied to the resource pool of skilled employees. The required skills across each of these nine categories are different. To some extent that may dictate how much emphasis is placed on each category. The enterprise will want to use its available skills, so the relative priority of each category can help or hinder that effort.

NOTE The Graham-Englund Selection Model (discussed later in this chapter) incorporates available staff capacity based on skills as part of its selection strategy.

Growth versus Survival Model

This way of categorizing projects is the simplest of all presented here. Projects are either focused on growth or survival. *Growth projects* are those that propose to make something better in some way. Obviously, these are discretionary projects. *Survival projects* are the "must-do" projects. These projects must be done or the enterprise will suffer irreparable damage. In short, survival projects are projects that must be done, and all other projects are growth projects.

How Are You Going to Allocate Your Resources?

If the budget is in a contracting phase, you will probably allocate most of your resources to the survival category. Conversely, if you are in an expansion phase, you will allocate most of your resources to the growth category.

Project Investment Categories

The Project Investment Categories Model is a close kin of the financial investment portfolio. It identifies categories of investments. These categories define types of projects, just as a financial portfolio defines types of investment instruments. In the case of projects, you define the following categories:

Infrastructure.   Projects that strengthen the hardware and software systems that support the business

Maintenance.   Projects that update existing systems or products

New products.   Projects that propose entirely new products or services

Research.   Projects that investigate new products, services, or systems to support the business

Each type of project will receive some percentage of the resource pool.

How Are You Going to Allocate Your Resources?

This model operates just like the BCG Products/Services Matrix discussed earlier in the chapter. Both models require the portfolio manager to establish a distribution across existing and new products and services. The distribution will most likely be directly related to whether the enterprise is in a growth or maintenance posture with respect to its upcoming investment strategy.

Choosing Where to Apply These Models

Depending on the particular application that you have in mind, you will want to choose the most appropriate model. This section helps you consider some of the possibilities.

Corporate Level

If your organization has an enterprise-wide project management office that has management responsibility for the project portfolio, then your choice of model is limited to two: Both the BCG Products/Services Matrix and the Strategic Alignment Model are good candidates. Both focus on the strategic goals of the organization at the highest levels and can directly relate a single project to how well it aligns with defined strategies. That provides a basis for prioritizing a project.

Functional Level

At the corporate level, dollars are allocated to strategic initiatives that affect the entire organization, whereas at the functional level — the information technology department, for example — the situation can be quite different. Resources are allocated to operational- or tactical-level projects. Rather than allocate dollars, it is more likely that the resource to be allocated is professional staff. In that case, the Project Distribution Matrix, Growth versus Survival Model, or Project Investment Categories will do the job.

> **NOTE** Later in this chapter I discuss the Graham-Englund Selection Model. It doesn't fit into the framework of the other models, so I treat it separately. In fact, the Graham-Englund Selection Model is built around the allocation of professional resources to prioritized projects as its basic operating rule. That makes the Graham-Englund Selection Model a good choice for functional-level projects.

Evaluating Project Alignment to the Portfolio Strategy

This evaluation is a very simple intake task that places a proposed project into one of several funding categories as defined in the model being used. The beginning of the project intake process involves determining whether the project is in alignment with the portfolio strategy, and placing it in the appropriate "bucket." These buckets are defined by the strategy that is used, and each bucket contains a planned dollar or resource amount. After all of the projects have been placed in buckets, each bucket is passed to the next phase, where the projects that make up a bucket are prioritized.

There are two ways that this intake process can take place:

- The person proposing the project does the evaluation.
- The intake person does the evaluation.

It can work well either way. If the person proposing the project does the evaluation, he or she needs a clear definition of each funding category in the portfolio strategy. The project proposal may be returned to the proposer for clarification or revision before being placed in a funding category. Some procedures may ask the proposer to classify the project, in which case this intake process is nothing more than an administrative function. This places the burden on the proposer and not on the portfolio manager. However, there is the possibility of biasing the evaluation in favor of the proposer. The bias arises when the proposer, having such intimate familiarity with the proposal, evaluates it subjectively, rather than objectively. There is also the strong likelihood that these types of evaluations will not be consistent across all projects. Having an intake person conduct the evaluations ensures that all proposals are evaluated using a consistent and objective criteria.

In other cases the process is more formal, and the project proposal is screened to specific criteria. This formal evaluation is now a more significant process and may involve the portfolio manager or a portfolio committee. Projects that do not match any funding category are returned to the proposer and rejected with no further action specified or requested. If the portfolio manager does the evaluation, the problem of bias largely disappears. In this scenario the proposer must follow a standard procedure for documenting the proposed project. I return to this topic at the end of this chapter in the section "Preparing Your Project for Submission to the Portfolio Management Process."

The deliverable from this phase of the process is a simple categorization of projects into funding categories.

Prioritizing Projects and Holding Pending Funding Authorization

The first tactical step in every portfolio management model involves prioritizing the projects that have been shown to be aligned with the portfolio strategy. Recall that the alignment places the project in a single funding category. It is those projects in a funding category that you prioritize. When you are finished, each funding category will have a list of prioritized projects. Dozens of approaches could be used to establish that prioritization. Some are nonnumeric; others are numeric. Some are very simple; others can be quite complex and involve multivariate analysis, goal programming, and other complex computer-based algorithms. My approach here is to identify those methods that can easily be implemented in the public sector and do not require a computer system for support, although sometimes a simple spreadsheet application can reduce the labor intensity of the process. I discuss six models:

- Forced Ranking
- Q-Sort
- Must-Haves, Should-Haves, Nice-to-Haves
- Criteria Weighting
- Paired Comparisons
- Risk/Benefit

See Chapter 14 for an additional discussion of these prioritization approaches.

Forced Ranking

This approach is best explained by way of an example. Suppose 10 projects have been proposed. Number them 1, 2, . . . 10 so that you can refer to them later. Suppose that the portfolio management team has six members (A, B, . . . F), and they are each asked to rank the 10 projects from most important (1) to least important (10). They can use any criteria they wish, and they do not have to describe the criteria they used. The results of their rankings are shown in Table 20-1.

Table 20-1 Forced Ranking of 10 Projects

PROJECT #	A	B	C	D	E	F	RANK SUM	FORCED RANK
1	2	5	3	2	1	6	19	2
2	4	3	2	7	9	10	35	6
3	7	4	9	8	6	3	37	7
4	1	8	5	1	2	2	19	3
5	3	6	8	4	7	5	33	5
6	8	9	10	9	10	8	54	9
7	5	1	1	3	3	4	17	1
8	6	2	4	5	4	1	22	4
9	10	10	7	10	8	9	54	10
10	9	7	6	6	5	7	40	8

The individual rankings from each of the six members for a specific project are added to produce the rank sum for each project. Low values for the rank sum are indicative of projects that have been given high priority by the members. For example, Project 7 has the lowest rank sum and is therefore the highest-priority project. Ties are possible. In fact, the preceding example has two ties (1 and 4, 6 and 9). Ties can be broken in a number of ways. For example, I prefer to use the existing rankings to break ties. In this example, a tie is broken by taking the tied project with the lowest rank score and moving it to the next lowest forced rank. For example, the lowest rank for Project 1 is 6, and the lowest rank for Project 4 is 8. Therefore, the tie is broken by giving Project 1 a rank of 2 and Project 4 a rank of 3.

Forced ranking works well for small numbers of projects, but it does not scale very well.

Q-Sort

When you use the Q-Sort (see Figure 20-5), projects are first divided into two groups: high priority and low priority. The high-priority group is then divided into two groups: high priority and medium priority. The low-priority group is also divided into two groups: low priority and medium priority. The next step is to divide the high-priority group into two groups: very high priority and high priority. The same is done for the low-priority group. The decomposition continues until all groups have eight or fewer members. As a last step, you could distribute the medium-priority projects to the other final groups.

The Q-Sort is simple and quick. It works well for large numbers of projects. It also works well when used as a small group exercise using a consensus approach.

Must-Haves, Should-Haves, Nice-to-Haves

This approach, and variations of it, is probably the most commonly used way of ranking. As opposed to the forced rank, in which each individual project is ranked, this approach creates three categories. The person doing the ranking only has to decide which category the project belongs in. The agony of having to decide relative rankings between pairs of projects is eliminated with this approach. The number of categories is arbitrary, as are the names of the categories.

TIP I prefer to use the naming convention "must-haves, should-haves, nice-to-haves," rather than categories like high, medium, low, or A, B, C. The names avoid the need to define what each category means.

This method is even simpler than the Q-Sort. If the number of projects is large, you may need to prioritize the projects within each of the three groups in order to make funding decisions.

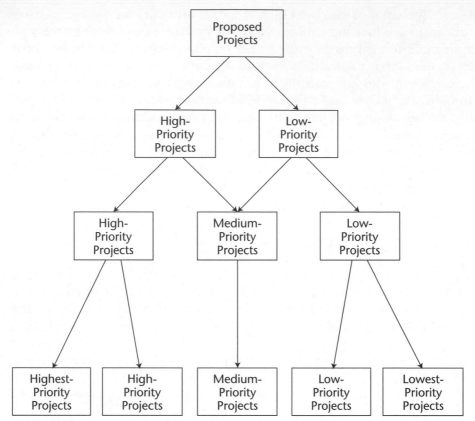

Figure 20-5 An example of the Q-Sort

Criteria Weighting

There are literally hundreds of criteria weighting models. They are all quite similar, differing only in the minor details. I give one example of criteria weighting, but several others apply the same principles. A number of characteristics are identified, and a numeric weighting is applied to each characteristic. Each characteristic has a scale attached to it. The scales usually range from 1 to 10. Each project is evaluated on each characteristic, and a scale value given to the project. Each scale value is multiplied by the characteristic weight, and these weighted scale values are added. The highest result is associated with the highest-priority project.

Figure 20-6 shows a sample calculation for one of the proposed projects for the portfolio. The first column lists the criteria against which all proposed projects for this portfolio will be evaluated. The second column lists the weight of that criterion (higher weight indicates more importance to the scoring algorithm). Columns three through seven evaluate the project against the given criteria. Note that the evaluation can be given to more than one level. The only restriction is that the evaluation must be totally spread across the levels. Note that each criteria level adds to one. The eighth column is the sum of the levels multiplied by the score for that level. This process is totally adaptable to the nature of the portfolio. The criteria and criteria weight columns can be defined to address the needs of the portfolio. All other columns are fixed. The last two columns are calculated based on the values in columns 2 through 7.

Paired Comparisons Model

The next scoring model is called the Paired Comparisons Model. In this model, every pair of projects is compared. The evaluator chooses which project in the pair is the higher priority. The matrix in Figure 20-7 is the commonly used method for conducting and recording the results of a paired comparisons exercise.

Criteria	Criteria Weight	Very Good (8)	Good (6)	Fair (4)	Poor (2)	Very Poor (0)	Expected Level Weight	Expected Weighted Score
Fit to Mission	10	1.0					8.0	80.0
Fit to Objectives	10	0.2	0.6	0.2			6.0	60.0
Fit to Strategy	10			1.0			4.0	40.0
Contribute to Goal A	8				1.0		2.0	16.0
Contribute to Goal B	6	0.2	0.8				6.4	38.4
Contribute to Goal C	4		0.5	0.5			5.0	20.0
Uses Strengths	10				0.6	0.4	1.2	12.0
Uses Weaknesses	10	0.7	0.3				7.4	74.0
								340.4

Figure 20-6 Criteria weighting

	1	2	3	4	5	6	7	8	9	10	SUM	RANK
1	X	1	1	0	1	1	0	1	1	1	7	2
2	0	X	0	0	1	1	0	0	1	1	4	6
3	0	1	X	0	0	1	0	0	1	1	4	5
4	1	1	1	X	1	1	0	0	1	1	7	2
5	0	0	1	0	X	1	0	0	1	0	3	7
6	0	0	0	0	0	X	0	0	1	1	2	8
7	1	1	1	1	1	1	X	1	1	1	9	1
8	0	1	1	1	1	1	0	X	1	1	7	2
9	0	0	0	0	0	0	0	0	X	0	0	10
10	0	0	0	0	1	0	0	0	1	X	2	9

Figure 20-7 An example of a paired comparisons

First note that all 10 projects are defined across the 10 columns and down the 10 rows. For 10 projects, you have to make 45 comparisons. The 45 cells above the diagonal contain the comparisons you make. First, Project 1 is compared to Project 2. If Project 1 is given a higher priority than Project 2, then a "1" is placed in cell (1, 2) and a "0" is placed in cell (2, 1). If Project 2 had been given a higher priority than Project 1, then you would place a "0" in cell (1, 2) and a "1" in cell (2, 1). Next, Project 1 is compared to Project 3, and so on, until Project 1 has been compared to all other nine projects. Then Project 2 is compared to Project 3, and so on. Continuing in this fashion, the remaining cells are completed. The final step is to add all the entries in each of the 10 rows, producing the rank for each project. The higher the score, the higher the rank. The rightmost column reflects the results of those calculations. Note that Project 7 had the highest overall priority.

NOTE This Paired Comparisons Model is a quick and simple method; unfortunately, it doesn't scale very well. For example, 100 projects would require 4,950 comparisons.

Risk/Benefit

The final scoring model is the Risk/Benefit Matrix. There are many ways to do risk analysis, from subjective methods to very sophisticated mathematical models. The one I am introducing is a very simple quasi-mathematical model. Risk is divided into five levels (1, 2, . . . 5). Level 1 has a very low risk (or high probability of success), and level 5 has a very high risk (or very low probability of success). Actually, any number of levels will do the job. Defining three levels is also quite common. In this model you assess two risks: the risk of technical success and the risk of business success. These are arranged as shown in Figure 20-8.

Each project is assessed in terms of the *probability of technical success* and the *probability of business success*. The *probability of project success* is estimated as the product of the two separate probabilities. To simplify the calculation, the graph shows the results of the computation by placing the project in one of three areas:

- Fund projects that fall in the lightly shaded cells.
- Consider projects that fall in the cells with no shading.
- Refer projects in the darkly shaded cells back to the proposing agency unless there is some compelling reason to fund them.

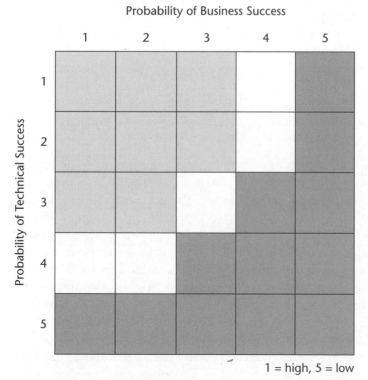

Figure 20-8 Risk/Benefit Matrix

When you have a large number of projects, you need to prioritize those that fall in the lightly shaded cells. A good start on that would be to prioritize the cells starting in the upper-left corner and working toward the center of the matrix.

Selecting a Balanced Portfolio Using the Prioritized Projects

You might think that because you have a prioritized list in each funding category and you know the resources available for those projects, the selection process would be simple and straightforward, but it isn't. Selection is a very challenging task for any portfolio management team. The problem stems from the apparent conflict between the results of evaluation, the ranking of projects from most valuable to least valuable, and the need to balance the portfolio with respect to one or more variables. These two notions are often in conflict. As a further complication, should partial funding of projects be allowed? You will examine this conflict later in the section "Balancing the Portfolio."

There are several approaches to picking the project portfolio. As you have already seen, this chapter deals with five portfolio strategies and six prioritization approaches. That gives you 30 possible combinations for selection approaches, and many more could have been covered. From among the 30 that I could examine, I have focused on three:

- Strategic Alignment Model and Weighted Criteria
- Project Distribution Matrix and Forced Ranking
- Graham-Englund Selection Model with the Project Investment Categories and the Risk/Benefit Matrix

This section shows the results of combining the previous sections into an approach for selecting projects for the portfolio. By choosing the BCG Products/Services Matrix, Strategic Alignment Model, Project Distribution Matrix, Growth versus Survival Model, or the Project Investment Category Model, you make a statement about how your resources will be allocated. Each one of these models generates some number of "buckets" into which resources are distributed. Those buckets with more resources are valued more than those with fewer resources. These buckets represent the supply of resources available to the projects that are demanding those resources. It would be foolish to expect a balance between the supply of resources and the demand for them. Some buckets will have more resources than have been requested, while others will not have enough resources to meet demand. This section explains how to resolve those differences to build a balanced portfolio.

Balancing the Portfolio

Unfortunately, there isn't a perfect or best way to build a balanced portfolio. There are basically two approaches and neither one ensures an optimal solution:

- The first approach is to make one master list of prioritized projects. However, if you simply use that prioritized list of projects using any of the models presented so far, you may end up with less than satisfactory results. For example, you could end up funding a number of short-term, low-risk projects with low organizational value. Alternatively, you could end up funding all long-term, high-risk projects with high organizational value. In either case the resulting portfolio would not be representative of the organization's strategy. In other words, you could end up with a portfolio that is not at all in line with the corporate strategy.

- The second approach, and the one that I have taken here, is to separate projects into buckets, and then prioritize the projects that have been placed in each bucket. While this certainly gives you a balanced portfolio, it may not give you the best portfolio because some buckets may have been very popular choices for proposed projects, and a very good project may not have reached high enough on the priority list to be funded. Yet that project may be a much better alternative than some project in another bucket that did receive funding. It's basically the luck of the draw.

Which approach should you take? I recommend the second, for two reasons

- Prioritizing a single list, which may be long, is far more difficult than working with several shorter lists. The work can be divided among several persons or groups in the second case, but not in the first case. Furthermore, when you first align projects with funding categories and then prioritize within funding categories, you are working not only with a smaller number of projects, but with a group of projects that are more homogeneous.

- Once the projects have been aligned within funding categories, the portfolio manager may then allocate the resources across the funding categories. That avoids situations in which there could be a wide variance between the resources that are being requested and those that are being offered in each category. The caution here is that the portfolio manager may try to honor the requests and abandon any portfolio strategy. You can't have it both ways.

The examples given in the sections that follow illustrate some of these ideas. These are but a few of the many examples I could give, but they are sufficient to illustrate some of the ways to mitigate against such outcomes and ensure a balanced portfolio that reflects the organization's investment strategy.

Strategic Alignment Model and Weighted Criteria

In this section, I use the Strategic Alignment Model to select projects for the portfolio. Figure 20-9 shows one variation that you might use.

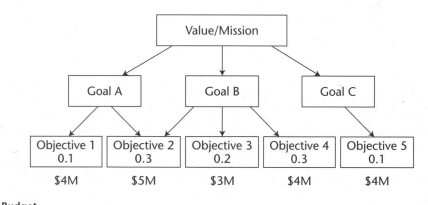

Budget Proposed		Objective 1 0.1 $4M	Objective 2 0.3 $5M	Objective 3 0.2 $3M	Objective 4 0.3 $4M	Objective 5 0.1 $4M	Score	Award
P#1	$2M	0.6 $1.2M		0.4 $0.8M			0.140	$2.0M
P#2	$2M	0.3 $0.6M	0.2	0.1 $0.2M		0.4 $0.8M	0.150	$1.6M
P#3	$4M	0.4 $1.6M	0.6 $2.4M				0.220	$4.0M
P#4	$1M	0.3 $0.3M	0.2 $0.2M		0.5 $0.5M		0.240	$1.0M
P#5	$3M				0.8 $2.4M	0.2 $0.6M	0.260	$3.0M
P#6	$4M		0.7		0.3 $0.3M		0.160	$0.3M
P#7	$3M		0.8 $2.4M		0. $0.6M		0.300	$3.0M
P#8	$3M			0.3 $0.9M		0.7 $2.1M	0.130	$3.0M
P#9	$1M		0.2	0.2 $0.2M	0.2 $0.2M	0.4 $0.4M	0.200	$0.8M
P#10	$2M	0.8 $0.3M		0.2 $0.4M			0.120	$0.7M

Figure 20-9 Achieving balance with the Strategic Alignment Model

Each objective is weighted with a number between 0 and 1. Note that the sum of the weights is 1. These weights show the relative importance of each objective compared against the others. Below each objective is the budget allocated to that objective. The total budget is $20M. Ten projects are being considered for this portfolio. The proposed budget for each is shown with the project number. The total request is for $25M. In this example, a project may be associated with more than one objective. You can do that by assigning to each project objective pair a weight that measures the strength of the relationship of that project to that objective. This weight is the result of evaluating the alignment of the projects to the objectives. The sum of the weights for any project is 1.0. To establish the priority order of the 10 projects, multiply the objective weight by the project weight and add the numbers. The result of that calculation is shown in the Score column for all 10 projects in the example. The higher the project's score, the higher the project should be on your list of projects to fund. For this example, Project 7 is the top-priority project, with a score of 0.300. Project 10 is the tenth priority, with a score of 0.120.

The awards to the projects are made by starting with the highest-priority project, which in the example is Project 7. The request is for $3M. Of that amount, 80 percent will come from the budget for Strategy 2 and 20 percent will come from Strategy 4. That reduces the budget for Strategy 2 from $5M to $2.6M and for Strategy 4 from $4M to $3.4M. The process continues with the next highest-priority project and continues until the budget for each strategy is allocated or there are no more requests for resources. In some cases, a project may receive only partial funding from a funding category. For example, Project 10 should have received $1.6M from Strategy 1 but when it came up for funding, there was only $0.3M left in that budget. Following the example to its completion results in the allocations shown in Figure 20-9. The requests total $25M, the budget totals $20M, and the allocations total $19.4M. The remaining $0.6M should not be redistributed to projects that did not receive their requested support. These resources are held pending performance of the portfolio and the possible need to reallocate resources at some later date.

This section gives you but one example of applying an adaptation of criteria weighting to the Strategic Alignment Model to produce a portfolio selection approach. This model is probably the best of those discussed in this chapter because it enables the portfolio manager to express the enterprise strategy in a direct and clear fashion through the weights chosen for each objective. It also shows how the proposed projects relate to that prioritization through the weighted scores on each objective. The model provides management with a tool that can easily adapt to changing priorities and that can be shared with the organization.

Project Distribution Matrix and Forced Ranking Model

To further illustrate the process of creating a portfolio selection approach, next I combine the Project Distribution Matrix and the Forced Ranking Model. Assume that the total dollars available for Major IT Projects is $20M and that the dollars have been allocated as shown in Figure 20-10. I'll use the same 10 projects from the previous section with the same funding requests. The projects are listed in the order of their ranking within each funding category.

The first thing to note in this example is that the investment decisions do not line up very well with the funding requests from the 10 projects. There is a total of $9M in four funding categories with no projects aligned in those categories. Your priorities as portfolio manager were expressed by your allocation of funds to the various funding categories. However, the project proposals do not line up with that strategy. Are you willing to make any budget changes to better accommodate the requests? You should, but with the stipulation that you do not compromise your investment strategy. Legitimate changes would be to move resources to the left but in the same row, or up but in the same column. If you agree that that is acceptable, then you end up with the allocations shown in Figure 20-11. $3M was moved from the Strategic/Maintenance category to the Strategic/Enhancement category, and $1M was moved from the Operational/New category to the Tactical/New category. Any other movement of monies would compromise the investment strategy.

Project Focus	New	Enhancement	Maintenance
Strategic	Budget $3M	Budget $3M P#2 $2M P#10 $2M P#6 $4M	Budget $3M
Tactical	Budget $3M P#1 $2M P#4 $1M P#9 $1M	Budget $2M	Budget $1M P#3 $4M
Operational	Budget $1M	Budget $2M P#8 $3M	Budget $2M P#7 $3M P#5 $3M

Figure 20-10 Project Distribution Matrix with budget and funding requests

Project Focus	New	Enhancement	Maintenance
Strategic	Budget $3M	Budget $6M P#2 $2M P#10 $2M P#6 $4M	
Tactical	Budget $4M P#1 $2M P#4 $1M P#9 $1M	Budget $2M	Budget $1M P#3 $4M
Operational		Budget $2M P#8 $3M	Budget $2M P#7 $3M P#5 $3M

Figure 20-11 Project Distribution Matrix with adjusted budget and funding requests

After the allocations have been made, you are left with the matrix shown in Figure 20-12. The balances remaining are also shown in Figure 20-12. These monies are to be held pending changes to project status as project work is undertaken.

Graham-Englund Selection Model and the Risk/Benefit Matrix

So far, in the examples shown, the only resource I have been working with is money. However, one of the most important resources, at least for information technology projects, is people. Staff resources are composed of professionals of varying skills and experience. As you consider the portfolio of projects, you need to take into account the ability of the staff to deliver that portfolio. For example, if the portfolio were largely new or enhanced strategic applications, you would draw heavily on your most experienced and skilled professionals. What would you do with those who have fewer skills or experience? That is an important consideration, and the Graham-Englund Selection Model is one model that approaches project selection with that concern in mind. Basically, it works from a prioritized list of selected projects, and staffs them until certain sets of skilled and/or experienced professionals have been fully allocated. In other words, people, not money, become the constraint on the project portfolio. Several related challenges arise as a result. I will briefly discuss some of the issues and staffing concerns that this approach raises.

Project Focus	New	Enhancement	Maintenance
Strategic	Budget $3M	P#2 $2M P#10 $2M P#6 $2M	
Tactical	P#1 $2M P#4 $1M P#9 $1M	Budget $2M	P#3 $1M
Operational		P#8 $2M	P#7 $2M P#5 0

Figure 20-12 Project Distribution Matrix showing budget balances and funding decisions

The Graham-Englund Selection Model is a close parallel to the models previously discussed, but it has some interesting differences. I added it here because of its simplicity and the fact that it has received some attention in practice. Figure 20-13 illustrates an adaptation of the portfolio project life cycle to the Graham-Englund Selection Model.

What Should We Do?

The answer to this question is equivalent to establishing the portfolio strategy. In the case of the Graham-Englund Selection Model, you are referring to the IT strategy of the organization. The answer can be found in the organization's values, mission, and objectives; it is the general direction in which they should be headed consistent with who they are and what they want to be. It is IT's role to support those goals and values. IT will do that by crafting a portfolio of projects consistent with those goals and values. Think of answering "What should we do?" as the demand side of the equation. You will use the project investment categories (infrastructure, maintenance, new products, and research) to identify the projects you should undertake. These categories loosely align with the skill sets of the technical staff and will give you a basis for assigning resources to projects. In fact, any categorization that allows a mapping of skills to projects will do the job. I have kept it simple for that sake of the example, but this approach can get very complex.

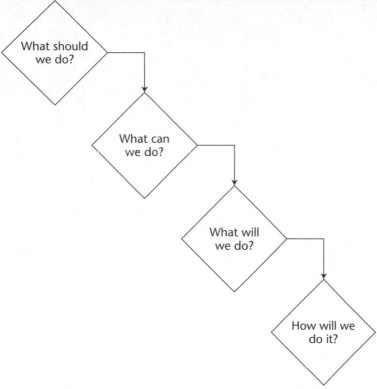

Figure 20-13 An adaptation of the Graham-Englund Selection Model

Figure 20-14 shows a list of the 10 projects and the skilled positions needed to staff them. The second column gives the number of staff in each position that is available for these 10 projects. Again, I have kept the data simple for the sake of the example.

What Can We Do?

The answer to this question is found by comparing project requirements to the organization's resource capacity. Current commitments come into play here, as the organization must look at available capacity, rather than just total capacity.

NOTE Dealing with the issue of what your organization can do raises the important issue of having a good human resource staffing model in place — one that considers future growth of the enterprise, current and projected skills inventories, training programs, career development programs, recruiting and hiring policies and plans, turnover, retirements, and so on.

	# Available	P#1 I	P#2 I	P#3 M	P#4 M	P#5 M	P#6 N	P#7 N	P#8 N	P#9 R	P#10 R
Senior Project Manager	2	X					X				
Project Manager	3		X	X				X	X	X	
Associate Project Manager	2				X	X					X
Systems Architect	4	X	X				X	X	X	X	
Database Architect	4	X	X				X	X	X	X	
Senior Programmer	2	X	X				X				
Programmer	3	X	X				X	X	X		
Associate Programmer	2			X	X	X					X
Test Technician	5	X	X	X	X	X	X	X	X		

Figure 20-14 Project staffing requirements

Think of answering "What can we do?" as the supply side of the equation. Figure 20-14 lists the projects that can be done with the staff resources available. Under each project number is the type of project (I = infrastructure, M = maintenance, N = new product, and R = research). However, it does not say which projects will be done. Not all of them can be done simultaneously with the available staff resources, so the question as to which ones will be done is a fair question.

What Will We Do?

The list of projects given in Figure 20-14 is longer than the list of projects you will do. The creation of the "will-do" list implies that some prioritization has taken place. Various criteria such as return on investment, break-even analysis, internal rate of return, and cost/benefit analysis might be done to create this prioritized list. In this example, I use the list that results from the Risk/Benefit Matrix, as shown in Figure 20-15.

The priority ordering of the projects based on the probabilities of success is P#1, P#4, P#5, P#2, P#7, P#3, P#6, P#8, P#9, and P#10. If you staff the projects in that order, you will be able to staff Projects 1, 4, 5, 2, and 7. At that point you will have assigned all resources except one senior project manager. Projects 3, 6, and 8 did fall in the acceptable risk categories, but no resources are left to staff them.

Probability of Business Success

1 = high, 5 = low

Figure 20-15 Projects prioritized using the Risk/Benefit Matrix

However, the example is oversimplified. You have assumed that a person is staffed 100 percent to the project. That is unlikely. In reality, a scarce resource would be scheduled to work on projects concurrently to enable more projects to be active. In practice, you would sequence the projects, rather than start them all at the same time. Projects have differing durations, and this difference frees up resources to be reassigned. In any case, the example has shown you how the process works.

How Will We Do It?

Answering this question is roughly equivalent to the selection phase in the portfolio project life cycle. In the case of resource management, "How will we do it?" is just a big staffing and scheduling problem. By scheduling scarce resources across the prioritized list, you are placing more projects on active status; that is, they will be placed in the portfolio. Detailed project plans are put in place, and the scheduling of scarce resources across the projects is coordinated. Performance against those plans is carefully monitored because the resource schedule has created a dependency between the projects. The critical chain approach to project management offers considerable detail on scheduling scarce resources across multiple projects. The interested reader should refer back to Chapter 12 of this book, which covers critical chain project management in more detail, and consult the book *Critical Chain Project Management* by Lawrence Leach.

Balancing Using Partial Funding or Staffing of Projects

Earlier in the chapter I asked whether partial funding would be allowed. The tentative answer to the question of partial funding or partial staffing is yes, because it yields a couple of key benefits: it puts more projects into active status and gives you a better chance to control the risk in the portfolio. If one of those partially funded projects doesn't meet muster, it can be postponed or cancelled and the remaining resources reallocated to other partially funded projects that are meeting muster. There is one major drawback that the portfolio manager must contend with: The delivery date of the partially funded projects will be extended into the next budget cycle. That may mean a delay in getting products or services into the market, thereby delaying the revenue stream. That has obvious business implications that must be taken into account.

Managing the Active Projects

In this last phase, you continuously compare the performance of the projects in the portfolio against your plan. Projects can be in one of three statuses: *on plan*, *off plan,* or *in trouble*. You will see how that status is determined and what action you can take as a result. Here, the challenge is to find performance measures that can be applied equitably across all the projects. Two come to mind:

- Cost schedule control
- Milestone trend charts

A detailed discussion of these is given later in this section. To bring closure to the final phase, projects can be postponed, cancelled, or, believe it or not, completed, and you will see exactly how these endings affect the portfolio going forward.

At this point, the project is under way. Regardless of the effort that was expended to put a very precise and complete plan in place, something will happen to thwart those efforts. In the 35 years that I have been managing projects, not a single project went according to plan. That wasn't due to any shortcomings on my part; it is simply a fact of life that unforeseen things will happen that will have an impact on the project. Corrective actions will have to be taken. This section introduces two reporting tools that enable an apples-to-apples comparison of the status of projects in the portfolio. The first tool is applied at the portfolio management level, while the second tool is applied at the project level.

Project Status

As mentioned, there are three categories for the status of active projects: on plan, off plan, or in trouble. The following sections take a look at each of these states and how that status might be determined.

On Plan

Even the best of plans will not result in a project that stays exactly on schedule. A certain amount of variance from the plan is expected and is not indicative of a project in jeopardy. The threshold between on plan and off plan is a subjective call. I offer some guidelines for this variance later in the chapter, in the section "SPI and CPI Trend Charts."

Off Plan

Once a project crosses that threshold value, it moves from on plan to off plan. For a project to be off plan is not unexpected, but what is expected is to get back on plan. If the project manager cannot show the corrective action that will be taken to get the project back on plan and when that event is likely to occur, there is a problem and the project has now moved to in trouble. The project can also move to in trouble if it passes a second threshold value that separates off plan from in trouble.

In Trouble

Regardless of the way in which a project reaches the in trouble condition, the implications are very serious. To be in trouble means that there is little chance the project can be restored. Serious intervention is required because the problem is out of control and out of the range of the project manager's abilities to correct it. However, just because a project is in trouble doesn't necessarily mean that the project manager is at fault. There may be cases where freak occurrences and random acts of nature have put the project in this category, and the project manager is unable to put a get-well plan in place and is asking for help that goes beyond his or her range of authority. The portfolio manager is considering canceling the project unless there is some compelling reason why that action should not be taken. A new project manager will not necessarily rectify the problem.

The Role of the Project Manager

Obviously, one of the project manager's key responsibilities is the status of the project. While there are many reasons why a project may drift out of plan, it is the responsibility of the project manager to institute corrective measures to restore the project to an on-plan status. The extent to which the project manager meets that responsibility will be obvious from the future status of an off-plan project.

The project manager can also be a cause of an off-plan status. That can happen in a number of ways. In my experience, one of the major contributing factors is the failure of the project manager to have a good system of cross-checking and validating the integrity of the task status being reported by the team. If the project manager does not have a visible process for validating task status, then that is a good indication that scheduling problems are sure to occur.

The second behavioral problem that you see is the failure of the project manager to establish a repeatable and effective communications process. The first place to look for that is in constant questioning from the team members about some aspect of the project that affects their work for which they have little or no knowledge. There should be full disclosure by the project manager to the team. That process begins at planning time and extends through to the closure of the project.

Reporting Portfolio Performance

Two well-known reporting tools can be used to compare the projects across a portfolio and assess the general performance of the portfolio as a whole: cost/schedule control (C/SC) and milestone trend charts. Both of these were discussed in detail in Chapter 10, and that discussion is not repeated here. What I will do is take those two reporting tools and show how they can be applied to measuring the performance of the portfolio.

Schedule Performance Index and Cost Performance Index

From C/SC I take the schedule performance index (SPI) and cost performance index (CPI):

Schedule performance index. The schedule performance index (SPI) is a measure of how close the project is to performing work as it was actually scheduled. If the project is ahead of schedule, its SPI will be greater than 1; if it is behind schedule, its SPI will be less than 1, which indicates that the work performed was less than the work scheduled.

Cost performance index. The cost performance index (CPI) is a measure of how close the project is to spending on the work performed compared to what was planned for spending. If you are spending less on the work performed than was budgeted, the CPI will be greater than 1. If not, and you are spending more than was budgeted for the work performed, then the CPI will be less than 1.

These two indices are intuitive and provide good yardsticks for comparing the projects in a portfolio. Any value less than 1 is undesirable; any value over

1 is good. These indices are displayed graphically as trends compared against the baseline value of 1.

SPI and CPI Trend Charts

The milestone trend charts introduced in Chapter 10 are adapted here to fit the SPI and CPI trends. This section tracks the SPI and CPI over time using the criteria established in Chapter 10.

Some examples will help. Consider the milestone trend chart for the hypothetical project shown in Figure 20-16. The trend chart plots the SPI and CPI for a single project at weekly reporting intervals. The heavy horizontal line has the value 1. That is the boundary value for each index. Values above 1 indicate an ahead-of-schedule or under-budget situation for that reporting period. Values below 1 indicate a behind-schedule or over-budget situation for that reporting period. Over time these indices tell an interesting story about how the project is progressing or not progressing.

For example, Figure 20-16 shows that beginning with Week 5, the schedule for Project ALPHA began to slip. The slight improvement in the budget may be explained by work not being done, and hence the cost of work that was scheduled but not done was not logged to the project. This type of relationship between schedule and cost is not unusual.

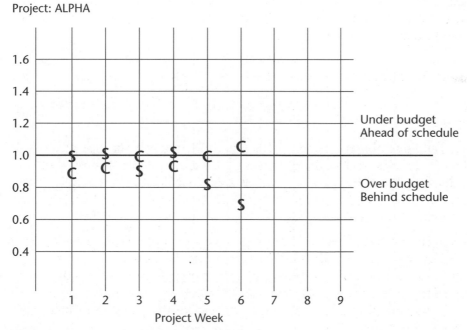

Figure 20-16 Example SPI and CPI trend chart

Spotting Out-of-Control Situations

Certain patterns signal an out-of-control situation. Some examples of this sort of situation are shown in Figures 20-17 through 20-20 and are described in this section.

Figure 20-17 depicts a project schedule slowly slipping out of control. Each report period shows additional slippage since the last report period. Four such successive occurrences, however minor they may seem, require special corrective action on the part of the project manager.

Figure 20-18, shows a minor over-budget situation. While this may not be significant by itself, that situation has persisted for the last seven report periods. The portfolio manager can fairly ask the project manager why he or she hasn't corrected the situation. The situation isn't serious, but it should have been fixed by now. There may be extenuating circumstances that occurred in the first few weeks of the project that have persisted without any possibility of correction. It is true that the CPI and SPI are fairly stable despite their negative performance.

Figure 20-19 shows both the SPI and CPI trending in the same direction. The fact that the trend is negative is very serious. Not only is the schedule slipping, there are consistent cost overruns at the same time. If the situation were reversed and the trend were positive, you would obviously have a much better situation. In that case not only would the project be ahead of schedule, but it would also be running under budget. Figure 20-20 illustrates that scenario.

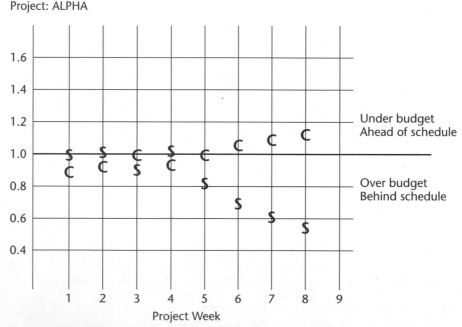

Figure 20-17 A run up or down of four or more successive SPI or CPI values

Project: ALPHA

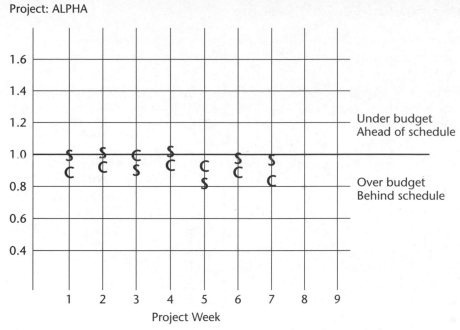

Figure 20-18 Seven or more successive SPI or CPI values above or below 1

Project: ALPHA

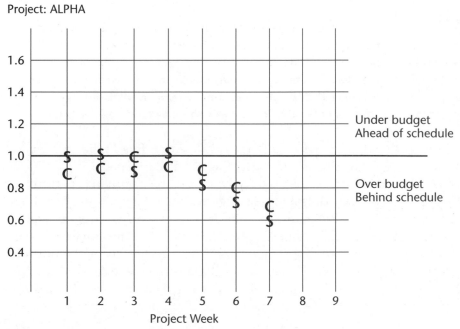

Figure 20-19 SPI and CPI trending in the same negative direction

Project: ALPHA

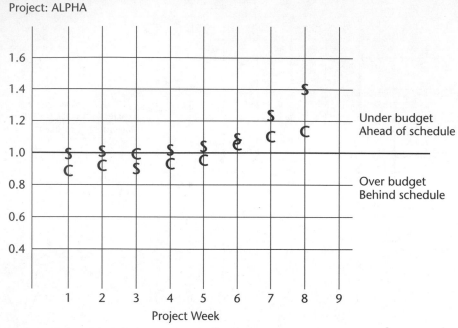

Figure 20-20 SPI and CPI trending in the same positive direction

NOTE Don't be too quick to congratulate the project manager because it may not be his or her heroic efforts that created such a positive trend. If the duration estimates were too generous and the labor needed to complete the activities was less than estimated, then the project may be ahead of schedule and under budget through no special efforts of anyone on the team. Nonetheless, give the project manager the benefit of the doubt; he or she may have been heroic.

In either case, whether trending to the good or trending to the bad, a good portfolio manager investigates to find out what has happened.

These same data plots can be used to show how the portfolio is performing with respect to both schedule and cost. Figure 20-21 illustrates the hypothetical data for the BETA Program Portfolio. It consists of five projects that all began at the same time. The solid lines are the SPI values for the five projects over the seven-week reporting period. The heavy dotted line is the portfolio average. Although the portfolio has been behind schedule for the entire seven weeks, it is trending upward and has nearly reached an on-schedule situation. The same type of plot can show budget performance for the portfolio as well.

Portfolio: BETA Program

Figure 20-21 SPI values for a hypothetical portfolio

Closing Projects in the Portfolio

Best practices include acceptance criteria, agreed upon by the client and the project manager during project planning, that clearly state when the project is considered finished. This acceptance criteria usually takes the form of a checklist of scope items or requirements. When all items on the checklist have been checked off as completed, the project is deemed finished. The work of the project, however, is not yet complete. What remains is what I call a *post-implementation audit*. The purpose of this section is to examine the activities and contents of a post-implementation audit and discuss why it is so important that one be done.

Attainment of Explicit Business Value

Each project was proposed based on the value it would return to the enterprise if it were funded and completed successfully. Was that value achieved? This is a question that may not be answerable until some time after the project is complete, but it is a question that deserves an answer. This proposed value was the justification for the project and a major factor in placing the project in the portfolio in the first place.

Lessons Learned

Following are several questions that might be asked about a project just completed:

- Were the project goals/objectives achieved?
- Was the project work done on time?
- Was the client satisfied with the project results?
- Was the explicit business value realized? (Check success criteria.)
- What modules were learned about your project management methodology? What worked? What didn't work?
- How well did the team follow the methodology?

All of these questions are important and should be answered. In some cases the particular nature of the project may render some questions more important than others, but that does not excuse the project team from answering all of them. Some of the most important information about the project management process can be found in these answers, so they should be shared with all other project teams.

Preparing Your Project for Submission to the Portfolio Management Process

Now that you understand the portfolio management process, you should have a pretty good idea of what you need to do to prepare your project proposal for submission and consideration as part of a portfolio. If your organization doesn't require you to follow a prescribed procedure for proposing your project, then I can suggest three ways to prepare your project proposal:

- Adapt the POS, which was discussed in detail in Chapter 3. The POS will work quite well but may need some additional information, such as cost and time estimates, that is traditionally not part of the POS.
- Try a two-step approach. Submit the POS first to determine the alignment of your project, and then prepare a detailed project plan to submit time and cost data to the prioritization and selection phases.
- Develop an entirely new submission process based on the five-phase portfolio management process.

The next three sections describe each one of these options.

A Revised Project Overview Statement

Chapter 3 already discusses the POS in great detail, so I won't repeat that discussion here. Recall that the POS is a short document (ideally one page) that concisely states what is to be done in the project, why it is to be done, and what value it will provide to the organization when completed.

When it is used in the portfolio management process, the main purpose of the POS is to have the portfolio committee evaluate the project and determine whether it is in alignment with the corporate strategy. Later it will be reviewed by the managers who are responsible for setting priorities and deciding what projects to support in the portfolio. For this reason, the POS cannot contain any technical jargon that generally would not be used across the enterprise. Once approved, the POS becomes the foundation for future planning and execution of the project. It also becomes the reference document for questions or conflicts regarding project scope and purpose.

Parts of the POS

The POS has five component parts:

- Problem/opportunity statement
- Project goal
- Project objectives
- Success criteria
- Assumptions, risks, and obstacles

Recall that its structure is designed to lead the reader from a statement of fact (problem/opportunity) to a statement of what this project will address (project goal). Given that senior management is interested in the project goal and that it addresses a concern of sufficiently high priority, they will read more detail about exactly what the project includes (project objectives). The organizational value is expressed as quantitative outcomes (success criteria). Finally, a summary of conditions that may hinder project success are identified (assumptions, risks, obstacles). The following list looks at each of these parts more closely as they apply to the project portfolio process:

Problem/opportunity statement.   The first part of the POS is a statement of the strategic objective(s) that the project is addressing. If appropriate, the statement should come directly from the company's strategic plan or be based on the portfolio strategy. This is critical because it provides a basis for the rest of the document. It also sets the priority with which the portfolio manager will view what follows. If you are addressing a high-priority area or a high-value area, your idea will get more attention and the reader will read on.

Project goal.   The second section of the POS states the goal of the project — what you intend to do to address the strategic objective(s) identified in the previous section. The purpose of the goal statement is to get senior management to value the idea enough to read on. In other words, they should think enough of your approach to the corporate strategy to conclude that it warrants further attention and consideration. Several other proposals will pertain to the same objective(s). Because yours will not be the only one submitted, you want it to stand out among the crowd.

The goal statement must not contain any language or terminology that might not be understandable to anyone having occasion to read it. In other words, no techie talk allowed. It is written in the language of the organization so that anyone who reads it will understand it without further explanation from the proposer. Under all circumstances, avoid jargon.

Keep the goal statement short and to the point. Keep in mind that the more you write, the more you increase the risk that someone will find fault with something you have said. The goal statement does not include any information that might commit the project to dates or deliverables that are not practical. Remember that you don't have much detail about the project at this point.

Project objectives.   The third section of the POS presents the project objectives. Here is your chance to show more breadth to your project and bind it even tighter to one or more of the strategic objectives.

Success criteria.   The fourth section of the POS answers the question "Why do we want to do this project?" It is the measurable explicit business outcome that will result from doing the project. It sells the project to the portfolio manager. This may be the most important part of the POS. The portfolio manager is trying to maximize the value that can be generated from the portfolio. Every project has to contribute to that value.

The question that you have to answer is this: What business value will result from successfully completing the project? The answer to this question will be a statement of the explicit business outcome to be realized. It is essential that the criteria be quantifiable and measurable, and, if possible, expressed in terms of business value. Remember that you are trying to sell your idea to the portfolio manager.

As an added value statement, consider quantifiable statements about the impact your project will have on efficiency and effectiveness, error rates, reduced turnaround time to service a customer request, reduced cost of providing service, quality, or improved customer satisfaction. Management deals in deliverables, so always try to express success criteria in quantitative terms. By doing this you avoid any possibility of disagreement later as to whether the success criteria were met and the project was successful. The portfolio manager will look at your success criteria and assign organizational value to your project. In the absence of other criteria, this success criteria will be the basis for his or her decision regarding whether or not to place the project in the portfolio.

Assumptions, risks, and obstacles.   The fifth section of the POS identifies any factors that can affect the outcome of the project and that you want to bring to the attention of the portfolio manager. These factors can affect deliverables, the realization of the success criteria, the ability of the project team to complete the project as planned, or any other environmental or organizational conditions that are relevant to the project. Record anything that can go wrong. Be careful, however, to put in the POS only those items that you want senior management to know about and in which they will be interested.

The project manager uses the assumptions, risks, and obstacles section to alert the portfolio manager to any factors that may interfere with the project work or compromise whatever contribution the project can make to the organization. Do not assume that everyone already knows what risks and perils to the project exist. Document them and discuss them.

POS Attachments

The best way I have found to provide the important time and cost information with your POS is through one or more selected attachments. As part of their initial evaluation and prioritization of your project proposal, portfolio management may want some measure of the economic value of the proposed project. They recognize that many of the estimates are little more than a guess, but they will nevertheless ask for this information.

TIP I recommend giving range estimates rather than point estimates. You don't have enough detail at this point to do any better.

In my experience, I recommend that you consider adding one of two types of analyses to your POS:

Risk analysis.   Risk analysis is the most frequently used attachment to the POS in my experience. In some cases, this analysis is a very cursory treatment. In others, it is a mathematically rigorous exercise. Many business decision models depend on quantifying risks, expected loss if the risk materializes, and the probability that the risk will occur. All of these are quantified, and the resulting analyses guide the portfolio manager in decisions on project approval. Risk management is discussed in detail in Chapter 2 and briefly in Chapter 3.

Financial analyses. Some portfolio managers may require a preliminary financial analysis of the project. Although such analyses are very rough because not enough information is known about the project at this time, they will still be useful. In some instances, they also offer criteria for prioritizing all of the POSs the portfolio manager will be reviewing. Some of the possible analyses are feasibility studies, cost/benefit analyses, and break-even analyses. These are all discussed in Chapter 3.

A Two-Step Submission Process

The first step in the two-step submission process is to submit the POS as described in the previous section. Once the alignment decision has been made and the project is aligned with the portfolio strategy, the second step can be taken. The second step is to prepare and submit the detailed project plan. The plan can contain information that would be useful for later decisions, and the information is generally not provided unless it will be used. The strategy in the two-step process is to do the extensive planning work only if the project is deemed to be in alignment with the portfolio strategy. An added benefit to the two-step process is that *how* the project is aligned may also be useful information for the planning work. In my experience, the planning effort can take a number of directions, and knowing specifically how the project relates to the portfolio strategy can produce better and more targeted business value.

A New Submission Process

If you are going to fashion a new submission process based on the five-phase portfolio management process, I advocate a single submission that contains all of the information needed to take the project up to the Selected stage of the project portfolio life cycle. What information is needed to reach that point? Here is a list for your consideration:

Project name. This should be a name that provides some indication of what the project is all about. Don't use code names like XP.47.

Sponsor name. This is the name, position title, and business unit affiliation of the sponsoring individual.

Project manager name. Add this if known.

Project funding category. This will attach the project to some part of the portfolio strategy. In some cases multiple categories may be given.

Project goal. This will be the same type of statement you would have used in the POS for this project.

Project objectives. This will be the same type of statements you would have used in the POS for this project.

CASE STUDY – PIZZA DELIVERED QUICKLY (PDQ)

The entire PDQ project could be viewed as a program consisting of several dependent projects. Once the component parts of the project have been identified through the initial changes, including those introduced by Dee, the project might be represented as shown in the accompanying figure.

Systems-level solution for PDQ

If one views this as a program consisting of five projects — one for each subsystem — there are a number of ways to approach finding the solution. The Order Entry and Inventory Control Systems should be available as commercial off-the-shelf products. An RFI or RFP can reach that conclusion quickly. The other systems are quite different. All three require some form of heuristic algorithms as part of their solutions. The difficulty with each of these is that order preparation can be at one of three sites. The stores and the pizza factories are fixed in place, whereas the pizza vans are moving locations. The same moving location problem complicates the Order Routing System and the Order Delivery System. So these three systems are highly interdependent and an optimal solution may not be possible. That is why a heuristics approach may be the best approach.

As far as a portfolio approach is concerned, this could be viewed as two separate submissions. One would be for the Order Entry and Inventory Control Systems. Together they provide an operational solution for the current store situation. The other would be the three projects all dealing with the complexities added by one moving component — the pizza vans that prepare pizzas. Even that solution could be done in stages. The first stage would incorporate the pizza factories as just another fixed location for preparation. The second stage would add the pizza vans as moving preparation locations. The APF works well regardless of the approach taken.

Explicit business value.   This is a very important piece of the submission. Here you have to establish the business value for this project. Make a quantitative statement about increased revenue, decreased cost, or improved service. It must be a measurable metric.

Risks.   Risk combined with project cost and explicit business value gives financial analysts the grist for their mill. This is where the true business validation of the project is made or lost.

Estimated total project cost.   You do not have a detailed project plan at this point, so all that you can give is a range estimate.

Estimated project duration.   You do not know when the project will begin, so you cannot give a completion date. The statement you want to make here is something like "This project will be completed eight months after the start date," or even better, "This project can be completed in six to nine months following its start date."

Putting It All Together

This chapter has shown you a model for project portfolio management and described several contemporary tools and processes that you might employ to implement it. In effect, I have given you a starter kit for building your own project portfolio management process. If you are a project manager and have to submit your project to a portfolio committee for approval, you now have a strategy for doing that, along with some hope for success.

Discussion Questions

1. In what ways, if any, would TPM, APF, and xPM projects affect your project portfolio management process? Be specific.

2. What criteria (time, cost, value, and so on) must a sequence of activities meet in order to qualify as a project for the portfolio?

3. What types of data will you need in order to evaluate, prioritize, and select projects for the portfolio?

4. How might you combine the C/SC approach with milestone trend charts to produce yet a third tracking method?

Project Support Office

*There is nothing more difficult to take in hand, more perilous
to conduct, or more uncertain in its success, than to take
the lead in the introduction of a new order of things.*

— Machiavelli, The Prince

CHAPTER LEARNING OBJECTIVES

After reading this chapter, you will be able to:

◆ **Describe a Project Support Office (PSO)**

◆ **Understand the signs that you need a PSO**

◆ **Know the missions, objectives, and structures of the PSO**

◆ **Know the functions performed by the PSO**

◆ **Know how to establish a PSO**

◆ **Understand the challenges to establishing a PSO**

◆ **Know how to grow and mature your PSO**

Your organization has put a project management methodology in place, and teams are beginning to use it. However, you are not satisfied. Your expectation was that with everyone using a project management methodology, a higher percentage of projects would be successfully completed. So far there has been no measurable impact on project success. What can you do?

The latest advancement in project management is the Project Support Office (PSO). It is established to support project teams and reduce the risk of project failure. The PSO has several different names and variations in terms of mission, objectives, functions, organizational structure, and organizational placement. These can become quite overwhelming for someone who is not familiar with the concept and its practice. In this chapter, I intend to help you understand all aspects of the PSO and to recognize the signs that you should establish one.

Background of the Project Support Office

Early in the life cycle of any process, there are always the early adopters who stumble onto it and are eager to give it a chance. Their enthusiasm may prove to be contagious, and soon others begin using the process, too. At some point, management begins to take notice because the various ways of understanding of the process is creating problems. Not everyone understands the process the same way, and there are many levels of expertise with the tool; while some misuse it, others don't take its use seriously.

If this sounds like the general topic of project management, it should. Previously, senior management intuitively understood they needed to do something about the problem, and the first reaction was to send people away for some project management training. This by itself didn't cause much improvement.

Next came the introduction of some standards and common metrics found in project management. A project management process was crafted and introduced with a lot of fanfare. All were expected to use it. Some did, some didn't. Some still held on to their old ways and managed projects the way they had been doing it all along. While all of this was going on, projects continued to be executed. There were so many projects under way and so much confusion that management recognized the seriousness of the problem. There was no way to manage across projects within the organization because of redundancy, wasted resources, and the lack of managed standards, and there was no leadership in making project management an asset to the organization. Effective project management was a recognized need in the organization. Senior management held high expectations that by having a standardized project management methodology the success rate of projects would increase. Considerable effort was spent getting a methodology designed, documented, and installed, but somehow it had little impact on project success rates. In fact, it was a big disappointment. Senior management realized that having a methodology wasn't sufficient. Something more was needed, and soon something appeared: the Project Support Office (PSO). The PSO created an opportunity to put an entity in place that ensured compliance. Project success would surely follow. Indeed, the PSO functions like an insurance policy to protect the adoption and spread of the methodology.

There are at least four reasons why an organization would choose to implement a PSO:

- As the organization grows in the number and complexity of the projects in its portfolio, it must adopt formal procedures for managing the volume. To do this, the organization establishes the procedures that are followed for initiating, proposing, and approving projects.

- With increased volume comes a need for more qualified project managers. Those who would like to become project managers will need to be identified and trained. Those who already are project managers will need additional training to deal effectively with the increased complexity. The PSO is the depository of the organization's skill inventory of current and developing project managers. Because managers using the PSO are aware of the types and complexity of current and forthcoming projects, the PSO is the entity best prepared to identify the training needs of project managers and their teams.

- A lack of standards and policies leads to increased inefficiencies and compromises productivity. The increasing failure rate of projects is testimony to that fact. Through the establishment and enforcement of standards and practices, the PSO can have a positive impact on efficiency and productivity.

- Finally, the increased complexity and number of projects places a greater demand on resources. It is no secret that the scarcity of information technology professionals has become a barrier to project success. By paying attention to the demand for skilled project teams and the inventory of skilled team members, the PSO can maintain the proper balance through training.

What Is a Project Support Office?

There are several varieties of PSOs in use in the contemporary organizations. Each serves a different purpose. Before you can consider establishing a PSO in your organization, you have to understand these differences. The purpose of this section is to describe those variations and ascertain what form is best suited for your organization. A good working definition of a Project Support Office is as follows:

> *A Project Support Office is a temporary or permanent organizational unit that provides a portfolio of services to support project teams that are responsible for a specific portfolio of projects.*

The next three sections look at each of the major components of the definition.

Temporary or Permanent Organizational Unit

Among the various forms of PSOs, some are temporary structures and some are permanent. That determination is made based on the types of projects that they support.

Temporary.   PSOs that are temporary are usually called Program Offices, and they support the administrative needs of a group of projects that are related by purpose or goal. When those projects are completed, the Program Office is disbanded. Many government projects have Program Offices affiliated with them. They are generally long-term arrangements and involve millions or billions of dollars of funding.

Permanent.   Those that are permanent are called by various names, as discussed in the section "Naming the Project Support Office" later in the chapter. These PSOs provide a range of support services for projects that are grouped by organizational unit, rather than goal or purpose.

Portfolio of Services

The fully functional PSO serves six major purposes. For now, I'll briefly list and describe them. Further discussion of these functions occurs later in the chapter in the section "Exploring PSO Functions."

Project support.   This includes preparing proposals, gathering and reporting weekly status information, maintaining the project notebook, and assisting with the post-implementation audit.

Consulting and mentoring.   Professional project consultants and trainers are available in the PSO to support the consulting and mentoring needs of the project teams. In this capacity, they are a safe harbor for the project manager and team members as well.

Methods and standards.   This includes such areas as project initiation, project planning, project selection, project prioritization, Work Breakdown Structure templates, risk assessment, project documentation, reporting, software selection and training, post-implementation audits, and dissemination of best practices.

Software tools.   The evaluation, selection, installation, support, and maintenance of all the software that supports project work is part of this function.

Training.   Training curriculum development and training delivery may be assigned to the PSO, depending on whether the organization has a centralized training department and whether it has the expertise needed to develop and deliver the needed programs.

Project manager resources.   Here the PSO provides a resource to project managers for advice, suggestions, and career guidance. Regardless of the organizational structure in which the PSO exists, the project manager does not have any other safe place to seek advice and counsel. The PSO is ideally suited to that role. A variety of human resource functions are provided. Some PSOs have project managers assigned to them. In these situations, the project managers are usually assigned to complex, large, or mission-critical projects.

Specific Portfolio of Projects

I have already identified one portfolio — those projects that have a link through their goals and purposes. In other words, collectively they represent a major initiative to accomplish some overall common purpose. A good example is the U.S. space program. Think of a single project as something that will accomplish a part of a greater overall mission. Together all of the projects represent a single focus and common purpose. As stated previously, these projects form a program and are administered under a Program Office. When the goal of the projects that are part of the program is accomplished, the Program Office is disbanded.

Another portfolio of projects that you can identify is one that organizes projects under a single organizational unit and is funded from the same budget, such as IT. The IT department's PSO will be a permanent structure that supports all IT projects now and into the future.

Still one more specific portfolio that deserves mention is made up of projects that are funded out of the same budget. They may have no other relationship with one another other than they share a finite pool of money. These projects are often linked through a PSO. Such a PSO will be primarily interested in ensuring the proper expenditure of the dollars in the budget that funds all of these projects. These PSOs generally have a project portfolio management process in place to manage the budgets for their projects.

Naming the Project Support Office

So far I have casually used the label PSO. In my experience, many different names have been used to identify the organizational unit that provides the functions just described, and you may have encountered some of these alternative terms for what I am calling the PSO. Some of these alternative names for a PSO are as follows:

- Project Office
- Program Office
- Project Management Office

- Project Control Office
- Project Management Group
- Project Management Center of Excellence
- Enterprise PMO
- Directorate of Project Management
- Development Management Office
- IT Project Support
- Mission Central

Some of these names are clearly attached to an enterprise-level unit, whereas others are more specific to the group they serve. An interesting one is the last one — Mission Central. A recent client for whom I designed and implemented a project management methodology and the accompanying Project Support Office was troubled by the word management and, in fact, wasn't too happy with the term project either. To that client, the term "management" suggested a kind of oversight or control function that wasn't intended. In addition, the term "project" had been overused in the company and carried a lot of baggage that needed to be left behind. They needed a name for this new entity they were commissioning. A naming contest was initiated by the chairman, who also selected the winning entry: Mission Central.

Despite the misgivings of the client just described, I have nevertheless chosen to use the name PSO for a reason. In my experience, the most successful project support units are those that are characterized as providing both proactive and reactive support services. They are ready to respond to requests for help in any way that the project manager or team members may need. These PSOs also have a responsibility to see that the organization practices effective project management. That happens through the provision of a standard methodology, training and documentation to support its widespread use, and a review function to ensure its correct usage.

However, I have had experience with PSOs that send a very different message. These are the units that have more of a monitoring and enforcement mission. They are seldom called a PSO and are more likely to be named Project Management Office, or Project Control Office, or simply Project Office. Such units have a spylike air about them and are unlikely to produce the usage that the organization expects.

Establishing Your PSO's Mission

If you have decided that a PSO will be established, the first order of business is to determine the mission of your PSO. The following list gives some examples of possible mission statements:

- Provide overall management and administrative support to the ALPHA Program

- Establish and monitor compliance with the project management methodology

- Provide a comprehensive portfolio of support services to all project managers on an as-requested basis

The first statement is the typical mission statement of a Program Office. It provides administrative support for a program, which comprises a group of projects related to something called the "ALPHA Program." This type of mission statement will be very common in organizations that operate large programs consisting of many projects.

The second statement is a very limited mission statement. Often such a statement doesn't find much favor with project managers. Even though this mission statement is not popular, it is necessary in any PSO that is worth the price. A standard must be established and there must be compliance with that standard, but it doesn't have to be couched in terms that suggest a Gestapo-like enforcement. Combining a strong statement of support in the mission statement will go a long way toward satisfying the project manager who is desperate for support and can live with it and with the standard.

The third statement is more to my liking. It seems to be more supportive of the things a project manager is looking for in a PSO. This is my choice, and its purpose fits comfortably with a name like Project Support Office. A PSO will still have some of those Gestapo-like functions to perform, but the mission statement suggests that they are surrounded by a comprehensive list of support services. It seems to define a package that can be sold to project managers and to senior managers as well.

Framing PSO Objectives

Assume that you have adopted the third mission statement as the mission statement of your PSO. (I use the name PSO from this point forward in the discussion.) Because the PSO is a business unit, its objectives should be framed in business terms. The following list illustrates some examples:

- Help project teams deliver value.
- Increase the success rates of projects to 75 percent.
- Reach PMMM Level 4.

The first statement is a bit vague in that it passes the business reason for the PSO to the project teams. They have to define value and make it happen. If you want to hold the toes of the PSO to the fire, then either the second or third statement will do the job. They are very specific and can be easily measured.

NOTE PMMM in the third statement stands for Project Management Maturity Model. It is discussed later in this chapter.

Exploring PSO Functions

The six functions mentioned earlier in the chapter and discussed in the following sections are fairly inclusive of those that a PSO might offer. A word of caution is in order, however. It would be a mistake to implement all of the listed functions at once even if that is the ultimate goal of your PSO. Introducing a PSO into the organization is asking management to absorb quite a bit. You will have a much better chance of success if the functions are prioritized and introduced piecemeal. I have more to say about this later in the chapter when I discuss the challenges of implementing a PSO. For now I will simply define what each of these functions involves and leave implementation for later.

Project Support

This function encompasses all of the administrative support services that a PSO might offer to a project manager and project team. They are as follows:

- Schedule updating and reporting
- Time sheet recording and maintenance
- Report production and distribution
- Report archiving
- Report consolidation and distribution
- Project notebook maintenance

The PSO project support services are an attempt on the part of the PSO to remove as much non-value-added work from the project team as it can and place it in the PSO. Obviously, you would rather have the project team focused on the work of the project and not be burdened by so-called administrivia. More important, the PSO staff will be much more knowledgeable about how to provide these services because they will be very familiar with them and with the use of the tools and systems that support them. Obviously the cost of providing the service is much lower if done by the PSO than if done by the project team. More to the point, the PSO staffs that will actually provide the service need minimal office skills, whereas the project team members' skill set is not likely to include the skills appropriate to provide these services. Therefore, the service will be provided by a less costly employee who is appropriately positioned for the assignment.

Consulting and Mentoring

The PSO professional staff members are available to project teams and project managers on an as-requested basis. They stand ready to help with any specialized assistance. The following is a list of the consulting and mentoring services they can supply:

- Proposal development support
- Facilitation of project planning sessions
- Risk assessment
- Project interventions
- Mentoring and coaching project managers
- Mentoring senior management

The PSO professional consultants are the senior-most project managers in the company. Their experiences are broad and deep. Because they have heard and seen most situations, nothing will surprise them. They are qualified to help the project manager even in the most complex of circumstances.

> **TIP** One practice that I have seen in a few PSOs is to rotate these consultants through the PSO. Think of it as a sabbatical from the front lines. One of the benefits of this rotation is that it continually infuses new ideas and best practices into the PSO as well as back out into the field.

The PSO is uniquely positioned to gather and archive best practices from around the company. That makes them particularly valuable as a resource to project teams. Those resources are made available to teams through the PSO professional consultants.

One service that I believe is particularly valuable is the facilitation of project planning sessions. The PSO consultant is the ideal person to conduct a project planning session. That relieves the project manager from the facilitation responsibility and enables that manager to concentrate on the project plan itself. The PSO consultant can concentrate on running a smooth planning session. This PSO consultant will have better planning facilitation skills than the project manager by virtue of the fact that he or she has conducted far more planning sessions. It is a win-win situation.

One other useful practice that I have seen is not having the PSO consultant actually attached to the PSO. Acting as virtual PSO consultants, they are out in the field running projects but have particular areas of expertise that they are willing to make available to others as needed. The PSO simply becomes the clearinghouse for such services. With this setup, confidentiality is critical. Project managers are not likely to bare their soul to other project managers if what they say will be the topic of conversation in the lunch room the next day.

Methods and Standards

Methods and standards represent a service that every PSO must provide. A good ROI from a PSO will not happen in the absence of a standard methodology and a means of monitoring and enforcing it. The following list contains the services included in this function:

- Establishing, monitoring, and enforcing standards
- Project selection for the portfolio
- Work Breakdown Structure construction
- PERT/CPM Network development
- Maintenance of tools/process library
- Bid preparation
- Risk assessment
- Status reporting
- Change management
- Documentation
- Change orders

The establishment, monitoring, and enforcement of standards are major undertakings for a newly formed PSO. Perhaps more than any other task the PSO will perform, this one affects the culture and operation of the organization. As I discuss later, a plan to put standards in place must involve as many stakeholders as possible. I am talking about a cultural change in every business unit that is involved with projects and project management. The affected parties must have an opportunity to be involved in establishing these standards or the whole effort will be for naught. I have a lot more to say on this point later in the chapter.

Software Tools

Every PSO should be looking for productivity improvements. As teams become dispersed, it is essential that they remain productive. In this technology-crazed business environment, you can't let time and distance erect barriers to performance. The PSO is the only organizational unit that can provide the support needed for the ever-changing set of tools available on the market. It is responsible for soliciting, evaluating, selecting, and contracting with vendors of these tools. The following list describes the services that the organization depends on the PSO to provide:

- Software evaluation
- Software selection

- Vendor negotiations
- Software training
- Software management and maintenance

Training

Training in project management has probably been around longer than any other methodology an organization is likely to have. Unfortunately, senior managers incorrectly assumed that the solution to their high rate of project failure could be found by giving everyone some training in project management. They were looking for that silver bullet, and there simply isn't one to be found. What has happened in many organizations is that several different project management training courses have been taken by the professional staff. Accordingly, there is no central approach that they follow as a result of their training. In a sense everyone is still doing his or her own thing. Some follow the approach they were taught, others do what they have always done, and yet others teach themselves. Under the PSO all of that needs to change.

NOTE To have maximum impact on the practice of project management in the organization, a project management curriculum must be built around an established project management methodology. You simply can't do it any other way.

One school of thought says that if you teach concepts and principles effectively, project managers will be able to adapt them to whatever situation they encounter. That sounds good in theory, but it doesn't work. I have found that most project managers don't want to think; they want to be told: "Just tell me what I am supposed to do. I'm not interested in the concepts and theory." That's a truly unfortunate attitude, but it's reality; you can't change it very easily. With that in mind, the PSO, in collaboration with the organization's training department, must jointly assume the responsibility of designing and implementing a curriculum that is aligned with the organization's project management methodology. Furthermore, the PSO must assume whatever responsibility the training department is unwilling or unable to assume. Whatever the case, the job must be done. The following list describes the training services provided by the PSO:

- Project management basics
- Advanced project management
- PMP exam preparation
- Specialized topics

- Support of the training department
- Development of courses and course content
- Delivering courses
- PM training vendor selection

When it comes to project management training, the relationship between the training department and the PSO must be a collaborative effort. The development of the project management curriculum should involve both the curriculum development experts from the training department and the subject matter experts from the PSO. Delivery of the curriculum can be done either by the PSO or by the training department. If it is to be done by the training department, then the curriculum design must have followed a facilitative design. That relieves the training department from having to find trainers who have project management practice expertise, which is difficult at best. In most cases I have seen, the trainers are project management subject matter experts, and this is the preferred method. There is no good substitute for frontline experience by the trainer. No amount of book knowledge can replace it.

Project Manager Resources

The final function in my PSO includes a number of human resource services revolving around project managers. The following list is quite comprehensive; it encompasses assessment, development, and deployment services:

- Human resource development
- Identification/assessment of skills
- Selection of team members
- Selection of project managers
- Assessment of project teams
- Professional development
- Career guidance and development

This function is delivered in two ways:

- In some cases project managers will be assigned to the PSO. They then receive their project assignments from the PSO.
- The more common arrangement is for the project managers to be assigned to a business or functional unit. Even in this case the PSO can still make project assignments and deliver the human resource services listed under this function.

Selecting PSO Organizational Structures

Different organizations have taken various approaches to the structure and placement of the PSO. In this section I comment on my experiences with each of the structures I have seen in practice. The following section considers the organizational placement of the PSO.

Virtual versus Real

A *virtual PSO* performs all of the functions of any other PSO except that its staff is allocated to the business units. These PSOs are mostly available when their services are needed. They do not perform any routine functions. Other than a director and perhaps an administrative support person, the virtual PSO does not have any other budgeted staff. Professional staffs from the business units that are involved with projects volunteer their services to the PSO. This is not a permanent volunteer position. These individuals, who are generally project managers themselves, agree to serve for some period of time and are then replaced. In many cases they volunteer to provide only a specified type of service or services.

A *real PSO* does have a budgeted staff of professionals, which probably includes several project managers. They perform several routine functions, such as project reviews and software evaluations. The project reviews are a good way to monitor the adoption of the methodology and uncover best practices. Their strength will probably be that they offer a healthy dose of project support services to project teams.

Proactive versus Reactive

The proactive PSO aligns very closely with the real PSO, and the reactive PSO aligns closely with the virtual PSO. The real PSO can be proactive because it has the staff to take leadership roles in a variety of projects to improve project management practices. The reactive PSO, conversely, does not have the staff and does well to just respond to requests for help.

Temporary versus Permanent

What I have called Program Offices in this chapter are the only temporary form of PSO that I know of. All other examples of PSOs are permanent and service an ever-changing list of projects.

Program versus Projects

I have already defined programs as collections of related projects. The related projects always have some dependencies between them, so there is a need for oversight such as a Program Office. Significant resource management problems will arise because of the interproject dependencies, and only oversight from the vantage point of a Program Office can be effective.

Enterprise versus Functional

PSOs can be attached at the enterprise level or functional level:

- At the enterprise level, they must provide services to all disciplines. They are generally well funded and well staffed. They have visibility at the project portfolio level and may be involved in strategic roles.

- At the functional level, they generally service the needs of a single discipline. They are generally not as well funded or staffed as their enterprise-level counterpart.

Hub — Hub and Spoke

In very large organizations the PSO may be organized in a hierarchical form. At the hub, or central office, if you will, is a high-level PSO that sets policy and standards for the enterprise. If only the hub form is in place, then all of the functions of the PSO will reside there. In time, as the organization grows in its maturity and dependence on the PSO, these functions may be carried out at the business unit or division level by regional PSOs (the spokes), who take their direction from the central PSO. The hub is typically staffed by high-level project executives whose focus is strategic. At the end of a spoke is a regional PSO, which has operational responsibilities for the unit it represents. Obviously, the hub-and-spoke configuration works best in those organizations that have a more mature approach to project management. It is not a structure for organizations new to project management.

Organizational Placement of the PSO

There are three organizational placements for the PSO, as shown in Figure 21-1.

At the enterprise level they are usually called by some name like Enterprise PSO (EPSO) that suggests they serve the entire enterprise. I have seen two variations of EPSOs — centralized or decentralized:

- In the centralized version, the EPSO provides all of the services to all project teams corporate-wide that any PSO would provide.

- The decentralized version often has a policy and procedure responsibility with satellite PSOs providing the actual functions in accordance with the established policy and procedures.

Both models can be effective. The size of the organization with respect to the number of projects needing support is the best determinant of structure, the decentralized structure favoring the larger organization. There really are no hard-and-fast rules here.

The PSO can also serve the needs of a significant part of the enterprise — such as at the division or business-unit level. The most common example is the information technology division. Here the PSO serves the needs of all the IT professionals in the organization (IT PSO in Figure 21-1, for example). Because this PSO is discipline-specific, it will probably offer project support services tailored to the needs of the information technology project. It may also offer services specific to the needs of teams that are using various systems development processes. In other words, a division-level PSO may offer not only project management support services, but also services specific to the discipline.

The PSO can also serve the needs of a single program. As shown in Figure 21-1, there may be several of these programs even within a single division. This is a common occurrence in the information technology division. These PSOs are temporary. When the program that they support is completed, the PSO is disbanded.

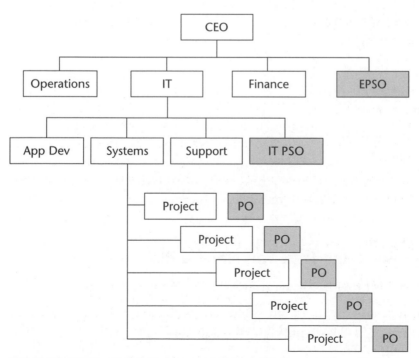

Figure 21-1 Organizational placement of the PSO

How Do You Know You Need a PSO?

However you slice it, the PSO is established for the sole purpose of improving the practice of project management for the group of projects and project managers over whom it has stewardship. The PSO is an investment, and its ROI is measured in terms of cost avoidance. That cost avoidance is a direct result of a significant reduction in project failures for which the PSO is held directly responsible and accountable.

The Standish Group Report

The reasons for project failure have been investigated and reported in detail for several years. One of the most thorough research efforts into the reasons for project failure is the work of the Standish Group. In Chronicles 2000 they surveyed several hundred IT executives, asking them why projects fail. According to this study, the top 10 reasons why IT projects fail were due to a lack of the following:

1. Executive management support
2. User involvement
3. An experienced project manager
4. Clear business objectives
5. Minimized scope
6. Standard infrastructure
7. Firm basic requirements
8. A formal methodology
9. Reliable estimates
10. Skilled staff

After reviewing the major functions that the PSO provides, you can see that a PSO is uniquely positioned to mitigate each of these 10 reasons for project failure. In fact, it is the only organizational entity that is so positioned.

Spotting Symptoms That You Need a PSO

Several symptoms provide you with clues that you might need a PSO:

Project failure rates are too high.   The data is all too familiar to me. Reports show 70 percent and higher regardless of how failure is defined. That is simply unacceptable. Many of the reasons for those high numbers are probably found in the list from the Standish Group. Those that relate to the project management approach that was used — namely, user involvement, clear business objectives, minimized scope, standard infrastructure, firm basic requirements, and formal methodology — can be addressed by choosing the correct approach (TPM, APF, or xPM). It is my contention that by choosing the appropriate approach, the organization can make a serious impact on failure rates.

Training is not producing results.   I am not aware of any systematic study of the root causes of training ineffectiveness. Possible causes are inappropriate materials, inappropriate delivery, no follow-through on behavioral changes after training, or no testing of skill acquisition. Training needs to be taken seriously by those who attend the training. Attendees must be held accountable for applying what they have learned, and there must be ways to measure that application. I am amazed at how many training professionals and curriculum designers are not familiar with Kirkpatrick's model. The interested reader can consult Donald L. Kirkpatrick's *Evaluating Training Programs, Second Edition* (Berrett-Koehler, 1998). In my experience, project reviews that are held at various milestones in the life of the project are excellent points at which to validate the application of training. If clear evidence isn't shown that training has been applied, some corrective action is certainly called for.

HR project staff planning isn't effective.   Organizations need to do a better job of defining the inventory of project staff skills and the demand for those skills by projects. A concerted effort is needed to match the supply to the demand and to make better staffing assignments to projects. The PSO is the best place for this responsibility to be carried out.

Inability to leverage best practices.   The PSO is the best place to collect and distribute best practices. Project status meetings and project reviews are the place to identify best practices. The PSO, through some form of bulletin board service, is the best place to distribute that information. In the absence of that service, the collection and distribution of best practices isn't going to happen.

Lack of control over the project portfolio.   Many senior managers don't know the number of projects that are active. They haven't made any effort to find out and to be selective of those projects that are active. That behavior has to change if there is any hope of managing the project work in the organization. The PSO is the clear choice for stewardship of that portfolio. At the least, it can be the unit that assembles project performance data and distributes it to the decision makers for their review and action.

No consistency in project reporting.   Without a centralized unit responsible for the reporting process, consistent and useful reporting isn't going to happen. Again, the PSO is the clear choice to establish the reporting structure and assist in its use.

Too many resource scheduling conflicts.   Most organizations operate with some form of matrix structure. Resources are assigned from their functional unit to projects at the discretion of the functional unit manager. In such situations resource conflicts are unavoidable. The individuals who are assigned to projects are torn between doing work for their functional unit and doing work for the project to which they have been assigned. None of this is news to you. One solution to resource scheduling conflicts is to use the PSO as the filter through which project staffing requests and staffing decisions are made. The major benefit of this approach is that it takes the project manager off the hot seat and puts the responsibility in the PSO where it can be more equitably discharged.

Gap between process and practice.   This is a major problem area for many organizations. They may have a well-documented process in place, but without any oversight and compliance function in place, they are at the mercy of the project manager to use or not use the process. The PSO is the only unit that can close this gap. The PSO puts the process in place with the help of those who will be held accountable for its use. The PSO, through project performance reviews, can determine the extent of that gap and put remedial steps in place to close it.

Establishing a PSO

When you are planning for a PSO, three critical questions must be answered. One of them deals with defining a desired future for your organization's PSO — the goal, so to speak. To reach that goal, however, you have to assess where you currently are with respect to it. The answer to that question identifies a gap between the current state and the future state. That gap is removed through the implementation plan for your PSO. This is the definition of a standard gap analysis. The three major questions, then, arranged chronologically, are as follows:

- Where are you?
- Where are you going?
- How will you get there?

Before you attempt to answer those questions, you need a foundation for answering them. The Software Engineering Institute (SEI) provides just the foundation you need. Their five-level model, described in the next section, also gives you a foundation on which you can plan for the further growth and maturation of my PSO.

PSO Stages of Growth

Over the past several years, the Software Engineering Institute at Carnegie Mellon University has developed a maturity model for software engineering. It has gained wide support and become a standard of the software development community. The model is called the Capability Maturity Model (CMM). It has recently been adapted to project management in the form of a Project Management Maturity Model (PMMM). I will use the five maturity levels of the PMMM to answer two of the questions: Where are you and where are you going?

Figure 21-2 offers a graphic depiction and brief description of each of the maturity levels of the PMMM.

Level 1: Initial

At Level 1, everyone basically does as he or she pleases. There may be some processes and tools for project management, which some people may be using on an informal basis. Project management training is nonexistent, and help may be available on an informal basis at best. There doesn't appear to be any signs of organization under project management.

Level 2: Repeatable

Level 2 is distinguished from Level 1 in that a documented project management process is available. It is used at the discretion of the project manager, and some training is available for those who are interested. The only sign of a PSO is through some part-time support who will help a project team on an as-requested basis.

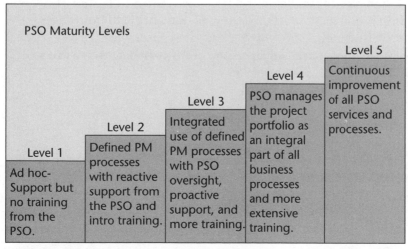

Figure 21-2 Project management maturity levels

Level 3: Defined

The transition from Level 2 to Level 3 is dramatic. The project management processes are fully documented, and project management has been recognized as critical to business success by senior management. A formal PSO is established and staffed and given the responsibility of ensuring enterprise-wide usage of the methodology. Enforcement is taken seriously, and a solid training curriculum is available. There is some sign that project management is being integrated into other business processes.

Level 4: Managed

At this level, successful project management is viewed as a critical success factor by the organization. A complete training program and professional development program for project managers is in place. The PSO is looked upon as a business, and project portfolio management is of growing importance. The project portfolio is an integral part of all business planning activities.

Level 5: Optimized

At Level 5, the PSO is the critical component of a continuous quality improvement program for project management. Progress in the successful use of project management is visible, measured, and acted upon.

Planning a PSO

You can now put the pieces of a plan together. Based on what I have discussed so far, your plan to establish a PSO might look something like what is shown in Figure 21-3. Before you can begin the activities shown in Figure 21-3, however, you have to write the Project Overview Statement (POS) for the PSO.

CROSS-REF For a more detailed discussion of the components of a POS and what goes into writing one, see Chapter 3.

The POS

Shown in Figure 21-4 is an example POS for a PSO implementation project submitted by Sal Vation.

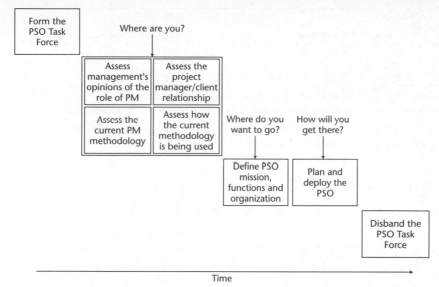

Figure 21-3 A plan to establish a PSO

The next sections take a quick look at what Sal submitted.

Problem/Opportunity

Note that the statement describes a business condition that needs no defense or further clarification. Anyone, especially the executive committee, who reads it will understand it and agree with it. The importance of this statement will determine whether or not the reader continues to the goal statement. In this case, the situation is grave enough that their continued reading is a foregone conclusion.

Goal

The statement is clean and crisp. It states what will be done and by when. Note that it is phrased so that the project is expected to deliver results before the expected completion date. Sal recognizes the importance of early results to the executive committee and doesn't want the stated timeline to shock them and perhaps jeopardize the project's approval.

Objectives

The objective statements expand and clarify the goal statement and suggest interim milestones and deliverables.

PROJECT OVERVIEW STATEMENT	Project Name **PSO Implementation**	Project No. **PSO.001**	ProjectManager **Sal Vation**

Problem Opportunity

To restore our lost market share, we must quickly develop our capabilities in the customized furnishings business but are unable to because our project management processes cannot support the needs of the product development teams.

Goal

Provide a fully mature and comprehensive portfolio of project management support services to all project teams in less than four years.

Objectives
1. Provide off-the-shelf and customized project management training.
2. Develop and document a standard project management process to support all of our project teams with special focus on product development teams.
3. Establish a projects review process to monitor and enforce compliance with our project management processes.
4. Establish a portfolio management process for all customized projects.
5. Create a professional development program for all project managers.
6. Design and implement a continuous quality improvement process for project management.

Success Criteria
1. Over 50% of all PMs will receive basic training by the end of 2007 Q1.
2. Project quarterly success rates will increase from current 35% to 70% by 2007 Q3.
3. At least 90% of all projects begun after 2007 Q3 will use the new O & P project management process.
4. 100% of all PMs will receive training in the O & P project management process by the end of 2007 Q4.
5. 90% of all PMs will have a professional development program in place by 2007 Q4.
6. The PSO will reach maturity level 2 no later than Q3 2007, maturity level 3 no later than Q4 2008, maturity level 4 no later than Q2 2010, and maturity level 5 no later than Q4 2010.
7. Market share will be restored to 100% of its highest level no later than Q4 2010.

Assumptions, Risks, Obstacles
1. Business unit managers will resist change in their operating procedures.
2. The customized furnishings market is not as strong as forecasted.
3. Project managers will continue to practice their old ways.

Prepared By **Sal Vation**	Date 1/3/2007	Approved By **Del E. Lama**	Date 1/6/2007

Figure 21-4 An example Project Overview Statement for a PSO implementation project

Success Criteria

Sal has expressed the success criteria in specific and measurable quantitative terms. This is very important. In this case the criteria will help the executive committee understand the business value of the project. It is the single most important criteria Sal can present to them at this time to help them decide whether the project is worth doing.

Assumptions, Risks, Obstacles

Sal has called to the attention of the executive committee anything that he feels can potentially compromise the success of the project. These statements serve two purposes:

- They highlight for senior managers some of the potential problems that they might be able to mitigate for the project team.
- They provide some risk data for the financial analysts to estimate the expected return on the investment in a PSO.

The executive committee will consider the success criteria versus risk to determine the expected business value that can result from this project. In cases where other projects are vying for the same resources, the analysts would have a comparable statistic to use to decide where to spend their resources.

Planning Steps

Sal will eventually get approval to move into the details of project planning in anticipation of getting executive committee approval of the plan so that he and his team can get to work. Sal might expect a few iterations of the POS before he gets that approval to proceed with planning. In my experience, senior managers often question success criteria, especially with reference to its validity.

Forming the PSO Task Force

The PSO task force forms the strategy group for this project. They are to be considered members of the project team. Their membership should include managers of those business units that will be affected by the PSO. The size of the enterprise determines how many members there will be. A task force of four to six should work quite well, whereas a task force of 15 would be counterproductive. Without the support and commitment of each task force member, the PSO it is unlikely to succeed. Because their operations are likely to be affected by the PSO, they must be a part of its mission and have an opportunity to be heard as decisions are made on the mission, functions, and services the PSO will provide.

Measuring Where You Are

Several metrics have been developed to quantitatively measure the maturity level of your project management processes. I have developed one that consists of over 800 yes or no questions. (The interested reader should consult me at rkw@eiicorp.com for details on this proprietary product.) These questions cover all five maturity levels for all 39 project management processes identified by PMI in their PMBOK. Figure 21-5 shows the results of a recent assessment for one of my clients. The data on each of the 39 processes have been aggregated to the knowledge area level.

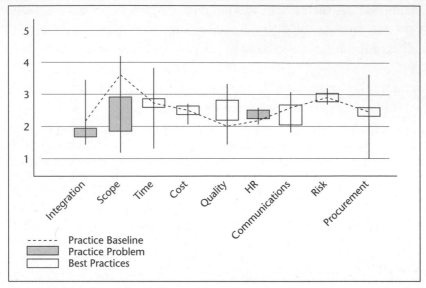

Figure 21-5 Maturity-level data for nine knowledge areas of PMBOK

This one graphic conveys a lot of information about this organization's project management maturity levels. First of all, the dashed line shows the maturity level of each knowledge area as documented in the organization's project management methodology. The box and whisker plots are maturity-level data reflecting how project management was practiced in several projects that were reviewed in the same quarter. The box and whisker plot is a summarized view of the data points for each project on a single knowledge area. Each box displays the middle 50 percent of the data. The endpoints of the whiskers denote the extreme data points. The color coding denotes the status of the knowledge area. A red box indicates a process whose practice is significantly below the maturity level of the baseline process. A yellow box indicates a process whose practice is significantly above the maturity level of the baseline process. For example, take a look at the Scope Management knowledge area. The projects that were reviewed demonstrate a maturity-level range from a low of 1.2 to a high of 4.1. The middle half of the data points range from 1.8 to 2.9. The Scope Management knowledge area was assessed at a maturity level of 3.5.

Any maturity level below target or above target indicates an area that needs further investigation. The investigation should look for solutions to the less than nominal maturity and take the necessary corrective steps to raise the level of maturity of that knowledge area. In those cases where the knowledge area is found to be performing above nominal, the investigation should try to reveal the reasons for that exemplary performance and for ways to share their findings with other project teams.

In determining where the organization is with respect to project management, there are two threads of investigation:

- The first is the organizational environment in which the PSO will function. This involves assessing the opinions of the managers whose business units will be impacted. Oftentimes this can be done with face-to-face interviews of key managers.

- The second is an attempt to assess the current relationship between project managers and the clients they serve. In this case the clients will be internal business units and external customers who buy their products.

An assessment tool that I have developed at Enterprise Information Insights, Inc., that has been quite successful in practice is the Project Manager Competency Assessment (PMCA). It is an assessment of a project manager's project management competencies. (Contact me at `rkw@eiicorp.com` for information about how to acquire the tool.) Figure 21-6 shows a report from that assessment tool.

This PMCA reports findings in four major areas (business competency, personal competency, interpersonal competency, and management competency) as they relate to the individual's project management behaviors. A total of 18 competencies are spread across these four areas. Each one uses the box and whisker plot to summarize the opinions of the assessors. In this case there were eight assessors. The endpoints of the box and whisker plots denote the extreme data points. The hollow rectangle is the middle half of the data. The filled rectangle is the average of all assessors. The bolded vertical line is the individual's self-assessment. This individual has a higher self-assessment of herself than do the managers who provided the competency data. This is especially evident in business awareness, business partnership, initiative, conceptual thinking, resourceful use of influence, and motivating others. This person should be advised to take a close look at how she sees herself relative to how others see her. This self-inflated phenomenon is not unusual. I have seen it time and time again in many of these assessments. People are simply not aware of how they affect others. As a group, her interpersonal competencies are held in high regard by her fellow workers. Her personal competencies, especially initiative, conceptual thinking, and self-confidence, may be problematic.

If either of these two assessments, either the maturity level of your project management processes or the project manager competency assessment, uncovers problems, an intervention may be needed prior to any further PSO planning. For the purposes of this exercise, the assessments have shown me that the organization is ready to move forward and strongly supports the creation of a full-service PSO.

Figure 21-6 An example project manager competency assessment

The next step is to take a look at the existing methodology. There are two areas of investigation:

▪ The first is to assess the maturity level of the project management processes that are in place. This can be done by using commercially available tools (such as the Project Management Maturity Assessment).

■ The second area of investigation is to assess how project teams are using that methodology. Again, there are commercially available tools for this assessment (the Project Management Competency Assessment, for one). Readers can contact me at rkw@eiicorp.com for more information on these and other similar assessment tools.

For this example, assume the assessments show that the organization is at Level 1 maturity both in terms of their project management processes and the practice of those processes.

Establishing Where You Want To Go

The future of the organization in the example seems to rest on its ability to restore market share. As expressed in the POS, Sal has as a long-term goal the achievement of Level 5 maturity in the PSO. His strategy will be to achieve that in phases, with each phase providing business value to the organization. The PSO is expected to be a full-service PSO. Its mission, functions, and organization are given in Table 21-1.

Table 21-1 Example PSO Mission, Functions, and Organization

MISSION
To provide the project management services and support needed to establish a market leadership position for the organization in the customized furnishings business

FUNCTIONS
All project administrative services
Project management processes to support all project types
Comprehensive software for all phases of product development
A customized and complete PM training curriculum
A revolving staff of consulting project managers
A professional development program for project managers

(continued)

Table 21-1 *(continued)*

ORGANIZATION
An enterprise-wide unit attached to the president's office
EPSO director will be a three-year renewable appointed position
Permanent staff consists of:
Project administrator to deliver support services
Manager of methods and tools
Senior project manager consultant
Project manager consultant
Curriculum development specialist
Senior trainer
Trainer

The long-term goal of the PSO is to ensure project success. It should be obvious that goal means at least the attainment of Level 3 maturity. Without a documented process in place and in use by all teams, it is unlikely that there will be any measurable increase in the rate of project success.

However, casually stating that Level 4 maturity is the goal of the PSO is not appropriate. That is clearly a business decision. Attaining Level 4 maturity is a big step. It is very costly in terms of the extent of change in the organization. I would liken that change to the evolution of the enterprise to a projectized organizational structure. To move from Level 4 to Level 5 is a matter of implementing a continuous quality improvement process within the PSO. That is far less traumatic and usually involves not much more than putting teeth into a project review process and a concerted effort to capture and implement best practices from the organization's projects, as well as projects external to the organization.

Refer back for a moment to the data in Figure 21-5 and you'll see that, because the middle half of the data points all fall below the average of 3.5, Scope Management needs some improvement. Such an area is where a continuous quality improvement effort would focus. The results of a continuous quality improvement effort in Scope Management might look something like the hypothetical data displayed in Figure 21-7. Note that not only has the process baseline maturity level improved from 3.5 to 4.1 during the period from 3/2006 to 12/2006, but the mid-range of the maturity level of the practice has moved from (1.8–2.9) to (3.9–4.3). The maturity level of the practice of Scope Management has increased significantly, and its range has decreased. This is a marked improvement! If this organization had set as its goal to increase the Scope Management maturity level of its process and its practice to 4.0, it would have achieved that goal.

Establishing How You Will Get There

It goes without saying that the lower your current project management maturity level is, the more challenging it will be to move to Level 3 or higher maturity. Level 3 is where the PSO can really begin to make an impact on the practice of project management. It is at this level that the organization has fully bought into project management. Teams must use it, and the PSO is monitoring that usage. Best practices are identified through project reviews and folded back into the methodology. All signs are positive. Figure 21-8 gives a brief description of what actions should be taken to move from one level to the next.

Sal's plan consists of four phases. Each phase ends with a milestone that signifies the attainment of the next level of maturity. Phase One is complete when the organization has reached maturity Level 2 in the PSO. Phases Two, Three, and Four are similarly defined. Within each phase are a number of deliverables that add business value. These deliverables have been prioritized to add business value as soon as possible. Figure 21-9 describes the high-level plan through all four phases.

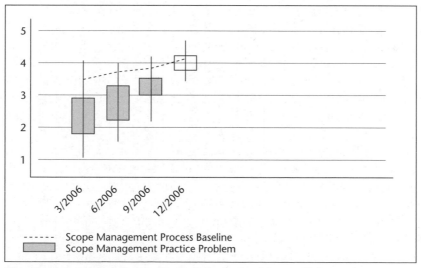

Figure 21-7 Continuous quality improvement of Scope Management

Current PSO Maturity Level	Characteristics of PSOs at This Maturity Level	Initiatives that Will Move the PSO to the Next Maturity Level
INITIAL (1)	• Some defined PM processes are available. • Informal support to teams as requested. • No PM training is available.	• Assemble a task force to establish a PM process. • Document the PM process. • Make PM training available.
REPEATABLE (2)	• A documented PM process is in place. • Part-time support to teams available. • Limited PM training is available.	• Establish programs to increase PM process usage. • Establish a full-time PSO staff to support teams. • Monitor and enforce compliance. • Increase available PM training.
DEFINED (3)	• Fully documented and supported PM process. • Full-time support to teams is available. • All project teams are using the PM process. • PM processes are integrated with other processes. • More extensive PM training is available.	• Projects are made part of the business plan. • Put project portfolio management in the PSO. • Give the PSO an active role in project staffing. • Offer more extensive training. • Create a career development program in the PSO. • Staff project managers in the PSO.
MANAGED (4)	• PSO responsible for professional development. • Complete PM training is available. • Project portfolio is managed as a business.	• PSO begins to identify and adopt best practices. • Metrics are defined to track process quality. • Project reviews are used to monitor compliance.
OPTIMIZING (5)	• A continuous improvement process is in place. • There is measured improvement in project success.	

Figure 21-8 How to move to the next maturity level

Figure 21-9 PSO plan overview

Challenges to Implementing a PSO

Too many executives have the impression that a PSO is mostly a clerical function and that establishing one is not too difficult. Nothing could be further from the truth. J. Kent Crawford provides a compelling discussion of some of those challenges in *The Strategic Project Office: A Guide to Improving Organizational Performance* (Marcel Dekker, 2001). Crawford's challenges are as follows:

- Speed and patience
- Leadership from the bottom up
- A systems thinking perspective
- Enterprise-wide systems
- Knowledge management
- Learning and learned project organizations
- Open communications

Speed and Patience

Effectively deploying a PSO can require two to five years for full implementation. That is a long time. According to the Standish Group research, the longer the project, the higher the probability of project failure. The way out of this apparent dilemma is to plan the PSO deployment in stages. Each stage must deliver visible and measurable value to the organization. To do otherwise is to court disaster.

Leadership from the Bottom Up

A major aspect of putting a PSO in place is a bottom-up strategy. At the department or project level, you must demonstrate value by showing the results that a PSO can achieve. Then, by way of example, others in the organization will see that success and ask how they can achieve it in their own areas. This grassroots effort will be contagious, and it is one of the keys to a successful PSO implementation over time.

A Systems Thinking Perspective

This goes to the very heart of a PSO contributing at the corporate level. At some point in the implementation of the PSO, senior managers will begin to see how an effectively managed project portfolio can contribute to corporate goals. Senior managers begin to think about the portfolio and not just the projects that comprise it. This transition from Level 3 to Level 4 maturity is the result of a major discovery by senior management as they begin to think in terms of a systems perspective.

Enterprise-Wide Systems

This characteristic is clearly one of a Level 4 organization. The integration of the project data into the other corporate databases provides senior managers with the tools they need to make enterprise-wide business decisions where projects are the strategic components of their business plans. Making this jump from a single-project focus to a strategic-portfolio focus is the sign of a Level 4 PSO.

Knowledge Management

To drive thinking to the enterprise-wide level requires sophisticated corporate databases, standardization of data capture, and the applications systems to extract knowledge from information. Even today, only a few organizations have implemented something as simple as a database of best practices and lessons learned. Part of the reason for the lack of those kinds of databases is because project management is in its infancy. Standards exist at the project level but there are few standards at the portfolio level.

Learning and Learned Project Organizations

Most organizations have not taken the education and training of project managers very seriously. That fact has to change if the PSO is expected to make an impact on project success. A comprehensive curriculum with a variety of delivery approaches is needed. Currently, career and professional development programs for project managers are few and far between. The PSO is positioned to deliver, but senior management must first make the commitment and provide the needed resources.

Open Communications

Communications between and among projects and from first-line managers through to executive levels must be open and free. The PSO can establish and maintain the channels of communications.

Putting It All Together

In this chapter, I introduced the PSO, discussed its roles and responsibilities, and gave a plan for establishing one. The five-level Capability Maturity Model is a good way to measure the maturity of your current PSO, and it provides a sound basis for a continuous quality improvement program.

Discussion Questions

1. Given that your PSO is going to support all three types of project management methodologies presented in this book, what advice would you offer about organizational structure, staffing, and functions provided? Be specific and back up your suggestions with valid reasons.

2. Senior management will always ask what business value they will realize from the PSO. How would you measure the return on investment for your PSO?

Putting It All Together Finally

I want to take this opportunity to make a few closing remarks about what I have shared with you throughout the course of this book.

This fourth edition has been a true labor of love for me. Even before the third edition was published, I realized there was so much more that I needed to say that I began making notes for the fourth edition. I am excited about the APF, and it will surely evolve as I continue to implement it with my clients and discuss it with my colleagues. I would value any input you care to pass on. E-mail me at `rkw@eiicorp.com`.

From the Third Edition

We are living and working in truly challenging and exciting times. Those in my generation can remember how times were before the computer became a social and business requirement. If someone had told me 20 years ago that within 25 years we would routinely talk to a computer and it would talk back, I would have thought he fell out of a tree and landed on his head. But here we are. The computer is pervasive. It has invaded every corner of our existence. There is no escaping it. And I doubt that anyone would want to escape it.

For the project manager it has been a boon, but it has also been a bust. Unfortunately, too many project managers have left the thinking to the software. I shudder when I hear senior managers say that they need to get some project management training for their people and in the same breath say they are looking for a good course on MS Project to help their people learn how to be project managers. Wow! I find it hard to believe that anyone would associate knowledge of project management with how to run a software package. The two are very different. I know of no project management software package that can teach you the concepts and principles of project management. That is not what they are designed to do.

As the project mix moves from traditional to adaptive to extreme, the set of tools also moves from process-oriented to people-oriented and from high-tech to low-tech. I have never really been a slave to the technology. I have always seen it as an enabler. I remind all of my colleagues that what we are all about as project managers is to deliver to our clients the maximum in business value for the money and time they place under our stewardship. Nothing else really matters. The emergence of the agile methods vividly reminds us of that fact. The introduction of APF and its guiding principles is another reminder.

All of my degrees are in mathematics. I was told very early on in that education that mathematics is the queen of the sciences. It exists to serve and support scientific advancement. In much the same way, project management is the queen of the business management disciplines. It exists to serve and support the growth and success of our business community. In that sense we have an obligation—a responsibility—to do the very best that we can.

For the Fourth Edition

It has been three years since the publication of the third edition, and I suspect that we are on the verge of yet another quantum change in project management. Effective project managers will be less likely to follow rigid processes and procedures and will instead assess the project at hand, weigh the alternatives, and take the appropriate actions. That means doing what makes sense and using or not using adopted processes as a result. We have all seen numerous examples of companies that expect rigid adherence to a project management process only to have a high incidence of project failures. It's time to use our brains to think through to an acceptable solution rather than follow some prescribed formula that may be totally ineffective. I have tried to open your minds to the possibilities. You be the judge.

What's on the Web Site?

He who would search for pearls must dive below.
— **John Dryden, English poet**

The Web site has been established to provide a ready source of useful information about the book's contents. It is designed to bring you quickly to some supporting materials for your reference and further study or for your use in presentations and other learning experiences.

The Web site can be accessed at `www.wiley.com/go/epm4e`.

Pleasantown Playground Project and Pizza Delivered Quickly (PDQ) Case Studies (MS Word File)

Pleasantown Playground and Pizza Delivered Quickly (PDQ) are new case studies for this edition. Throughout the book I draw on these case studies for examples that demonstrate how to apply the tools, templates, and processes discussed. The Web site contains copies of the case study materials from the book involving these two examples.

Figures Master File

This file contains a printable and reproducible file for every figure used in the text. This file is made available for those readers who are teaching a course from this book and for anyone who might find some use for the figures in their presentations. You have my permission to embed the figures in your slide presentations. All I ask is that you give the appropriate attributions whenever you use one of the figures.

Tables Master File

This file contains a printable and reproducible table for each table used in the text. This is made available for those readers who are teaching a course from this book and for anyone who might find some use for the tables in their presentations. You have my permission to use the tables in your presentations. All I ask is that you give the appropriate attributions whenever you use one of the tables.

A NOTE ON THE ANSWER FILE FOR THE DISCUSSION QUESTIONS

Each chapter ends with a few discussion questions that might be used by instructors to create a dialogue with the class or for use with written assignments. It is hoped that these questions are thought-provoking. There are no right answers, although there are plenty of wrong answers. An answer file has been created for instructors. Just e-mail me at rkw@eiicorp.com, identify yourself as a legitimate instructor or faculty member, and I'll send you the answer file. I'd love to hear from you and learn how you are using the book and its materials.

Bibliography

Ignorance never settles a question.
— **Benjamin Disraeli**

Those who have read of everything are thought to understand everything, too; but it is not always so — reading furnishes the mind only with materials of knowledge; it is thinking that makes what is read ours. We are of the ruminating kind, and it is not enough to cram ourselves with a great load of collections; unless we chew them over again, they will not give us strength and nourishment.
— **John Locke**

The following books represent a collection of current publications from my project management libraries. Nearly all the books included here were published in the last 10 years. The few exceptions are titles that were written by leaders in our field or have a particularly valuable contribution to the literature. They are classics. All of these books will be of particular interest to professionals who have project management responsibilities, are members of project teams, or simply have a craving to learn about the basics of sound project management. The focus of many of the books is systems and software development because that is our primary interest, although several also treat the basic concepts and principles of project management. Also included are books on closely related topics that I found to be of value in researching and writing this book. You might find value in them, too.

For your ease in finding specific sources, I arranged the bibliography topically according to the major areas covered in the book.

Traditional Project Management

Bainey, Kenneth R. 2004. *Integrated IT Project Management: A Model-Centric Approach*. Boston, MA: Artech House. (ISBN 1-58053-826-2)

Baker, Sunny, and Kim Baker. 1998. *The Complete Idiot's Guide to Project Management*. New York: Alpha Books. (ISBN 0-02-861745-2)

Barkley, Bruce T., and James H. Saylor. 1994. *Customer-Driven Project Management: A New Paradigm in Total Quality Implementation*. New York: McGraw-Hill, Inc. (ISBN 0-07-003739-6)

Bechtold, Richard. 1999. *Essentials of Software Project Management*. Vienna, VA: Management Concepts. (ISBN 1-56726-085-3)

Belanger, Thomas C. 1995. *How to Plan Any Project: A Guide for Teams (and Individuals)*. Sterling, MA: The Sterling Planning Group. (ISBN 0-9631465-1-3)

Bennatan, E. M. 1992. *On Time, Within Budget: Software Project Management Practices and Techniques*. Wellesley, MA: QED Publishing Group. (ISBN 0-89435-408-6)

Berkun, Scott 2005. *The Art of Project Management*. Sebastopol, CA: O'Reilly Media. (ISBN 0-596-00786-8).

Blaylock, Jim, and Rudd McGary. 2002. *Project Management A to Z*. Columbus, OH: PM Best Practices, Inc. (ISBN 0-9719121-0-6)

Block, Thomas R., and J. Davidson Frame. 1998. *The Project Office*. Menlo Park, CA: Crisp Publications. (ISBN 1-56052-443-X)

Burr, Adrian, and Mal Owen. 1996. *Statistical Methods for Software Quality*. London, England: International Thomson Computer Press. (ISBN 1-85032-171-X)

Cable, Dwayne P., and John R. Adams. 1997. *Principles of Project Management*. Upper Darby, PA: Project Management Institute. (ISBN 1-880410-30-3)

Capper, Richard. 1998. *A Project-by-Project Approach to Quality*. Hampshire, England: Gower Publishing Limited. (ISBN 0566079259)

Center for Project Management. 1995. *Managing Advanced IT Projects*. San Ramon, CA: Center for Project Management.

CH2Mhill. 1996. *Project Delivery System: A System and Process for Benchmark Performance*. Denver, CO: CH2Mhill. (ISBN 0-9652616-0-3)

Chapman, Chris, and Stephen Ward. 1997. *Project Risk Management: Processes, Techniques and Insights*. New York: John Wiley & Sons. (ISBN 0-471-95804-2)

Cleland, David I., et al. 1998. *Project Management Casebook*. Upper Darby, PA: Project Management Institute. (ISBN 1-880410-45-1)

Cleland, David I., et al. 1998. *Project Management Casebook: Instructor's Manual*. Upper Darby, PA: Project Management Institute. (ISBN 1-880410-45-1)

Cleland, David I., et al. 1998. *Annotated Bibliography of Project and Team Management*. Newtown Square, PA: Project Management Institute. (ISBN 1-880410-47-8)

Conway, Kieron. 2001. *Software Project Management: From Concept to Deployment*. Scottsdale, AZ: The Coriolis Group. (ISBN 1-57610-807-4)

Crawford, J. Kent. 2002. *Project Management Maturity Model: Providing a Proven Path to Project Management Excellence*. New York: Marcel Dekker, Inc. (ISBN 0-8247-0754-0)

Darnell, Russell W. 1996. *The World's Greatest Project: One Project Team on the Path to Quality*. Newtown Square, PA: The Project Management Institute. (ISBN 1-880410-46-X)

Davidson, Jeff. 2000. *10 Minute Guide to Project Management*. Indianapolis: Macmillan. (ISBN 0-02-863966-9)

DeGrace, Peter, and Leslie Hulet Stahl. 1990. *Wicked Problems, Righteous Solutions*. Englewood Cliffs, NJ: Yourdon Press Computing Series. (ISBN 0-13-590126-X)

DeMarco, T. 1982. *Controlling Software Projects*. New York: Yourdon Press.

DeMarco, Tom. 1997. *The Deadline: A Novel About Project Management*. New York: Dorsett House. (ISBN 0-932633-39-0)

DeMarco, T., and T. Lister. 1999. *Peopleware, Productive Projects and Teams*. 2d ed. New York: Dorsett House. (ISBN 0-932633-43-9)

Dettmer, H. William. 1997. *Goldratt's Theory of Constraints: A Systems Approach to Continuous Improvement*. Milwaukee, WI: ASQ. (ISBN 0-87389-370-0)

Dobson, Michael S. 1999. *The Juggler's Guide to Managing Multiple Projects*. Newtown Square, PA: The Project Management Institute. (ISBN 1-880410-65-6)

Dymond, Kenneth M. 1998. *A Guide to the CMM: Understanding the Capability Maturity Model for Software*. Annapolis, MD: Process Transition International, Inc. (ISBN 0-9646008-0-3)

Fleming, Quentin W. 1992. *Cost/Schedule Control Systems Criteria*. Chicago: Probus Publishing. (ISBN 1-55738-289-1)

Fleming, Quentin W., John Bronn, and Gary C. Humphreys. 1987. *Project and Production Scheduling*. Chicago: Probus Publishing. (ISBN 0-917253-63-9)

Fleming, Quentin W., and Quentin J. Fleming. 1993. *Subcontract Planning and Organization*. Chicago: Probus Publishing. (ISBN 1-55738-463-0)

Fleming, Quentin W., and Loel M. Koppelman. 2000. *Earned Value Project Management*. 2d ed. Newtown Square, PA: The Project Management Institute. (ISBN 1-880410-27-3)

Friedlein, Ashley. 2001. *Web Project Management: Delivering Successful Commercial Web Sites*. San Francisco: Morgan Kaufmann Publishers. (ISBN 1-55860-678-5)

Fuller, Jim. 1997. *Managing Performance Improvement Projects: Preparing, Planning, Implementing*. San Francisco: Jossey-Bass Publishers. (ISBN0-7879-0959-9)

Goldratt, Eliyahu M. 1997. *Critical Chain*. Great Barrington, MA: North River Press. (ISBN 0-88427-153-6)

— — — . 1992. *The Goal: A Process of Ongoing Improvement*. Great Barrington, MA: North River Press. (ISBN 0-88427-061-0)

Goodpasture, John C. 2002. *Managing Projects for Value*. Vienna, VA: Management Concepts. (ISBN 1-56726-138-8)

Hallows, Jolyon. 1998. *Information Systems Project Management: How to Deliver Function and Value in Information Technology Projects*. New York: AMACOM. (ISBN0-8144-0368-9)

Harrington, H. James, et al. 2000. *Project Change Management: Applying Change Management to Improvement Projects*. New York: McGraw-Hill. (ISBN 0-07-027104-6)

Haugan, Gregory T. 2002. *Project Planning and Scheduling*. Vienna, VA: Management Concepts. (ISBN 1-56726-136-1)

— — — . 2002. *Effective Work Breakdown Structures*. Vienna, VA: Management Concepts. (ISBN 1-56726-135-3)

Hiebeler, Robert et al. 1998. *Best Practices: Building Your Business with Customer-Focused Solutions*. New York: Simon & Schuster. (ISBN 0-684-83453-7)

Hill, Peter R. 2001. *Practical Project Estimation: A Toolkit for Estimating Software Development Effort and Duration*. Warrandyte, Victoria, Australia: International Software Benchmarking Standards Group. (ISBN 0-9577201-1-4)

Hiltz, Mark J. 1994. *Project Management Handbook of Checklists*. Vol. 1, *Conceptual/Definition and Project Initiation*. Ontario, Canada: MarkCheck Publishing. (ISBN 0-9697202-2-X)

— — — . 1994. *Project Management Handbook of Checklists*. Vol. 2, *Organizations/Communications/Management*. Ontario, Canada: MarkCheck Publishing. (ISBN 0-9697202-3-8)

— — — . 1994. *Project Management Handbook of Checklists*. Vol. 3, *Project Planning and Control*. Ontario, Canada: MarkCheck Publishing (ISBN 0-9697202-4-6)

— — — . 1994. *Project Management Handbook of Checklists*. Vol. 4, *Implementation/Termination*. Ontario, Canada: MarkCheck Publishing. (ISBN 0-9697202-5-4)

Humphrey, Watts S. 1997. *Managing Technical People*. Reading, MA: Addison-Wesley. (ISBN 0-201-54597-7)

Huston, Charles L. 1996. *Management of Project Procurement*. New York: McGraw-Hill. (ISBN 0-07-030552-8)

Ibbs, C. William, and Young-Hoon Kwak. 1997. *The Benefits of Project Management: Financial and Organizational Rewards to Corporations*. Newtown Square, PA: The Project Management Institute. (ISBN 1-880410-32-X)

Jalote, Pankaj. 2000. *CMM in Practice: Processes for Executing Software Projects at Infosys*. Reading, MA: Addison-Wesley. (ISBN 0-210-61626-2)

Jensen, Bill. 2000. *Simplicity: The New Competitive Advantage in A World of More, Better, Faster*. Cambridge, MA: Perseus Books. (ISBN 0-7382-0210-X)

Kaydos, Will. 1999. *Operational Performance Measurement: Increasing Total Productivity*. Boca Raton, FL: St Lucie Press. (ISBN 1-57444-099-3)

Keen, Peter G. W., and Ellen M. Knapp. 1996. *Business Processes: A Glossary of Key Terms and Concepts for Today's Business Leader*. Cambridge, MA: Harvard Business School Press. (ISBN 0-87584-575-4)

Kerzner, Harold. 1998. *In Search of Excellence in Project Management*. New York: Van Nostrand Reinhold. (ISBN 0-442-02706-0)

— — —. 2001. *Project Management: A Systems Approach to Planning, Scheduling, and Controlling*. 7th ed. New York: John Wiley & Sons, Inc. (ISBN0-471-39342-8)

Kirkpatrick, Donald L. 1998. *Evaluating Training Programs*. 2d ed. San Francisco: Berrett-Koehler. (ISBN 1-57675-042-6)

Kliem, Ralph L., and Irwin S. Ludin. 1997. *Reducing Project Risk*. Hampshire, England: Gower Publishing Limited. (ISBN 0-566-07799-X)

Kloppenborg, Timothy J., and Joseph A. Petrick. 2002. *Managing Project Quality*. Vienna, VA: Management Concepts. (ISBN 1-56726-141-8)

Kolluru, Steven, et al. 1996. *Risk Assessment and Management Handbook For Environmental, Health, and Safety Professionals*. New York: McGraw-Hill, Inc. (ISBN 0-07-035987-3)

Kopelman, Orion et al. 1998. *Projects at Warp-Speed with QRPD: The Definitive Guidebook to Quality Rapid Product Development*. Palo Alto, CA: Global Brain, Inc. (ISBN 1-885262-16-0)

Kyle, Mackenzie. 1998. *Making It Happen: A Non-Technical Guide to Project Management*. Toronto, Canada: John Wiley & Sons, Canada Ltd. (ISBN 0-471-64234-7)

Lambert, Lee R., and Erin Lambert. 2000. *Project Management: The Commonsense Approach*. Columbus, OH: LCG Publishing. (ISBN 0-9626397-8-8)

Laufer, Alexander. 1997. *Simultaneous Management: Managing Projects in A Dynamic Environment*. New York: AMACOM. (ISBN 0-8144-0312-3)

Laufer, Alexander, and Edward J. Hoffman. 2000. *Project Management Success Stories: Lessons of Project Leaders*. New York: John Wiley & Sons, Inc. (ISBN 0-471-36007-4)

Leach, Lawrence P. 1997. *The Critical Chain Project Managers' Fieldbook*. Idaho Falls, ID: Quality Systems.

— — —. 2000. *Critical Chain Project Management*. Boston: Artech House. (ISBN 1-58053-074-5)

— — —. 2005. *Critical Chain Project Management*. 2d ed. Boston: Artech House. (ISBN 1-58053-903-3).

Levine, Harvey A. 2002. *Practical Project Management: Tips, Tactics, and Tools*. New York: John Wiley & Sons, Inc. (ISBN 0-471-20303-3)

Lewis, James P. 1995. *Project Planning, Scheduling, and Control*. Chicago: Irwin. (ISBN 1-55738-869-5)

— — —. 1998. *Mastering Project Management*. New York: McGraw-Hill. (ISBN 0-7863-1188-6)

— — —. 2000. *The Project Manager's Desk Reference*. 2d ed. New York: McGraw-Hill. (ISBN 0-07-134750-X)

Maguire, Steve. 1994. *Debugging the Development Process*. Redmond, WA: Microsoft Press. (ISBN 1-55615-650-2)

Martin, Paula. 1995. *Leading Project Management into the 21st Century: New Dimensions in Project Management and Accountability.* Cincinnati, OH: Martin Tate. (ISBN 0-943811-04-X)

McConnell, Steve. 1996. *Rapid Development.* Redmond, WA: Microsoft Press. (ISBN 1-55615-900-5)

— — —. 1998. *Software Project Survival Guide.* Redmond, WA: Microsoft Press. (ISBN 1-57231-621-7)

— — —. 2004. *Professional Software Development: Shorter Schedules, Higher Quality Products, More Successful Projects, Enhanced Careers.* Boston: Addison Wesley. (ISBN 0-321-19367-9)

Milosevic, Dragan Z. 2003. *Project Management ToolBox: Tools and Techniques for the Practicing Project Manager.* New York: John Wiley & Sons. (ISBN 0-471-20822-1)

Muller, Robert J. 1998. *Productive Objects: An Applied Software Project Management Framework.* San Francisco: Morgan Kaufmann. (ISBN 1-55860-437-5)

Muther, Richard. 2000. *More Profitable Planning: Six Steps to Planning Anything.* Kansas City, MO: Management and Industrial Research Publications. (ISBN 0-933684-193)

Neuendorf, Steve. 2002. *Project Measurement.* Vienna, VA: Management Concepts. (ISBN 1-56726-140-X)

Newbold, Robert C.1998. *Project Management in the Fast Lane: Applying the Theory of Constraints.* Boca Raton, FL: St Lucie Press. (ISBN 1-57444-195-7)

Nielsen, Jakob. 2000. *Designing Web Usability.* Indianapolis: New Riders Publishing. (ISBN 1-56205-810-X)

Paulk, Mark C., et al. 1994. *The Capability Maturity Model: Guidelines for Improving the Software Process.* Reading, MA: Addison-Wesley. (ISBN 0-201-54664-7)

Phillips, Jack J. et al. 2002. *The Project Management Scorecard: Measuring the Success of Project Management Solutions.* Boston: Butterworth-Heinemann Ltd. (ISBN 0-7506-7449-0)

Pritchard, Carl L. 1998. *How to Build A Work Breakdown Structure: The Cornerstone of Project Management.* Arlington, VA: ESI International. (ISBN 1-890367-12-5)

— — —. 2001. *Risk Management: Concepts and Guidance.* Arlington, VA.: ESI International. (ISBN 1-890367-30-3)

Pritchett, Price, and Brian Muirhead. 1998. *The Mars Pathfinder: Approach to Faster-Better-Cheaper.* Dallas: Price Pritchett & Associates. (ISBN 0-944002-74-9)

Project Management Institute. 1997. *Principles of Project Management.* Upper Darby, PA: Project Management Institute. (ISBN 1-880410-30-3)

— — —. 1997. *The PMI Book of Project Management Forms.* Upper Darby, PA: Project Management Institute. (ISBN: 1-880410-31-1)

— — —. 1999. *Project Management Software Survey.* Newton Square, PA: Project Management Institute. (ISBN 1-880410-52-4)

— — —. 1999. *The Future of Project Management.* Newtown Square, PA: Project Management Institute. (ISBN 1-880410-71-0)

— — — . 2000. *A Guide to the Project Management Body of Knowledge.* Newtown Square, PA: Project Management Institute. (ISBN: 1-880410-23-0)

— — — . 2000. *Project Management Experience and Knowledge Self-Assessment Manual.* Newtown Square, PA: Project Management Institute. (ISBN 1-880410-24-9)

— — — . 2001. *Practice Standards for Work Breakdown Structures.* Newtown Square, PA: Project Management Institute. (ISBN 1-880410-81-8)

Putnam, Lawrence H., and Ware Myers. 1992. *Measures for Excellence: Reliable Software On Time, Within Budget.* Englewood Cliffs, NJ: Yourdon Press Computing Series. (ISBN 0-13-56794-3)

Rad, Parviz F. 2002. *Project Estimating and Cost Management.* Vienna, PA: Management Concepts. (ISBN 1-56726-144-2)

Raferty, John. 1994. *Risk Analysis in Project Management.* London, England: E&FN SPON. (ISBN 0-419-18420-1)

Raynus, Joseph. 1999. *Software Process Improvement with CMM.* Boston: Artech House. (ISBN 0-89006-644-2)

Robertson, Suzanne and James Robertson. 1999. *Mastering the Requirements Process.* Boston: Addison Wesley. (ISBN 0-201-36046-2)

Robertson, Suzanne and James Robertson. 2005. *Requirements-Led Project Management: Discovering David's Slingshot.* Boston: Addison Wesley. (ISBN 0-321-18062-3)

Royce, Walker. 1998. *Software Project Management: A Unified Framework.* Reading, MA: Addison-Wesley. (ISBN 0-201-30958-0)

Royer, Paul S. 2002. *Project Risk Management: A Proactive Approach.* Vienna, VA: Management Concepts. (ISBN 1-56726-139-6)

Schuyler, John. 2001. *Risk and Decision Analysis in Projects.* 2d ed. Newtown Square, PA: The Project Management Institute. (ISBN 1-880410-28-1)

Schwalbe, Kathy. 2000. *Information Technology Project Management.* Boston: Course Technology. (ISBN 0-7600-1180-X)

Siegel, David. 1997. *Secrets of Successful Web Sites: Project Management on the World Wide Web.* Indianapolis: New Riders. (ISBN 1-56830-382-3)

Smith, John M. 2001. *Troubled IT Projects: Prevention and Turnaround.* Herts, United Kingdom: The Institution of Electrical Engineers. (ISBN 0-85296-104-9)

Sodhi, Jag, and Prince Sodhi. 2001. *IT Project Management Handbook.* Vienna, VA: Management Concepts. (ISBN 1-56726-098-5)

Stellman, Andrew and Jennifer Greene. 2006. *Applied Software Project Management.* Sebastopol, CA: O'Reilly Media (ISBN 0-596-00948-8)

Taylor, James. 2004. *Managing Information Technology Projects.* New York, NY: AMACOM. (ISBN 0-8144-0811-7)

TechRepublic. 2001. *IT Professional's Guide to Project Management.* Louisville, KY: TechRepublic. (ISBN 1-931490-16-3)

Toney, Frank, and Ray Powers. 1997. *Best Practices of Project Management Groups in Large Functional Organizations.* Upper Darby, PA: Project Management Institute. (ISBN 1-880410-05-2)

Verzuh, Eric. 1999. *The Fast Forward MBA in Project Management*. New York: John Wiley & Sons, Inc. (ISBN 0-471-32546-5)

Ward, J. LeRoy. 2000. *Project Management Terms: A Working Glossary*. Arlington, VA: ESI International. (ISBN 1-890367-25-7)

Whitten, Neal. 1995. *Managing Software Development Projects*. 2nd ed. New York: John Wiley & Sons. (ISBN 0-471-07683-X)

— — —. 2000. *The EnterPrize Organization: Organizing Software Projects for Accountability and Success*. Newtown Square, PA: The Project Management Institute. (ISBN 1-880410-79-6)

— — —. 2005. *Neal Whitten's No-Nonsense Advice for Successful Projects*. Vienna, VA: Management Concepts. (ISBN 1-56726-155-8).

Wysocki, Robert K., Robert Beck, Jr, and David B. Crane. 2000. *Effective Project Management*. 2nd ed. New York: John Wiley & Sons. (ISBN 0-471-36028-7)

Wysocki, Robert K. 2006. *Effective Software Project Management*. New York: John Wiley & Sons. (ISBN 0-7645-9636-5).

Yourdon, Edward. 1999. *Death March: The Complete Software Developer's Guide to Surviving "Mission Impossible" Projects*. Upper Saddle River, NJ: Prentice Hall. (ISBN 0-13-014659-5)

When I introduced the APF in the last edition of this book, there weren't any other published references to speak of at the time. Since then, several related titles have been published.

Extreme Project Management, and more generally agile project management, are products of the software development discipline. They remain there today. For that reason the references dealing with it that follow are almost exclusively focused on software development.

Adaptive Project Framework and Extreme Project Management

Ajani, Shaun. 2002. *Extreme Project Management: Unique Methodologies, Resolute Principles, Astounding Results*. San Jose, CA: Writers Club Press. (ISBN 0-595-21335-9)

Ambler, Scott W. 2000. *The Unified Process Elaboration Phase: Best Practices in Implementing the UP*. Lawrence, KS: R&D Books. (ISBN1-929629-05-2

— — —. 2002. *Agile Modeling: Effective Practices for Extreme Programming and the Unified Process*. New York: John Wiley & Sons, Inc. (ISBN 0-471-20282-7)

— — —. 2004. *The Object Primer: Agile Model-Driven Development with UML 2.0*. 3d ed. New York: Cambridge University Press. (ISBN 0-521-54018-6)

Ambler, Scott W., and Larry L. Constantine. 2000. *The Unified Process Inception Phase: Best Practices in Implementing the UP*. Lawrence, KS: CMP Books. (ISBN 1-929629-10-9)

— — —. 2000. *The Unified Process Construction Phase: Best Practices in Implementing the UP*. Lawrence, KS: CMP Books. (ISBN 1-929629-01-X)

Anderson, David J. 2004. *Agile Management for Software Engineering*. Upper Saddle River, NJ: Prentice Hall PTR. (ISBN 0-13-142460-2)

Augustine, Sanjiv. 2005. *Managing Agile Projects*. Upper Saddle River, NJ: Prentice Hall PTR. (ISBN 0-13-124071-4)

Beck, Kent, and Martin Fowler. 2001. *Planning Extreme Programming*. Reading, MA: Addison-Wesley. (ISBN 0-201-71091-9)

Boehm, Barry and Richard Turner. 2004. *Balancing Agility and Discipline: A Guide for the Perplexed*. Boston: Addison Wesley. (ISBN 0-321-18612-5)

Chin, Gary. 2004. *Agile Project Management: How to Succeed in the Face of Changing Project Requirements*. New York: AMACOM. (ISBN 0-8144-7176-5)

Cockburn, Alistair. 1998. *Surviving Object-Oriented Projects*. Boston: Addison-Wesley. (ISBN 0-201-49834-0)

— — —. 2001. *Writing Effective Use Cases*. Boston: Addison-Wesley. (ISBN 0-201-70225-8)

Cohn, Mike. 2004. *User Stories Applied for Agile Software Development*. Boston: Addison Wesley. (ISBN 0-321-20568-5)

Fowler, Martin. 2000. *Refactoring: Improving the Design of Existing Code*. Boston: Addison-Wesley. (ISBN 0-201-48567-2)

Highsmith, James A. 2000. *Adaptive Software Development: A Collaborative Approach to Managing Complex Systems*. New York: Dorset House. (ISBN 0-932633-40-4)

Highsmith, Jim. 2002. *Agile Software Development Ecosystems*. Boston: Addison-Wesley. (ISBN 0-201-76043-6)

Highsmith, Jim. 2004. *Agile Project Management: Creating Innovative Products*. Boston: Addison Wesley. (ISBN 0-321-21977-5)

Jeffries, Ron, Ann Henderson, and Chet Hendrickson. 2001. *Extreme Programming Installed*. Boston: Addison-Wesley. (ISBN 0-201-70842-6)

Koch, Alan S. 2005. *Agile Software Development: Evaluating the Methods for Your Organization*. Boston: Artech House. (ISBN 1-58053-842-8)

Kruchten, Philippe. 2000. *The Rational Unified Process: An Introduction*. 2d ed. Boston: Addison-Wesley. (ISBN 0-201-70710-1)

Larman, Craig. 2004. *Agile and Iterative Development: A Manager's Guide*. Boston: Addison Wesley. (ISBN 0-13-111155-8)

Newkirk, James, and Robert C. Martin. 2001. *Extreme Programming in Practice*. Boston: Addison-Wesley. (ISBN 0-201-70937-6)

Poppendieck, Mary and Tom Poppendieck. 2003. *Lean Software Development: An Agile Toolkit*. Boston: Addison Wesley. (ISBN 0-321-15078-3)

Schwaber, Ken. 2004. *Agile Project Management with Scrum*. Redmond, WA: Microsoft Press. (ISBN 0-7356-1993-X)

Stapleton, Jennifer. 1997. *DSDM: Dynamic Systems Development Method*. Harlow, England: Addison-Wesley. (ISBN 0-201-17889-3)

Succi, Giancarlo, and Michele Marchesi. 2001. *Extreme Programming Examined*. Boston: Addison-Wesley. (ISBN 0-201-71040-4)

Thomsett, Rob. 2002. *Radical Project Management*. Upper Saddle River, NJ: Prentice Hall. (ISBN 0-13-009486-2)

Wake, William C. 2002. *Extreme Programming Explored*. Boston: Addison-Wesley. (ISBN 0-201-73397-8)

Organizational Considerations

Block, Thomas R., and J. Davidson Frame. 1998. *The Project Office*. Upper Darby, PA: Project Management Institute. (ISBN 1-56052-443-X)

Cooper, Robert G., Scott J. Edgett, and Elko J. Kleinschmidt. 1998. *Portfolio Management for New Products*. Reading, MA: Perseus Books. (ISBN 0-201-32814-3)

Crawford, J. Kent. 2002. *The Strategic Project Office: A Guide to Improving Organizational Performance*. New York: Marcel Dekker. (ISBN 0-8247-0750-8)

Dinsmore, Paul C. 1999. *Winning in Business with Enterprise Project Management*. New York: AMACOM. (ISBN 0-8144-0420-0)

Dye, Lowell D., and James S. Pennypacker, editors. 1999. *Project Portfolio Management: Selecting and Prioritizing Projects for Competitive Advantage*. West Chester, PA: Center for Business Practices. (ISBN 1-929576-00-5)

Graham, Robert J., and Randall L. Englund. 1997. *Creating an Environment for Successful Projects*. San Francisco: Jossey-Bass. (ISBN 0-7879-0359-0)

Hallows, Jolyon. 2002. *The Project Management Office Toolkit: A Step-by-Step Guide to Setting Up a Project Management Office*. New York: AMACOM. (ISBN 0-8144-0663-7)

Kerzner, Harold. 2001. *Strategic Planning for Project Management Using a Project Management Maturity Model*. New York: John Wiley & Sons, Inc. (ISBN 0-471-40039-4)

Rad, Parviz F., and Ginger Levin. 2002. *The Advanced Project Management Office: A Comprehensive Look at Function and Implementation*. Boca Raton, FL: St Lucie Press. (ISBN 1-57444-340-2)

Raynus, Joseph 1999. *Software Process Improvement with CMM*. Boston: Artech House. (ISBN 0-89006-644-2)

Index

Coventry University Library

